CURRENTS OF ENCOUNTER

*Studies on the Contact between Christianity and
Other Religions, Beliefs, and Cultures*

Religions and the Truth

Philosophical Reflections and Perspectives

by

Hendrik M. Vroom

Translated by

J. W. Rebel

WILLIAM B. EERDMANS PUBLISHING COMPANY
GRAND RAPIDS, MICHIGAN

EDITIONS RODOPI, AMSTERDAM

Copyright © 1989 by William B. Eerdmans Publishing Co.,
255 Jefferson Ave. SE, Grand Rapids, MI 49503.

This edition first published jointly 1989 by Wm. B. Eerdmans Publishing Co. and
Editions Rodopi, Amsterdam

Originally published as *Religies en de Waarheid,* © 1988
Uitgeversmaatschappij J. H. Kok, Kampen, the Netherlands.

Library of Congress Cataloging-in-Publication Data

Vroom, H. M., 1945–
[Religies en de waarheid. English]
Religions and the truth : philosophical reflections and perspectives /
Hendrik M. Vroom ; translated by J. W. Rebel.
p.   cm.
Translation of: Religies en de waarheid.
ISBN 0-8028-0502-7
1. Religion—Philosophy.   2. Religions.   3. Truth.   4. Religions—Relations.
I. Title.
BL51.V7613   1989
200′.1—dc20   89-39188
                                                              CIP

Contents

5

Part 2: DESCRIPTION 101

Preface

This study is an account of an enquiry into what people understand by 'truth' in religion. It has been a long journey, often along perhaps well-frequented roads, but also through an often rather unfamiliar landscape. Religions claim that they know man and the world as these really are, yet they differ in their views of reality. Question therefore arises as to how the claims to truth by various religions are related. Are they complementary? Do they contradict or overlap one another? These questions couch a yet more fundamental question: What —according to the religious traditions themselves— is the nature of religious knowledge? How ought one to conceive of claims to truth by religions? This question has been considered by people within all the major religious traditions. Critical and profound thinkers have shed their light on such questions. It is to such classical exponents that we must address our questions, rather than to 'popular religion,' for they have left us a witness to their thought through writings, writings which, moreover, have themselves contributed to further development within their respective traditions. In this manner our enquiry reached further and further. The road first led from what certain currents of Western philosophy think about 'religion and truth' to what people in religious studies believe they can maintain concerning this theme. From there, our enquiry carried us to classical thinkers within various religions. Much can be learnt from the classical exponents of the various traditions; they became 'classic' because many people in subsequent generations found inspiration in their insights. A selection had to be made of theologians and philosophers who we would choose to treat. An enquiry such as the present one requires the imposition of many limitations. Such selections and limitations are always debatable. Friendly colleagues were prepared to offer advice on what approach to take for this study, as well as on its general plan. The long line of religious thinkers which have passed under review came about accordingly. The last part of this enquiry is an attempt to learn as much as possible from the insights of the figures discussed. We have dealt in detail with the experiential basis for faith. Our voyage ends with the central question of how the various religious claims to truth are related.

In studying the thinkers discussed, we have generally used (translations of) their writings. The very breadth of this study makes one dependent upon secondary literature. If it were otherwise, the aim —an overview of the thought within the major religious traditions concerning 'truth,' followed by philosophical reflection on our presentation— could not be achieved. Philosophy cannot be nourished by specialized studies alone. The concern is ultimately with general orientation and insight.

Specialists in various areas were fortunately prepared to read various chapters, guarding me from error and offering advice for improvements to the text. I owe them much thankfulness. This study has emerged within a group of scholars from various disciplines, all students of the encounter between religions. Chapters II, VIII, and IX were discussed in this group. I would like to thank a number of specialists for their competent and critical commentary on the chapters of the second part of this study: Prof. R. Fernhout (Free University of Amsterdam), Prof. T. E. Vetter (Leiden), Prof. A. van der Heide (Free University of Amsterdam/Leiden), and Prof. A. Wessels (Free University of Amsterdam). I would also like to express gratefulness to Prof. H. de Wit for his comments; our paths display a marked parallel, since he too, as a psychologist, has extended his research to consulting the religious traditions themselves, owing to his interest in the discussion in Western psychology about religious growth. I would particularly like to mention the advice by Prof. D. C. Mulder and Prof. A. F. Droogers in connection with Chapters II, VIII, and IX. I have made grateful use of all their comments; they are naturally not to blame for the shortcomings of this study.

A substantial enquiry demands time. I was twice granted additional opportunity for research. A sabbatical in 1983 spent at the Center for the Study of World Religions at Harvard University was very inspiring because of the earnestness and integrity which marked discussion with adherents of other religious traditions. The subject of this study, as well as its aims and limitations, were discussed with Wilfred Cantwell Smith. I also received valuable advice from Professors David Eckel, Diana Eck, and later on, from John Carman. My stay in the U.S.A was made possible by the Vereniging voor Christelijk Wetenschappelijk Onderwijs to whom I am accordingly very grateful.

I also wish to express heartfelt thanks to John Rebel, who translated the book from Dutch into English and did all the work involved in preparing a camera-ready text. The translation accords well with the author's intentions, and I am pleased to be able to present it. I would also like to thank John Medendorp for many suggestions to improve the English text.

It is at present not general custom in the philosophy of religion to consult the philosophical reflection present in other religious traditions, although interest is rapidly increasing. The beliefs of the different religions have therefore been briefly described, even though some readers and students of religions will already be familiar with them. Our purpose was to make the book accessible to a broad group of readers. In our transcription of foreign terms, we have been as faithful as is possible for a general study. I hope the readers will follow the presentation with as much interest as possessed the author while carrying out his research. May this study help the reader to orient himself (or herself) with respect to the questions raised by religious pluralism.

Amsterdam
April 15, 1989

PART 1

INTRODUCTION

Chapter I

The Question of Truth
in Interreligious Perspective

§ 1   Religion and truth: posing the problem

1.1   Relevance of the issue

Religious convictions have displayed a sweeping diversity since time immemorial. In ancient India, Buddhism and Hinduism existed next to Jainism and materialistic currents. Zen, Confucianism, and Taoism have lived side by side in China since living memory. Judaism marked off its own identity over against the fertility cults and the religions of Babylon. In the Hellenistic world wherein Christianity made its appearance, many religious options existed alongside of each other; until long after the time of Augustine, all kinds of religious currents had their own place next to Neo-Platonic and Stoical philosophies of life. Sometimes cultures with a more uniform religious culture emerged. Islam exerted itself to bring the whole of culture under the impress of Islam, of religious surrender and obedience. Christianity identified itself with the whole of Western culture, even though the roots of Western culture also lie in ancient Athens. Philosophies of life abound, and thus it has been since ancient times.

Questioning the mutual relationship of the various religious currents is today a very relevant issue. Relevance however is never an objective datum; it is felt, more strongly by some than by others. For the Western part of Christianity in particular, the issue of how religions are related to each other is a relatively new problem. Was the superiority of Western culture in Europe not taken for granted? Though it was truly a voyage of discovery to make acquaintance with the teachings of oriental wisdom, even in the previous century, it did not involve a serious confrontation with the question of truth. People regarded their own culture and faith as superior. Already in the last century, however, many people did see fit to adapt their own faith to circumstances. As a result modernism, liberalism, and liberal theology made their appearance. Still, the notion of Western superiority remained unchallenged. In Protestant circles, Barthianism gained ground in the decennia succeeding the second world war; in America, many fundamentalist and orthodox currents have flourished. The attitude of the Christian churches, including the largest of all, the Roman Catholic Church, remains characterized by an unquestioning acceptance of the 'absoluteness of Christianity.'

A number of new developments have cast a different light on the question of how religions are related in Western culture as well. The Western sense of superiority has begun to falter in the past twenty years. The limits of Western culture have been encountered; pollution, various addictions, and feelings of uneasiness and doubt regarding the meaning of existence are spreading. The mutual contact between cultures has been extended exponentially due to the emergence of the global village. In North America and Europe people intermingled from many religious traditions live together. The exclusive claims to truth which were formerly taken for granted within the limited circle of one's own culture now have to make good in the encounter with the claims of other faiths. For many, especially for the young, this means a breach with the old self-evident faith.

According to many people in Western secularized culture the abundance of religions trivializes religion. Many people think: If people everywhere think so differently, religion cannot be true. Others reach a different conclusion. They consider the differences between persuasions to be secondary; what is central is what all religions have in common. That is where the truth lies; the rest is incidental and probably untrue.

Thus the issue of how religions are related has again become a question in our time, for Western culture too — a question which no religious person can elude. To study the questions surrounding the relationship of religions is therefore one of the first tasks of contemporary philosophy of religion. Eastern religions have been familiar for centuries with a plurality of philosophies of life. Confrontation with exclusive religions such as Christianity and Islam is sometimes problematical for less exclusive religions. They have the tendency to open-mindedly clear a place for Christianity, for example; yet they will experience no reciprocity. Islamic and Christian claims to absolute truth have sometimes given rise to regrettable practices. The question of the mutual relationship between religions is urgent, practically as well as intellectually.

1.2   The question of truth

People have been defining their attitude towards non-believers and followers of other faiths since days of old. Most everyone has his own view on the relationship of his own faith —whichever that may be— to other faiths. Closer investigation teaches us that the view one holds concerning other faiths is related to one's own experience of faith and to one's interpretation of one's own tradition. It is untrue that each religion has one specific view of other religions. Rather, each current within a tradition gives its own appraisal of other traditions and of the various currents within it. This issue will be raised in more detail in this enquiry.

One of the crucial topics related to the relationship of religions is the question of truth. That question is central to this study. People think very differently about the importance of the question of truth. In the dialogue between adherents of various traditions, such as that broached by the World Council of Churches, actual practice indicates an attitude of great reticence with respect to the question of truth, for experience proved that raising this question quickly disturbed arduously built-up relationships. Consequently, primarily topics which could lead to a meaningful discussion were sought. To some, this approach is a matter of respect for one's neighbour, a matter of patience and wisdom; to others, it implies a more basic rejection of the question of truth; still others take the position that if one faith is true, then others are untrue. This third stance is understandable: If doctrine is considered to be central to religion, and if doctrine is conceived of as corresponding (in some fashion) to reality, then the truth of religion *A* must exclude that of religion *B.* Many find this position to be an oversimplification. This issue will also be raised in more detail.

Examination of the question of truth is rather complicated. Various religions not only have specific truth claims, but also have their own theories about the nature of religious truth. The 'dialogue,' in other words, must be concerned not only with the content of religious beliefs, but also with the concept of truth present in various traditions. Are they comparable or not? We will try to acquire more insight on this point.

1.3   Comparative philosophy of religion

A number of people have relatively recently arrived at a more or less elaborated view in the area of interreligious relations. We have in mind the work of such people as Wilfred C. Smith, William A. Christian, John Hick, Derek Z. Phillips, Shivesh Ch. Thakur, and Donald Wiebe, but also the ideas of such men as D. T. Suzuki, Radhakrishnan, and Mahatma Gandhi. Nine names also means nine conceptions, however. These authors not only have differing opinions; they also have divergent approaches to the subject. Christian primarily analyzes the 'logic' of religion; Smith pairs personal involvement with people from many religions with a considerable knowledge of religious studies. After training in the tradition of analytical philosophy, Hick made profound acquaintance with non-Christian religions. These and other factors determine the angle from which they approach and 'resolve' the problem. Most of the authors mentioned are conversant with the beliefs of the major religious traditions.

Reflection on the question of truth has, on the one hand, become more complex due to the contributions of comparative religious studies and the philosophy of religion. On the other hand, however, it has also come more to the point. Enquiry has become more difficult because it is no longer possible to arrive at a conception of religious truth merely and simply in terms of one's own cultural and religious tradition; acquaintance must also be made with living notions present in other traditions. Although this has made enquiry into the question of truth more complex, it also preserves a closer proximity to the reality it is attempting to clarify because one is thus forced to take the uniqueness of each religion seriously. Philosophical study of the concept of truth has come a long way as a result.

The theme of 'religion and truth' has been raised many times in the Western philosophy of religion. The issue of religious truth is raised implicitly whenever religion and knowledge are spoken of, for the problem of what one understands by 'truth' always entails the question: When is it permissible to speak of 'real knowledge'? Related to this is the problem of criteria by which truth claims must be assessed. Another related issue is of course the problem of the pre-conditions for knowing truth. These questions have also been continually raised in the history of the Western philosophy of religion. We can refer to only a very small segment of this ongoing discussion. In the next chapter we will present several moments from the Anglo-Saxon discussion concerning religious truth. We will see that the discussion is determined primarily by a Western, secularized-Christian representation of matters. The Christian tradition also forms the point of reference for the European continent. This holds equally for Christian and for non-Christian thinkers. Yet such a limitation of philosophical religious enquiry no longer seems possible for two reasons:

(1) The confrontation between the major cultural traditions in our world needs to be considered.

(2) Scholarly integrity demands that in an endeavour to acquire insight into the theme of religion and truth, philosophy of religion carried out from perspectives other than that of Western (post) Christian culture not be left out of consideration.

This is not to deny the full right to philosophical reflection within the context of a religious tradition. It is permissible to practise the philosophy of the Christian tradition or philosophical theology within a tradition if one so desires.[1] But philosophy of *religion* in the strict sense of the word cannot be exercised within the context of a specific religion. We employ the term philosophy of religion here in a particular sense: the philosophical analysis of the phenomenon of religion. Account must be taken of the data of religious studies in such analysis. The attempt must be made to develop a view which is not distinctive for a specific religion.

---

[1] Compare the 'philosophical theology' in England, e.g., T. F. Torrance, *Theological Science* (Oxford ²1971); R. Swinburne, *Faith and Reason* (Oxford 1981). Swinburne's chair (and that of his predecessors, B. Mitchell and I. T. Ramsey) is called, 'Philosophy of the Christian Religion.' Also compare V. Brümmer, *What Are We Doing When We Pray?* (London 1984).

In so-doing, it is important to keep in mind that no purely neutral description of phenomena is possible, let alone of religion. Hermeneutical philosophy has convincingly demonstrated to what extent knowledge is linked to the context or horizon in which one lives.[2] Yet even when that is taken into account, there is still a difference between a study which tries as much as is possible to adduce philosophical arguments for a specific religious position, and a study which tries as much as is possible to glean its insights from the data of comparative studies in order to reach a theory of religion and truth in terms of those insights. The latter is the aspiration of this study.

1.4 General outline of this enquiry

We will attempt to draw several universally valid conclusions from a description of what is said about religious truth within religious traditions themselves. We must therefore peruse what people in various religious traditions have thought concerning the nature of religious knowledge, truth, and criteria. To this end, we will consult the *thinkers* of the traditions which we consider. The first of the many limitations which we have had to impose on ourselves in this enquiry surfaces here. There are many people within the various traditions who have reflected on the nature of their religious understanding, the methods by which insight is attained, and the criteria for assessing insights. We have limited ourselves to a few of the many great thinkers within these traditions. We have chosen to treat influential and representative thinkers. Since their reflection stands within the context of their respective religious traditions, we have tried to sketch their views within the context of that tradition by describing a few of the characteristic beliefs. The link existing between these beliefs and the concept of truth will appear in the description of the insights which they attained.

Another of the severe limitations which we have had to impose upon ourselves in this enquiry is to draw the line at a particular number of religious traditions which will be taken into account. We have chosen a pragmatic solution on this point. We will limit ourselves to the five world religions: Hinduism, Buddhism, Judaism, Christianity, and Islam. It is regrettable, but limitations must be imposed in order to reach conclusions. Many things have been left unmentioned in this study which could have been studied and treated; they have often been omitted out of sheer necessity. Although the author is painfully aware of these limitations it is impossible to avoid them. Restricting ourselves to a description of figures from the five traditions mentioned is not unusual, as comparison with the works of Wilfred Smith and the design of the Center for the Study of World Religions established by him shows. Comparison could also be made

---

[2] Cf. H. M. Vroom, *De Schrift Alleen?* (Kampen [2]1979), pp. 188ff.

with the choice of religious traditions primarily taught in continental European theology. Consequently, the framework chosen seemed responsible to us. Further account of why certain representative thinkers from these traditions have been described is offered in the chapters dealing with the various traditions. The selection of these thinkers has also been discussed with experts in the area of the religion concerned. Various chapters have been read by specialists in those traditions and grateful use has been made of their comments. They share no blame for the defects of this study, however.

This enquiry has been organized as follows: The **introductory Part** raises introductory issues: aspects of the concept of truth as these have emerged within Western philosophical discourse; a short exposition on the concept of religion; some of the outlines of discussion about religion and truth in the tradition of analytical philosophy; a number of views from the discussion on the European continent; and finally, a description of the positions of people who have occupied themselves extensively with the relationship between religious truth claims.

The **second Part** discusses the concept of truth within the five religious traditions mentioned, in five chapters. These five chapters have been structured in the following manner:

1) Introductory comments and preamble, along with a brief survey of the developments which have taken place — this to avoid speaking too monolithically of 'Buddhism,' etc.
2) A description of several central insights from these traditions.
3) A description of reflection on the concept of truth within the respective tradition; representative thinkers will be brought up here.
4) Views within the tradition on the plurality of religious insights.

In the **third, analytical Part** of the enquiry, we will try to garner the fruits of this study. Multiplicity in speaking about the truth of religion will be raised, as well as the role of knowledge in religion, the religious interpretation of the experiences which underpin religions, the universality and exclusivity of the traditions, and the issue of criteria for evaluating religious truth. Accordingly, we will sketch a theory of religion inasmuch as the cognitive aspect of religion is concerned. At the conclusion of this study we will return to the charter of the philosophy of religion as practised in this study.

1.5   The preconditions of this enquiry

To close this section (§ 1) we will examine the conditions for the possibility of this enquiry. The big question here is whether there is a 'something' called 'truth' which (a) is encountered in all these religious traditions (b) can be compared. One might also ask whether (c) the question of truth can be settled in an interreligious context.

The various currents of religious thought do not always have one and the same concept of truth. The 'truth' is not always localized in the same 'places.' By way of illustration we could cite the saying that in Judaism the truth is not a theory but is something which one must do. Sometimes one speaks of a true person, a true way, etc. People are not univocal in what type of 'reference' they have in mind when utilizing the concept of truth. We can express this notion as follows: People's concept of truth differs. There are still other complications. Much has been said within religious traditions about the conditions for the possibility of obtaining profound religious insight. Mention is often made of the moral qualities of the person who knows, and of susceptibility and preparation for receiving insight. Differences of opinion also prevail as to the prerequisites for the possibility of acquiring religious insight. On the basis of the foregoing, we can already ascertain that (c) the question of truth cannot be settled in an interreligious context in a simple way. A separate chapter will be devoted to the questions of assessment and criteria in the analytical part, Part 3. Our study can help to map out the field of meanings which are ascribed to the term 'religious truth.' In Chapter VIII we will distinguish between five ways of speaking about religious truth which occur in various traditions.

If it is true that religious traditions have divergent concepts of truth, how can we be sure that we are speaking about 'the same thing' when the 'truth' is spoken of in various traditions? To put it differently: Do *ĕmet, satya, alètheia,* and *ḥaqq* always connote 'truth'? This question resembles the basic question which continually confronts the phenomenology of religion: How do you know that when dealing with prayer, meditation, *ṣalāt,* etc., you are always dealing with one phenomenon, viz. 'prayer' (or 'worship')? Van der Leeuw defined a phenomenon with the familiar phrase: *was sich zeigt* 'what manifests itself,' i.e., to the investigator.[3] In response to this question as to the legitimacy of the classification of religious phenomena in a single category, one could ask with reason whether it is not the investigator himself who is establishing the categories, so that he conceptually maps out a pluralistic reality without being able to claim that what is thus being described is a true phenomenon.[4] Whatever may be the case here, in respect of 'truth' matters are in any event different. This is already apparent from the fact that in English the expression 'as it is' is a generally accepted definition for 'truth.' We will comment on this current definition below. We advance this common translation here of various concepts in different religions by 'as it is' and 'truth' to evince the communality of *the quest for truth.* This can be understood in terms of anthropology: People generally ask themselves whether what they think is true, just as all are familiar with the question of whether what they

---

[3] G. van der Leeuw, *Phänomenologie der Religion* (Tübingen 1933), p. 634.
[4] See R. D. Baird, *Category Formation in the History of Religions* (Den Haag 1971).

do is good. It is an anthropological fact that people evaluate and assess their knowledge, that they seek truth and discuss it with one another. Anyone who believes everything that occurs to him and everything that he is told does not live long and happily. People appraise their knowledge: they ask themselves what the nature of knowledge is and whether their own knowledge is correct. This phenomenon is encountered everywhere, religion included.

The fact that people speak of truth in respect of religion signifies that they appraise and assess, and indicate ways of reaching the truth. No matter how people may localize the truth, it appears that everywhere knowledge plays a role — regardless of whether it is thought that at a later stage such knowledge ought to be transcended. This is borne out by investigation. One could subsequently pose the question of whether it is possible to speak in a general way of religious truth. By the expressions 'religious truth' and 'truth and religion' we expressly do *not* mean anything like *the* religious truth. It is very well possible to have one's own thoughts about whether 'the religious truth' exists or not; arguments to corroborate an opinion on this matter will have to draw —at least partially— on detailed investigation of the beliefs and concepts of truth present in various religious traditions.

This study is a query of 'religion and truth.' The concept of truth will be investigated broadly. We can be brief with respect to the *concept of religion*. As is well known, many definitions of religion have been given. However not all of the elements mentioned in such definitions are immediately relevant to our enquiry. We are concerned in the first place with the cognitive aspect of religion. Common to the religions described is that all contend that people in the customary, earthly 'condition humaine' are lacking in insight and are in need of moral perfection. In religious traditions the concern is always for *genuine* reality, which is usually this empirical reality, but seen from a radically different *perspective*. The concern is for perfecting man and possibly the world, for happiness and salvation, for goodness and for the realization or the finding of a purpose. In this sense, to quote D. C. Mulder's definition, the concern of religion is with *a relationship to an other, decisive reality*.[5] What a religion or a current within a religion actually may say about the *nature* of that other reality (other than the one at hand) differs. This definition of religion

---

[5] D. C. Mulder, *Religie, Religies, Religiositeit* (Kampen 1973), p. 7; cf. Mulder, "Het Einde van de Religie?" *Rondom het Woord* 13 (1971): 294 ff., and "Mogelijkheden en Grenzen van een Fenomenologie der Religie," *Gereformeerd Theologisch Tijdschrift* 73 (1973): 34. The problem with this definition lies in the term 'other'; it would be more appropriate to say with respect to some traditions that religion is about this reality, but then seen from another perspective (i.e., such as śūnyatā or creation). On the occasion of defending my doctoral dissertation, I conveyed some of the difficulties with this definition in thesis XIX (see n. 2 above). If 'other' is interpreted as 'other than the reality normally experienced' (and precisely this is Mulder's intention), then this definition of religion is useful.

could therefore be called a *chameleon-like term*, describing phenomena which are not alike, but which do show family resemblances.[6] As in the whole of religious studies, an investigation of 'comparative religious epistemology' often runs across striking parallels and similarities on the one hand, but also across drastic differences on the other. The issue of the nature of religion is raised in passing on numerous occasions throughout this study. This enquiry, however, primarily addresses the question of *truth* in religion.

As to the question posed at the beginning of this section (§ 1.5), whether 'truth' is a 'something' which one encounters in all religions, we can answer that (a) religions do not have in common a kind of 'something' called 'truth,' but knowledge and insight and their evaluation do always play a role in religion. To pose the question of truth is human.

The second question asked (b) whether the 'concepts' of 'truth' present in various religions could be compared? The answer is that traditions lend content to their concept of 'truth' from within the context of their own tradition, so that they do not have entirely the same view on the *nature* and importance of religious knowledge.

In comparing the beliefs of different traditions, it is necessary to take into account differences regarding the nature and function of religious knowledge. We will examine these in detail. Since knowledge and evaluation of knowledge always play a role, however, concepts of truth are comparable. To what extent they are comparable must be shown by concrete investigation.

In concluding this introduction, we will add one last question here: Is it possible to comprehend the beliefs of other religions? This too is a precondition of this enquiry; one must have access to religious insights. This problem has been much discussed, as is well known. With reference to my extensive treatment published elsewhere of how to understand writings, a few remarks will suffice here.[7]

(1) In the first place, an understanding of other persons and writings is always a partial understanding. Understanding occurs in terms of and within a horizon of understanding in which one stands and lives; this 'horizon' is not a permanent given but is fluid.

(2) Secondly, understanding occurs in terms of one's own interest for the concern to which the text (or spoken word, or image) refers. Religion is a question of what will ultimately bring people well-being ('Heil') and salvation, and of the nature of reality, mankind, and the transcendant (however conceived). One can apprehend something of what stirs other people in their religion and of what they have experienced in terms of one's own interest for these concerns.

---

[6] See H. M. Vroom, "De Waarheid in het Geding," in *De Dialoog Kritisch Bezien: Studies over de Waarheidsvraag in de Dialoog met Gelovigen uit andere Kulturen,* ed. A. W. Musschenga (Baarn 1983), p. 46.

[7] See Vroom, *De Schrift Alleen?* pp. 188-202; 223 ff.

In our opinion this forms an adequate basis for this enquiry. The kinds of obstacles which people must overcome in order to attain profound religious insight will become apparent in the course of describing various concepts of truth. The insight of outsiders remains very limited and insufficient according to most religious currents. It is precisely for that reason that knowledge of various concepts of truth is of importance to any substantial philosophical or theological dialogue about religious beliefs.

§ 2   Basic aspects of the theory of truth

2.1   Introduction

In preparation for presenting the insights into truth in the various religious traditions, we will first present several highlights from the history of Western philosophy; we will subsequently give a summary of elements from the discussion about theories of truth; and finally, we will give a brief characterization of several philosophical views on truth.

Ever since Plato the concept of truth has been one of the central concepts in Western philosophy. For Plato truth is transcendental. People seek truth by thinking: truth is approached by thought. Truth is related to being itself, the highest Being, the One, the Good, the True, and the Beautiful. The yearning to contemplate the Truth is actually the quest for the Divine.[8] For Aristotle, by way of contrast truth does not abide beyond the visible world in the realm of ideas but in statements. Here is the root of the definition of truth which has been most influential in the history of Western philosophy: truth is the correspondence between thought and (the form of) things.[9] The views of Plato and Aristotle have both been very influential in the history of Western philosophy. For many thinkers the emphasis has come to rest on formulated knowledge, due in large measure to the modern emphasis on systematically acquired scientific knowledge. No matter how much people have thought about the structuring of knowledge by human reason and culture, the idea of correspondence between thought (or speech) and being was rarely called into question. Thus, in the *Critique of Pure Reason,* Kant writes concerning truth:

---

[8] Plato, *The Dialogues of Plato,* tr. B. Jowett (Oxford ⁴1953), II, 371 ff. (no. 504 ff.); I, 415 ff. (no. 65 ff.). Cf. C. J. de Vogel, *Plato* (Baarn 1968), p. 89; for later developments in Plato's thought, see pp. 112 f.; cf. also A. P. Bos, *Wetenschap en Zinervaring* (Amsterdam 1985), pp. 28 ff.

[9] Aristotle, *Über die Seele,* German translation by W. Theiler (Darmstadt ³1969), p. 62 (no. 431b/8); see L. B. Puntel, *Wahrheitstheorien in der neueren Philosophie* (Darmstadt 1978), p. 1, *n.* 1.

The nominal definition of truth, that it is the agreement of the cognition with its object, is granted. What is wanted is to know a general and safe criterion of the truth of any and every kind of knowledge.[10]

Kant here stands in the tradition of Thomas Aquinas' classic definition: truth is *adequatio rei et intellectus* (correspondence between the subject matter and the mind). This definition and the content given it by Thomas will be raised below. How much depth their conception harbours will appear in the sections on Thomas and Maimonides.[11] Kant assumes that agreement or *correspondence* exists in one way or another between cognition and what is known; against the backdrop of his reflections on the structuring of knowledge by human understanding and reason, he regards the chief question to be what the *criterion* for truth is.

One of the discoveries of the 19th century was the insight into the historicity of knowledge, its determination by time and culture. This insight was fundamental for later phenomenological philosophy on the European continent. In the later work of Wittgenstein, and in later analytical philosophy in England as well, the *connection of the meaning of statements to their context* (or 'language-game') was taken into account. Austin's definition of truth exhibits the impact of this development:

A statement is said to be true when the historic state of affairs to which it is correlated by the demonstrative conventions (the one to which it 'refers') is of the type with which the sentence used in making it is correlated by the descriptive conventions.[12]

The conventions have here taken the place of the permanent structure which Kant thought to discern in human cognition. A definition such as Austin's yields a problem for the philosophy of religion in that religious traditions, as we will see, are not satisfied by language conventions and common sense. Common sense was equally suspect to Martin Heidegger: People are 'generally and commonly inauthentic.' The truth is concealed. It must be re–vealed, as Heidegger described it in relation to the Greek word *alètheia*. Heidegger placed more emphasis on the event character of the truth in his later work.[13] The historicity and the intangible and normative transcendental character of the truth have also been underscored by H. -G. Gadamer in his analysis of the understanding of texts, as appears from the following quote:

---

10 Immanuel Kant, *Critique of Pure Reason*, tr. F. Max Müller (New York 1966), p. 48 (B:82).
11 On Maimonides, see below, Ch. V § 3.3; on Thomas, VI § 3.3.
12 J. L. Austin, "Truth," in *Truth*, ed. G. Pitcher (Englewood Cliffs, N.J. 1964), p. 22, and the discussion concerning this by D. W. Hamlyn, *The Theory of Knowledge* (London 1971), p. 133.
13 M. Heidegger, *Sein und Zeit* (Tübingen [11]1967), pp. 218 f.; "Vom Wesen der Wahrheit," in *Wegmarken* (Frankfurt 1967), esp. pp. 96 f.; cf. also Th. de Boer, "De Eindigheid van de Mens en de Oneindigheid van de Waarheid: De Geschiedenis van het Fenomenologisch Waarheidsbegrip van Brentano tot Levinas," in *De Eindige Mens: Essays over de Grenzen van het Menselijk Bestaan* (Bilthoven 1975), pp. 78 ff.

> In understanding we are drawn into an event of truth and arrive, as it were, too late, if we want to know what we ought to believe.[14]

Knowledge of truth always stands within the subject's horizon of understanding. On the other hand, knowledge is always knowledge of the subject-matter ('die Sache'), which retains its own value and normativity for the subject as the 'over against' of the subject. At the end of his description of the modern discussion of truth theory in Western philosophy, L. B. Puntel comes to the conclusion that the concept of truth always comprises two poles: the claim to *validity* and the articulation of the *matter*. The two poles are unmistakably what is known (in a certain context) and the subject (who claims to have knowledge). I have spoken elsewhere in this connection of the 'at once' character of the subjective and the objective moment of cognition: Cognition is always knowledge on the part of a person who knows, but it is simultaneously also knowledge of matters which retain their own independence with respect to the person(s) who knows.[15] Puntel says that whatever definition one may give, what is decisive is whether one does justice to both these poles. He himself gives the following definition of truth, wherein he first defines the truth of a statement and subsequently delineates both sides of the 'truth.'

> (1) Statement x is true $=_{def}$ the claim to validity made by statement x can be discursively integrated into a coherent whole.
> (2-1) Truth $=_{def}$ the coherence of the subject-matter which articulates itself in the mode of a discursively integrable claim to validity.
> (2-2) Truth $=_{def}$ the discursively integrable claim to validity which articulates the coherence of the subject-matter itself.[16]

On the one hand, one must take into account the immanent coherence of the matter known, and on the other, the coherence within the knowledge which one possesses. Another element in his definition is discursiveness. Given the comprehensive discussion of religious language usage, and given what is said in various religious traditions about the nature of religious insight (as we will see), one must ask oneself to what extent a definition of truth as *discursive truth* will do for religious knowledge. It is one of the most important objectives of our enquiry to achieve more clarity on this score.

These few fragments from the history of reflection on the concept of truth in Western philosophy will suffice here. In the remainder of this section we will give an overview of several elements of the concept of truth as they have played a role in recent discussion of truth. Acquaintance with these elements is serviceable for understanding nuances which religious epistemology also introduces.

---

[14] H. -G. Gadamer, *Wahrheit und Methode* (Tübingen ²1965), p. 465.

[15] See Vroom, *De Schrift Alleen?* pp. 28f., 269f.

[16] L. B. Puntel, *Wahrheitstheorien* (Darmstadt 1978), pp. 215f.

2.2 Key elements in theories of truth

In more recent discussion on the concept of truth it has been posited that the statement " 'p' is true," means no more than 'p'. 'P' is repeated with more stress; someone confirms that 'p' really is thus, but the meaning of 'p' does not thereby change;[17] otherwise the confirmation of the truth of statement 'p' would no longer refer to 'p', but would refer to 'q'. " 'P' is true" is conceived of as a confirming repetition of 'p' in this view. In answer to the question of when the word 'true' is used correctly, it has been said, by way of example, that: " 'New York is a large city' is true if and only if New York *is* a large city." The background for such a suggestion is formed by the demand for *correspondence* between assertion and fact. Such simple examples are in fact ill-suited to obtaining insight into the complexity of the concept of truth. We will indicate various elements of the theory of truth by extending an example. The discussion already obtains a somewhat broader character if one takes into account the fact that there is always a person who *claims* to have true knowledge: "A says to B that 'p' is true." A claims to possess a certain knowledge concerning a *matter* x, which is denoted by 'p'; p runs as follows, for instance: 'x is y'. We can therefore rewrite the last statement as follows: "A says to B that 'x is y' is true." If we rewrite the statement thus, then not only is the 'truth' of 'p' (i.e., x is y) at stake, but also the *truthfulness* of A. If one does not wish to separate the content of assertion 'p' (i.e., proposition p) from the communication between A and B, then one must distinguish more elements. We will summarize them:

a) A's *commitment*: A confirms 'p'.
b) The implicit presupposition that A has the *authority* to confirm 'p'.
c) The *personal knowledge* which A has of x.
d) The *provisional knowledge* which B has of x.
e) The *communication situation* wherein A says to B that 'p' is true.
f) The common knowledge which A and B have of the *language conventions* in which 'x', 'y', and 'p' obtain meaning.
g) The *context* in which A and B stand, wherein the elements mentioned possess a certain value.
h) The idea that 'p' really says something about x: the *correspondence* of p to x.
i) The expectation that A has formed a proper assessment of 'p' on the basis of relevant *criteria*.

---

[17] For what follows, see Hamlyn, *Theory of Knowledge*, pp. 126 ff.; cf. the reader on truth by G. Pitcher, *Truth*.

a) Commitment

Someone who says that " 'p' is true" arrogates a judgment. This is actually already the case when someone asserts 'p'. If someone explicitly confirms the truth of an assertion, 'p', he assumes more responsibility for it. What is misleading about *common sense* examples such as 'New York is a large city' is that the commitment and the responsibility of the speaker do not become apparent. Another example can make this clear. If someone declares before a court that C was in his presence on a certain evening (and, consequently, not in the presence of D), and someone else confirms that this assertion is true, then a personal *commitment* comes into play. If the assertion is untrue, then A has committed perjury; such a declaration could have implications for C and D. Communication normally takes place between people within a certain situation. There is a connection between what people say and what people (can) do. Therefore not only assertion 'p', but even more so the confirmation of 'p' implies that the speaker assumes responsibility for this assertion and is accountable to a certain degree for the consequences that the 'belief that p' could have. A person who speaks commits himself, particularly when he confirms the truth of a statement.

b) Authority

The confirmation of the truth of 'p' by A presupposes that A is in a position to confirm 'p'. Were a tourist in Amsterdam to ask someone: "Is this the right way to the Begijnhof?" and the other said, "yes" (in other words: "It is true that this is the right direction to the Begijnhof"), then the speaker lets it be known, by what he does in speaking, that he has the *authority* to confirm the correctness of 'p' ("this street leads to the Begijnhof"). In asking for confirmation of 'p', the concern is for accuracy; to formulate the situation more sharply: Are we accurate? Do we really know for sure? Whoever confirms 'p' implicitly claims the authority to confirm 'p'. That is why it can be painful to ask of someone who possesses a certain authority, when speaking of matters in which he is competent, whether what he says is indeed true. Dependence on the authority of others plays a greater role to the degree in which the topic falls within the province of specialization and is less generally accessible.

Confirmation of the truth of a statement presupposes in principle that the one person has more knowledge of the matter than the other. If B asks of A: "Is it true that God exists?" and A were to respond: "It is true that God exists," then it is assumed that A, due to a personal familiarity with the matter, is capable of confirming (or denying) the question. If a skeptic, C, comes along who says to A: "Is it really true that God exists?", then C casts doubt on A's knowledge, and thus on his authority to confirm the question without further ado. C demands grounds;

discussion could arise. As soon as the question of truth is raised between people, however, the *possibility* is accepted that one person may know something that the other does not. This also applies when a person does not believe what another asserts; such a person then disputes that the aforementioned possibility has been realized. The possibility that A has more knowledge of x than B has is logically presupposed in raising the question of whether 'p' is true. As we shall see, the issue of authority plays a major role in religious epistemology.

c) Personal knowledge

Someone who confirms that "'p' is true," implicitly claims the authority to confirm 'p'. Someone's familiarity with matter x, which is raised in 'p' ('x is y'), is presupposed. A must be acquainted with x because x is what we are dealing with. The manner in which A must know x depends on statement 'p'. To indicate the direction to the Begijnhof, for instance, a person need not have walked there himself; but he ought to have consciously seen a sign with 'Begijnhof' on it, or something of that nature. Authority to confirm a statement may be claimed only if one has personal knowledge of the matter concerned. In many situations it is not always possible for a person who has personal knowledge of a matter to make his knowledge fully explicit. Polanyi has used the expression 'personal knowledge' in connection with tacit components of knowledge incapable of being explicated.[18] Knowledge is always *someone's* knowledge; it is knowing within the context of personal commitment. This could be expressed as follows, with reference to Gadamer's view: Each human being has, in part, the same horizon of understanding as people from his time and culture, but each has his own personal horizon as well. People have much in common, but they also have their own experiences. Van Peursen likes to express this personal commitment as follows: Knowledge is relation; it arises and exists in a relation between the subject and the matter known.[19] As a result, knowledge concerning a matter is not wholly capable of being made explicit. Personal experience can, to a great extent, be put into words, but not entirely. There is always an element of *tacit knowing*, as Polanyi called it.[20]

---

[18] M. Polanyi, *Personal Knowledge: Towards a Post-Critical Philosophy* (London 1958), passim, see esp. pp. 300 ff., 311 f., 139.

[19] The expression 'relational concept of truth' is used in a Report by the Reformed Churches in the Netherlands on the nature of biblical authority, *God met ons* (Leusden 1981), Chapter 1. For the philosophy behind this expression, see C. A. van Peursen, *Wetenschappen en Werkelijkheid* (Kampen 1969); *De Opbouw van de Wetenschap* (Meppel 1980).

[20] Cf. Polanyi, *Personal Knowledge*, p. 86; compare among others M. Polanyi and H. Prosch, *Meaning* (Chicago 1975), pp. 34 f.

d) Provisional knowledge

Just as it is assumed that one party in a discussion about the truth of a statement give account of his knowledge of the matter, and that he confirm his statement regarding the matter, so it is assumed that the other party attaches importance to the truth of what is discussed. If B were to ask A: "Is 'p' true?", then B has a provisional relation to matter x. This provisional relation to x can be improved by knowledge of assertion 'p'. Coming back to the example given above, if B were to ask of A, "Is it true that this is the way to the Begijnhof?", then B has a provisional relation to the street in which he is walking, as well as to the Begijnhof. He desires that his hunch (that this is the way to the Begijnhof) be verified. Were B to ask of A: "Is it really true that God exists?", then B has a (provisional) idea of what is involved by the concept of 'god.' If people raise the question of truth, then it is thereby posited that they have a relation to the matter whereof they speak. In the example of the question as to God's existence, this can be either a relation to God or the theism of others. Such a relation is present in any normal conversation.

e) Communication

To confirm that 'p' is true is a certain form of communication between people. The question of whether a certain pronouncement is true is of a different order than the communication of facts. The question of truth indicates a meta-level. The conversational partner who asks, "Is 'p' true?" is asking for an additional confirmation of assertion 'p'. Other motives could be present in the demand for confirmation. It could be that someone doubts the truth of 'p'; it could be that 'p' has important implications for a person's conduct so that the conversational partner wants more certainty about 'p'. Were someone to say: "*Nirvāṇa* is a state of peace and bliss in which suffering is past," then the other would perhaps ask, before turning onto the long road which can lead to *nirvāṇa*: "Is it true that *nirvāṇa* is such a state?" The situation in which people speak to each other presupposes, certainly in the case of weightier subjects, a certain relation between the conversants which we could indicate by terms such as trust and obligation.[21] We shall see that many religious traditions contend that their insights must be expressed in such a manner that people can understand them at the level which those people have reached. In other words, the aim of communicating insight is also vital for the truth of its formulation. The truth is often regarded as relative or relational in this sense as well: A communicates insight to B by means of statements.

---

[21] Th. de Boer, "Hermeneutiek en Ideologiekritiek," *Wetenschap en Ideologiekritiek*, ed. H. Kunneman (Meppel 1978), pp. 114f.

f) Use of language

In Austin's definition, quoted in the previous sub-section (§ 2.1), reference was made to language conventions. Communication between A and B regarding x can succeed only if A and B have enough common language at their disposal. Statement 'p' must be sufficiently clear to B to bring something of matter x to light. In making the statement, 'x is y', the conversants must both think of matter x and ascribe predicate y to it. If people do not speak a common language they can still point out things. But then they still need certain conventions in order to be able to refer to them. It is not a requirement, however, that the conversants know all the meanings of words and language conventions. The requirement is only that they possess *sufficient* common language and knowledge to make something clear to one another. Not only language conventions are at issue in Austin's definition, but also conventions of denotation: If someone confirms, " 'p' is true," then it is presumed that he has made a careful appraisal and is competent in the matter. What is judged to be 'careful' depends on how people in a particular cultural context think and to what they are accustomed. A reservation has already been made in referring to conventions. The 'truth' is normally ascertained according to the conventions of a community. And yet the conventions do not ultimately dictate what is true. The situation is actually the reverse: priority lies not with the conventions but with the truth. If, for example, all the conventions in the world were to say that the sun revolves around the earth, then it still remains a fact —scientifically speaking— that the earth revolves around the sun; that is why the conventions had to be adapted to accommodate this fact within the whole of human knowledge. On the one hand, conventions do not have the last word; otherwise a 'revolution of scientific theory' would be excluded from the start.[22] On the other hand, a revision of existing knowledge can occur only if there is a certain link to existing knowledge. We will see that religious traditions are intent upon adapting current language usage to their subject matter, and to try to bring about a kind of 'revolution' in the 'conventional world-view.'

g) The context

We have already drawn attention to the situation wherein the question as to the truth of an assertion is posed. The context in which people discuss truth has yet more aspects.

(1) In the first place, the context plays a constitutive role in determining the meaning of statements. They have meaning only within a certain frame of reference, a certain horizon of understanding, a 'language-game,' world-view, or whatever one may call it. Setting aside the nuances which various thinkers intended to introduce by using these terms (and

---

[22] Th. S. Kuhn, *The Structure of Scientific Revolutions* (Chicago ²1970), pp. 205 f.

the differences among them), it could be stated that it is an accepted insight (by many) that experiences are 'theory-laden,' and that the meaning of statements is determined by their context.[23]

(2) Second, the context is formed not only by ideas about the world, etc., but also by collective patterns of action and by 'forms of life' — as Wittgenstein expressed it. This has been emphasized in constructivist views on the nature of scientific practice, for example by Holzkamp in the very title of his study, *Science as a Form of Action*.[24] Van Peursen states that scientific endeavour belongs to the category of human action.[25] Brümmer also connects the nature of truth to human action: True statements indicate possibilities for action.[26] The examples are familiar enough: The meaning of the sentence, "The door is open," depends on the situation; it could indicate that there is a draught, but could also urge someone's earlier than anticipated departure. Observations are not made in complete separation from action and experience.

(3) Third, the relationship between knowledge and action implies that there are interests at stake — a fact that has been pointed up in Neo-Marxism. Why the question of truth is posed at certain junctures but not at others can indeed be answered in large measure by referring to the interests of people. What is here understood by interests is that in which those concerned (think they) have an interest, regardless of whether that interest is legitimate, fancied, or real. Religions, as we shall see, usually regard people's erroneous interests as obstacles which prevent them from facing the truth.

h) Correspondence

The notion of correspondence brings us to the topics which are central to the theory of truth. Truth theory belongs to the area of epistemology. In truth theory the manner in which knowledge is related to reality is questioned — whether it is believed that true knowledge is in some way knowledge of reality, or whether it is thought that knowledge is a construct of the human mind. In this study, we will proceed from the notion that true knowledge is in some way knowledge of reality, even though the constructive, culturally determined aspect of discursive knowledge must be taken into account. Even after taking into account what many people have written regarding horizons of understanding, frames of reference, world-views, etc., the idea of an 'object side' to reality persists nonetheless — a 'resistance' in things, the 'matter' which one knows, which is normative for knowledge.

---

[23] J. P. M. Geurts, *Feit en Theorie* (Assen 1975), pp. 105 ff.; 84 ff.; cf. Van Peursen, *Wetenschappen en Werkelijkheid*, p. 38.

[24] Kl. Holzkamp, *Wissenschaft als Handlung* (Berlijn 1968).

[25] Van Peursen, *De Opbouw van de Wetenschap*, pp. 135 f.

[26] See below, Ch. II § 2.1.

This aspect of 'being over against' is what the correspondence theory is all about. The term 'correspondence' suggests a simple one-to-one relation between a statement and the thing described. Such a simple correspondence is out of the question. Nor can statements be isolated from the context of people making them; a *hermeneusis* of statements is indispensable in determining what they refer to. The sheer fact that statements are understood in terms of the matter described —even though no thing can ever be known as uninterpreted fact— signifies that there remains nonetheless the normativity for knowledge in the reality known. This moment of reference to the permanent that is known cannot be lacking, even if one has long ago left the picture theory of language behind.[27] This 'referring to' can be expressed by the term correspondence.

It was precisely in order to introduce some nuance to the theory of correspondence that it was necessary to mention a number of other aspects of speaking about the truth before raising the concept of correspondence. Statements about truth always occur in the broader context of human action and experience.

i) Criteria

If someone confirms that assertion 'p' is true, one might expect, as we have seen, that he has first made a proper assessment of 'p' according to generally accepted standards. The criteria often mentioned in connection with scientific statements are coherence, compatibility, intersubjective verifiability, and empirical fit.

Coherence demands that statements be plausibly related to other statements on the same subject; compatibility demands that statements in one sector of human knowledge not conflict with those from others; intersubjective verifiability demands that others (besides the speaker or author) be able to test the research and reasoning, since true statements are universally valid, in principle. We have added empirical fit to this series, because it is essential for true knowledge that it applies to reality and springs from experience. The demand for empirical fit is in agreement with what we have written about correspondence.

In terms of the study of religion, much discussion has focussed on the applicability of these criteria. Many questions arise here which we will scrutinize in the follow-up to our expositions in Part 2, where we will give a description of concepts of truth in various religious traditions. Chapter XI has been set aside for the question of criteria valid for religious truth.

---

[27] See L. Wittgenstein, *Philosophische Untersuchungen* (Oxford ³1968), esp. no. 241 f.; cf. below, Ch. II § 1.1.

§ 3   Some leading theories of truth

As a follow-up to our exposition of basic elements in the discussion of the theory of truth —broadly conceived— we will now characterize several of the more prominent Western theories of truth.

3.1   The correspondence theory

As we have just indicated, the term correspondence refers to an agreement between knowledge and reality. The correspondence theory has ancient roots. They stem from the notion of *adequatio intellectus ad rem* (correspondence of mind to matter). This theory is adumbrated by the common sense idea of truth as 'knowledge of things as they are,' or more briefly, 'as it is.'

So many qualifications are usually introduced with respect to the term correspondence that the term is almost too naive to be used. Later on we shall see that it is precisely these qualifications that play a role in religious epistemology. Let us give a single example to illustrate the limitations of the correspondence theory: The statement, 'water is wet,' does not portray water 'in itself,' but a human experience of water. 'Water is H_2O' indicates a structure of water molecules which does not present itself 'in itself,' but in chemical analysis. It is generally accepted in the philosophy of science that observations are at least partially determined by theory; and it is largely accepted in Western hermeneutics and epistemology that neither uninterpreted experience nor neutral, culturally independent articulation of experience exist.

Insights related to a philosophy of life present yet another problem in connection with the correspondence theory of truth. World and life views attempt to interpret reality according to its deepest nature. Often the intent, on the one hand, is to articulate how things *really* are; on the other hand, interpretation tends to occur in terms of a larger context. It is therefore a particular problem for philosophy, religion, and (other) views of life that they are not so much concerned with as exact a description of the details of scientific investigation as possible, but their concern is for a telling characterization of what is essential to man and the world. The metaphorical character of language must be taken into account here.[28] How can one continue to speak in such cases of giving a *description* of reality which corresponds in one way or another to reality? Some people have relinquished the correspondence theory due to such critical questioning. They regard the notion of 'correspondence' as too vague a term to maintain. The term nevertheless makes it plain that *a claim is being made to insight into reality*. Writing with reference to Strasser, De Boer says, "And yet, that which is not without us is not yet

---

[28] Cf. J. J. van Es, *Spreken over God: Letterlijk of Figuurlijk?* (Amsterdam 1979).

by us."[29] The aim of statements, in a very qualified manner, is knowledge of reality as it really is in the deepest sense. We therefore see no overruling objection to maintaining the term correspondence theory, albeit within the framework of a very sophisticated conception. We shall see, however, that some religious currents want to transcend discursive knowledge altogether because it does not, in their view, conform to reality.

3.2 The coherence theory

As a result of the problems surrounding the correspondence theory truth has sometimes been defined as the coherence of statements. This view can be encountered in epistemological idealism (compare Berkeley's *esse est percipi*) and with some positivists (who abandoned the connection between coherent scientific theories and reality).

Problems arise here as well. The notion of coherence is no more entirely lucid than that of correspondence. If human knowledge ought to form a coherent whole, in what fashion must the various sectors of knowledge be related? How is knowledge concerning hormones coherent with knowledge of gravity? Why should it be that man's knowledge attains a coherent totality? Is it imparted by virtue of the nature of human cognition? Such are the many questions which could be raised.

Critics of the coherence theory often presume that the demand that theories be consistent issues from the experience that reality itself manifests order and relationship.[30] In reply, however, one could comment that coherence is in effect not a description of the nature of truth but a criterion to ascertain the truth of statements. We will return to this topic below.[31]

3.3 Truth as intersubjectivity

Still others have defined truth in terms of knowledge concerning which inter-subjective agreement exists. We have already quoted Austin's definition. Hamlyn more or less concurs with this in his reflections on truth.[32] No matter what one might further wish to add about the relation between fact and reality, knowledge cannot be explained without reference to its factuality. Knowledge of factuality, however, is intersubjectively and culturally determined. The world is a *collective world*. That is why agreement between people is the touchstone of a statements's truth.

The strong point of this conception is that it pays heed to factuality as well as to the cultural, constructive component in knowledge. The problem

---

29 Th. de Boer, "De Eindigheid van de Mens en de Oneindigheid van de Waarheid," p. 81; cf. S. Strasser, *Fenomenologie en Empirische Menskunde* (Arnhem 1962), p. 86; 2nd edn. (1965), p. 89.

30 Thus Pannenberg, for instance; see below, Ch. II § 2.3.

31 We will return to this later in Ch. XI § 2.2.

32 Hamlyn, *Theory of Knowledge*, p. 135.

with the intersubjective theory, however, is that it in fact offers a *common sense* theory which basically glosses over man's personal commitment to his knowledge concerning other people, nature, and the world. If it were said, for example, that love and compassion are prerequisites for knowledge, then personal, committed knowledge has an edge on inter-subjective, more or less impersonal knowledge. If, moreover, one desires to see things in the larger context in which they stand, or to designate them according to their deepest nature, then one cannot adopt the demand for intersubjective agreement without further qualification. The reverse side to such reservations regarding intersubjective validation is that without being answerable to others and without intersubjective substantiation, one can state anything at all.

3.4 A pragmatic view of truth

The so-called pragmatic theory states that truth consists in the circumstance that knowledge squares either with the practice of the totality of scientific investigation, or with practical life. The difficulty of this conception comes to light soon enough when pause is taken to recall that the whole question of what truth is arises precisely because people do not always agree with one another.[33] It is precisely at the point at which they no longer agree with one another that people differ about what fits in with the whole of scientific theory, about what 'works,' and about what valid knowledge is. Often something does not work at all, or at least not satisfactorily. The question regarding what works is whether it works *well* and is *justifiable*; the question is also which insights are true regardless of human conduct. Brümmer expresses this criticism as follows: It is not permitted to make the truth relative to current scientific opinion, nor to the individual human being who experiences life as meaningful seen in a particular manner, nor to the problems which the investigator poses.[34] At stake is reality as it *really* is.

A short exploration of several of the better known modern theories of truth in the Western world must suffice here. In the rest of this enquiry we will make acquaintance with distinctively different concepts. We will not delve into the manifold issues here. Numerous matters will be brought up later in connection with religious epistemology. It seems appropriate in a study about religion and truth, however, to mention several modern theories by way of introduction to the problematic. We shall see how some of the themes broached above, such as commitment, authority, and the defectiveness of common sense, resurface time and again in religious epistemology.

---

[33] See H. M. Vroom, "Geloofswaarheid als Kennis van de Weg," in *Geloofsmanieren*, ed. J. M. Vlijm (Kampen 1981), p. 210.

[34] V. Brümmer, *Wijsgerige Begripsanalyse* (Kampen 1975), p. 173 (cf. *Theology and Philosophical Inquiry* [London 1981], pp. 177f., 181).

Chapter II

The Debate over 'Religious Truth' in Western Philosophy

In this introductory Part of our enquiry, we will be presenting a number of conceptions regarding 'religion and truth.' In the first section (§ 1, below) we will direct our attention to the tradition of analytical philosophy, a rather motley aggregate of views. The classical representatives from this school have been presented often: the early Wittgenstein, Sir Alfred Ayer, and Braithwaite. The post-war discussion has been influenced in significant part by the later Wittgenstein; D. Z. Phillips applied his insights to the philosophy of religion. We will briefly mention a few more names from that continuing discussion.

In § 2 we will present the 'continental' views of Brümmer, who seeks to link up with analytical philosophy, and of Pannenberg and Kuitert, who develop a model for argumentative theology.

In § 3 the voices of several people will be heard who have approached the questions surrounding 'religion and truth' in terms of religious studies and the philosophy of religion: William A. Christian, Wilfred C. Smith, John Hick, Donald Wiebe, and Shivesh Ch. Thakur.

One could ask to what extent such conceptions transcend partiality. Were the ideas of these authors developed with the variegated world of religious traditions in mind? Or do they —mostly from their own Western, Christian or post-Christian points of view— in effect prescribe for religious currents how things should be according to their own conviction? On what grounds and with what argumentative force? These and other questions were what gave rise to a more penetrating investigation of what is said about truth in the religious traditions themselves. In § 4 we will summarize the most prominent of the questions under discussion. In the second, descriptive Part of this study we will be gathering material in the hope of making headway with these issues in the third, analytical Part.

§ 1 The debate in analytical philosophy

1.1 The position assigned to religion
in early analytical philosophy

From 1900 onwards, idealistic philosophy in England was slowly but surely displaced by the common sense philosophy of G. E. Moore and by logical atomism.[1] An attempt was made to establish what knowledge was certain. In the *Tractatus,* Wittgenstein submitted the idea that names refer to elementary states of affairs. In the names of things, language finds its foundation in reality.[2] In order to say something about the state of reality, one must relate the names of things to elementary propositions.[3] More complex statements can then be derived from combinations of atomistic statements. These owe their cognitive meaning entirely to the atomistic statements from which they have been derived.[4] No knowledge exists, therefore, of things which cannot be immediately referred to in experience. It is impossible to speak about them meaningfully. This must not be so construed that Wittgenstein regarded as unimportant those domains of life about which knowledge was impossible. On the contrary, it has been pointed out that the province of the ineffable was of utmost importance to Wittgenstein. Nuchelmans states that there can be no doubt that one of Wittgenstein's chief incentives was to open up the outlook on the transcendent side to æsthetics, ethics, and religion.[5] It is in this light that the last paragraph of the *Tractatus* may be understood: "Wovon man nicht sprechen kan, darüber muss man schweigen." (Whereof one cannot speak one must be silent.) It is of no little significance that this forms an independent paragraph: the remainder cannot be meaningfully said. In this way Wittgenstein allows room for the inarticulable, the mystical, which *manifests* itself.[6]

Logical positivism established itself in the following years. Typical for Wittgenstein, whose own conception otherwise differed from that of the logical positivists, is the statement: "Einen Satz verstehen, heißt, wissen was der Fall ist, wenn er wahr ist."[7] (Understanding a statement means knowing what the case is, if it is true.) The logical positivists take this statement to mean that the *meaning* of a statement consists in the

---

[1] Cf. G. J. Warnock, *English Philosophy Since 1900* (London ²1969), pp. 1 ff.

[2] G. Nuchelmans, *Overzicht van de Analytische Wijsbegeerte* (Utrecht 1969), p. 113.

[3] *Ibid,* pp. 112 f.

[4] *Ibid,* pp. 121, 119.

[5] *Ibid,* pp. 124 f. See also L. Wittgenstein, *Notebooks 1914–1916,* eds. G. H. von Wright and G. E. M. Anscombe (Oxford ²1979), pp. 74 f.; cf. W. D. Hudson, *Wittgenstein and Religious Belief* (London 1975), esp. pp. 86 ff.

[6] L. Wittgenstein, *Tractatus Logico-Philosophicus* (1921; rpt. London ³1966), § 7; cf. § 6.522.

[7] Wittgenstein, *Tractatus,* § 4. 024; cf. Nuchelmans, p. 142; Hudson, pp. 87, 116.

manner in which it is verified.[8] We will limit ourselves to the view of Ayer in his early work, *Language, Truth, and Logic* (1936). Ayer construes the theory of truth as the furnishing of criteria. In the statement, " 'p' is true," 'is true' is logically superfluous.[9] The truth of a proposition is determined by reference to sense experience:

> I adopt what may be called a modified verification principle. For I require of an empirical hypothesis, not indeed that it should be conclusively verifiable, but that some possible sense-experience should be relevant to the determination of its truth or falsehood. If a putative proposition fails to satisfy this principle, and it is not a tautology, then I hold that it is metaphysical, and that being metaphysical, it is neither true nor false but literally senseless.[10]

Statements about God do not satisfy the verification principle because they are not based on empirical experience of God. Statements about God are therefore without meaning. Ayer points to the distinction between his view, and atheism and agnosticism. An atheist denies the assertion that God exists; his mistake is that the statement 'God exists' is not an assertion, and can therefore be neither confirmed nor denied. The same applies to the agnostic who, according to Ayer, thinks that the existence of God is possible but that there is no good reason to believe that he either does or does not exist. Ayer's own view is that all statements about God are meaningless; they contain neither propositions nor knowledge.[11] If someone were to assert that one experiences God in a purely mystical experience, without being able to verbalize that experience in comprehensible terms, then one in effect admits, according to Ayer, that it is impossible for a sentence both to be about God and to be meaningful.[12] Ayer thus gave a relatively simple account of religious truth. His view on the assessment of valid knowledge does not admit of the notion that religion is concerned with knowledge. These and similar such views have not been without repercussions in Anglo-Saxon philosophy. Sundry attempts have been made to show that religious statements indeed cannot be empirically tested and yet nevertheless are not devoid of meaning. A familiar example of such a posture is that of Braithwaite. Empirical statements derive their meaning from the fact that they can be tested empirically. The meaning of other statements is not empirical. Whatever meaning they do have must then be inferred from *the function* which they fulfill. For empirical thinkers, then, the core of the problem regarding the nature of religious belief is to explain how a person *uses* religious

---

[8] Nuchelmans, p. 142; cf. Hudson, pp. 117ff.
[9] A. J. Ayer, *Language, Truth, and Logic* (1936; rpt. Harmondsworth 1972), p. 117.
[10] *Ibid*, p. 41.
[11] *Ibid*, p. 153.
[12] *Ibid*, pp. 155ff.

statements.[13] According to Braithwaite's understanding, religious assertions are used as recommendations for moral action. The intention of acting in a certain way is expressed with the aid of moral statements.[14] Religious statements give expression to such moral intentions. By sorting out which principles of behaviour people regard as being implied by their faith, one can trace which intentions they express in their religion.[15] Religious people live by their stories. By religious *story*, Braithwaite understands "... a proposition or a set of propositions which are straightforwardly empirical propositions capable of empirical test and which are thought of by the religious man in connection with his resolution to follow the way of life advocated by his religion."[16] Braithwaite assumes that the manner of life in various religious currents is not different. Divergent religious stories can express the same moral outlook:

> On the assumption that the ways of life advocated by Christianity and by Buddhism are essentially the same, it will be the fact that the intention to follow this way of life is associated in the mind of a Christian with thinking of one set of stories (the Christian stories) while it is associated in the mind of a Buddhist with thinking of another set of stories (the Buddhist stories) which enable a Christian assertion to be distinguished from a Buddhist one.[17]

We will leave Braithwaite's identification of the Buddhist and the Christian way of life for what it is. The religious traditions have the same essential meaning as their stories, according to him; their meaning stands free of any empirical reference which they could have were one (wrongly) to take them literally. The stories have a psychological and causal function; they influence one's life. A person can resist certain natural inclinations by conducting his life according to certain stories.[18] For Braithwaite it is not imperative that the person who tells and 'uses' such stories believe that they entail true affirmations about reality.[19] Braithwaite notes in this context that he uses the term *story* where others who intend the same thing use terms such as allegory, fable, tale, and myth.

His view does not stand on its own. Many discussions have taken place about whether religious stories regarding the hearing of prayers, the nearness of God, resurrection of the dead, heaven and hell, and the last judgment are not myths which serve to regulate life after a certain

---

[13] R. B. Braithwaite, "An Empiricist's View of the Nature of Religious Belief," in *The Philosophy of Religion*, ed. B. Mitchell (Oxford 1971), pp. 77f.
[14] *Ibid*, p. 78.
[15] *Ibid*, p. 81.
[16] *Ibid*, p. 84.
[17] *Ibid*, p. 84.
[18] *Ibid*, p. 86.
[19] *Ibid*, pp. 85 f.

fashion.[20] On the European continent, Bultmann distanced himself from pretty near the whole cognitive content of the Bible; what remained was a most radical transition from inauthentic to authentic existence: not 'what,' but 'that.' Faith does not refer to beliefs, according to him, but to the manner in which one takes a stance in life.[21] The view articulated by Braithwaite in 1955 has served as a model for a whole series of people who accept that cognitive statements ought to be empirically testable, and who sought the meaning of religious statements not in knowledge, but in morality, or sometimes in how reality is experienced.

This line of thought was reinforced by the publication of works written by Wittgenstein after the *Tractatus*. There he proffers a different view on knowledge and language usage than previously given. This view led to an elaborate debate within the philosophy of religion.

In the *Philosophical Investigations*, Wittgenstein no longer traces the meaning of statements from names and atomistic statements, but describes their meaning from the perspective of the function which language has in people's lives. He utilized the notion of language-game, as is well known:

> Here the term 'language-*game*' is meant to bring into prominence the fact that the *speaking* of language is part of an activity, or a form of life.[22]

Wittgenstein gives examples of how the analysis of language-games can, in his view, help to rid the world of philosophical problems which originate from a confusion of language-games. The notion of language-games is not completely clear.[23] With respect to religion, one of the points on which there are differing opinions is whether one should think in terms of smaller units within religion —such as prayer, singing, speaking— in conjunction with language-games, or whether whole religious traditions should be thought of as separate language-games. Wittgenstein does not address these questions, although in his delineation of 'language-game' he does give as an example: asking, thanking, cursing, greeting, praying.

In 1966 Cyrel Barrett provided an edition of lectures which Wittgenstein had held for a small group of students. From students' notes he reconstructed Wittgenstein's lectures and the ensuing discussions. Among the material included are classes about religious belief from 1938 or thereabouts. In the respective lecture, Wittgenstein speaks of belief —one of his examples is belief in the last judgment— as a *picture* which regulates

---

[20] As dealt with at the VIth European Conference on the Philosophy of Religion, Hatfield College, Durham, 31st August 1986, in papers by Cyril Barrett and Reijo Työrinoja.

[21] R. Bultmann, "Zum Problem der Entmythologisierung," in *Kerygma und Mythos*, II, ed. H. W. Bartsch (Hamburg 1952), pp. 179-208; see H. M. Vroom, *Naar Letter en Geest* (Kampen 1981), pp. 52f.

[22] L. Wittgenstein, *Philosophische Untersuchungen* (1953; Oxford [3]1968), no. 23.

[23] Cf. H. M. Vroom, *De Schrift Alleen?* pp. 117f.

life.[24] Somebody who believes in the last judgment has another *picture* than somebody else. Several statements of Wittgenstein follow which contain important implications for the issue of the relationship between religious traditions, for Wittgenstein delves into the question of whether one can compare different beliefs, and whether the one 'belief' contradicts the other.

> Suppose someone is ill and he says: "This is a punishment," and I say: "If I'm ill, I don't think of punishment at all." If you say: "Do you believe the opposite?" —you can call it believing the opposite, but it is entirely different from what we would normally call believing the opposite.
>
> I think differently, in a different way. I say different things to myself. I have different pictures.
>
> It is this way: if someone said: "Wittgenstein, you don't take illness as punishment, so what do you believe?" —I'd say: "I don't have any thoughts of punishment." ...
>
> What we call believing in a Judgement Day or not believing in a Judgement Day —The expression of belief may play an absolute minor role.
>
> If you ask me whether or not I believe in a Judgment Day, in the sense which religious people have belief in it, I wouldn't say: "No. I don't believe there will be such a thing." ...
>
> I can't say. I can't contradict that person.
>
> In one sense, I understand all he says —the English words "God," "separate," etc. I understand. I could say: "I don't believe in this," and this would be true, meaning I haven't got these thoughts or anything that hangs together with them. But not that I could contradict the thing.
>
> You might say: "Well, if you can't contradict him, that means you don't understand him. If you did understand him, then you might." That again is Greek to me. My normal technique of language leaves me. I don't know whether to say they understand one another or not. ...
>
> The point is that if there were evidence, this would in fact destroy the whole business.[25]

Several issues emerge in this passage:

(1) The possibility of understanding people with another religious world-picture.

(2) The question whether contradiction between religious world-pictures is possible.

(3) The question of the demonstrability of world-pictures.

Regarding the first issue, understanding people with another world-picture, Wittgenstein thinks that we are able to understand each other in a certain sense, but in another sense are not. The essence —living within a world-picture— remains remote to our understanding. Perhaps it can be put thus: according to Wittgenstein, one can understand the words, but not the essence: living and experiencing in accordance with such a world-picture. His view on the second point issues from this. Contradiction may exist at the level of beliefs; but concerning the essence —living with and within such a world-picture— it is not a question of contradiction but of

---

[24] L. Wittgenstein, *Lectures and Conversations on Aesthetics, Psychology, and Religious Belief*, ed. Cyril Barrett (1966; rpt. Oxford 1970), p. 54; cf. Hudson, *Wittgenstein*, pp. 165 ff.

[25] Wittgenstein, *Lectures*, pp. 55 f.

living and experiencing *differently*. People have different horizons in which things come into view in a different light. Thus one could understand what Wittgenstein meant by the expression, "My normal technique of language leaves me." The third point is the *evidence* for *beliefs*. Wittgenstein's idea is that evidence is valid only within a world-picture (aside from the issue of whether a religion is a world-picture). He worked this out in his later notes about *certainty*. A world-picture is the basis for what counts as evidence; it has not itself been founded on evidence. This implies that 'the whole business' of verification, argumentation, and reflection on a world-picture takes place within that world-picture and is thus of *necessity* never neutral and cannot be completely intersubjective. The concept of truth doesn't exist on its own either, but functions within language-games.[26] Within a world-picture some insights and 'facts' are regulative and foundational; the world-picture cannot itself be further grounded. "Es muss uns etwas als Grundlage gelehrt werden." (It is inevitable that we be taught something as Foundation.)[27] Something similar holds true for a religious picture as well. Religious beliefs regulate life; they cannot be proven; they describe a way of living and experiencing.[28] Työrinoja takes this to mean that belief in a last judgment does not imply that the believer believes in the last judgment as a future event, but does accept it as a regulative idea.[29]

Many questions can be posed regarding the view Wittgenstein presents. If one enters further into this discussion one encounters the nuances of Wittgenstein interpretation. Within the context of this study, it will suffice to show the kind of questions raised by Wittgenstein. These questions were discussed in the decennia after his death time and again. A well-known reputedly 'Wittgensteinian' position is that taken by Derek Z. Phillips. We will deal with his work in somewhat more detail.

1.2 The view of Derek Phillips

Continuing in Wittgenstein's tradition, Phillips wanted to offer another approach to religion than customary in an important current of Anglo-Saxon philosophy of religion. We have seen how people such as Ayer and Braithwaite contended that beliefs are not cognitive. Theistic thinkers tried to construct arguments to make it plausible that belief really is about God. Reasons to believe are then spoken of. By arguing thus, one forgets the proper nature of religion, according to Phillips. The basic error being made is that religion is confused in this manner with the rest

---

[26] J. H. Gill, "Wittgenstein's Concept of Truth," *International Philosophical Quarterly* 6 (1966): 74.

[27] L. Wittgenstein, *Über Gewissheit* (Frankfurt 1971), no. 449.

[28] L. Wittgenstein, *Culture and Value* (1937; rpt. Oxford 1980), p. 29; R. Työrinoja, "The Last Judgment: Myth or Prediction...," VIth Eur. Conf. Phil. of Rel, August '86, p. 5 (unpublished).

[29] Työrinoja, pp. 6f.

of human knowledge. Religious belief then in(de-)clines towards a kind of hypothetical knowledge about special facts, such as the soul, immortality, and God.[30] As a matter of fact, the concern in religion is not with factual knowledge, not with the *how* of each thing by itself, but with the fact *that* they exist.[31] Religion does not concern itself with a part of life but with life itself. Phillips adopts certain of Wittgenstein's notions to make this clear: language-game, world-picture, and forms of life.

In *The Concept of Prayer* Phillips states that religious traditions are distinct from all other language-games; they have their own rules. These rules have an intrinsic relation to their context, the religious language-game.[32] One cannot, therefore, justify the religious language-game by referring to what falls outside of its domain without detracting from the absolute character of religion.[33] Phillips introduced a few nuances in response to criticism of his conception. A world view is a way of seeing the world. Religion has significance for an appreciation of the whole of life; religion determines one's attitude with respect to living and experiencing events. Religion does respect certain facts; a religion may accordingly not explain away the reality of suffering and evil.[34] In a later work, *Religion without Explanation,* Phillips still uses the concept of language-game; more often he speaks of a world-picture, a term borrowed from Wittgenstein's *On Certainty.* One of the functions of a world-picture is that it yields criteria which determine what may be said and done within a religious tradition.[35]

Phillips gives a theory of religion. He arrives at a certain view of what religion *really* is. How does he know what right faith is? According to Phillips, it is the task of philosophy (of religion) to analyze what the nature of faith is. Philosophy of religion does not yield a theological deliberation on faith (inasmuch as that is possible), but a philosophical one. The philosopher does not describe what people actually believe; that is done by the 'science of religion.' Philosophy tries to understand right faith, and to thus find an answer to the philosophical questions which can be asked regarding faith.[36]

What is genuine faith? How does philosophy decide which faith is *true* faith? Phillips contends that it becomes clear from analysis of faith that

---

[30] D. Z. Phillips, *The Concept of Prayer* (London ²1968), p. 13; *Religion Without Explanation* (Oxford 1976), pp. 163 ff. For the description of Phillips' views, I owe much to papers by Chris de Valk.

[31] Phillips, *Concept of Prayer,* p. 102, with reference to the *Tractatus,* § 6. 44, cf. p. 130.

[32] Phillips, *Concept of Prayer,* p. 22; cf. also *Without Explanation,* pp. 143, 145 ff.

[33] D. Z. Phillips, *Faith and Philosophical Enquiry* (London 1970), p. 108.

[34] Phillips, *Faith and Enquiry,* pp. 97 ff.

[35] *Ibid,* pp. 7, 11 f., 90, 132; A. Keightley, *Wittgenstein, Grammar, and God* (London 1976), p. 80, cf. p. 78.

[36] Phillips, *Faith and Enquiry,* pp. 67 ff.; cf. *Concept of Prayer,* pp. 1 ff.; *Without Explanation,* pp. 188 f.

faith such as Kierkegaard and Simone Weil described is genuine and true.[37] It might not be orthodox faith, he comments in reference to Simone Weil, but the authenticity is plain.[38] Phillips objects to orthodox-dogmatical belief because it represents God as (a) being within the world. True faith is the subjective, unconditional surrender in faith and love to God "in *whatever* is the case."[39] This holds consequences for his view of prayer, for example. Phillips rejects the prayer of supplication as superstition. True prayer is praise, the unconditional *worship* of God. One sees what faith is in the life in which it *functions,* in commitment. Faith is not subscribing to a theory, but it is loving God.[40]

Although he does not clearly define it, the notion of language-game is apparently very important to Phillips. In answer to criticism that he has not clearly delimited the boundaries of the religious language-game, Phillips relates the story of someone who once tried to establish the boundary between day and night, and, unsuccessful, thereupon contended that day and night are no different.[41] The boundaries are vague; one can nonetheless speak of the independence of religion. Religion makes it possible to deal with reality in a way that would be impossible without religion. A religious tradition is a 'family of language-games' which itself determines criteria for the meaningfulness of its statements and practices.[42] The meaning of sentences and words must be established within this language-game.

Phillips uses the notion of world-picture more than that of language-game, in his later work.[43] This argues in favour of also taking what he writes about language-games as being meant to refer to the religious world-picture as whole. Phillips writes about 'inter-religious relations' only in passing. The reproach that doctrinal contradictions between religions deal his theory a death blow has been levelled against Phillips, it being supposed that he could neither explain them nor indicate how they should be dealt with.[44] There is no prima facie certainty that religions do contradict one another, however, according to Phillips, nor that they should discuss their beliefs among each other. Whether this is true or not must become apparent from further investigation of those beliefs. If certain religions have enough in common, then there is a basis for discussion. If not, then the basis for such a discussion is lacking.[45] Are we

---

37 Phillips, *Concept of Prayer*, pp. 158 ff.; cf. pp. 101 ff., 109 f.; *Faith and Enquiry*, pp. 204 ff.
38 Phillips, *Concept of Prayer*, p. 156; *Faith and Enquiry*, p. 245.
39 Phillips, *Concept of Prayer*, pp. 130, 102.
40 Phillips, *Concept of Prayer*, pp. 126 ff.; *Faith and Enquiry*, pp. 26, 29, 32; *Without Explanation*, pp. 172, cf. p. 178.
41 Phillips, *Faith and Enquiry*, p. 65.
42 *Ibid*, p. 71.
43 Phillips, *Without Explanation*, pp. 166 f., 168, 145, 140; see his index for 'language-games.'
44 P. Sherry, *Religion, Truth, and Language-Games* (London 1977), p. 43.
45 Phillips, *Concept of Prayer*, pp. 25 f., *Faith and Enquiry*, pp. 11, 73; cf. *Without Explanation*, p. 165, for the passage by Wittgenstein.

then still speaking of the same thing when we use the word 'religion'? One should bear in mind here what Wittgenstein wanted to make clear: another world-picture is not so much contradictory as fundamentally *different*. Religions are apparently not completely closed units, according to Phillips.

Phillips has elsewhere expressed himself in somewhat more detail on the view which one should hold of other religions in terms of a Christian background.[46] One cannot call Christianity a better religion; such a judgment presupposes an objective norm whereas precisely the content of faith is what constitutes the norm. Phillips believes that attempts to convert others to one's own religion are unjustifiable. He holds that a religion does not have the whole truth at its disposal. By thinking that one has the whole truth at one's disposal, one would be trading in neighbourly love for dogma.[47] Phillips acknowledges that he is applying a certain standard here: the criterion for true religion lies in love.[48] As an aside, we add at this juncture that Phillips regards some beliefs as incorrect or as non-essential.[49]

The nature of a religion's truth depends on the religion concerned. Criteria for determining what is true and what is false belief are therefore intrinsically related to the context concerned.[50] Religion cannot be proven to others; but they can be shown what religion entails by one's way of life and conduct. The concept of truth is inherent to a religion. Phillips states that 'truth' in religion is related to its usage in Jesus' saying: "I am the truth, the way, and the life."[51]

A few final remarks with reference to Phillips' views are now in order. (1) First, Phillips states that the philosophical analysis of religion is neutral. One ought not apply a standard which one has obtained from outside of religion. A norm to determine what true religion is within a tradition must be derived from that religion itself. When Phillips himself points out what true (Christian) faith is, he refers to a few portions of the Bible, as well as to the thought of Kierkegaard and Simone Weil. His conception clearly lies in the direct extension of Wittgenstein's annotation, "Theology as Grammar."[52] Philosophy of religion describes the (true) grammar of religion. Phillips thereby invokes the same set of problems entailed by Wittgenstein's view. He describes, yet at the same time he evaluates. He is neutral, yet at the same time he takes sides. How can the philosophy of religion preclude taking a theological position? Is a neutral philosophy of religion possible?

---

[46] Phillips, *Faith and Enquiry*, pp. 245 ff.
[47] *Ibid*, p. 246.
[48] *Ibid*, pp. 242, 247 f.; cf. *Concept of Prayer*, pp. 159 f.; God should be seen as 'supernatural.'
[49] Phillips, at the end of *Concept of Prayer*, cf. pp. 76 f.; cf. *Faith and Enquiry*, pp. 238 f.
[50] Phillips, *Concept of Prayer*, pp. 22, 27.
[51] Phillips, *Faith and Enquiry*, pp. 158, cf. 239.
[52] Wittgenstein, *Philosophische Untersuchungen*, no. 373.

(2) Second, Phillips underscores the specific nature of religion and the distinctiveness of the religious experience-of-the-whole. Every religion should be taken as it is and should be understood from within. A religious tradition has its own picture of reality. Phillips uses the term religion with a prima facie meaning. He gives no definition. He contends that the boundary of a language-game is vague. As for inter-religious relations, he says that this must be examined a single case at a time. That seems right to us. This said, however, it cannot be rigorously maintained that each religious tradition forms a unit. It remains true that religious traditions shows cohesion and that one must try to understand a religion from within rather than from without. But whether religions are indeed entities with a totally internal concept of truth and internal criteria becomes problematical. It occurs to us that Phillips ends up contradicting himself here. On the one hand he evaluates religion by the criterion of (Christian?) love; on the other hand he rejects taking a specific position. Questions are also raised by his concurrence with a remark of Simone Weil's, that religions are "different reflections of the same truth."[53] How is one to know that? If one defends this, then does one not have a view of all religion(s) after all? If so, religions stand less side by side than Phillips otherwise suggests, and are then not such independent units after all!

(3) Third, Phillips puts all the emphasis on the transcendence of God. Due to the absolute character of faith, Phillips records his protest against the statement that God 'exists.'[54] The peculiar nature of religion carries with it the fact that religion has its own truth and reality. God is divine reality; He is 'divinely real.' Phillips thus maintains the distinctive nature of religion. Keightly has called into question whether Phillips is still in a position to accomodate Christian discourse in which the basis for faith is laid by certain events.[55] Here again we are confronted by the question of whether Phillips can sustain his views: Is his concept of (good) religion merely a description of religion rather than his own perception?

(4) Fourth, Phillips makes a distinction between the religious language-game and other language-games. At issue, in fact, is a variation on the dichotomy between the empirical and the religious to which we have already drawn attention in the introductory chapter. The intent of such dichotomies with respect to religion is clear: the peculiar nature of religious knowledge can thereby be accomodated. The way in which religious insight is related to the rest of life is left unclarified though — a perennial difficulty. Religion has a universal pretension; it says something about the whole of life, or so Haikola's criticism of Phillips runs.[56] That is why one must

---

[53] Phillips, *Faith and Enquiry*, p. 246.

[54] Phillips, *Without Explanation*, pp. 172ff.; *Faith and Enquiry*, pp. 59f., 63; cf. *Concept of Prayer*, p. 13.

[55] Keightley, pp. 118, 121, 127.

[56] L. Haikola, *Religion as Language-Game: A Critical Study with Special Regard to D. Z. Phillips* (Lund 1977), pp. 93ff.

indicate how the one kind of knowledge is related to the other. Religion must, says Phillips, take certain facts from (hard) reality into account. His concern here is the relation between religion and the rest of life. It does not become clear what this relation is.

We do not wish to diminish Phillips' justified championing of the distinctive nature of religious knowledge by raising such critical questions. Moreover, he is right in saying that the relationship between religions must be examined in terms of how matters actually stand.

1.3   Some other voices in this discussion (Sherry and Trigg)

Patrick Sherry shares the opinion that Wittgenstein's thought contains important initiatives towards an accurate analysis of religion. He regards it as a shortcoming of Wittgenstein that he (like many of his followers) did not peruse more deeply the historical background of ideas.[57] Sherry contends that Phillips has let cultural relativism catch up with him.[58] Religious truth cannot be localized within an autonomous religious language-game, according to him. In such a view the doctrinal differences within a tradition as well as the conflicting truth claims of the various religions cannot be explained. He holds that Phillips conceives of truth as 'true for me' — a usage of the word truth which Haikola also detects in Phillips.[59] Sherry rejects such a subjective truth (although we have already seen that Phillips' concern is ultimately not with a trite 'true for me'). Sherry maintains that one cannot relinquish the propositional element in faith.[60]

Sherry describes the peculiar nature of religion by pointing to the *context,* or the *surroundings,* of faith.[61] He refers to situations in which people live. Experiencing different sorts of facts demands divergent reactions. Sherry distinguishes four kinds of 'facts' which present themselves:

    (1)   unrepeatable historical events
    (2)   regularities in the world and the universe
    (3)   the world as a whole
    (4)   transcendence.[62]

These four kinds of 'facts' are always experienced in a distinctive manner. These experiences have led people to the veneration of a transcendent being. They have developed concepts to put these experiences into words. These religious concepts have undergone development. Together they form a complex conceptual scheme.[63] They no longer refer to certain experiences

---

[57] Sherry, *Religion, Truth, and Language-Games,* pp. 192 ff.
[58] *Ibid,* p. 28.
[59] Haikola, *Religion as Language-Game,* p. 118; Sherry, pp. 63, cf. p. 167.
[60] Sherry, p. 43.
[61] *Ibid,* pp. 68 f.
[62] *Ibid,* pp. 71 ff.
[63] *Ibid,* p. 107.

or events in a univocal way because they all stand in relation to each other within that network. That is why the meaning of religious terms lies anchored in the context of the religious life as a whole.

Sherry holds that religious terms can be understood by those who do not belong to a religion. For a deeper understanding, however, a *transformation* of the person is necessary.[64] He refers to Newman's distinction between 'notional assent' and 'real assent.' Personal religious experience helps someone to achieve 'real assent.' The difference between the believer and the unbeliever is that the unbeliever will reject the terminology of the believer since he rejects the ontology which is presupposed by those concepts.[65] Religious experience presupposes certain beliefs, yet, in his view, these beliefs can to a large extent be comprehended by outsiders.

With respect to the concept of truth in religion, Sherry discusses, among other things, Wilfred Smith's view, which will be brought up in § 3. Smith closely relates truth to personal religious experience, to faith. Sherry retains the doctrinal element here too. At issue in doctrine is how things are.[66] Religions have different, incompatible claims in this regard. Following Austin's line of argument, Sherry wants to read, " 'p' is true" as, "things are as 'p' says they are." He understands the expression 'as they are' as a circumscription of the moot term correspondence.[67]

People do refer to their own concepts of religious truth, e.g., the 'biblical concept of truth.' Sherry points out that the word *ĕmet* in the Bible, in addition to usages to which we are not accustomed, also has the meanings familiar to us from our own daily language.[68] It cannot be maintained, in his view, that different religions have different kinds of truth. Instead of speaking about different kinds of truth, it would be better to distinguish various *strata* of religious beliefs. States of affairs can be called true, but so can statements. Religious ideas are expressed in myths, parables, poetry, and symbolic statements or analogies.[69] This does not indicate a special religious concept of truth, but points up a multitude of "relationships of 'picturing' and 'projection.' " The significance of these religious terms must be seen in terms of the grammar of their usage. This grammar is learnt by looking at the historical emergence of a theological system, and by taking into account that it is connected with a religious way of life.[70]

In terms of the relationship between religions, Sherry puts a lot of emphasis on spirituality. There must first of all be appreciation for the

---

[64] *Ibid*, pp. 110 ff.
[65] *Ibid*, p. 133, cf. p. 132.
[66] *Ibid*, p. 171.
[67] *Ibid*, p. 179.
[68] *Ibid*, p. 180, 'rightly'; see also Ch. VI § 3.1.
[69] *Ibid*, p. 183.
[70] *Ibid*, p. 184.

important role which experience plays in each religion. Only then can the question of truth be raised:

> If a religion is a way of life (rather than a 'form of life') in which men attempt to achieve spiritual self-transformation by prayer, meditation, and holy living, then we will come to understand the concepts, language-games, activities, institutions and so forth which constitute religion only by recognizing the purpose which they serve.[71]

Below we shall see to what an extent the transformation of life plays a part in religious epistemology, and Sherry rightly accentuates this. It seems to us questionable, however, whether much headway can be made by substituting the term 'as it is' for 'correspondence.' This definition strikes us as no improvement upon the common sense notion of correspondence. We shall see the idea of various strata of speaking about truth confirmed in our investigations. While Sherry contends that inter-religious truth is at issue, he leaves it at that; he does not indicate how one might attempt to settle the question of truth. Sherry maintains the element of knowledge susceptible to formulation and its concomitant truth claims, but he does not elaborate how one might raise the discussion about truth in religion. He also neglects to mention that there are religions which seek to transcend the propositional element. He does, however, rightly point out that one must first be familiar with the spirituality of other traditions.

One of the people who accentuates the cognitive nature of religious belief is Roger Trigg. His worry is that if belief cannot be true or untrue, then the commitment of believers is arbitrary.[72] People are personally involved in faith. They assume that their belief is true. This perspective leads him to object to a conception such as that of D. Z. Phillips. Phillips allows that *within* a religion, Christianity for example, one may speak of true faith. Christianity as such cannot be true or untrue; criteria by which the truth can be established inhere in a religion itself. Truth is no longer subject to discussion in this view.[73] Trigg cites a remark by Phillips about people who lose their faith. Phillips notes that believers talk of turning one's back on God.[74] That expression, says Trigg, presupposes that for believers God exists, regardless of people's (un)belief. Trigg is not, however, of the opinion that philosophy can adjudicate what is true in religion. One can only argue in terms of one's own view of the world. There is no neutral, mutually acceptable basis which could serve as starting point.[75] That yields problems. Yet if it does not matter to which insights people commit themselves then everything is permitted, and not a

---

[71] *Ibid*, p. 195.
[72] R. Trigg, *Reason and Commitment* (Cambridge 1973), pp. 92, 121, 139.
[73] Cf. Trigg, p. 87.
[74] Phillips, *Death and Immortality* (London 1970), pp. 78 f.; Trigg, pp. 89 f.
[75] Trigg, p. 96.

single belief is wrong —remarks Trigg, and rightly so in our opinion.[76] If people have no reasons for considering their ideas true then their ideas must be otherwise explained, in terms of psychological and other causes.[77] One of the conditions for the possibility of language use, however, is that people talk *about* something. They speak about 'what is the case.'[78] If the distinction true/untrue is relinquished, the possibility of communication is abandoned. Anything can then be said with impunity. Trigg thus arrives at his thesis: "Language must be understood to be about one world open to public inspection."[79] The world has a certain stability, which makes communication and agreement between people possible. 'Forms of life' appear to overlap. The relativist himself denies the possibility of truth, to be sure, but at the same time he claims that his view is objectively true. He apparently does not preclude objective truth completely. Trigg thus maintains that religious knowledge is knowledge of the world and of God.

We concur with Trigg, in that knowledge is knowledge of reality. We too assert that the question of truth is at stake. The truth pointed out by the such people as Wittgenstein and Phillips as well, however, remains: Religious traditions point to a certain access to reality which is related to a whole way of life. As Trigg himself states, there is no neutral access to reality. Precisely that fact makes the question of truth in and among religions so fascinating and exciting.

Herewith we conclude our exposition of how the concept of truth in religion is treated in the tradition of analytical philosophy. Many more authors could be mentioned, but we have reviewed these thinkers because Wittgenstein's language-game concept and its application by Phillips to religion bring to the fore angles which are of key importance to the issue of the relationship between religions. These concerns are also raised by other philosophical schools, such as the issues of contextuality, horizon of understanding, and the inter-wovenness of theory and practice. In the following sections of this chapter, other philosophers from the analytical tradition will be brought up for discussion: Brümmer and Hick. In this chapter our concern was the discussion which resulted in and stemmed from Wittgenstein's concept of language-game.

§ 2   Insistence on the truth claims of religions

In this section we will discuss a few continental authors who stress the cognitive component in faith. Brümmer developed his view in dialogue with the tradition of analytical philosophy, but he has also assimilated insights from continental European philosophy. Kuitert engages in dialogue

---

[76] *Ibid*, p. 121.
[77] *Ibid*, p. 139.
[78] *Ibid*, p. 154.
[79] *Ibid*, p. 156.

with German as well as Anglo-Saxon authors. He concurs in Pannenberg's thought in various respects. Pannenberg developed his ideas within the context of a broad discussion of hermeneutical philosophy and studies in the philosophy of science.

2.1   Vincent Brümmer: impressive experiences

Brümmer's work stands in the tradition of analytical philosophy. In the previous section (§ 1), we dealt mainly with that strain of analytical philosophy in which an attempt is made to illumine the distinctive nature of religious knowledge by distinguishing it from other knowledge. Brümmer, however, is more an heir to the other line of the analytical philosophy of religion which could be designated by the term, 'philosophical theology'; he reflects philosophically on the insights and problems of Christian theology. He compares the task of the philosopher with that of the jurist who does two things: he describes current standards of justice in a society, but at the same time tries to better delineate their meaning with regard to its future use.[80]

Brümmer contends, as is customary in analytical philosophy, that the question of truth is preceded by the question of meaning. One must know what is being asserted before one can examine whether it is true. In analyzing the meaning of statements, the concern, in his view, is not the meaning in itself since language always functions within the course of human action. He therefore links analysis of meaning to philosophical anthropology.[81]

Brümmer regards religious statements to be cognitive; they can thus be either true or untrue. Religious statements spring from experiences of aspects of reality which have acquired religious significance. Within the normative context of a view of life, religious assertions acquire a prescriptive significance as well. They appeal to certain attitudes and certain behaviour.[82] Taken by themselves, they describe reality.

The Christian faith, like other religious conceptions, is a persuasion concerning life. The core consists in a personal relationship to God and hope in his promises. This belief presupposes the conviction that the facts give grounds for this faith. Belief thus presupposes a conviction regarding the state of affairs.[83] Brümmer puts a lot of emphasis on the fact that a religious persuasion is based not on the will to believe but on the recognition of facts.[84]

---

[80] V. Brümmer, *Theology and Philosophical Inquiry* [Eng. version of *Wijsgerige Begrips-analyse.*] (London 1981), pp. 77ff.

[81] V. Brümmer, *Wijsgerige Begripsanalyse* (Kampen 1981), p. 69; cf. *Theology*, pp. 59ff.

[82] Also V. Brümmer, *Wat Doen wij als wij Bidden?* (Kampen 1985), pp. 152ff.; = *What Are We Doing When We Pray?* § 7.2.

[83] Brümmer, *Wat Doen Wij . . .*, pp. 40f.; concerning Braithwaite, cf. p. 149.

[84] Compare R. Swinburne, *Faith and Reason* (Oxford 1981), pp. 25f.; W. Pannenberg, "Einsicht und Glaube," in *Grundfragen systematischer Theologie*, I (Göttingen 1967),

Subsequent to these introductory remarks, we will examine more closely Brümmer's conception of a 'view of life,' the manner in which they are related to experience, and the concept of truth.

Taken by themselves, descriptive statements are neutral, Brümmer contends. His example is "Nelson's column stands on Trafalgar Square."[85] This statement is true or untrue regardless of the significance which Nelson might have.[86] A particular fact can acquire a certain significance within a view of life, e.g., Nelson is worthy of praise or trust. Life-view statements describe characteristics of things. Brümmer distinguishes three such characteristics: directly observable characteristics (such as 'the cat is *black*'), dispositional characteristics (such as 'the cat is *mean*'), and impressive characteristics (such as, "I find the panorama from the Zugspitze *impressive.*")[87] Impressive characteristics are empirical; if one notices and voices them, confirming them is expressive ("I find that . . . ").[88]

Certain things, events, and people can make a deep impression; they are impressive (for certain people). Religious belief is based on the impressive character of empirically observable phenomena:

> A commitment to a view of life . . . involves responding to whatever inspires one as being more important or more determinant of meaning than anything else.[89]

The unity in someone's persuasion is usually determined by a certain basic conviction. A basic conviction distinguishes a certain thing from other things by marking that thing as unique. That thing is so special that the meaning of all others things is determined by their relation to that unique thing: that thing is the primary determinant of meaning.[90] The classical views of life are characterized by the thing to which they have attributed the status of primary determinant of meaning.[91] That thing can be an experiential given or a metaphysical entity. Following this line of thought, Brümmer contends that the acts of God in the Christian religion —as these are described in the Bible— are experienced as impressive. A Christian bases his claim that God exists "on the impressive acts of God in His works."[92] Brümmer admits that the impressive characteristics of events are not without ambiguity; not everyone experiences them in this

---

pp. 223-36. Compare with Montsma's discussion of the debate in the Netherlands about Brümmer's views, J. A. Montsma, *De Exterritoriale Openbaring* (Amsterdam 1985), pp. 113-24; see also H. van Luijk, "Het Recht op een Overtuiging: Balans van een Diskussie," *Bijdragen* 41-42 (1980–81): 141-57.

[85] Brümmer, *Wijsgerige Begripsanalyse*, pp. 122 f.; *Theology*, p. 123, "Nelson's column stands on Travalgar Square."

[86] Brümmer, *Theology*, p. 124.

[87] *Ibid*, p. 120.

[88] *Ibid*, p. 119.

[89] *Ibid*, p. 143, cf. also p. 210.

[90] *Ibid*, p. 133.

[91] *Ibid*, pp. 133 ff.

[92] *Ibid*, p. 282.

manner. In this regards, the whole of a view of life plays a part. The things which are experienced as impressive are possessed of impressive significance only within the context of a view of life. Brümmer defines a view of life as follows:

> ...the total set of norms, ideals, and eschatological expectations in terms of which someone directs and assesses his way of life.[83]

Everyone is forced to introduce a certain consistency into his view of life, because everyone poses normative questions. For many people, though, there is no single primary determinant of meaning in their life but rather several central interests.[94]

According to Brümmer it is not possible to justify a view of life externally. If one were to ask someone who believes in God to demonstrate that God justifiedly has the status of primary determinant of meaning, then the answer will be problematical: "We would have reached the ultimate criterion, the end of a series of justifications of justifications of justifications. I could advance no grounds to justify my final ground. I could merely *testify* that this was my final ground."[95] At this point one ends up in a circular argument according to Brümmer.[96] This does not imply, however, that it is impossible to give grounds for one's conviction. Brümmer eschews the rationalistic demand that only assertions whose grounds are evident to all may be held for true. Proofs and arguments remain personal in the sense that they may or may not be persuasive to a certain person: "The concept of 'evidence' is also person-relative."[97] How is it possible, one could ask, that the same 'evidence' convinces one person while another remains unconvinced? Why does one person experience certain events as impressive while another does not?[98] A person learns to see the impressive character of events, things, and people by the interpretation which the tradition of a life-view imparts to them. Religious traditions themselves emerged due to the fact that certain people once had certain experiences of the impressiveness of things, etc.[99]

In a discussion of various theories of truth Brümmer gives the following definition of the nature of constatives (assertions about states of affairs): "Our *constative beliefs* are expectations held by us with regard to the way our possibilities of action are determined."[100] Brümmer rejects the correspondence theory of truth because it postulates an agreement between propositions and facts; he does, however, recognize that truth

---

[83] *Ibid*, pp. 132f.
[94] *Ibid*, p. 135.
[95] *Ibid*, p. 136.
[96] *Ibid*, pp. 137, 273, cf. p. 210.
[97] *Ibid*, p. 196.
[98] *Ibid*, pp. 272ff., p. 210.
[99] *Ibid*, pp. 209f.
[100] *Ibid*, p. 167.

exists in relation to facts. The term 'truth' is an evaluative term.[101] In order to avoid the question of how propositions correspond to states of affairs and the idea that language 'pictures' things, Brümmer speaks of describing possibilities for action: "A statement is false if our possibilities for action are not determined as assured in the statement."[102] Thus Brümmer adopts Wittgenstein's notion of life-forms in his reflection. This view of truth is also applicable to views of life. If one believes that God exists then this determines one's possibilities for action in the most comprehensive way.[103]

Religious traditions each have their own interpretation of reality. It is based on experiences which are experienced as impressive. The traditions contradict one another because they attribute the status of primary determinant of meaning to different things. This does not exclude agreement regarding a number of items on the basis of different views of life. But as comprehensive views of life they do contradict each other.[104] One cannot be Buddhist and Christian simultaneously. Brümmer contends that views of life are comparable because they fulfil a similar function, i.e., they seek to provide an answer to ultimate questions. Religions must be subject to the same criteria since they fulfil the same function. Brümmer contends that these criteria are valid for views of life in general. In order for people to differ about a view of life, they must necessarily be in agreement on four items:

(1) the fact that their respective views of life exclude each other;
(2) the fact that their respective views of life seek to fulfil the same function by providing answers to the same questions, thus also;
(3) on the function of a view of life;
(4) on the common criteria that a doctrinal scheme has to meet in order to fulfil that function.[105]

Here we encounter what is called the issue of the common ground in the literature on interreligious relations. Brümmer apparently claims that his view of religion is universally valid and thus applies to all religions and views of life. He regards as universally valid his definition of view of life, primary determinant of meaning, concept of truth, and the function of the cognitive content of a religion.

Whether the views of life which people hold in esteem are good views of life can be measured by these characteristics. It is possible to reject someone else's view of life, Brümmer says, because . . .

(1) it formulates and provides a basis for a way of life that cannot be accepted in terms of one's own basic conviction, thus providing unacceptable

---

[101] *Ibid*, p. 179.
[102] *Ibid*, p. 180; cf. Chapters 2 and 3 on language, *ibid*.
[103] *Ibid*, p. 280.
[104] *Ibid*, p. 138.
[105] *Ibid*, pp. 138f.

> alternative answers to the questions to which one's own view of life
> provides correct answers; and because
> (2) it cannot be a functional view of life since it does not meet the
> common criteria for the fulfillment of the function of a view of life.[106]

The first reason to reject an(other) religion is interreligiously non-negotiable, since the reasons why one rejects another religion are connected to a specific religion. The second reason is open to discussion since the criteria intended are common to all religious traditions. At issue here are the following five criteria: (1) freedom from contradiction, (2) unity, (3) relevance, (4) universality, (5) impressiveness.[107] We will examine the issue of criteria more closely in Ch. XI. Brümmer contends that these five external criteria do not provide sufficient grounds to choose one view of life or another as the only right one.[108] In comparing religions one cannot stand at a neutral point, in Brümmer's view. Someone who belongs to a religion has not chosen that faith: one can but profess to be impressed by something or someone as being more important than anything else.

Brümmer's conception is interesting and well-considered. He attempts to describe the constitution of a view of life, and does not give a view of his own purely on the grounds of certain philosophical premises. He recognizes, as we have seen, that there are no strictly neutral grounds for the evaluation of religions. A number of questions may be posed in connection with his view:

(1) First, Brümmer speaks about the primary determinant of meaning. For the Christian tradition God is the primary determinant of meaning. Certain things and events are experienced as 'acts of God.' In terms of the Christian tradition, Brümmer has the following four things in mind: (1) God is the Creator of all that exists; (2) God is the origin of the order and regularity that we find in nature; (3) in the course of history God has revealed himself . . . (4) as Christians we experience the power of God's regenerative grace, by which He changes our lives and makes 'new beings' of us.[109]

These four points —as we have here presented them— are not specifically Christian. People in any monotheistic religion could accept this. Brümmer refers to Christ in connection with the third point regarding history. A Muslim would refer to the prophet's revelation. In other words, referring to God as the primary determinant of meaning is not exclusively Christian. Reference to one exclusive primary determinant of meaning in a religious tradition should be reconsidered. Brümmer admits that overlapping between religious traditions can occur, as we have seen. They appear to be numerous. We will return to this issue in the analytical part of this study.

---

[106] *Ibid*, p. 139.
[107] *Ibid*, p. 139.
[108] *Ibid*, p. 143.
[109] *Ibid*, pp. 269f.

(2) Second, the five criteria mentioned by Brümmer lie readily at hand in the Western philosophy of religion. It is important for a valid argument to see the extent to which religious traditions themselves accept such criteria. That is precisely what we wish to verify in this enquiry.

(3) Third, the definition of truth as indicative of real possibilities for action has been prompted by long and drawn out debates in Western philosophy. Brümmer avoids difficulties with the notion of correspondence by speaking of possibilities for action. This maneuver strikes us as problematical nevertheless. Although it is correct that I can go to see Nelson's column on Trafalgar Square only if Nelson's column is on Trafalgar Square and that such truth has implications for the possibilities for action, the point of such confirmation lies not in the implied possibilities for action, but in the possibility of *experiencing and sensing reality*. The constative, "The panorama from the Zugspitze is impressive," aims to say something about the panorama as it is (and not merely that one can travel there). Reason for speaking of possibilities for action is provided by the relatedness of experience and by the culture-related interpretation of experience; one does not know reality *in itself*, but within the context of human culture. This relatedness of experience and culture can be expressed by saying that knowledge is relational, and precisely for that reason, is knowledge of reality.[110]

Aside from this caveat regarding the concept of truth, the question remains whether Brümmer's view of 'truth' is Western and Christian, or whether he can with reason claim universal validity for it within the philosophy of religion. That must be verified with reference to what thinkers in various religious traditions have themselves said about truth.

(4) Fourth, the question could be posed whether all religions wish to meet the demands which Brümmer —and many with him— make of religion, and whether they all wish to fulfil the same function and to provide answers to the same ultimate questions. In referring to the function of religion in providing answers to ultimate questions, Brümmer broaches an essential point. There are indeed anthropological constants involved; people put certain questions to themselves: the concern is with life and death, well-being and calamity ('Heil and Unheil'), guilt and purification, and such like. A further analysis of the impressive experiences to which religions refer can perhaps provide further help here (Ch. IX).

---

[110] See what I have written elsewere about the entanglement of the 'subjective' and the 'objective' in knowledge, *De Schrift Alleen?* pp. 28 ff.; 269 ff.; and "Waarheid als Kennis van de Weg," in *Geloofsmanieren*, ed. J. M. Vlijm (Kampen 1981), pp. 202 ff. Use of the expression 'relational' is not uncommon nowadays, e.g., in the expression 'relational concept of truth,' in *God Met Ons: Report by the General Synod of the Gereformeerde Kerken in Nederland* (Leusden 1981); the term can easily be mis-understood in a relativistic way.

2.2   Harry Kuitert: religion as a search paradigm

Kuitert also inists on the cognitive nature of religious knowledge. Faith is much more than a mere holding-for-true, although it is that as well. There must be something true, otherwise one cannot with good grounds have any experience of it, be motivated by it in one's actions, and be legitimately sure of it. Trusting in God is a different matter if God exists and is trustworthy, than is the purely psychological act of trusting the divine if God did not exist. Religious experience presupposes 'is'-statements, and thus doctrine: religious belief ultimately stands or falls (...) with the existence or non-existence of God.[111] The doctrines must be true. Kuitert conceives of the word 'truth' in such a manner that some reality must answer to is-sentences. He avoids the concept of correspondence with this definition but maintains the element of describing the world 'as it is' — the cardinal point in the correspondence theory.

Knowledge of reality always contains a moment of interpretation for Kuitert as well. In that sense every reference to experience is subjective. People are personally involved in the ordering and naming of their experiences. When speaking of religion, Kuitert does not in particular have in mind inner, mystical experiences, but primarily experiences which are in principle public.[112] What everyone can see in principle, however, is not actually seen by everyone. To see things (as they are) one needs proper access to the facts. Such access is afforded by religious traditions. They serve as a framework of interpretation for the individual, within which certain experiences have been designated as experiences of the reality of God. The experience of former generations reverberates in religious traditions. People have designated their experiences in a creative fashion. Human experience thus speaks in religious traditions but it always speaks as experience of something.

Kuitert endeavours as much as possible to account for faith. He begins his legitimation with Ericson's concept of basic trust. It is basic trust which kindles religious experiences and convictions in human beings. It is an anthropological constant which never occurs uninterpreted but always appears 'clothed' in the garb of concrete religions. On the basis of this universal datum of human existence, people arrive at the various religious (and other) *search paradigms* regarding the transcendent.[113] They follow the traces of God's imprint which they believe they have encountered, but they differ in their interpretation of the experiences which direct them towards the transcendent.[114] Various religions give divergent answers to the question of which reality answers to our basic trust. Since truth

---

[111] H. M. Kuitert, *Wat Heet Geloven? Structuur en Herkomst van de Christelijke Geloofsuitspraken* (Baarn 1977), p. 150.

[112] *Ibid*, pp. 151 f.

[113] *Ibid*, pp. 147 f., cf. also pp. 83 ff.; referring to Wilfred Smith, Kuitert too uses the description of religions as cumulative traditions.

[114] *Ibid*, pp. 142 f., 231, 134.

always contains reference to 'how it is,' the various religions cannot be simultaneously true if they make conflicting statements about Ultimate Reality. The truth is thus open to discussion.

Like Brümmer, Kuitert steps from certain religious experiences to a religious persuasion as a whole. He allows that some events and states of affairs are experienced as impressive, but in distinction to Brümmer, Kuitert does not hold that *impressiva* are concerned with invisible characteristics of things as opposed to visible characteristics. Kuitert rejects the distinction between the visible (observable for all) and invisible characteristics (experienced by some) of things and events,[115] for everything which is known is perceived interpretatively. Impressive characteristics ('The view from the Zugspitze is impressive') are not distinguishable from directly observable characteristics ('the cat is black') in this regard. Given a framework of interpretation, some events and states of affairs are impressive to some people. One claims within that framework that they *are* impressive. For the experience of transcendental reality, Kuitert thus refers to worldly experience which is in principle open to anyone's observation. The emergence and continued existence of religious traditions depends on our world of experience.[116] Basic trust is actualized by specific occasions; it takes the form of is-sentences.[117] The meaning of is-sentences, however, lies within the context of the search paradigm of religion.

Kuitert contends that faith is far more comprehensive than the knowledge advanced in propositions. His point is that faith *also* includes knowledge and makes claim to the truth.[118] For the assessment of religious truth claims, Kuitert refers to the concept of God. God must be conceived minimally as "power which is not outstripped by yet another power."[119] Trust in God always presupposes God's ultimate superior power. A criterion can be inferred from this: "A God who is not power over everything cannot remain in existence, and in his fall, he will drag with him the religious belief which held his existence for true all that time."[120] Thus only time will tell whether people's belief in God will stand up to developments. Kuitert calls the notion of God's omnipotence an eschatological predicate; in the end it will appear that He is power over everything.[121] Since God is experienced as power over everything, here lies the criterion by which one may assess a tradition. A search paradigm proves itself true, says Kuitert, if one by its aid *finds,* that is, finds the power which people

115 *Ibid,* p. 143 *n.* 6.
116 *Ibid,* p. 143.
117 *Ibid,* p. 135.
118 *Ibid,* p. 149.
119 *Ibid,* p. 145.
120 *Ibid,* p. 145.
121 *Ibid,* p. 146 *n.* 17.

with reason call God."[122] In connection with this finding the traces of God, Kuitert speaks of *actes de présence* by the one who has become the content of the basic conviction.[123] God has power over everything — no matter how many questions can be posed about the relation between God's power and the many unsavoury events in this world. Kuitert therefore refers to the myriad human experiences for assessing a search paradigm. A life-view should place a maximum of experiential givens in a meaningful ordered context. In this way Kuitert connects finding God with discerning relations in reality. One finds traces of the one sought in the light of the search paradigm and such finding in turn confirms the search paradigm. If no one were to find anything anymore, the search paradigm would have lost its power. Thus the fertility religions of Western Asia have disappeared.[124] In like manner, one sees a continual process of development and revision of the search paradigm in religious tradition.[125]

Kuitert's view contains many insights which we can use to good advantage: the interpretation of experience in *search paradigms,* the rootedness of faith in knowledge of reality, and his view of the basis for faith in basic trust. The rootedness of religion in basic trust can be complemented by other anthropological constants, whereby overlapping and contradiction between religions can be further clarified. On the basis of the results of Part 2, however, we will have to introduce important qualifications on the extent to which Kuitert thinks that a neutral public discussion about religious assertions is possible.[126]

2.3 Wolfhart Pannenberg: truth as the totality of meaning

Wolfhart Pannenberg also aspires to adduce arguments for the truth of belief statements. Our exposition on Pannenberg will borrow heavily upon an earlier consideration of his thought in another context.[127] Statements about God cannot be directly tested by comparison to their 'object.' Assertions may also be tested by their implications, however. Pannenberg says that God is the all-determining reality, although he himself reserves a fuller, more differentiated explanation. If God —ultimately— determines reality then it must be possible to experience reality as determined by

---

[122] *Ibid,* p. 169.

[123] *Ibid,* p. 159.

[124] *Ibid,* pp. 153f.

[125] *Ibid,* pp. 154f.

[126] See H. M. Kuitert, "Het Vrije Veld van de Theologie," in *In Rapport met de Tijd: 100 Jaar Theologie aan de Vrije Universiteit (1880–1980)* (Kampen 1980), pp. 236-51; and his "Theologie Moet Blijven," in *Maatschappelijke Relevantie van Wetenschap: Nonsense of No-Nonsense?* eds. M. C. Doeser and A. W. Musschenga (Kampen 1985), pp. 145-57; cf. Kuitert, "Is Belief a Condition for Understanding?" *Religious Studies* 17 (1981): 233-43.

[127] See Vroom, *De Schrift Alleen?* pp. 181ff.

God.[128] Thus, the universal meaning claimed for the message of Jesus Christ demands, *per implicationem,* confirmation by the totality of experienced reality. Yet no one can have an overview of the totality of experience. When giving an account of faith and theology —and like Brümmer and Kuitert, Pannenberg thinks in terms of the Christian tradition— one can proceed from the traditions in which people have given expression to their experience of the totality of existence. These traditions are world and life views, particularly religions and philosophies. Over against philosophies which leave no room for God, theology can argue that the 'hypothesis' that God exists accords better with reality than a view which takes no account of God. Moreover, by comparison with other religions, Christian theology must endeavour to demonstrate the truth of Christian faith. The religion which conforms most with human experience can be considered the best.

According to Pannenberg, such a discussion is inevitable if we are to honour the claim by religions of being in agreement with reality. Due to the radical differences between them, religions cannot just be put on a level with each other. These religious differences themselves evoke the question of the comparative value of the various religions; only by comparing them can one take them seriously.

How is such an enquiry possible? The criterion which Pannenberg wishes to use in evaluating religion and philosophy is the same one discussed earlier in the exposition on Kuitert. Since God is the all-determining power, religious conviction must create coherence within the diversity of human experience. Religions must therefore be compared for their *integrative force.* With this term, Pannenberg means the capacity of a religion to provide a place within a consistent whole for the abundance of human experiences. In applying this criterion, one in fact operates with the same standard imposed on religion through the ages; people have always questioned their faith on the basis of experiences which they have undergone. Developments have occurred within religious traditions due to the influence of new experiences. Just as people have in actual practice assessed religion for its integrative capacity, philosophy of religion can attempt now to assess religious and philosophical systems by the same standard. With respect to Christianity Pannenberg therefore states that theology has the task of demonstrating that the 'integrative nucleus' of Christianity, the history of Jesus of Nazareth, has the capacity to integrate elements of truth from foreign provenance into its own tradition.

What is constantly at issue in religious truth claims is the larger context in which things stand.[129] Truth pertains to reality as it is. For Pannenberg truth is fundamentally the correspondence of statements to

---

[128] See W. Pannenberg, esp. *Wissenschaftstheorie und Theologie* (Frankfurt 1973), pp. 304 ff. and "Erwägungen zu einer Theologie der Religionsgeschichte," in *Grundfragen,* I (Göttingen 1967), pp. 252-95, esp. pp. 285 f.

[129] See Vroom, *De Schrift Alleen?* pp. 214 ff.

reality. Pannenberg wants to account for truth claims through inter-subjective discussion. This aspiration to inter-subjective agreement presupposes, however, that there is a reality which can be discussed by people, a thought which we have encountered in Roger Trigg as well. Reality must manifest coherence; otherwise people cannot speak coherently of it. People in fact assume meaningful relationships in reality, tacitly regarding reality as a coherent whole. From this, Pannenberg infers on the one hand the necessity for inter-subjective assessment, and on the other, the notion that inter-subjective consensus cannot be the ultimate criterion of truth. That criterion lies in the agreement of statements with reality, or more precisely, with comprehensive reality. The truth —the real, comprehensive truth— coincides, as he puts it, with the "all-experience-encompassing totality of meaning in its inner coherence."[130] The truth is thus the sum of statements in their inner coherence. One only knows the truth, in effect, when one knows the totality of experiential facts. The whole of experience, however, is tied to history. History is not yet final. It is therefore impossible to know the whole truth, but the future can be anticipated; one has an idea of the truth. Knowledge of truth is historically determined, and given the unfinished character of history, the manifold human anticipations of truth have historical legitimacy. Yet a definite judgment of the truth can come to pass only in the eschaton.

People are confronted with the need to judge for themselves concerning religious and philosophical paradigms of totality. Pannenberg mentions four criteria by which one can try to reach a judgment:[131]

(1) The first criterion concerns the relation between a statement and the tradition in which the person making the statement stands. It must be possible to conceive of a statement as a formulation of the implications of (Biblical) tradition.

(2) The second criterion is that theological statements must be regarded as incorrect if they are not related in a relevant manner to reality as a whole, and, moreover, if they cannot be defended with reference to the philosophical problems which have arisen in their own time.

(3) Third, theological propositions must be capable of integrating the experiences to which they refer.

(4) Fourth, they can be regarded as falsified if they have less explanatory force than other hypotheses and do not contribute anything to the discussion of the boundaries of existing hypotheses.

Regarding this presentation of Pannenberg's view, we will now pose a few questions:

(1) The first issue is whether Pannenberg does not speak too monolithically about the unity of experience. Particularly with regard to the Jewish and

---

[130] Pannenberg, *Wissenschaftstheorie*, p. 219; see Vroom, *De Schrift Alleen?* p. 215. Compare the quote from Bruno Puntel in Ch. I § 2.1.

[131] Vroom, *De Schrift Alleen*, pp. 217 ff.

the Christian traditions, the problem which immediately arises is how assertions about God's goodness and power are to be squared with the reality of evil. The weight which Pannenberg and Kuitert attach to God's power as starting point immediately evokes the question of how one can then speak of the love of God. Precisely the love and the faithfulness of God are important to both in connection with basic trust: Power is trustworthy because it is powerful *and* loving. Reality is too multi-faceted to fit all aspects of God as omnipotent power and love into one coherent scheme.

(2) A second question is related to this. Just as Brümmer speaks of the basic conviction of a religious persuasion, so Pannenberg speaks of the integrative force of a tradition on the basis of the integrative nucleus (with regard to Christianity, Jesus of Nazareth). On the basis of our investigation, as recounted in Part 2, it seems questionable to us whether it is entirely plausible to sustain this way of speaking about the unity, consistency, and integration of a religious conviction. Important qualifications must be introduced here.

(3) In the third place, Pannenberg, like Kuitert, presupposes that it is basically possible to describe reality in terms of propositions. Pannenberg demands that what is tacitly intended in a statement, though left unsaid, be explicated. One must of course attempt to do so. But whether all that which is intended is also capable of being said is a problem which hermeneutical studies have already brought up for debate. I have levelled criticism at Pannenberg's view on this point.[132] Within the context of this study, the question arises: Does not this demand betoken a Western overvaluation of 'objective knowledge'? In Part 2 of this study, this issue emerges time and again.

§ 3 Approaches by the philosophy of religion in terms of the encounter between religious traditions

The relationship of the religious traditions cropped up incidentally in the previous two sections. In this section we will examine this issue more deeply by presenting the positions of those who have occupied themselves explicitly with the question of interreligious relations. The positions of Christian, Smith, Hick, Wiebe, and Thakur will set before us a number of the most important elements in the modern discussion.

---

[132] *Ibid*, pp. 198 ff.; 208 ff.

3.1   William A. Christian: opposition between religions

William A. Christian contends that the theme of 'religion and truth' can be approached from two sides: first, from a comprehensive conception of all types of truth; and second, from a study of the disparate terrains where one speaks of truth. He opts for the second approach in his own studies, an approach in which one procures much data from religious phenomenology.[133] Proceeding from religious phenomena, he tries to clarify the *logic* of religious convictions. Christian gives the following definition of religion:

> A religious interest is an interest in something more important than anything else in the universe.[134]

Similar to Brümmer's exposition, the recognition of something which is more important than everything else leads to the conclusion that factual contradiction exists between the various religions.[135] It is essential for religion that what is acknowledged to be most important exist. Religion holds consequences for the believer since it concerns what is regarded as most important. True religion encompasses a reorientation and change in the life of the believer, as well as a view of *life as it ought to be*.[136] Religion is far more than rationality; but since religion is concerned with insight into reality, it also includes doctrine. Religious beliefs are transmitted in a number of ways; one finds them in books or in confessions, but they are also implied, for example, in rituals.[137] Where one comes across them depends on the nature of the religious tradition. There are often reservations in religion with respect to the importance of propositions. Yet even though a person's heart cannot be reached by reason alone, *something* must be said, explained, and understood, if only for the purpose of acquiring a proper view on being human. Religion therefore also includes beliefs. Religious doctrine furnishes insight into the conditions of existence and the conditions of existence determine possibilities for behaviour.[138] A religion gives an interpretation of experiential givens. In so doing, religions ascribe 'unrestricted primacy-ranking force' to certain concerns and these stand at the centre of the life-orientation of those religions.[139] Just as certain matters are basic within the context of a religious tradition, so too the doctrinal tenets which correspond to them.

---

[133] W. A. Christian, *Meaning and Truth in Religion* (Princeton 1964), pp. 8f.

[134] *Ibid*, p. 60.

[135] *Ibid*, pp. 134ff.

[136] *Ibid*, p. 62; also his *Oppositions of Religious Doctrines: A Study in the Logic of Dialogue among Religions* (London 1972), pp. 43ff. Christian points to differences and to shared views with respect to the way of life which is seen as desirable, *Oppositions*, pp. 84f.

[137] Christian, *Meaning and Truth*, p. 81.

[138] Christian, *Oppositions*, p. 40.

[139] Christian, *Oppositions*, pp. 73f.; *Meaning and Truth*, pp. 217f., 234f.

A basic doctrinal proposal recapitulates the truth claims of an entire doctrinal system.[140]

Christian examines how the various religious convictions are related to each other. It is apparent that there are similarities and differences between the various religions. This means, on the one hand, that religions are not diametrically opposed on all points, and on the other hand, that it betrays scanty knowledgeability to equate them. An important problem in comparing religious traditions lies in the paucity of common concepts.[141] Yet if one is willing to take for granted that terms from a single philosophical tradition are utilized in making such comparisons, then the problem can be resolved as follows: One reduces the unique terms of a religious tradition to abstract terms. Thus discourse regarding *nirvāna* (which does not 'exist') and the God of the Torah (who does 'exist') can be made comparable by presenting statements which employ comparable terms:

> There is no actual existent of such a character that, by relation to it, life can include a mode of satisfaction deeper than joy or sorrow.
> There is an actual existent of such a kind that, by relation to it, life can include a mode of satisfaction deeper than joy or sorrow.[142]

The 'opposition of religious doctrines' becomes apparent through such a reformulation of beliefs. Christian searches out what religious traditions regard as central in this fashion. The mere fact that religions value certain matters highly does not of itself mean that one belief excludes the other (e.g., Buddhists too can value Mohammed highly). But if primacy is ascribed to dissimilar subjects, then there is a point of difference between traditions.[143] And if the valuations are incompatible, then there is a point of disagreement.[144] Disagreements exist not only in terms of valuations of things, events, or persons, but also in terms of propositions. Someone who makes an assertion is speaking of how reality is. The concern of those who make assertions is an "interest in knowing what is the case, knowing what existents there are, and what conditions of existence are."[145] Assertions about states of affairs are related to valuations; such assertions are presupposed by any appraisal. For this reason there are conflicts between religious traditions with regard to both the central points of various religions and to less comprehensive points. Examples of disputed beliefs are faith in a creator, supernatural beings (angels, etc.), nirvāna, and the inspiration of sacred writings. On many points there is no direct opposition, but at first glance, it must be said that things are seen *otherwise,* and that *other* concepts are used. Christian does, however, describe a method for showing that opposition between

---

[140] Christian, *Meaning and Truth*, p. 109.
[141] Christian, *Oppositions*, p. 99.
[142] *Ibid*, p. 97.
[143] *Ibid*, p. 73.
[144] *Ibid*, p. 84.
[145] *Ibid*, p. 88.

doctrines is indeed at stake, although he notes emphatically that conflicting beliefs are not tantamount to opposition between persons.[146] One can regard others very highly, respecting their person and their way of life, and still hold different views. Respect does not demand that others are always right. It does demand that one is prepared to learn from others in discussion, and, if necessary, to revise one's own notions.[147] He presents a fitting quote from Dogen (13th cent.) in connection with this proposition:

> Those who are lax in their thinking are saying that the essence of Taoism, Confucianism, and Buddhism is identical, that the difference is only that of the entrance into the Way, and also that the three are comparable to the three legs of a tripod. Many Buddhist monks of the great Sung (dynasty) have quite often said this. If people say such things, Buddhism has already gone from them.[148]

If one accepts the conception that beliefs can be in conflict, the next question is whether they can be discussed. Christian reviews a number of reasons which are advanced to clarify why beliefs cannot be discussed, e.g., the need for paradoxical language, the analogical character of religious language, or the nature of the transcendent which eludes all formulation (we will encounter all of these qualifications in Part 2 of this study). The most important of the objections against the articulation of propositions within the bounds of religion, according to Christian, is that the formulation of propositions is not a religious activity.[149] One cannot make meaningful assertions about the infinite. Christian points out, however, that if one is entirely incapable of giving descriptive statements, it becomes impossible to explain the *context* of religion.[150] In actuality there are methods to help people along. Nevertheless, says Christian, it is important to realize that discourse concerning Brahman, *nirvāṇa*, or God is not about physical objects.[151] Christian claims that such a misconception of religious language usage can be obviated by speaking of 'open concepts' which are in principle susceptible to improvement. He thus maintains the cognitive aspect of religious language. Beliefs *can* be discussed to a certain extent.

To what extent can decisions be reached about the truth of religious propositions? The problem which hampers discussion between religious traditions about conflicting views is that such conflicts are accompanied by different insights regarding the value of argumentation; there are 'different rules for relevance and consistency.'[152] An internal doctrinal dispute can be settled in a tradition using the internal rules of that

---

[146] *Ibid*, p. 85.
[147] *Ibid*, pp. 117ff.
[148] In Christian, *Oppositions*, pp. 115f., cf. p. 5.
[149] Christian, *Meaning and Truth*, pp. 256, cf. pp. 155, 100.
[150] *Ibid*, p. 257.
[151] *Ibid*, pp. 258f.
[152] Christian, *Oppositions*, p. 12; compare, " ... the doctrines of religion have their own consistency-rules, their own way of hanging together in a scheme," p. 34.

tradition.[153] External differences, however, cannot be settled with the aid of neutral, supra-religious rules. No 'master-norm' exists, providing a foundation for other norms, with which all other persuasions could then be assessed.[154] This does not imply, however, that no discussion about doctrinal differences is possible. In the first place, traditions themselves apply norms. These norms are not arbitrary. There is a difference between assertions which are supposedly unbound by criteria, and assertions bound by the norms observed within the context of a life-view.[155] This latter type is not arbitrary. In the second place, it appears upon closer inspection that people decidedly do observe certain norms. These norms can be discussed. Arguments can apparently be tendered.[156] The lack of a 'master-norm,' however, entails that a final decision can never be made.[157]

The question of truth entails a certain *harmony between thought and reality,* Christian says.[158] That is why religious traditions claim universal validity as soon as they allege something about the nature of reality. If one claims universal validity, but discussion about such propositions is indecisive, the question emerges as to how one can be sure of such a belief. In connection with the certitude of faith, Christian distinguishes three strata in a religious persuasion:

(1) 'Basic proposals' and 'doctrinal propositions' that are believed to be reasonably certain.

(2) 'Illuminating suggestions' which one accepts whole-heartedly.

(3) 'Basic suppositions' which are 'unquestioned.'[159]

Religious knowledge thus occurs at various levels. The certainty is not of a similar nature at all levels. At the third and deepest level lie convictions of which one is assuredly convinced. The basic suppositions form the basis of the process of thought by which people arrive at conclusions.[160] Recall here Wittgenstein's remarks about religious pictures by which people live. At the level of formulations and dogmas, discussion is possible; yet this discussion and openness to alternative formulations poses no threat to the deeper certainty. A portion of the beliefs of a religion belong to these basic suppositions; if one does not share them, says Christian, then one is not religious. The level of the basic suppositions is more closely connected to the whole of experience than is the level of the

---

[153] *Ibid*, p. 3.

[154] Christian, *Meaning and Truth*, p. 252; cf. *Oppositions*, p. 4.

[155] Christian, *Meaning and Truth*, p. 251. He gives four criteria to test truth-claims by religious traditions, on p. 24: (a) self-consistency; (b) the proposal should make disagreements possible; (c) reference to the subject-matter under discussion should be possible; (d) the proposal should allow support to be given for ascribing certain qualities to the subject-matter under discussion.

[156] *Ibid*, pp. 236 f.

[157] *Ibid*, p. 159.

[158] *Ibid*, p. 238.

[159] *Ibid*, p. 245.

[160] *Ibid*, p. 247.

propositions.[161] Experience plays a major role in religion, in Christian's conception. He regards propositions as secondary to experience in this context. Propositions are *attempts* to define the reality experienced. He notes that it is thus possible to affirm the figure of Christ with all one's heart without being certain of each dogma, for the presence of Christ (or, e.g., the Buddha) in the believer's experience is beyond question. No matter how high his esteem for propositions, Christian does recognize that we rely on experience for our basic orientation.[162]

William A. Christian's view is illuminating in more than one respect. Among the ideas which we will elaborate in the analytical part of this study, some are akin to his: the distinction between levels of knowledge, prominent reference to experience, and the idea of an unrestricted primacy of certain subjects above all others. On the basis of our account of religious epistemology in Part 2, we will distinguish five ways of speaking about truth in religion; we will above all elaborate the anthropological basis of those experiences which sustain religion. We will introduce important nuances to the discussion of 'primacy' in religion. Another correction which must be inserted into Christian's view is that religious traditions do not have such clear rules for settling internal differences of opinion as he purports. This too can be clarified by introducing some nuance to the idea of 'primacy.' In this chapter we will now move on to discuss the view of Wilfred Smith, which is more or less contrary to that of Christian. Smith places all emphasis at the point at which all religions agree (insofar as they conform to their intention): *faith*.

3.2   Wilfred C. Smith: 'faith as a generic category'

Ever since his study, *The Meaning and End of Religion* (1962), Wilfred Smith has tenaciously championed an open encounter between people from various religious traditions. As opposed to a rigid conception of religion, he underscores the mobility of religious traditions; over against an objectifying view of religion, he stresses the personal elements in faith; rejecting an antithetical attitude towards other religions he encourages an approach of dialogue to followers of other faiths. It was his aspiration to promote an interreligious discussion in which people would no longer write about other religions from the perspective of their own without first listening to others or even consulting them. Smith thus endeavoured to discover an attitude for believing people who are conscious of the fact that there are many religious traditions and that each religious tradition itself is a quilted conglomeration.[163] He favours global theology; not a neutral theology, but a form of theological reflection conducted from the

---

[161] *Ibid*, p. 246.

[162] *Ibid*, p. 246.

[163] Wilfred Cantwell Smith, *Towards a World Theology* (London 1981), pp. 5f.: The unity of a religious tradition lies in the historical relations within a tradition.

perspective of one's own tradition, attempting as much as possible to learn from the insights which other traditions have attained. Proceeding from one's own (exclusive) rightness is parochial. Those who have truly met people from other traditions know that they can have sincere faith and find well-being in their religion, just as people from one's own tradition do.[164] Religious experience is determined by context and situation; religious traditions are subject to cultural influences.[165] Such an insight moderates differences as being relative.[166] Smith demands respect for followers of other traditions: Let the one regard the other as pre-eminent. Next to loyalty to fellow believers, however, stands loyalty to one's own tradition. Smith is not evasive on this score; he himself stands within the Christian tradition.[167] Both these loyalties are voiced when Smith states that it is his intention to participate in the whole of history in a Christian way:[168] in other words, God's history with all people.[169]

In this way, Smith aims to connect the unity of 'faith' with the multitude of expressions and experiences of faith. For this he utilizes the distinction between the terms faith and belief. Faith is generic, a trait of the human genus. People have —each in their own fashion— worshipped God, even if in the form of idols.[170] Everywhere people speak the truth and everywhere they do good, the hand of God can be recognized, because He is the Truth.[171] God has spoken to people everywhere, Smith believes.[172] Religions are the varied human responses to God's speaking. Religious traditions form the accumulated deposit of human reactions to God's initiative.[173] One can never come to know the revelation of God apart from its concomitant human response and human interpretation.[174] The history of religions is a divine-human complex.[175] Thus, God does not reveal himself exclusively in one revelation. He does not reveal a revelation, but he reveals himself, to people, in the midst of their existence.[176] People can hear the voice of God in their sacred writings, as Muslims do in the Koran and Christians do in the Bible.[177]

---

164 Smith, *World Theology*, pp. 170f., 168; *Religious Diversity: Essays*, ed. W. G. Oxtoby (New York 1976), pp. 14f.
165 Smith, *The Meaning and End of Religion* (1962; rpt. New York 1964), pp. 171f.
166 Smith, *World Theology*, p. 90; cf. his *Belief and History* (Charlottesville 1977), p. 33.
167 Smith, *World Theology*, p. 44; *Religious Diversity*, pp. 136; see also his *Faith and Belief* (Princeton 1979), p. 12.
168 Smith, *World Theology*, pp. 129; cf. pp. 177ff.
169 Smith, *Faith and Belief*, p. 140; *World Theology*, pp. 3f., 164f., 154ff.; *Religious Diversity*, p. 137.
170 Smith, *Meaning and End*, p. 127.
171 Smith, *Questions of Religious Truth* (London 1967,) p. 85.
172 Smith, *Religious Diversity*, p. 21; Smith, "On Dialogue and 'Faith': A Rejoinder," *Religion* 3 (1973): 112.
173 Cf. Smith, *Meaning and End*, pp. 139ff.
174 Smith, *World Theology*, pp. 127f.
175 Smith, *Religious Diversity*, pp. 120, 123.
176 Smith, *Meaning and End*, p. 116; *World Theology*, pp. 173f.
177 Smith, *Questions*, pp. 55f., 84; *World Theology*, p. 164; *Faith and Belief*, p. 4.

Throughout the variegated entirety of a religious tradition, the concern is ultimately with the nucleus of the matter, which is personal belief: faith. One can never come to know a person's beliefs separately from the forms of its expression in ritual, prayer, and confession.[178] Faith is thus the primary phenomenon; beliefs are secondary.[179] People don't believe in propositions; they believe in God. They hold God to be true; God is the truth.

How can faith be further defined? Smith holds that a definition cannot in principle be given.[180] As soon as one says something substantial about faith, one becomes entangled in the differences which accompany beliefs. He is willing to give an open circumscription: faith is everything that a tradition means to an insider.[181] In his work, Smith gives several other indications of what he understands by faith, such as: faith is what the universe means for someone (in the light of the tradition in which the believer stands); faith is man's participation in God's dealing with humankind; faith is the capacity of people to devote themselves to the transcendent.[182] Faith includes insight into all of reality, into the universe. Everything in life is thus bound up with faith. Religious commitment is accompanied by a certain attitude towards life.[183] Taking into account the whole of human history, Smith thinks it possible to state that faith is a universal quality. Actually it is *the* essential human quality, according to Smith; this quality is constitutive for human existence.[184] Thus, on the one hand, Smith points out something universally human; on the other hand, he wants to maintain the pluriformity of religions — the faith of the one is not the same as the faith of the other.[185] That is why he refers both to the transcendent as well as to tradition in his profile of faith. Smith has been criticized on this point. For example, Sharp has opposed Smith by pointing out that no uniform faith exists right across the board for all religions. In response, Smith could say that this is precisely his own perspective. He does not wish to speak of the essence of religion.[186] In his

---

[178] Smith, *Meaning and End*, p. 152; cf. pp. 155 ff.

[179] Smith, *Belief and History*, p. 51; *Faith and Belief*, p. 125, et passim.

[180] Smith, "On Dialogue . . . ," pp. 108 ff.; *Religious Diversity*, pp. 104 f.

[181] Smith, *Religious Diversity*, pp. 104 f.; *Meaning and End*, p. 143; *Faith and Belief*, pp. 6 ff.; *World Theology*, p. 47; "On Dialogue . . . ," p. 109.

[182] Smith, *World Theology*, p. 47; *Faith and Belief*, pp. 103, 140. Other circumscriptions can be found in *Meaning and End*, p. 116; *Belief and History*, pp. 79 f., 83; *Faith and Belief*, pp. 11 f., cf. pp. 40, 60 ff., 87, 101; *World Theology*, pp. 110 f., 113.

[183] Smith, *Belief and History*, p. 93.

[184] Smith, *Faith and Belief*, p. 129.

[185] Passim; plainly so in Smith, "On Dialogue . . . ," pp. 108 f.

[186] Smith, *Meaning and End*, p. 130. E. J. Sharpe remarks, in "Dialogue and Faith," *Religion* 3 (1973): 89-105, that faith is always determined by the subject of faith; a uniform, abstract faith, identical throughout all religion therefore cannot exist. Sharpe thinks that this amounts to a critique of Smith, see esp. pp. 97 ff. Smith could assure him that he agrees fully, however. Cf. "On Dialogue . . . ," pp. 108 ff. Compare also Smith's critique of 'essences,' *Meaning and End*, p. 130. Smith's views have been discussed many times. Further critiques: A. R. Gualtieri, " 'Faith, Belief,

reflections on faith, he aims to do justice both to its plurality as well as to its universally human quality. Sometimes he places the emphasis on the similarities of human faith; at other times on the differences between them. Sometimes he says that the faith of the one resembles that of the other more than is commonly thought; faith is a relative constant.[187] At other times he stresses the many kinds of religious experience. What is constant in religious commitment is that one enters into a relation with the one God; what varies is that right up to the point at which one meets God, the religious experience is continually determined by circumstances and tradition. That is why there is both universality as well as plurality in faith.[188] It is due to this universality that Smith wishes to speak of faith only in the singular.[189]

Nonetheless, Smith does not regard what religious traditions have to say as unimportant. The issue of mutually exclusive, or perhaps complementary, propositions is extraordinarily complicated, however.[190]

(1) A first complicating factor is that cumulative traditions have a comprehensive character, the whole of which influences the meaning of words and statements.[191] As an aside, one can also find this observation in the work of Hendrik Kraemer.[192] Although Kraemer, on the basis of this insight, decides that *bhakti* and *pistis,* for example, are entirely different categories,[193] Smith regards the faith of the one as comparable to the faith of another; the differences between the traditions are primarily situated in the beliefs.

(2) A second complication in comparing religious statements is that propositions are not in themselves true or untrue. Assertions acquire their meaning within the context of the communication which they serve. People do not know propositions but rather the reality to which the assertions refer (contextually).[194] Religious symbols, myths, and metaphors do not obtain their significance from themselves but receive content from the process of becoming aware of reality.[195] Comparison of religious beliefs is difficult because of these two factors.

---

and Transcendence' according to Wilfred Cantwell Smith," *Journal of Dharma* 6 (1981), esp. p. 249; and P. Slater, D. Wiebe, and T. Horvath, "Three responses to Faith and Belief: A Review Article," *Studies in Religion* 10 (1981): 113-26.

[187] Smith, *Religious Diversity,* p. 10; cf. *Faith and Belief,* pp. 11, 13.

[188] Smith, *Faith and Belief,* p. 151; "On Dialogue . . . ," pp. 108 f.

[189] Oxtoby, in the Introduction to *Religious Diversity,* p. xix; cf. Smith, *World Theology,* p. 118; in one passage, faith is written as a plural, 'faiths,' *Religious Diversity,* p. 151.

[190] Smith, *Questions,* pp. 81 ff.; *Faith and Belief,* p. 153.

[191] Smith, *Belief and History,* p. 43; see also his "Conflicting Truth-Claims: A Rejoinder," in *Truth and Dialogue: The Relationship between World Religions,* ed. J. Hick (London 1974), pp. 157 f.; *World Theology,* p. 82.

[192] H. Kraemer, *Godsdienst, Godsdiensten en het Christelijk Geloof* (Nijkerk 1958), pp. 38, 66, cf. p. 112; *The Christian Message in a Non-Christian World* (London 1938), pp. 148 f.

[193] Kraemer, *The Christian Message,* p. 172, 'cannot be compared.'

[194] Smith, *Belief and History,* p. 51.

[195] *Ibid,* pp. 88, cf. pp. 23, 97; *World Theology,* p. 64.

Smith does not deny the importance of beliefs.[196] Yet faith is and remains primary; Smith writes that 'believing,' and related words such as 'belief,' come from 'to love,' just as 'credo' comes from *cor do* (I give my heart to God)[197]. The primary issue is to love God, and faith only secondarily involves propositions. This awareness has been obscured in Western culture. The image of what faith is has undergone a long development in which it has shifted from loving God —via holding doctrines to be true— to holding uncertainties and absurdities for truths.[198] In order to come to the point and to speak responsibly and directly about faith, beliefs have to be rejoined to faith again. Buddhists do not believe that *dharma* is true, but perceive that things in their life happen in accordance with what is expounded in *dharma*.[199] In studying assertions by religious traditions, the proper question is therefore not precisely which views people hold to be true, but to what form of religious commitment a certain belief-system has conferred structure and by what this faith was generated.[200]

This does not mean that Smith regards the choice for one or another belief-system as trivial.[201] Beliefs do matter; faith does not occur apart from conceptualization,[202] and intellectual integrity makes demands.[203] We will return to this matter again later.

With reference to the study of religions, Smith thinks that one ought to appreciate the mutual influence religions have on one another. It is in fact not very accurate to speak of religions as cumulative traditions — a term which he himself forged and which many have adopted. The term still suggests too strongly that religions are separate entities, which they are not. In actuality there is a single history of humankind, which is simultaneously the history wherein God grants his grace to people,[204] and all believers participate in this one history.[205] These currents are so interrelated, and there is so much interaction, that one must learn to think in terms of the whole when studying religion. Smith considers it unwarranted to construct a view of other religions in terms of one religious point of view.[206] That is reasoning too much in terms of the one bulwark going out to meet the other. Theology must become global and comparative. The comparative religion of which he is a proponent is "the

---

[196] Smith, *Faith and Belief*, pp. 124 f., cf. p. 82.
[197] Smith, *Belief and History*, p. 41.
[198] *Ibid*, pp. 51-65.
[199] Smith, *Faith and Belief*, p. 31.
[200] Smith, *Belief and History*, p. 88.
[201] Smith, *Faith and Belief*, pp. 167, 51 f.; *Meaning and End*, p. 166; *Questions*, p. 67.
[202] Smith, *Faith and Belief*, pp. 168 ff.
[203] Smith, *World Theology*, p. 82; *Faith and Belief*, pp. 82, 168.
[204] Smith, *World Theology*, pp. 33, 169 ff.; *Religious Diversity*, p. 137.
[205] Smith, *World Theology*, p. 172, cf. pp. 39, 43.
[206] *Ibid*, pp. 110, 152.

profound self-awareness of man in his and her unintegrated wholeness."[207] A global theology will ensue from this comparative approach to the study of religion; here the question of truth comes into view, because in the study of the faith of others as it is lived, one automatically confronts the question of what one can learn from others.

In this context, Smith raises the problem of the conditions for the possibility of understanding people from other religious traditions. One ought to try and get into the other's skin and to see with the other's eyes.[208] Smith regards such comprehension to be possible.[209] His assumption is that human beings, no matter how different, are ultimately one.[210] People live in the same world; whoever tries to understand something of the *Gita* will learn something about the world in which he himself lives as well. The conditions for the possibility of understanding others lie in human *corporate self-consciousness*.[211] This self-consciousness is transcultural, critical, and global.[212] Since it is focussed on common humanity, it is implicit in this idea that in the study of the many forms of faith one must endeavour to enrich one's own faith.[213] If one succeeds in reaching a synthesis of other's insights with one's own faith, then dormant facets of one's own existence will be brought to light.[214] It is in this cautious manner that the question of truth is at issue in the study of religious traditions.

One must, however, realize that the goal in the dialogical study of religions upon which one has embarked cannot be reached; one is always underway. No one can oversee all religions and single-handedly rule on what is and is not true![215] One can attempt to approach the truth as nearly as is possible in such a dialogical process, but each participant stands within his own religious tradition.[216] Participation in religious history is even a precondition for understanding the faith of others, and one can therefore engage in the study of religion as a Muslim or as a Christian without qualms. Smith himself says in his studies that he wants to preserve the insight that the salvation of humanity has been effectuated through Jesus Christ.[217] Precisely because it becomes manifest in Jesus that

---

[207] *Ibid*, p. 49.

[208] Smith, *Meaning and End*, p. 125.

[209] Smith, "Comparative Religion: Whither and Why?" in *The History of Religions: Essays in Methodology*, eds. M. Eliade and J. M. Kitagawa (1959; rpt. Chicago ⁵1970), p. 56.

[210] Smith, *Religious Diversity*, p. 88.

[211] Smith, *World Theology*, pp. 59ff., 55; cf. *Religious Diversity*, pp. 160-80.

[212] Smith, *World Theology*, pp. 62, 59f., 102.

[213] *Ibid*, p. 103.

[214] *Ibid*, p. 79.

[215] Smith, *Questions*, p. 74; cf. *Belief and History*, p. 2; *World Theology*, p. 65.

[216] Smith, *World Theology*, pp. 191, 135.

[217] Smith, *Religious Diversity*, p. 16; cf. pp. 123, 136f. On the 'Christian' character of his pronouncements, cf. *World Theology*, pp. 177f.; there Smith says that he has experienced a change of mind regarding salvation, which is not to say, in my

God is a God of Love, the salvation of God extends to Buddhists, Hindus, and Muslims.[218]

In conclusion, we will examine Smith's view on the question of truth. Oxtoby notes that three conceptions of truth occur in the work of Smith.[219] Oxtoby calls it *existential* truth when the participants in a religious tradition find that the religious commitment which that tradition mediates rings true. He calls it *moral* truth when observants believe that their religious tradition agrees with the will of God. And *propositional* truth is the truth of beliefs if they agree with reality and experience. Oxtoby adds that Smith increasingly speaks about God as the Truth from whom all other truth is derived. Smith's view is indeed related to that conception of truth in the Western tradition which calls God *ens verum*.[220] God is the Truth.[221] Faith, so says Smith, is "saying 'yes' to the truth."[222] A religious tradition can be called true if it mediates well the experience of God, the Truth.[223] Smith is extremely reluctant to spell out criteria for good or true religion. He suggests that one criterion for appraising religious systems could lie in the degree to which a particular system helps a person to reach a right relationship to oneself, one's neighbour, and the universe — including (inasmuch as this occurs at the level of ideas) relationship by virtue of intellectual apprehension.[224] Even though Smith places all the emphasis on faith, beliefs also matter. He writes:

> If it is to be faithful, (it must) be the closest approximation to the truth of which one's mind is capable.[225]

Not all religion and not all beliefs are equally true, according to Smith.[226] If consideration is given to the fact that propositions do not possess such truth as they have in and of themselves, then Smith is willing to say: "some potential beliefs are truer than others."[227]

Smith is of course extremely reluctant to speak about contradictions between religions. Above all, he does not wish to speak monolithically about 'a religion,' which then asserts this or that. Religious traditions are insufficiently uniform for that. He subsequently objects to the pretension

---

opinion, that he no longer relates salvation to Jesus.

[218] Smith, *Religious Diversity*, p. 20.

[219] Oxtoby, in the Introduction to *Religious Diversity*, p. xx (f.).

[220] Smith, *Belief and History*, p. 83; cf. *Faith and Belief*, p. 82 *'prima veritas'*; "Conflicting Truth-Claims . . . ," pp. 21 f.; *Questions*, p. 78; see below, Ch. VI §§ 3.2 and 3.3.

[221] Smith, *World Theology*, pp. 123 f.; *Questions*, p. 85; *Al-Haqq: Faith and Belief*, pp. 42 f.; 'transcendental conception of truth,' p. 157.

[222] Smith, *Faith and Belief*, pp. 163 f.; cf. p. 168.

[223] Cf. Smith, *Questions*, pp. 68, 70: religion becomes true; the criterion lies in the example of true religion.

[224] Smith, *Belief and History*, p. 28.

[225] Smith, *Faith and Belief*, p. 168; Smith's italics; cf. pp. 169 f.

[226] Smith, *Meaning and End*, p. 166.

[227] Smith, *Faith and Belief*, p. 142; *Belief and History*, p. 51.

in the term truth *claims*.[228] People bear witness to the truth, they continually indicate aspects of the multi-faceted truth, which on later examination do not appear as contradictory as they first seemed. Smith advocates a dialogical study of religion in which people together search further for the Truth.

One can question Smith's view. He is open-minded. Every claim to exclusive knowledge concerning God is foreign to him, and yet he confers uniqueness upon the tradition in which he stands. If one were to ask him whether he is not being inconsistent here, his answer would presumably be that every tradition has unique insights. Sometimes he has been interpreted as though he ascribes no value to beliefs. Actually, in his view faith never occurs without beliefs. He does, however, sometimes *accentuate* faith to the detriment of beliefs. Smith advances some exceedingly important insights, but it occurs to us that he places religions all on a par more than accords with reality.

3.3 John Hick: religions as outlooks upon God and the world

Hick was one of the first post-war philosophers of religion to point out the importance of the confrontation between religions. For more than a century, the most important challenge to Christianity was the upsurge of the natural sciences and technology. Now that the various cultures increasingly have more contact, determining the position of Christianity in the world of the religions is the first task. The danger in the profusion of religious traditions to which Hick repeatedly draws attention is the trivialization of religion: If it is possible to say so many different things about God, can they then be true? What one believes depends on where one was born — this can be read many times in Hick's work. One cannot persist in the view that there is no salvation outside of one's own religion. As a Christian, Hick warns —again, repeatedly— about the parochialism of the expression *extra ecclesiam nulla salus*. There is salvation outside the church and Christianity; everyone can see that. Many Christians reluctantly do acknowledge that; but to retain the uniqueness and exclusivity of Christianity, all manner of improbable hypotheses are built onto the edifice of one's own theology. Whether one speaks of the hidden Christ of the Hindus, or of followers of other faiths as anonymous Christians, it bespeaks a desire to combine the incompatible: on the one hand, the exclusivity of Christian salvation is maintained; on the other hand, one acknowledges salvation among other religions. Just as the Ptolemaic world view could not be rescued by contrived accretions, so this 'Christianity-centered' world view cannot be retained. It must be replaced. Christianity is not the centre of the religions, but God. Hick argues for a 'God-centered'

---

[228] Smith, "Conflicting Truth-Claims," p. 158; *Faith and Belief,* p. 163.

reorientation within religions, in which it is open-mindedly acknowledged that there are many roads which lead to salvation.

Hick distinguishes between *fides* and *fiducia* within faith. Confident faith bases itself on the belief (*fides*) that God exists and is trustworthy.[229] On many points, Hick agrees with Smith, but not with his concept of truth, which Hick considers too personalistic Hick defines truth thus: "right relationship to reality."[230] In Hick's view, this personalistic concept of truth does not resolve the problem of colliding religious views. Hick can go along with Smith on many scores, yet he retains the claim to true knowledge. When Smith says that Christianity and Hinduism *are* not true, but that they can *become* true for someone because they help them to experience God, Hick judges this to be insufficient:

> For surely 'Christianity' or 'Hinduism' can only *become* true in the personalistic sense because they are already true in another, more universal and objective though less existential sense.[231]

Although knowledge has a subjective aspect, its character is objective. Knowledge is objective in the sense that it is 'the same for everyone.'[232] Hick accordingly does not allow the claim to be dropped that religion provides knowledge. He defines faith as follows: "Religious faith is seeing and experiencing the world as being under the ultimate control of sovereign personal Love."[233] We will now present Hick's view proceeding from this definition of faith.

It appears from this definition that faith is based on experience. God is transcendent; the experience of God for the ordinary believer is therefore not immediate.[234] People have a 'sense of the presence of God.'[235] This experience is based on the human capacity for perceiving a situation as a whole.[236] One then perceives the significance of a situation. In this experience of 'significance,' one experiences "... that fundamental and all-pervasive characteristic of our conscious experience which de facto constitutes for us the experience of a 'world' and not of a mere empty void or churning chaos."[237] Thus, there are certain experiences in which and by which human beings experience the transcendent; existence is experienced as meaningful then. The transcendent —as infinite—

---

[229] J. Hick, *Faith and Knowledge* (London ²1967), pp. 3f.
[230] Hick, "The Outcome: Dialogue into Truth," in *Truth and Dialogue*, p. 143.
[231] Hick, "The Outcome . . . ," p. 146.
[232] Hick, *Faith and Knowledge*, p. 207.
[233] *Ibid*, p. 263.
[234] *Ibid*, pp. 95f.
[235] Hick, *God and the Universe of Faiths* (London 1973), p. 47; *Faith and Knowledge*, pp. 146f.
[236] Hick, *Faith and Knowledge*, pp. 81f.
[237] *Ibid*, p. 98.

cannot be experienced immediately; the experience of God is therefore always mediated by other experiences.[238]

Since the experience of God is mediated by other experiences, human knowledge of God is always an *interpretation* of the religious experience.[239] Religion is a way of seeing reality. Hick harks back to the view of Ludwig Wittgenstein.[240] He concurs with Wittgenstein that things can be experienced in more than one way. Hick objects to D. Z. Phillips' elaboration of Wittgenstein's view because Phillips fails to appreciate that religious statements claim the status of knowledge; they presume to have a factual character;[241] at issue is the truth. Yet at the same time, Hick regards all knowledge of reality as an interpretive knowledge. The events which one experiences are fundamentally ambiguous; they allow of more than one interpretation.[242] Believers experience the presence of God in certain situations. These experiences are sometimes accompanied by a sense of moral obligation, and sometimes by a sense of majestic beauty.[243] Faith is not based on intellectual reasonings, but on a way of experiencing reality. All experience is 'experiencing *as*...' Religious experience shares the general structure of human knowledge, although faith includes an interpretive moment: one learns to experience reality as sustained by the transcendent.[244]

Such a *view* of reality arises through a " 'divine-human encounter,' a mediated meeting with the living God."[245] Hick regards the history of religions as the history of God with all people and increasingly insists on accomodating all religious traditions. All religious movements form part of one great divine movement of self-revelation to humanity.[246] The various religious traditions are not really rivals, but divergent ways in which people have conceived of God's revelation.[247] Hick defines *religion* as follows:

> the understanding of the universe, together with an appropriate way of living within it, which involves reference beyond the natural world to God or gods or to the Absolute or to a transcendent order or process.[248]

Since the transcendent is the concern, one cannot speak about it literally. Concepts must be coined in order to signify this distinctive reality. Such concepts have two sides. Hick calls them icons through which one knows

---

[238] *Ibid*, pp. 95 f.; cf. *Universe*, p. 44. Hick says that mystical experience of God is relatively independent of external circumstances, *Universe*, p. 47.

[239] Hick, *Faith and Knowledge*, p. 43.

[240] Hick, *Faith and Knowledge*, p. 142.

[241] Hick, *Universe*, pp. 25 ff.; 33 ff.

[242] *Ibid*, p. 43.

[243] *Ibid*, p. 47.

[244] Cf. Hick, *Universe*, p. 50.

[245] Hick, *Faith and Knowledge*, p. 115.

[246] Hick, *Universe*, p. 138.

[247] *Ibid*, p. 137.

[248] *Ibid*, p. 133.

God, but he also calls them idols, since they are themselves easily revered.[249] They are necessary since the Ultimate can only be worshipped in terms of a particular appearance.[250]

Various religious traditions see reality from different perspectives. The 'infinite divine reality' is named and experienced differently in terms of various cultural frameworks.[251] As diverse as cultures are, so divergent are religions. Thus, on the one hand, Hick regards experienced reality as fundamentally ambiguous; there *is* room for more than one interpretation. On the other hand, one of the reasons why people interpret differently lies in the plurality of cultural traditions.[252] All religions have undergone ample developments. One cannot point out an 'essence.' The fixed element in a tradition is the beginning, the original inspiration on which the tradition is based. Religions have grown outwards in many directions from this starting point due to the influence of various circumstances. It is not impossible in our time that they now grow towards each other through more mutual contact.[253] Perhaps, in the course of time, people will look at the various religious traditions in much the same manner as they view the divergent Christian denominations of Europe and North America today.[254]

Is every religion then equally good? No one would say that, according to Hick. Everyone knows how thoroughly the good and the bad are blended in religions, as in all of human existence. Not all religion is good, but religions in which people have found salvation for ages must boast something of value. Hick believes it probable that any conception from an old and eminent tradition which has for ages sustained human faith can mediate a real encounter with divine reality.[255]

The question arises how such a view of reality emerged. Hick ascribes great importance to the founders of religions. They have experienced something of divine reality as few others have; a religion emerged due to their contagious experience of God. Great minds later consolidated the new movement.[256] Hick thoroughly examines the grounds on which people allow such 'mediators' to lead them. He mentions three. (1) They envisioned a concept of God and of how people must live; their *morality* linked up to that of the culture in which they lived —otherwise they would have been unintelligible; they lived in accordance with their teaching, and the affinity between their teaching and their life made an impression. Hick thus contends that one can recognize a 'mediator' by an ethical criterion. (2) A second reason to believe a religious founder lies in the promising, deep, and compellingly new view of reality which he provides. Also

---

[249] Hick, *God Has Many Names* (London 1980), pp. 48f.
[250] Hick, *Universe*, p. 178.
[251] *Ibid*, p. 145.
[252] *Ibid*, p. 141.
[253] *Ibid*, p. 146.
[254] *Ibid*, p. 147.
[255] *Ibid*, p. 141.
[256] Hick, "On Grading Religions," *Religious Studies* 17 (1981): 457ff.

present with reference to this new view, was a close relationship between the new message and the basic perceptions of the culture concerned.[257] The new message would otherwise have been incomprehensible. (3) A third element which made the founders plausible was the transformational force of the new view of reality.[258] Hick also points out the bipolarity of the experience of the 'mediators' between divine reality and the rest of the people; their experience concerned the transcendent, yet no matter how special, it remained the experience of people determined by their own time and culture.

Since religions make a claim to truth, it is inevitable that people try to think through the implications of their faith. In this way doctrine emerges. Hick opposes a reification of doctrine over against faith. God did not reveal propositions but himself — as one can read repeatedly in Hick's work. Religious reflection and systematic formulation is always secondary. Theology is the work of mortals. As such, theology is conditioned by time and influenced by the culture in which it exists.[259] Hick more than once deals with Christology; he has undergone an important development on this point, precisely due to the influence of his study of other religious traditions and his practical activity on behalf of the Birmingham Council of Religions.[260] Initially he wrote about the faith of Jesus and faith *in* Jesus, and about Jesus Christ as in one sense or another both God and man.[261] In later publications Hick regards Christology as a later dogmatic construction.[262] Christology is the myth that Jesus Christ is God incarnate. Myths are not literally true; they evoke a certain attitude on the part of the hearer; they have practical significance. People who have found God the heavenly Father through Jesus Christ express that mythologically by saying that he is the incarnate son of God.[263] Conceived thus, the story of Jesus does not invoke exclusive truth claims on behalf of the Christian tradition.

Hick quotes a Hindu adage with approval: "Whatever path men choose is Mine."[264] Despite all the differences between religions, what people are actually doing in the diverse forms of worship is essentially the same.[265] People pray to the divine One.[266] All religions belong to the one history of the divine with humanity, and they could learn much from each other

---

[257] *Ibid*, p. 459.
[258] *Ibid*, p. 460.
[259] Cf. Hick, *Faith and Knowledge*, pp. 218f.
[260] Hick, *Many names*, Chapters 1 and 2.
[261] Hick, *Faith and Knowledge*, p. 220.
[262] Hick, *Many names*, pp. 68ff., 87f., 56.
[263] Hick, *Universe*, p. 172.
[264] Hick, *Many names*, pp. 43ff., 58; *Bhagavadgītā*, IV. 11; cf. J. P. K. Sukul, *De Bhagavad-gītā: Nederlandse vertaling en enkele Hoofdstukken Beschouwingen* (Utrecht 1958), p. 27, cf. p. 124.
[265] Hick, *Many names*, p. 45.
[266] *Ibid*, p. 48.

in a 'global theology.'[267] Hick believes that religions differ too much ever to become one. Each religion should desist from making exclusive claims to the truth, however. This is not to deny that each religion is unique. The gift of Christianity to other people, for instance, is that they can deepen their relationship to God through awareness of the person of Jesus Christ.[268] In every religion something of great value has come to light — even if the faith of most of the adherents of a religion is rather mediocre and even though aberrations crop up time and again. It is possible to learn from one another without converting one another.[269]

Despite all of the wonderful things there are to report about the fellowship of the various religions, Hick contends that conflicting views are possible and do in fact exist, referring at this juncture to the work of W. A. Christian.[270] Although religions do indeed hark back to experiences of the same divine reality, they interpret this in different ways. This is what opens up the possibility of contradiction. Hicks summarizes three kinds of possible differences between religions:[271]

(1) Differences as to the manner in which one experiences the divine, e.g., personally or impersonally.

(2) Differences in the philosophical and theological theories of reality or the implications of faith. As noted earlier, this reflection is secondary; it has also been subject to enormous development; recall, for example, the changes Christianity has undergone during the past 150 years.

(3) The third difference lies in the 'key-experiences' which form the basis of various religions. These experiences stem from the founders and the sacred writings. It is precisely because these people and books are regarded as sacrosanct that adherents start to claim exclusivity.

Certain experiences lie at the basis of a religion. Hick declares that religious founders such as Buddha, Jesus, and Mohammed each had their own distinctive 'encounter with reality.' Their 'root-experiences' were so overwhelming that others accepted them as authentic.[272] Religious convictions in turn sprouted from these 'root-experiences.' Such systems must be surveyed with a view to their inner consistency and to the question of whether they do justice, first, to the distinctive experiences from which they stem, and second, to human experience in general.[273] Each religious system focusses its attention on a few aspects of human experience, but is relatively indifferent with respect to other aspects of human

---

[267] Hick, *Universe*, p. 106; *Philosophy of Religion* (Englewood Cliffs, N.J. ²1973), p. 127.
[268] Hick, *Many names*, p. 75.
[269] *Ibid*, p. 85.
[270] Hick, *Philosophy*, pp. 119 ff.
[271] *Ibid*, p. 127.
[272] Hick, "On Grading Religions," p. 461.
[273] *Ibid*, p. 462.

existence. This view seems correct to me, although it requires some shading and further elaboration.[274]

Hick poses the question of whether, given the nature of religious traditions, one can speak of 'better' or 'worse.' Some people would put their religion at the head of the list without hesitation. Others would refuse to speak in terms of better or worse. Hick agrees with neither position. Sadly enough, it is obvious that there is good and bad religion. How can one tell the difference? For that one must look at the spiritual and moral fruit which various religious currents —in all their branches and offshoots— yield. In the article concerned, Hick limits himself to Hinduism, Buddhism, Christianity, and Islam. Each of these four religions springs from fundamental experiences. One can test the veracity of these experiences as follows:

> The test of the veridical character of such an experience must thus be the test of the larger religious totality which has been built around it. And such a test can only be pragmatic: is this complex of religious experience, belief, and behaviour soteriologically effective? Does it make possible the transformation of human existence from self-centeredness to Reality-centeredness?[275]

As views of reality or 'maps of the universe,' religious traditions do test themselves in practice; are they exercising their soteriological function or not? One cannot carry out this test theoretically. Who will judge which 'religious civilization' is best? How does one weigh the passivity of the Eastern religions in the face of socio-economic problems against Western greed and the exhaustion of the earth's natural resources? Even though in principle one religious civilization is possibly better in moral terms than another, no practical possibility exists for such weighing.[276]

In spite of his opposition to belief in one's own rightness Hick nonetheless reaches the verdict that quite possibly not every religious view of reality is true. It could always become apparent, he remarks, that of the many 'maps' of reality which have been designed only one is true or that they are all distorted projections of the same reality. Only the future will tell.[277] The ultimate verification (if there is one) is eschatological, Hick comments.[278]

Knowledge ultimately remains knowledge *of* reality for Hick. The truth of personal faith depends on reality really being as one says it is.[279] The question of truth therefore ultimately remains, in his view of the relationship between the religions. He distinguishes three levels of knowledge:

---

[274] See below, Ch. IX.
[275] Hick, "On Grading Religions," p. 461.
[276] *Ibid*, p. 465.
[277] *Ibid*, p. 462.
[278] Hick, *Philosophy of Religion*, pp. 100f.; *Faith and Knowledge*, pp. 176f.
[279] Hick, "The Outcome," pp. 147f.

(1) The experience of divine reality; disparate experiences of the Infinite are not contradictory per se.

(2) Conscious, transmitted *knowledge* concerning divine reality, or doctrine; though secondary, it is necessary. A global theology is required with respect to doctrine.

(3) Key —or revelation— experiences which provide unity to the various traditions. This is where the greatest problems exist with regard to the differences between religious traditions.[280]

We can concur with many of Hick's perceptions, although a number of points in his view are not entirely convincing. We will list three points:

(1) The manner in which Hick declares the incarnation to be mythology is too facile a resolution of the problem of the relationship between religions. Is it permissible in philosophical debate over interreligious relations to present an interpretation of a Christian dogma which is at odds with what most Christian thinkers believe? Does Hick here not confuse philosophy of religion with theology?

(2) Hick's threefold division of knowledge evokes questions. Throughout his exposition he utilizes a twofold division, viz. between the experience of the transcendent and the philosophical-theological articulation thereof. The key-experiences are added with reference to the founders of religious traditions. These, however, are experiences of another sort than those which Hick designates as experiences of divine reality. Questions such as the following can be raised here: Do key-experiences exclude each other, or are they complementary, or are they incomparable? What is the relationship of the key-experiences to the doctrines and to the experience of divine reality itself? We propose, in connection with these (fundamentally) universal human experiences, to speak of *basic experiences*: experiences which fundamentally affect human beings because they dovetail with the fundamental characteristics of human existence. The fundamental experiences which people must necessarily sustain are not similarly construed by different religions.

(3) If the criterion for evaluating religion is situated in the degree to which they bring well-being/salvation, one ought to realize that different conceptions of salvation are present. In Part 3 we will attempt to further elaborate a number of Hick's observations.

---

[280] *Ibid*, pp. 152ff.; cf. "On Conflicting Religious Truth-Claims," *Religious Studies* 19 (1983): 461f., where Hick indicates three levels of contradiction: 1. with respect to historical facts (e.g., Jesus did/did not die on the cross); 2. quasi- or transhistorical differences (e.g., reincarnation); 3. the mannner in which divine reality is conceived of (esp. (un)personal). Compare also H. A. Netland, "Professor Hick on Religious Pluralism," *Religious Studies* 22 (1986): 255ff. He levels two points of criticism against Hick: 1. our first point in the text; 2. Hick's use of the distinction between God in Himself and God in human cognition.

3.4 The perceptions of Wiebe and Thakur

In conclusion, we wish to mention a few perceptions of two authors who have also written on our subject: Donald Wiebe and Thakur.

In *Religion and Truth,* Donald Wiebe addresses extensively the question of whether religion yields truth, and if so, where such truth must be localized. The aim of his study is to demonstrate that the study of religion cannot skirt the question of truth. It must deal with the truth content of religions. Only if religion can in principle be true is it even possible for religious studies to run across the question of truth; and it can only occupy itself with the question of truth if religious truth is in some way accessible. Wiebe raises both issues: the nature and the accessibility of religious truth.

Wiebe thinks that religion is a 'belief-system,' albeit not primarily.[281] Smith emphasized the personal character of religion; Wiebe regards this correct, so long as this is not applied to the detriment of the epistemic side of faith (as does Smith, in his view). Smith makes a radical separation between the subjective and the objective side to religion, says Wiebe.[282] We have seen that Smith goes far in this direction, but not all the way. To support the notion that religion is concerned with truth, Wiebe refers to a statement by Ninian Smart: The world religions owe their strength partially to the success with which they give a 'total picture of reality,' a 'coherent system of doctrines.'[283] Even if human knowledge does not offer a simple reflection of reality, religious doctrine refers to reality nevertheless. Knowledge always seeks to be knowledge of external reality.[284] Wiebe also mentions the teaching of the two truths, which we will encounter in more detail in the description of Hindu and Buddhist concepts. The real religious truth, as it is then put, lies on a higher plane, unattainable for the ordinary person; only those initiated know the higher truth. In a profound sense, religious doctrine is not 'true'; viewed from a higher perspective, it is situated in the domain of worldly truth.[285] Wiebe points out that this view is in fact also familiar to Western Christian theology which sometimes speaks of 'theological truth.'[286] Such truth is personal and is not susceptible for reasonable proof.[287] Wiebe objects to these views:

> The claim, that 'religious truth' wholly transcends questions of 'ordinary' truth and falsity involves such severe difficulties that it can hardly be taken seriously as support of the claim that questions of the truth of

---

[281] Donald Wiebe, *Religion and Truth: Towards an Alternative Paradigm for the Study of Religion* (Den Haag 1981), p. 123.

[282] *Ibid,* p. 135.

[283] See Wiebe, p. 135.

[284] *Ibid,* p. 141.

[285] *Ibid,* pp. 99-105.

[286] *Ibid,* p. 145.

[287] *Ibid,* p. 146.

religion cannot legitimately be raised by the scientific (and possibly non-religious) student of religion.[288]

It appears that the doctrine of the double truth actually involves three levels of knowledge, says Wiebe: the objective, worldly truth; subsequently a mediating level; and finally, an immediate truth.[289] Wiebe contends that religious experience, no matter how esoteric it may be, is always brought to expression in ritual, ceremonies, music, and also in beliefs and philosophical systems.[290] Otherwise a discussion about religion could never take place. Faith also includes a cognitive, theoretical component.[291] Wiebe concurs with Polanyi that there is a personal involvement in knowledge of the truth; this does not mean, however, that the idea of correspondence and the objective nature of the truth must be rejected.[292] The idea of correspondence —however it should be explained— remains fundamental for all theories of truth.[293] Wiebe presents a critical appraisal of quite a number of authors on 'religion and truth' who situate religious truth in an area other than the propositional. He then demonstrates how they must nevertheless presuppose the 'truth' of a number of propositions.[294] Whether one says that religious truth is symbolically true (as distinct from propositionally true), or that religious truth is a truth inherent in reality, or that it is a (true) transformation of the person, or a personal truth, one always presupposes assertions about reality.[295] Wiebe admits, with reference to the findings of hermeneutical philosophy, that an important personal element is present in knowledge. This does not mean that the truth is entirely subjective, however. Wiebe approvingly quotes: "There can be no domain of truth that supersedes all principles of judgment."[296] Religious truth includes more than the truth of beliefs, but this 'more than' is *based* on 'rational correctness.'[297] Even if there were different 'domains' of truth accompanied by differing principles of forming judgments, there cannot be a domain without principles.[298] It would indeed be strange, says Wiebe, if the study of religion could say nothing about one of the most important aspects of religion, viz. the truth.[299] He is convinced, as mentioned, that the study of religion cannot circumvent giving a verdict regarding the (un)truth of a religion, since religious phenomena are of a different nature depending on whether the beliefs

---

[288] *Ibid*, pp. 144 f.
[289] *Ibid*, p. 148.
[290] *Ibid*, pp. 148 f.
[291] *Ibid*, p. 150.
[292] *Ibid*, pp. 183, 179.
[293] *Ibid*, p. 178.
[294] *Ibid*, pp. 193 ff.
[295] *Ibid*, p. 222.
[296] *Ibid*, p. 218.
[297] *Ibid*, pp. 223, 227.
[298] *Ibid*, p. 228.
[299] *Ibid*, p. 221.

which are presupposed are either true or untrue. Real clarification of religious phenomena cannot bypass the question of truth.[300]

In his study, Wiebe examines in detail the issue of truth in religion. He considers a succession of authors from the study of religion who have given their views on the nature of religious truth. He also mentions the so-called doctrine of two truths of Hinduism and Buddhism and makes some valuable observations, such as the idea that the doctrine of the two truths (sometimes, we would say) assumes a mediating in-between level. We shall see how that occurs when dealing with Jñānagarbha. The limitation of Donald Wiebe's book, however, is that he scarcely consults what the classics of the various religions themselves have said about the nature of religious truth (in their own tradition). His investigation therefore remains too limited. One must patiently peruse what religious people themselves say and not hasten to introduce one's own (Western, (post-) Christian) ideas about religion. This limitation of Wiebe's study makes itself felt at several points.

(1) In the first place, Wiebe does not examine the obstacles along the way to religious insight indicated by the religious traditions themselves. Religious traditions require of people a certain behaviour —as we shall see again and again; otherwise they are unable to see the truth. This is even the essence of the stricter form of the doctrine of the two truths: at the lower level, people are alienated and perceive things wrongly. Wiebe acknowledges, to be sure, that knowledge requires commitment, but the issue reaches further than he allows.

(2) Secondly, Wiebe legislates for religious traditions that their truth be propositional. He identifies the idea of correspondence (or reference to reality) with propositional truth.[301] Yet there are religious traditions which state that it is precisely propositional truth which disables an open experience of things. One must therefore pass beyond propositional thinking. Wiebe rejects this notion, for its acceptance would leave little opportunity for the critical and evaluative study of religion (sometimes conducted by unbelievers) which he advocates.

It occurs to us, in sum, that Donald Wiebe draws attention to several important points, such as the personal component in knowledge and the commitment demanded by religious knowledge; but he errs in passing over the moral transformations which religious traditions require and in too easily prescribing a Western propositional model of religious knowledge.

Shivesh Chandra Thakur distinguishes three kinds of 'commitments': belief-commitments, attitude-commitments, and action-commitments.[302] One assumes, among other things, the existence of certain metaphysical

---

[300] *Ibid*, pp. 222, 159, 3ff.
[301] *Ibid*, p. 193.
[302] Shivesh Chandra Thakur, *Religion and Rational Choice* (London 1981), p. 29.

existents. He defines religion thus: "A religion is a metaphysical theory rooted in experience and commanding deep, personal, commitment to certain beliefs, attitudes, and actions on the part of its follower(s), such commitment being (or being seen as) entailed by the theory in question."[303] Thakur regards the reference to experience as being of great importance. The major religious traditions bring to expression special experiences. Religion in this sense provides an explanation of experiences, paralleling the scientific explanation of experiences. The experiences explained by religion are special experiences, undergone by unique individuals. People such as Buddha, Jesus Christ, and Mohammed have made possible a new way of perception for other people by their extraordinary experiences.[304] Religion helps people in 'coming to terms with the world.'[305] After discussing several views of religion and language, Thakur concludes that there is no autonomous religious language; there is only religious language *usage*. There are many kinds of language usage within religion, including 'fact-stating' as well. A number of the assertions which are made in religious traditions are empirical.[306] Other assertions about 'facts' are of another order; one could call these 'metaphysical facts.' From a list of nine theses in which Thakur summarizes his view, we quote what he says about metaphysical facts and experiences:

> 3. These metaphysical facts constitute the primary statements of the theory underlying a specific religion.
> 4. The complete theory consist of these primary statements plus many secondary utterances, including empirical assertions, moral, and ritual exhortations, etc.
> 5. What turns the theory into religion is the background of relevant experiences and the deep, personal commitment of the believer to a specific policy of behaviour (seen by him to be) entailed by the theory.[307]

Thakur points out that 'asserting' is a language act by a speaker at a certain moment.[308] A language act can be successful or unsuccesful; its content can be true or untrue. Since it concerns metaphysical assertions, the truth value is undetermined. Sometimes the possibility of empirical evidence can suddenly arise, as recently perhaps appeared in connection the idea of reincarnation.[309] But even if the truth of an assertion cannot strictly be proven, it can be regarded as true if it meets certain specific criteria.[310] First, a theory must be comprehensible. One must understand the meaning of religious assertions within the context of certain religious

---

[303] *Ibid*, p. 32.
[304] *Ibid*, pp. 49, 83.
[305] *Ibid*, p. 58.
[306] *Ibid*, p. 77.
[307] *Ibid*, p. 78.
[308] *Ibid*, p. 79; see above, Ch. I § 2.2.e.
[309] *Ibid*, p. 80.
[310] *Ibid*, p. 81.

theories.[311] The second demand required of theories, whether metaphysical or not, is that they be consistent. Thakur contends that no a priori criteria exist according to which consistency is defined.[312] Paradoxes and puzzles do occur in religious theories. Religious theories undergo changes in the course of time. Their consistency is not so obvious. It has always been the task of 'theological' reflection, however, to mold religious dogma in a consistent and coherent form.[313] He mentions in passing that paradoxes also occur in the natural sciences. As Kuhn has shown, just as scientific investigators readily hold on to existing paradigms within their own subject, believers grow attached to their theories. Beliefs constitute one's fundamental conceptual 'framework.'[314] This framework is then subject to a kind of 'subterranean' test; it is open to all sorts of influences, new experiences, and important events.[315] In this fashion, theories are adapted or abandoned. The 'dialectic' of religious faith comprises an interplay of three factors: conjecture (intuition, speculation, et al.), commitment, and critique. These are framed by a 'basically rational logic' which provides a basis for (conceivably) rejecting faith.[316] Thakur contends that the pattern of growth and development in religions is similar to the pattern in the development of the natural sciences, even though this process of growth and change is not stated explicitly in the theories.[317] Religious traditions contain a 'body of truths' in this way.[318]

Every religious system proceeds in terms of its own truth, is inhospitable towards other perceptions, and is reluctant in adopting other perceptions. The practice of religion is not relativistic. Religious 'belief-systems' contest the truth with each other. Each religion presupposes that there is a 'body of truths' which is true independent of that religious system. The transcendent reality which is spoken of exists independently of beliefs. Religions do not allow that their truth claims be evaluated by purely secular criteria.[319] Thakur himself proposes a less 'inhospitable' exclusive view, which he denotes by the term 'moderate form of relativism': "The many competing religions can all be seen as alternative descriptions of reality, no particular one of which is *known* to be true."[320] Thakur thinks reality so complex that each religion designates certain aspects. No single religious system need be entirely rejected. They all describe the same reality and know it in part. He refers here to the *Ṛg Veda*, which says: The truth is one, but the wise call it by different names. The Jains

---

[311] *Ibid*, pp. 85, 96.
[312] *Ibid*, p. 86.
[313] *Ibid*, p. 87.
[314] *Ibid*, p. 103.
[315] *Ibid*, p. 104.
[316] *Ibid*, p. 106, see also p. 105.
[317] *Ibid*, p. 107.
[318] *Ibid*, p. 108.
[319] *Ibid*, p. 112.
[320] *Ibid*, p. 113.

developed the doctrine of the multifaceted quality of reality.[321] In practice, the test of a religion is a pragmatic: people make personal choices, they develop an outlook on reality. Although the rules for the criticism and development of religious perception are not made explicit, they surely exist.[322]

In this fashion, Thakur gives his own approach to *Religion and Rational Choice*. Among the important elements in his view are the idea that religion is not autonomous and impervious to criticism; that in the practice of life, confronted by all kinds of experiences, a 'subterranean' test takes place; that religions do not allow for assessment by secular criteria; that certain metaphysical entities have a central significance within a religious theory; and that faith in these existents is related to other experiences. It remains a matter of closer investigation to discern which experiences are involved; how such a 'theory' is put together; what its consistency is; and what its development possibilities are. We hope to offer a little more clarity on this score. With regard to the problem of the relationship between religions, Thakur's view evokes the question of whether he has not in effect chosen the Hindu view as the true solution. The question of whether this view is in agreement with the beliefs of all the great traditions calls for more elaborate scrutiny.

§ 4   The main issues in current discussion regarding 'religion and truth'

On the basis of this survey of conceptions of religious knowledge and our discussion of religious truth, we will now state the main problems currently under discussion.

4.1   Is religious truth concerned with states of affairs?

A recurrent theme is whether religious knowledge yields knowledge of reality, and, if so, how. Most of the authors discussed assume that religion does in some way refer to reality. If faith entails trust in the transcendent, or in any case, directing one's gaze towards it, then the transcendent must 'exist' — however one wishes to further qualify the word 'exist.' We have encountered this argument a number of times. Religious knowledge is concerned not only with the transcendent; the 'knowledge' of the transcendent has implications for the outlook which one has on the rest of reality. Religion has to do with the whole of reality. Various kinds of facts have therefore been distinguished. Sherry gives a classification of four kinds of facts: (1) historical events, (2) uniformities in the world and the universe, (3) the world as a whole,

---

[321] *Ibid*, p. 114.
[322] *Ibid*, p. 115.

(4) transcendence. Thakur speaks of empirical and metaphysical facts. The question then arises how experience of the transcendent is related to experiences in finite reality.

4.2 Primacy of concern

Several authors strongly emphasized the fact that certain concerns are of central significance within a religious persuasion. Thakur speaks of metaphysical facts to which the primary statements of a religion refer. Brümmer speaks of the primary determinant of meaning, Christian of unrestricted primacy, and Pannenberg of the integrative nucleus (of Christian tradition, in any case). We have already raised in passing the question of whether one does not in this way speak too monolithically about a belief-system. We must examine how knowledge regarding the 'unique, central' concern is attained. Is it experienced directly, or via other, mediating experiences? Hick uses the term 'root-experiences.' Which experiences lie at the basis of insight according to the authoritative writings or authors of the major religious traditions themselves?

4.3 Contradiction and overlapping of religions

If one regards religions as separate language-games, or if one assumes that religions are determined by one primary determinant of meaning, then it is obvious that religions stand side by side, each occupying their own isolated space. In Phillips' view they stand side by side as 'different worlds'; in Brümmer's view as alternative persuasions of life. And yet there are many similarities between religious perceptions, right across all religious demarcations. We have stated that both the contradictions as well as the overlappings of religions must be explained. The truth of one religion seems not entirely to exclude that of other religions. Thakur, Hick, and others also point out the 'partial' character of religious knowledge. Whether and how religious traditions can ascribe unrestricted primacy to a certain entity is thus a matter for discussion. If things become more complicated than this, questions arise regarding the unity of a religious tradition. These questions are brought up in Ch. IX and XII.

Brümmer noted that all religions aim to answer ultimate questions. On the basis of that statement one could ask oneself what those questions are. Can this talk of ultimate questions be related to essential experiences which necessarily belong to being-human? This too shall be examined in Ch. IX.

4.4 Levels of religious knowledge

We ran into the notion of levels of religious knowledge many times. Christian spoke of three levels (basic proposals, etc.), Smith distinguished between the level of faith and that of belief, and Hick too makes distinctions, namely between knowledge of divine reality, transmitted knowledge, and the key-experiences of various traditions. Two matters come up for discussion here:

(1) To what extent is religious knowledge public? Kuitert speaks of theological knowledge as public knowing; Wiebe demands that religious truth claims be tested by the study of religion. Thakur points out, to the contrary, that religions refuse assessment by secular criteria. Can an uninitiated person assess religion? Is assessment public?

(2) Ought one to distinguish layers of knowledge? If one introduces such a distinction, then how must one speak of truth at the various levels? We will bring up this question in Ch. VIII, after enquiry into how classical thinkers in various traditions have spoken of truth.

4.5   Frames of reference and assessment

A religious view of the world cannot be wholly explicated —an issue which we have encountered several times— because it serves as a frame-of-reference. It cannot be grounded, because it is itself the ground. This was emphasized by D. Z. Phillips with reference to the relevant passage in Wittgenstein. It is often pointed out that separate doctrines in different religions gain their significance within the whole of such a religious conviction. The interpretation of experiences is dependent on the whole of a persuasion, say Kuitert and Pannenberg. Hick too points to the interpretation of experience by religious tradition when he states that the founders of religious traditions have had very special experiences which inaugurated a different view of reality.

Several questions arise with respect to the relation between experience and the interpretation given it by a tradition. The point under discussion is above all whether a frame of reference which serves as ground can itself be tested. We have seen that Thakur speaks of a 'dialectical' process by which people test, attune, or surrender their convictions in practical life instead of offering clear criteria by which to evaluate truth claims. Several other authors also pointed out the practical testing which takes place, such as Kuitert, Pannenberg, and Hick. Others mentioned criteria which are presumed to be independent of life-views, such as obviousness, coherence, freedom from contradiction, unity, relevance, etc. Phillips, who insisted on the distinctive nature of religion in distinction to scientific knowledge, mentions love as criterion. Smith used as criterion the notion that a religion should help people find a right relationship to themselves, their neighbour, and the universe. There is a clear difference of perception here. Some aspire to finding criteria external to the separate traditions; others think that religions imply their own rules. This issue will be further examined in Ch. XI.

4.6 Personal transformation

Some authors emphasize that religion ideally leads to personal transformation. It is beyond question that religion concerns action, but for some that is not enough. They point out that religions mean to change people for the good. Sometimes acquiring insight is linked to the transformation of the person. This aspect obtains prominence in Patrick Sherry's work. One misses it in Donald Wiebe's work, who does not exclude the possibility that the question of truth be posed by someone who does not himself believe. This is therefore also a matter of discussion. In the second part of this enquiry this will prove to be one of the most essential questions.

4.7 The transcendent

Some authors contend that all religions focus on the same (divine) reality. This reality is interpreted in divergent ways. Sometimes it is said that every religion is acquainted with part of the truth concerning transcendent reality.

The following question must then be asked, in our view. Can one rule on philosophical grounds alone that all religions focus on the same transcendent reality? Such a conclusion lies at hand more readily if one takes a single religion as starting point. Then maybe one can state that the other religions have the same transcendent reality in mind. If one tries to argue as neutrally as possible, however, this becomes more difficult. We will return to this question at the conclusion our study.

4.8 The truth of religion

Difference of opinion also exists concerning the concept of truth. The truth is 'localized' in disparate places; in beliefs, in persons, in God. Question then arises as to which position is correct. One might also ask whether the philosophy of religion can settle the matter or even whether a single conception of 'religion and truth' can be developed. Precisely these questions form the incentive for the second part of our investigation: a description of conceptions of truth within the framework of the great traditions, on the basis of classical conceptions within those traditions. We shall now set about this task.

PART 2

DESCRIPTION

Chapter III

The Concept of Truth in Hindu Tradition

§ 1 Introduction

1.1 Preamble

The Hindu tradition is a most variegated phenomenon in the world of religions; it is almost a collection of religions.[1] It is an old tradition, whose roots go back to the second millennium before the common era. The Hindu tradition has undergone drastic change, such as the blending of the religious conceptions of the original inhabitants with those of the Aryans, the emergence of monistic thought, and the emergence of *bhakti*-devotion among the common people. The welter of divine images, the exuberant and long-lasting religious festivities, and the abundance of stories about the gods also add to its variegation.

It seems futile even to begin to present in brief some of the profound perceptions of the Indian religious world. The obvious path of flight is to resort to a few of the more philosophical traditions which Hinduism includes. But in this introductory section we will nonetheless first give a brief overview of some of the most important lines in the development of the Hindu tradition. Section 2 examines a number of central insights. In § 3 we will have reached the concept of truth. We will then first present insights from the Vedānta School; we will subsequently deal with two more modern views, viz. Radhakrishnan's and Gandhi's. Our aim is to present somewhat divergent concepts of truth which are more or less representative for currents in Indian thought, or, as is the case with Radhakrishnan and Gandhi, views which have obtained familiarity in the West. Section 4 raises the problem of how the divergent perceptions outlined in this chapter are mutually related according to Hindu views.

---

[1] E.g., P. Bowes, *The Hindu Religious Tradition: A Philosophical Approach* (London 1977), p. *ix*.

1.2 Developments in the Hindu tradition

It is established fact that the oldest religious writings in India, the *Vedas,* originated from the circle of the Aryans who penetrated India from the north-west.[2] The Vedic writings are comprised, among other things, of hymns to the gods and magical incantations. The *Vedas* have been assigned various dates. The coming of the Aryans is usually dated between 1500 and 1000 B.C.E., although any date remains a guess, according to Zaehner.[3] The *Vedas* emerged in the ensuing period, as well as collections of hymns, verses, and aphorisms for use in sacrificial rites. The Vedic period represents the polytheistic phase in Hinduism. Later portions of the *Ṛg Veda* adumbrate the notion that a deeper unity lies at the basis of the plurality in created reality and in the world of the gods.[4] Here lies the basis for the later so-called *henotheism.* This term is used to indicate that even though many gods were revered —one at a time— the unity which forms the basis of all plurality is what is ultimately intended by this worship.[5] The One and the inclusive is approached in many ways; in fact, it *must* be approached in many ways in order to do justice to its inexhaustible riches. This central idea of later Hinduism is already seminally present in the *Ṛg Veda.*

Writings which describe the rituals and which offer *commentary* on the *Vedas,* such as the *Brāhmaṇas* and the *Upaniṣads,* date from a somewhat later time. Along with the *Vedas,* they belong to the *śruti* (listened to), the sacred books of the Hindus. The *śruti* are revered as eternal. Sacred writings from later times, the *smṛti* (remembrance), possess less authority.[6] Radhakrishnan characterizes the *Upaniṣads* as meditations by philosophers.[7] The trend towards a monistic view of reality establishes itself here. The quest for the unity which lies at the basis of all plurality can be discovered at work here. Zaehner comments that many pantheistic passages are already to be found in the *Upaniṣads.*[8] A well-known example is the expression *Thou are That* which is repeated emphatically several times in the *Chāndogya-Upaniṣad.*[9] The individual human-being ultimately participates

---

[2] R. C. Zaehner, (London ²1966), p. 14.

[3] *Ibid,* pp. 14 f.

[4] *Ibid,* p. 39; Bowes, pp. 27 ff.

[5] D. L. Eck, *Banaras: City of Light* (New York 1982), p. 40, "kathenotheism: the worship of many gods, one at a time"; cf. Bowes, pp. 102 f.; D. L. Eck, *Darśan: Seeing the Divine Image in India* (Chambersburg 1981), p. 19; H. Zimmer, *Myths and Symbols in Indian Art and Civilization,* ed. J. Campbell (1946; rpt. Princeton ²1974), pp. 135 f.

[6] *A Sourcebook in Indian Philosophy,* eds. S. Radhakrishnan and Ch. A. Moore (Princeton ⁵1973), pp. 350 f., *xxvi,* consult the editors' commentary; see also Zaehner, p. 10; D. C. Mulder, "Het Hindoeisme," in *Antwoord,* ed. J. Sperna Weiland (Amsterdam ²1982), pp. 51 f.

[7] *Sourcebook,* p. *xviii.* 'Radhakrishnan' stands for both editors.

[8] Zaehner, p. 52.

[9] E.g., *Sourcebook,* pp. 68 f.; cf. *Chāndogya-Upaniṣad,* VI, 9 ff.

in the Highest. The greatest blessing consists in one's realization and experience of this.

Traces of the original indigenous religion are plain in the later phases of the history of Hinduism. In the course of time, large shifts occur in the world of the gods. Some gods lose significance while others move into the foreground, until at last the 'Hindu trinity' emerges: Brahmā, Viṣṇu, and Śiva, of whom the latter two are especially revered.[10] Numerous elements from the old folk religion were preserved in the popular religion, according to many commentators.[11] People point out the worship of Śiva's liṅga, a practice still widespread in modern India; it is a phallic symbol which, in combination with the female symbol, is seen as an expression of the encompassing unity of all things. Thus, writes Diana Eck, it is *the* symbol of the unity of the Hindu Universe.[12] In later mythology, numerous elements from the earlier indigenous religion can be discovered.

A subsequent period in Hindu history is the epoch in which the great heroic poems emerge: the Epic period. Radhakrishnan and Moore attach as dates to this period 500 B.C.E. to 200 C.E. in the introduction to their anthology of Indian philosophy.[13] The famous *Bhagavadgītā* —one of the most important texts in Indian thought— has been inserted into the great epic poem, the *Mahabharata*. The *Upaniṣads* spoke already of the Absolute from which everything has come forth and to which everything returns. In the *Bhagavadgītā* (the song of the Lord), the personal side of the Absolute was now illuminated. The Most High is both transcendent and encompassing as a personal reality which can be venerated.[14] As a personal God, the Most High is responsible for the creation, sustaining, and destruction of the universe. Especially impressive is the revelation of the Lord before the eyes of Arjuna. Arjuna receives a supernatural eye to see God, that is, to see the whole universe — all that moves and all that does not move.[15] He sees the All in the person of the Most High. All things are suffused with the Highest, yet the Highest is not contained by things. God is immanent in the world, yet he remains transcendent. God may be approached in veneration, love, and worship (*bhakti*); that is what the *Bhagavadgītā* reveals.

---

[10] See for instance the chapter called "What Happened in India" in N. C. Chaudhuri, *Hinduism: A Religion to Live By* (New York 1979), pp. 84-100; cf. pp. 237-93; Zaehner, p. 86; cf. Eck, *Banaras*, pp. 60 f.

[11] Eck, *Banaras*, pp. 5 f., 61, 96; Zaehner, p. 16; critical of the idea of melting together is Chaudhuri, pp. 96 ff.

[12] Eck, *Banaras*, p. 105; cf. Chaudhuri, p. 229.

[13] *Sourcebook*, p. xviii.

[14] *Sourcebook*, p. 101; Bowes, pp. 30 f.

[15] *Bhagavadgītā*, XI. 7 ff.; Dutch translation and explanations by J. P. K. Sukul (Utrecht 1958), at XI. 7 ff.; *Sourcebook*, pp. 138 ff.

Systematic treatises by philosophical schools emerge in a subsequent period, the third of the Hindu tradition, often known as the *Sūtra* period.[16] The *sūtras* are exceedingly terse summaries of the traditions, fashioned in a systematic and logical manner, but not elaborated much beyond aphorisms. The philosophical schools too conveyed knowledge with the aid of *sūtras*. The *Vedānta* or *Brahma Sūtra*, on which the Vedānta Schools are based, is so succinct that understanding is impossible without commentary. It is therefore usually published along with a commentary by a later author.[17] We will return to these systems of Hindu philosophy below. The Sūtra period, in which many of the classical texts were written, is dated in the first centuries of the common era.[18]

The fourth period, it is assumed, begins in the first centuries of the common era although there are great difficulties with regard to the dating.[19] This period is indicated as the Scholastic period. It is the period in which the commentaries on the *sūtras* were written. Radhakrishnan has little praise for some of the commentaries, some of which deal with futilities according to him. The influential and profound reflections of such people as Śaṅkara (approx. 8th cent.) and Rāmānuja (11th cent.), who both belong to the Vedānta Schools —that is, the schools which appeal to the authority of the *Upaniṣads*— also stem from this time, however.[20]

After the 11th century, Hinduism suffered under the occupation by Turkish Moslems, who were replaced in the 18th century by British Christians.[21] Under British rule temples were no longer destroyed and the Hindu religion became an object of study. Colonialism and Christian missions unwittingly contributed to a revival of Hinduism starting at the end of the 19th century.[22]

A great movement of renewal had already sprung forth from the so-called *bhakti*-religion between the 14th and 17th centuries.[23] God was represented and venerated as a person, and He was worshipped in the statues of three gods (and the *avatāras* of Viṣṇu). The believer himself was free to choose which path he wished to travel to God, by worshipping one of the gods in particular. The three religious currents within *bhakti*-religion did attempt to expand the number of their adherents but acknowledged that all worship is basically and ultimately directed towards the

---

[16] *Sourcebook*, pp. *xix* (f.). A different division of eras is given for example by Zaehner, pp. 6 f.: 1. polytheism; 2. pantheistic monism; 3. *bhakti*; 4. modern revival. And Chaudhuri, p. 27, suggests: 1. vedic; 2. classical; 3. modern. Cf. E. Frauwallner, *Geschichte der indischen Philosophie*, 2 parts, I (Salzburg 1953), pp. 275 ff.

[17] *Sourcebook*, p. 506.

[18] Since explicit reference to the Christian tradition is to be avoided as much as possible, we prefer the term Common Era (C.E.).

[19] *Sourcebook*, pp. xx (f.).

[20] *Sourcebook*, pp. 506 ff.

[21] Zaehner, pp. 137 ff., 147 ff. Much of Hindu life was quietly going on under British occupation. Some of the British studied the Hindu tradition.

[22] See Zaehner, pp. 147-69.

[23] Zaehner, pp. 125 ff.

one God. There is a great distance, of course, between the beliefs present among the common people in their daily worship, *darśana* (seeing the divinity, especially in the temple)[24] and their great feasts, and the philosophical systems (or theological reflection). Yet even in popular religion, there is a realization that everything is sustained and pervaded by the Most High, indeed, even that one is ultimately one with the Absolute. The great theme of Hindu philosophy is the relation between the Absolute on the one hand and man and the world on the other. The thoughts of the philosophers may appear incomprehensible to the common man; nevertheless, the basic concern of philosophical reflection is with the vital beliefs of the common people. Philosophy retained its bond with religion.[25] Hindu religion is permeated by the realization of the ultimate unity of all things.

Bhakti-religion, on the basis of certain passages in the *Bhagavadgītā*, found a way to God through simple religious commitment, uninhibited by the difficult training of the yoga. The Absolute received a face — the face of one of the gods. It was not the statues which were worshipped, for ultimately one does not venerate wood or stone when worshipping one of the three main gods or, for that matter, any of the other 330 million depictions of gods in India, but one worships God, who can rule all things through his might.[26] Renon notes that *bhakti*-religion originated between 600 and 800 C.E. According to Zaehner, it flowered in central and northern India between the 13th and the 18th century. It continues to flourish until this very day.[27] Having given a general exposition of the Hindu tradition, we will now first say something about the six schools of philosophy.

1.3 The six schools of philosophy

Outlines of Hindu thought mention the emergence of six schools of philosophy in the flourishing classical period. Radhakrishnan and Moore mention seven insights which the various schools share and which are thus characteristic of Hindu thought in general. We will present their characterization here with the caveat that it betrays a so-called neo-Hindu conception, advancing a certain interpretation of the Advaita Vedānta. Yet since this view is quite familiar and widespread in the 'West,' we have chosen to present it. We would like to remark in passing that the unanimity of Hindu philosophy described by Radhakrishnan is certainly not present in the degree which he suggests; we will return to this topic in the concluding section. Particular elements of the following

---

[24] Cf. Eck, *Darśan*, pp. 1, 3.

[25] Chaudhuri, p. 88.

[26] Eck, *Darśan*, pp. 19-21; cf. G. Richards, *The Philosophy of Gandhi: A Study of His Basic Ideas* (London 1982), p. 5.

[27] L. Renon, "Introduction," in *Hinduism*, (Englewood Cliffs, N.J. 1960), p. 17; Zaehner, pp. 127, 139.

points do not at all apply to schools other than those of the Advaita Vedānta.[28]

(1) Concentration on the spiritual is prominent.

(2) Philosophy is closely related to life; the concern is for truth which liberates, not for items of knowledge, analysis for the sake of analysis, or aimless scholarship. The truth is not so much something one must know as something one must *realize*; a certain attitude in life is demanded in this regard.

(3) The truth is not to be sought in the external world, but within, in one's self.

(4) Most Indian philosophy is idealistic and monistic. Monistic idealism admits of considerable mutual difference in the articulation of insights.

(5) Reason is not unimportant, but the deepest truth must be perceived. The word for philosophy is *darśana* (from *dṛś* 'to see'); this perception is a direct, intuitive awareness of its object, or better, a realization of becoming one with it.

(6) The authority of the *śruti* is accepted, to wit, the *Vedas* and the *Upaniṣads*. Appreciation exists for the fact that trust in the wisdom of those who have realized the truth is needed. The acceptance of truth has not led to rigid doctrines since the purpose of wisdom is the realization of truth rather than its formulation.

(7) What the *Ṛg Veda* articulates as follows is generally accepted: God is one, but people call Him by many names.[29] This realization forms the basis for an attitude of tolerance towards those of other persuasions.

Aside from these seven points, Radhakrishnan and Moore single out several other common insights. They contend that all Indian schools are concerned with salvation, that is, liberation from the cycle of rebirth, and that all have the same view of life on earth; they preach the need to be free of attachment.[30] In addition, the four stages of life were recognized in classical times (student, father, forest inhabitant, and mendicant monk).

It is apparent from our presentation of their exposition that Radhakrishnan and Moore believe that the six schools of philosophy have much in common. Actually —if one reads historical expositions— there was far more opposition and conflict than appears from Radhakrishnan's characterization, no matter how widespread this representation of matters and of the philosophy of religion implied by it is.

The general acceptance of the authority of the Vedic scriptures elicits the following question: To what extent are we concerned with philosophy

---

[28] Radhakrishnan–Moore, *Sourcebook*, pp. *xxiii* (f.); for a description of the classical philosophical systems and their disagreements, see Frauwallner, 2 parts, II (1956).

[29] Cf. *Sourcebook*, p. 21 (*Ṛg Veda*, § To Viśvedevas, no. 46).

[30] Cf. point 2 of the summary in our text. In the introductory literature these issues are stressed many times.

here? Are we not rather dealing with theology? This question has been discussed by S. S. Raghavachar, for example, in his small study on Rāmānuja. He would rather not speak of theology here. By theology he understands a dogmatic exposition which admits of little room for debate and controversy.[31] He therefore calls it philosophy, although he acknowledges that Hindu thinkers, particularly those of the orthodox schools of the Vedānta, wish to stay within the bounds which the *Vedānta Sūtra* permit. John Carman does speak of theology in the title of his study on Rāmānuja.[32] It is indeed striking —as we shall see again— that Rāmānuja raises many questions which are also discussed in Christian dogmatics. Whatever the case, be it theology or philosophy, many themes come to the fore which would be considered philosophical in the West, such as epistemology.

The introductory literature generally characterizes the six philosophical systems in groups of two, as follows:[33]

(1) The *Nyāya* School and the *Vaiśeshika* School

The Nyāya School focusses particularly on the study of the methods of valid reasoning, or logic. Perception, deduction, analogy, and trustworthy witness are accepted as valid sources of knowledge.

The Vaiśeshika School analyzes the nature of earthly reality; this school counts a proportionately large number of unorthodox thinkers among its ranks, according to K. M. Sen.[34]

Both these schools accept one another's conclusions.

(2) The *Sāṁkya* School and the *Yoga* School

The Sāṁkya School proceeds in its analysis of reality from the notion that all experience is based on the duality of the knowing subject and the object known.[35] It analyzes the process of cosmic evolution. The actual, empirical individual is the real 'self' but has the limitations which the body and the senses impose. One can achieve freedom through insight, but virtuous conduct and yoga must also be practised to this end.

The Yoga School analyzes and teaches the way to salvation and freedom via meditation and concentration. It accepts the Sāṁkya School's view of reality at face value. Moreover, the School mentions a highest God who is merciful to towards humankind; belief in God does not, however, occupy a prominent place within the Yoga School.

---

[31] S. S. Raghavachar, *Introduction to the Vedarthasangraha of Sree Rāmānujacharya* (Mangalore 1957), p. 5.

[32] J. B. Carman, *The Theology of Rāmānuja* (New Haven 1974).

[33] K. M. Sen, *Hinduism* (Harmondsworth [12]1981), pp. 78ff. *Sourcebook*, the Introduction to the texts; cf. Frauwallner, I, 273, II.

[34] Sen, p. 79.

[35] *Sourcebook*, p. 424.

(3) The *Pūrva-Mīmāṃsā* School and the *Vedānta* School

The Pūrva-Mīmāṃsā School is in the first place interested in the rites. With an eye on the efficacy of the rites, a philosophy was constructed which has much in common with the Nyāya and Vaiśeshika Schools. It is a relatively orthodox school with predominantly practical interests.

The Vedānta Schools are perhaps the most influential of the six philosophical traditions. We will delve into the views held within these schools in more detail in the third section. The Vedānta itself has a number of currents, as one would expect of a large movement. Controversial points are the (im)personality of the Absolute and, in relation to this, the nature of knowledge of the Absolute. The latter point also relates to the concept of truth. Much discussed has been the so-called doctrine of non-dual truth or non-discriminatory knowledge. The problematics resemble to some extent the Mahāyāna Buddhist doctrine of non-duality.

This short characterization of the six systems must suffice here; the object of this characterization is merely to indicate that Hindu thinking is a variegated aggregate; in § 3 we will discuss only a number of these currents. We would like to interpose but a single remark concerning their mutual relationship. Section 4 of this chapter will examine this issue in greater depth. We will here mention the issue only in terms of the mutual relationship between various currents. Radhakrishnan and Moore supply the following picture. Indian philosophy tends to be more synthetic than the analytically minded philosophy of the West.[36] The Most High cannot be adequately defined. It therefore admits of more than one approach. Every philosophical current has a certain perspective, and the truth of any conception is always related to such a perspective. When another person takes a different point of view, it is not a contradiction which ensues, but merely a difference in perspective. This forms the basis —it is then stated— for the generous tolerance within Hindu philosophy. All groups and communities seek the one truth. In like manner, Diana Eck also accentuates the necessity for multiple approaches to do justice to the inexhaustibility and the incomprehensibility of the All. This view, whether it is based on a neo-Hindu philosophy of religion or on a description of popular religion, represents one view. In the more philosophical current one also encounters a different attitude. Controversies and conflicting views exist, and people oppose one another, attempting to justify their own conception by demonstrating the deficiencies of other views.[37]

---

[36] *Sourcebook*, pp. xxvii (ff.).

[37] Eck, *Darśan*, pp. 17-22; see T. Vetter, *Studien zur Lehre und Entwicklung Sankaras* (Vienna 1979), pp. 101f. Discussion with other schools is already present in Śaṅkara's

Regardless of which view one adopts, the profusion of currents and sects designated by the term Hinduism does in fact harbour a few boundaries nonetheless. It used to be that one was not permitted to travel across the sea on pain of losing one's caste.[38] Whoever does not acknowledge the authority of the *śruti* falls outside of the orthodox schools. Moreover, those who like the Buddhists deny the existence of the self (*ātman* or *atta*), exceed the bounds of Hinduism. Since we will later return to the relationship between the various currents and their tolerance of other views, this short characterization of the current view will suffice.

§ 2 Central insights

2.1 The Absolute

We have already seen how in the course of the ages, monistic thought arose and advanced into the centre of Hindu tradition. We will now pursue this a little more closely. We will begin our presentation with a few samples from mythology of the awareness of the essential unity of all things.

One of the best known narrative cycles is about Kṛṣṇa, one of the *avatāras* (earthly form of appearance) of Viṣṇu among mankind. Kṛṣṇa was born in a miraculous fashion and was saved from the hand of the enemy. He grew up among shepherds, and, not to be overlooked, shepherdesses. His many remarkable deeds were but so many notches on his belt for the young hero. The most familiar narratives, however, concern his encounters with *gopis,* the wives of the shepherds. He entices them out of their homes with his admirably beautiful flute playing. Roused by longing for Kṛṣṇa they abandon mop, brood, husband, and honour. He dances with them. He steals their clothes while they are taking a sacred bath in the river. He leaves them in the lurch. The love scenes with one of the *gopis,* Radha, are elaborately described and have been narrated and depicted countless times. Their unification is more than romantic love or fornication. For Kṛṣṇa is in reality the Most High. That is how the myth relates it as well: Madhusudana (that is, Kṛṣṇa), whose nature is immeasurable, appeared as a young man in this fashion and played with the shepherds' wives, day and night. He whose real form is as pervasive as the wind lives as the Lord in these women, and in their spouses, as in all creatures. Just as ether, fire, earth, water, and wind are in all creatures, so the Lord Himself, who permeates the universe, abides in all things.[39]

---

work itself.

[38] Zaehner, p. 149.

[39] C. Dimmitt and J. A. van Buitenen, *Classical Hindu Mythology: A Reader in the Sanskrit Purānas* (Philadelphia 1978), p. 127; cf. also *In Praise of Krishna: Songs from Bengali,* tr. Edw. C. Dimock and Denise Levertov (1967; rpt. Chicago 1981), passim.

Radha is Kriṣṇa; God is in everyone. According to some currents, the love of Radha and Kriṣṇa symbolizes the unity of all worldly plurality in God. It simultaneously points up the longing of the human soul to experience spiritual union with God.[40]

The mystery of reality becomes more tangible through the myth; it is expressed in a more colorful and multi-faceted way than a philosophical theory could do it. The realization of the ultimate union of all things with God is vitalized by the myths, stories, statues, and portraits of folk religion. Another example of this awareness: The wild goose, like all earthly things, has a twofold nature, Zimmer relates.[41] It lives on the water, but is not confined to it. It can fly and meander wherever it wants. Thus it represents the Divine. The Divine Self is the goose of the macrocosmos. It manifests itself through a melody. It is the melody of human breathing, which occupies such a pre-eminent position in meditation technique. He who controls his breathing hears the 'inner goose.' Inhaling sounds like 'ham'; exhaling like 'sa.' Together they are haṃsa, Sanskrit for goose. By continually naming its own name, the inner goose reveals its permanent presence to the yoga practioner.

Since the Absolute is the all-encompassing, it is indeterminate in a certain sense. All experiences and all events in life can be related to the influence of good or evil powers through which the Absolute manifests itself. The rites carried out by the Brahmans serve not only to comply with the cosmic order, the *dharma*, but also to integrate people into that order.[42] The influence of the powers is great and not entirely subject to calculation. The gods have more than one side to them. They are not only strong and helpful, but can sometimes be terrifying, hostile, and intent on destruction as well. It is characteristic of Śiva, one of the three main gods, that He unifies contradictions within Himself. He is an ascetic whose knowledge and concentration may not be disturbed by love and sexuality. His ascetic personality, however, can do an about-face in a wild dance in which He destroys the world at set times. Yet at the same time, He is worshipped as Creator. He unifies the good, creative element and the destructive element in Himself. Sometimes He is portrayed in union with the goddess. Together they form a unity and are portrayed as a single being: Ardhanarinara, half god, half goddess.[43] The polarity of the feminine and the masculine has one source and essence at bottom. Śiva's worshippers represent Him as Creator of the universe. In His union with the goddess, from whom life energy emanates, Śiva-Śakti portrays the unity of the universe. Dimmitt and Van Buitenen note that the image of their union

---

[40] Dimmitt and Van Buitenen, p. 104.
[41] Zimmer, pp. 48 ff., cf. p. 46.
[42] Cf. Zaehner, pp. 31, 59; cf. Bowes, p. 126, cf. also pp. 128, 135.
[43] Dimmitt and van Buitenen, p. 153; Zimmer, p. 216.

can best be understood as a symbolical reconciliation of the monistic and dualistic conception of the world's beginning.[44]

This same search for the unity of all things amidst a sometime fascinating, sometime terrifying reality, is reflected by the myths about the origin of suffering and misfortune. Here too things melt and blend. The gods are not constantly good and the devils are not constantly bad.[45] In the *Purāṇas* (collections of myths), it becomes apparent that all things are intermingled. The gods have no clearly circumscribed functions; their characters contain oppositions. The 'answers' to the question of the origin of suffering are not univocal: "We must face the disquieting ability of Indians to believe several seemingly contradictory tenets at once," remarks O'Flaherty.[46] But enough here on the multiplicity of perspective in popular religion.

2.2 'Many names'

The awareness that plurality in the world is sustained and suffused by the One and Absolute is also to be found in the more philosophical strata of the Hindu tradition. As early as the *Ṛg Veda*, we read: "To what is one, sages give many a title: they call it Agni, Yama, Matarisvan."[47] It is the selfsame divine reality which people indicate by different names. In the *Bhagavadgītā*, we read: "Along whatever path they travel, in the end it leads to Me."[48] This is not to say that all forms of religion are of equal value. We also read:

> But these are men of little wisdom, and the good they want has an end. Those who love the gods go to the gods, but those who love me come unto Me.[49]

Be that as it may, the absolute is the goal which all people pursue, in whatever form of religion:

> Even those in faith worship other gods, because of their love they worship me, although not in the right way.[50]

Hindus are capable of appreciating other religions on the basis of such perceptions. Which elements in another religion are valuable, though, is determined in terms of their own outlook. But given the presence of the One in the many, all people in all religions are ultimately seeking the

[44] Dimmitt and van Buitenen, p. 153.

[45] W. D. O'Flaherty, *The Origins of Evil in Hindu Mythology* (1976; rpt. Berkeley 1980), p. 58.

[46] *Ibid*, p. 19.

[47] *Ṛg Veda*, I, 164. 48; see *Sourcebook*, p. 21.

[48] *Bhagavadgītā*, IV. 11; according to Dutch tr. by the School voor Filosofie, Amsterdam; cf. tr. with Intr. by Juan Mascaró, "For many are the paths of men: But they all in the end come to me" (Marmondsworth 1986), p. 62.

[49] *Bhagavadgītā*, VII. 23.

[50] *Bhagavadgītā*, IX. 23; cf. Sukul, p. 47; Mascaró, p. 82.

same: a relationship to the Highest Being. This view keeps resurfacing in Hindu publications. It is the typically Hindu approach to the problem of the multitude of religions. This concept is also fundamental to the views of Hindu philosophers on the issue of (inter)religious truth.[51]

2.3 The world

Brahman —no matter how it is signified— is beyond all thought. It is inexhaustible. It is being (*sat*), consciousness (*cit*), and blessedness (*ananda*).[52] His being has no beginning or end. In dealing with the world, the Highest is represented as one of the gods. Brahmā, the Creator, has produced the world. It will be destroyed when the four eras through which each world abides have passed.[53] Then there will be a new world. In eternal play (*līlā*), God takes pleasure in forming new worlds and watching people live.[54] The world is transitory. Joy and suffering are mixed in it. The world is the antipode of God; in the essence of its existence it is nevertheless one-in-being with the Highest. People and animals live in the world. They are all material beings imbued with spirit, governed by the laws of nature. Their essence is their self, *ātman*. By means of their self, they have their being in God, since their *ātman* is God. God is, to be sure, infinitely more than all the 'selves' of people and animals taken together, but all living beings participate in God through their *ātman*. In reality, their being is God's being.[55] The entire creation is essentially related to God.

2.4 Man

People form part of the world which God has created. They have name and form. Their soul lives in the matter of mother earth. They derive their energy from their food — from all that mother Nature as goddess gives them. Human existence therefore has two aspects. On the one hand, it is not a state of happy union with Brahman. One is bound by the shackles of temporality and finitude. On the other hand, nature too is permeated by Brahman's power. The earth produces rice and life. It follows the laws which have been established in it.[56] People observe rites, particularly in connection with special events such as birth, marriage, and death, in order to live in harmony with the order which suffuses all being. But Brahman is greater than the structure in creation. The gods can make exceptions. They bestow their gifts to whom they please. That

---

[51] See § 4.

[52] Bowes, p. 153; Zaehner, p. 63.

[53] On Hindu cosmology, see for instance Bowes, pp. 45 ff.

[54] Zaehner, pp. 99, 103; cf. Śankara, in *Sourcebook*, p. 533 (II. i. 33).

[55] H. von Strietencorn, "Hinduistische Perspektiven," in *Christentum und Weltreligionen*, ed. H. Küng (Munich 1984), pp. 280 ff.

[56] Zaehner, p. 31.

is why people implore them and bring sacrifices. They want God to see them through the many, many eyes of the gods. People seek strength through their worship of God. They hope that God will employ his power to influence the course of their lives.

All people have their existence in Brahman. In this sense they are all equal, no matter how separated by the boundaries of their castes. They form part of Brahman and participate in his oneness. They will be reincarnated in another creature after this life, each in a place which is in accordance with the merits which he or she has accumulated during a series of lives.[57]

2.5 *Dharma, karma,* and *mokṣa*

The causality in this world is *dharma* (duty), the cosmic order which spans the whole world.[58] People must fulfill their *dharma* within the domain of the natural order. They ought to live in conformity with the order which God has established. That is how rites have found their way into life.[59] No matter how much time the prescribed rituals cost, until recently even secularized Hindus observed them.[60] *Dharma* may not be contravened, for the regulations were instituted by God himself.

People are responsible for their deeds. They reap what they sow, and thus accumulate a *karma* (literally 'work')[61] which determines their point of departure in a subsequent life. If someone behaves badly but things go well for him, then he will pay the penalty in a subsequent life. If someone is deprived of the happiness for which he has worked, he will receive his portion when he is reincarnated. A person is thus free to act on his own responsibility and to influence his *karma*. And yet he is also a plaything, at the mercy of the forces governing this world. Life can be good, but it can also be harsh and bitter. These two sides to life give rise to differing attitudes toward God and life in the Hindu tradition, just as they presumably do in all religions. Chaudhuri says that people in India do not bother themselves with liberation from existence in the way that some philosophers fuss about it.[62] People hope for something good in life. They are not constantly preoccupied with distant coasts across the sea but with life on this side of the great water. At least, that is how life tends to proceed as long as all goes well or prospects for improvement are still present. There is also another side to existence, though. Just as the problem of ultimate salvation is present in other religions, Hindus too search for a happiness which cannot be affected by circumstances. Here they speak of *mokṣa,* or liberation from the bonds with which the world constrains the

---

[57] Mulder, pp. 53 ff., 65 ff.
[58] Zaehner, pp. 102 ff., 192; Mulder, p. 63; Chaudhuri, p. 16, concerning *ṛta.*
[59] Bowes, pp. 126 ff.
[60] Chaudhuri, p. 156.
[61] Zaehner, pp. 103, 107 f., 59.
[62] Chaudhuri, pp. 10, cf. 17, 152 ff., 164 ff., 186.

soul.[63] This liberation can only be attained when the *karma* which determines this life has spent itself. In other words, the thought of the *Upaniṣads* seems to be that one must oneself earn salvation. After the appearance of the *Bhagavadgītā* and the emergence of *bhakti*-religion, people latched onto the possibility of asking God to influence *karma* through his grace.[64] What constitutes ultimate liberation? Liberation has to do with the soul's relation to God. Man is ultimately *ātman*, but *ātman* is God. Therefore man is ultimately God. The ground of his existence contains eternal happiness, and this must be realized.[65] One must know this in order to become more and more deeply aware of it. Thus one can grow in this awareness. The Self is then *realized*, and one can achieve *mokṣa* in this way. There are conflicting views in the various currents within Hindu tradition concerning the concrete paths which lead to self-realization. Which remedy is recommended for the ailment depends on the diagnosis.

Bowes mentions five causes for the wrong approach to reality.[66]

(1) In the first place, there is *ignorance*. People do not properly distinguish spirit and matter. People think that they are identical with their body and their 'name and form.' One thus focusses on what is of no real importance and takes care of the outside of the person one is.

(2) Second, people are *egoistic*. They tend to experience everything in terms of their 'I'.

(3) Third, *attachment* to what people find pleasant.

(4) Fourth, aversion to people or to *circumstances* which are unpleasant.

(5) Finally, the *hankering for life* and the fear of death are a source of misery.

The way out of this bind indicated by the various schools and currents is related to the factors which are responsible for the brokenness of human existence. Three ways are pointed to. Some philosophical schools teach the *way of knowledge*. By concentrating on the bond which binds man to God, and on the soul, and by reflecting on the unreality of the world of 'name and form,' the Hindu philosophers are enabled to realize themselves. "While they abide in Wisdom and realize my Godhead," says the Lord in the *Bhagavadgītā*, "they will not be reincarnated when the universe is created anew ... nor will they be destroyed when the universe is again dissolved."[67] Through knowledge one can attain self-realization.

Other philosophical schools focus their attention not on fighting ignorance, but on the *way of yoga and meditation*. Attachment can be obliterated along the way of meditation on the soul and disengagement

---

[63] Zaehner, pp. 63ff.

[64] Zaehner, p. 66.

[65] See R. Kranenborg, *Zelfverwerkelijking* (Kampen 1974), p. 301.

[66] For what follows, see Bowes, pp. 188f., 98f.; cf. the *Yoga sūtras* by Pantajili, a fragment with commentary in *A Sourcebook*, pp. 462f., 468.

[67] *Bhagavadgītā*, XIV. 2, tr. Mascaró.

from worldly existence. This is particularly the approach of the *Yoga Sutra* by Patanjali.[68]

Next to meditation and theoretical discipline, the *Bhagavadgītā* adds a third possibility for those who wish to be without attachment to this world: right action.[69] The *way of action* consists in simply fulfilling one's duty, or *dharma,* while being utterly without attachment. One can renounce the desire for reward and recognition by freeing oneself of attachment. One can conquer the antipathy one feels towards people. Only in this way, states Gandhi, is love possible.[70] Only he who has conquered himself can be loving. Thus, self-realization does not demand withdrawal from the world. Some modern Hindu thinkers take great pains to make it clear that Hinduism is not hostile towards the world. It demands a proper attitude towards life.[71] If we see it correctly, the life of Hindus in the *bhakti* movement is more or less an extension of the way of action. They worship God and try to fulfill their task in life. Not everyone attains freedom from attachment, however. Yet they pray that Kṛṣṇa, or Śiva, or even Durgā as well, will be merciful and influence their *karma* for the good.[72] This sketch of the main concepts in the Hindu tradition must suffice here.

§ 3   Truth

3.1   Prelude

The Sanskrit word for truth is *satya,* which is derived from *sat,* concerning which the *Bhagavadgītā* states:

> '*Sat*' means Reality or the Highest Good, and is also used to signify deeds of uncommon merit.[73]
> Everything done without faith, be it sacrifice, strict asceticism, bestowal of gifts, or whatever, is called '*Asat*' (which means 'unreal') ... [74]

What is true is real, and what is real is true. One could sum up the consequences of our outline of the Hindu world view thus: Hinduism is concerned with being true, not being right. People approach true being. They think about or meditate on it. All exertions, along whatever way, are attempts to approach the Ineffable, the True. The true is the Highest; it

---

[68] Cf. *Sourcebook,* pp. 453-85; cf. Bowes, p. 196.

[69] *Bhagavadgītā,* XIII. 24, tr. Mascaró; Dutch tr., no. 25, School voor Filosofie, Amsterdam, p. 81.

[70] D. M. Datta, *The Philosophy of M. Gandhi* (1953; rpt. Madison 1972), pp. 80 f. M. Gandhi,

is Reality. The human aspiration which corresponds to this reality and approaches it can be called *sat* (authentic). What is done without faith, in attachment or ignorance concerning the origin of human existence, is *asat* (inauthentic and unreal).

People are unable to communicate without words. The question therefore arises as to what the right words are which can accommodate this lofty reality. What is there that is true? What is understood by the truth of the notions which we have presented? Or is there another truth?

We will now focus our attention on a few Hindu thinkers' conceptions of these issues, a procedure which will be repeated in the subsequent chapters of the descriptive part of our enquiry. We will refer first to a modern representative of Śaṅkara's Advaita Vedānta School, Swami Satprakashananda, who of course gives his own interpretation of the Advaita tradition, and then to the view of Rāmānuja. Both positions represent the Vedānta current. The focus within this tradition was especially directed to Brahman and to the manner in which people are related to Brahman. The school goes back to the *Brahmā* or *Vedānta Sūtra* of Badarayana, which is dated between 500 and 200 B.C.E.[75] The text is very compact and apparently susceptible to multiple interpretations. The *Vedānta Sūtra* tries to recapitulate the religious and philosophical speculations of the *Upaniṣads*. The text contains 555 *sūtras* of two or three words. Translations are customarily published with explanatory insertions in the text and commentary by a later thinker from the Vedānta Schools. Śaṅkara is undoubtedly the best-known exponent of this Hindu current, although his thought is controversial. He contends that discursive knowledge is transcended in the unification with Brahman. We are faced here with thoughts which are to a certain extent comparable to the doctrine of the two truths in Buddhism, as we will see in Ch. IV.[76]

Śaṅkara's philosophy has obtained great influence among Hindu thinkers even though it was quite distant from the religious experience of common people.[77] His work is accessible to the foreigner since there are translations of some of his writings. There is also a contemporary study about the epistemology of the Advaita Vedānta by Satprakashananda. In presenting the thought of the Advaita Vedānta, we shall focus on this study. The other classical thinker whose thought we will present is Rāmānuja. He also belongs to the Vedānta School, but was unconvinced by what Śaṅkara wrote concerning total unification. In his thought, Rāmānuja also sought union with Brahman, but a unification which preserves some distance. His theology, or philosophy, has obtained much influence in the

---

[75] *Sourcebook*, p. 506; Sen, p. 82.

[76] F. J. Streng, *Emptiness: A Study in Religious Meaning* (Nashville 1967). He stresses the difference between Nāgārjuna and the Advaita Vedānta; see his comment on Murti's interpretation of Buddhism (*The Central Philosophy of Buddhism*), p. 148.

[77] Cf. Zaehner, p. 73.

bhakti movement. Several of his works have also been translated. There are several studies on Rāmānuja: we will focus chiefly on John Carman's.

After we consider these two classical Hindu views, we will present several of Radhakrishnan's and Gandhi's ideas. Radhakrishnan stands in the tradition of Śankara, whose view has become familiar in the West, partly through other modern Hindu thinkers.[78] Gandhi is more difficult to classify. He himself has not written anything systematic or philosophical about the concept of truth but his ideas have been summed up systematically by others. In view of Gandhi's influence and great appeal, we will also pay notice to his view. In the final section we will examine more closely questions concerning the plurality of views and their complementarity or possible mutual contradiction.

3.2 The Advaita Vedānta according to Satprakashananda

Śankara lived between 650 and 800 C.E.[79] He produced a commentary on the *Vedānta Sūtra*. There are of course doctrinal differences within the Advaita School. This does not diminish the fact that they are agreed on one fundamental matter, the non-discriminatory character of the awareness of the Highest Truth. To this the School owes its name: *advaita* means not-many, not-two, 'non-duality.'[80] In our text we will follow Satprakashananda's exposition; we stress, however, that he offers a personal interpretation of the Advaita tradition.

a) Epistemology: means of cognition

According to Satprakashananda, the Advaita School recognizes six valid ways of knowing.[81] The six methods (*pramāṇas*) which can lead to valid knowledge are: perception, deduction, testimony, comparison, postulation, and non-perception (of something or someone). The latter three *pramāṇas* are characteristic of the Advaita School; other orthodox schools occasionally consider them forms of deduction. The fact that the Advaita School accepts them as independent means of cognition is due partially to their analysis of the means of cognition in question, and partially to other Advaita Vedānta insights. In the context of our study we must briefly deal with perception, testimony, and comparison.

Perceptions can refer to the external world beyond man or to one's inner world. Sensations of pain, pleasure, love, and hate belong to inward experience, but so do knowledge and ignorance. One perceives whether one knows something or not. Knowledge can be either direct or indirect. Knowledge which comes about directly and without mediation is certain,

---

[78] Cf. Zaehner, pp. 168f.
[79] *Sourcebook*, p. 506; Küng, p. 208; Vetter, p. 11.
[80] Sen, p. 19; Vetter, pp. 28ff.
[81] For the following section, see Satprakashananda, *Methods of Knowledge: According to Advaita Vedānta* (London 1965), pp. 35ff.

according to Satprakashananda.[82] Since inner perception is immediate, it follows in principle that it is certain. If one perceives that one dislikes something, then one does dislike it. If one is uncertain whether one dislikes something or whether one finds something to be right, then the uncertainty arises not from perception, but from what is perceived. To put it differently, one can be certain that one does not yet know something. Inner perception itself is certain.

The *testimony* of others is accepted as a valid means of knowledge by the orthodox schools. They recognize the authority of the Vedic Scriptures. They point out that in daily life, people assume an awful lot on the basis of hearsay.[83] *Sabda-pramāṇa* (verbal testimony) may be accepted only on the authority of a competent person. Various demands are made of valid testimony: (1) the words in the sentence must be related; (2) the statement must be consistent; (3) the words and sentences must form a whole, no lacuna are allowed; (4) the intent of the sentence must be comprehensible in terms of the sentence itself.[84]

Another demand of valid testimony is that what is thus purported may not be contradicted by knowledge acquired through one of the other means of cognition.[85] We will return to this demand for consistency in discussing valid knowledge. It is clear that the step taken here functions not only to explain that one does well to listen when a reliable person raises alarm, but also that the Vedic Scriptures ought to be highly regarded since they pass on visionaries' knowledge of supersensory realms which would otherwise remain unknown. Without the knowledge which one obtains from the Vedic Scriptures, one cannot attain to deep truth.[86] The lofty, supersensory awareness which one receives from the Vedas is no immediate knowledge.[87] One obtains it through a means — the testimony. Since it is knowledge of a higher plane, it cannot be contradicted by other knowledge. Thus it can still be certain. Two insights are basic to the Vedic Scriptures:

(1) The insight that the individual self is in effect the Highest Self.[88]

(2) The insight that the ultimate or genuine reality is non-dual Brahman – Being, Consciousness, and Blessedness.[89]

Since these insights are not contradicted by other experiences, they can be adopted with certainty.

---

[82] *Ibid*, p. 73, cf. p. 83.

[83] *Ibid*, pp. 173-92.

[84] *Ibid*, pp. 178 ff.

[85] Cf. also N. K. Devaraja, *An Introduction to Śaṅkara's Theory of Knowledge* (Delhi ²1972), p. 70.

[86] Satprakashananda, pp. 212 f.

[87] *Ibid*, p. 37; Devaraja, p. 66.

[88] *Sourcebook*, p. 514 (Śaṅkara's text, I. iii. 19). The *Sourcebook* has Śaṅkara fragments from *The Vedānta sūtras of Badarayana with the Commentary by Śaṅkarakaṛya*, tr. Thibaut, Sacred Books of the East 34/38 (Oxford 1890/1896; rpt. 1962).

[89] *Sourcebook*, p. 512, cf. pp. 525 f., 530.

One also procures valid knowledge by *comparison*.[90] This particular means of cognition is of importance with reference to metaphysics, since it opens the possibility of conveying to others knowledge concerning the Highest. Brahman is without name or form.[91] If one wants to speak of Him, one must make comparisons with the rest of experience in order to indicate the correspondences and differences between it, one the one hand, and Brahman and the Self on the other.

b) Knowledge of things

People acquire knowledge of the world with the aid of the senses. What in the West is designated as extrasensory perception is also recognized.[92] Four factors play a role in perception: the object, the specific organ for knowledge of a particular object, the mind, and the knowing self.[93] The concept of the Advaita Vedānta, as Satprakashananda understands it, is that certain subtle material substances are connected with the senses.[94] Two of them, connected with hearing and seeing, have the ability to perceive outside the body.[95] The human mind can reach outside the body through the cognitive activity of these subtle substances and converge with the object known.[96] In this way, there can be direct experience of things. These organs (*indriyas*) belong to the 'subtle body' which, together with the soul, migrate to a subsequent body upon death. We will skip the variations defended within the Advaita tradition with regard to such cognition, since religious knowledge is our primary concern.[97]

c) Self

Satprakashananda distinguishes between the mind and the (knowing) self. The person, or the self, has an instrument at its disposal: the mind. The 'I' which is conscious of itself, is the Self. This 'I' cannot be made an object of analysis, because it is the 'I' which is conscious of the analysis. The Self eludes any objectification.[98]

---

[90] Satprakashananda, pp. 155 f.
[91] Cf. *Sourcebook*, pp. 530 f. (Śaṅkara's text, II. i. 4).
[92] Satprakashananda, p. 44.
[93] *Ibid*, pp. 46 f.
[94] *Ibid*, p. 49; cf. Devaraja, pp. 94 f.
[95] Satprakashananda, p. 53.
[96] *Ibid*, pp. 102 f.; on knowledge, cf. esp., pp. 61 ff.; pp. 75, 90 ff.; cf. Śaṅkara, in *Sourcebook*, p. 537 (III. ii. 21); cf. also J. F. Staal, *Advaita and Neoplatonism: A Critical Study in Comparative Philosophy* (Madras 1961), pp. 102 ff.; Devaraja, pp. 95 f.
[97] Satprakashananda, p. 50. See the description of various views within the Advaita Vedānta in L. Schmithausen, "Zur ādvaitischen Theorie der Objekterkenntnis," *Wiener Zeitschrift für die Kunde Süd- und Ostasiens*, XII/XIII, Fests. E. Frauwallner (Vienna 1968), esp. pp. 339, 359 f.; cf. also S. Mayeda, "The Advaita Theory of Perception," in *WZKSOA* (1968), pp. 221 ff.
[98] Satprakashananda, p. 41; Devaraja, p. 103.

We can now take a step in the direction of non-duality. In epistemology, one must always deal with the distinction between subject and object. Śaṅkara and his School want to transcend the subject-object dichotomy which is always present in any consciousness of things. The subject of cognition is the mind, while its object is what is known; the Self, however, is the 'silent witness' which —itself eternal and immutable— is conscious of mental processes and the state of the body which it sustains.[99] The self is limited by the body, by 'name and form,' but the Self itself is untouched, being related to the Eternal. The Self is thus actually beyond the duality of subject and object. The Self is pure and free.[100] One can view the Self in two perspectives: (1) In relation to the limitations of body and mind, the Self undergoes experience and undertakes action. (2) As a transcendent witness to earthly processes, the Self participates in immutable, Pure Consciousness.[101]

The problem is that people are seldom aware of their true self. It is not something which can simply be explained to everyone; more is needed in order to attain true insight. *Ajñāna* (ignorance) must be overcome.[102] What does *ajñāna* consist in? Satprakashananda describes the two sides of *ajñāna*.[103] (1) *Ajñāna* covers the existence of the (real) object with a veil. People do not see that the world —in a certain sense— is appearance (*māyā*). People do not see things as manifestations of Brahman due to their ignorance. (2) *Ajñāna* covers over the manifestations of Brahman so that people no longer see the divine, even if they become convinced at a certain moment that all things are manifestations of Brahman. *Ajñāna* nourishes egoism.[104] It is because of ignorance and egoism that people no longer see that Pure Consciousness is everything which exists, and that it assumes multifarious forms in things and in people.[105]

d) The world

Things are not what they appear to be. It appears that earthly reality is replete with many, many things, but at bottom there *is* only Brahman. On account of this perception, Śaṅkara has been accused of not taking the everyday experience of the world seriously, everyday experience being 'illusionary.'[106] Śaṅkara is alleged to be diametrically opposing all common sense. Satprakashananda explains, however, that at its own level, the

---

[99] *Ibid*, pp. 63, 82, 140, 241.
[100] *Ibid*, p. 233.
[101] *Ibid*, p. 233.
[102] *Ibid*, p. 79.
[103] *Ibid*, pp. 109, cf. 134, 278f., 281; cf. Staal, pp. 115f., 121f.
[104] Satprakashananda, p. 138.
[105] *Ibid*, p. 83.
[106] *Ibid*, pp. 134ff.; cf. Staal, p. 122, who renders *māyā* not as 'illusion,' but as 'magically-creative activity'; cf. also Bowes, p. 152, 'magic-like creative potentiality.'

world is as it is experienced. It is valid in its own sphere.[107] From an *absolute* point of view, the world does not exist. Seen from an everyday point of view, however, it does exist and is known as it is. From the absolute point of view, again, the world is a mixture of *satya* (reality/truth) and *anṛta* (unreality, that which does not conform to the cosmic order).[108] The entire world exists by virtue of ignorance and egoism.[109] Cognitive consciousness (the self) ascribes 'name and form' to things, and identifies itself with body and mind. It thus assigns boundaries to the boundless self; *"Avidyā* [ignorance] . . . limits the limitless."[110] Individuality is an 'illusion.'[111]

Satprakashananda does acknowledge the relative legitimacy of everyday experience. Given this illusion, the world is real. Due to the coincidence of the mode of mind with the consciousness in things, knowledge is the unity of cognition with its object.[112] Satprakashananda thereby rejects the conception of knowledge as representation of its object. An object is not reflected in cognition but is actually present in perception. Knowledge is simple awareness of its object. Knowledge is 'from within' in a certain sense; more reliable still is hardly possible.

But what of the mistakes which people make then? Satprakashananda deals extensively with this, following time-honoured custom in Hindu philosophy. Here too the emphasis is put on the objective circumstances which lead the subject astray. Illusory perceptions, such as the rising of the sun, have an objective basis; they depend not on thought, but on the facts as these occur to man, concealed, however, by *ajñāna*.[113] Illusion —a piece of rope on the street is mistaken for a snake, or mother of pearl for silver— stems from a vague sensation of what is perceived.[114] The error does not lodge in thought, but in the unclearness of the object. The other side of this is that anything which is perceived clearly is also certain.

When is knowledge valid? What are the *criteria* by which cognition may be tested to sort out what is true? It should be borne in mind that true knowledge bears in itself the characteristics of validity.[115] In true knowledge, the truth is evident. Therefore one is automatically certain of true insight. Satprakashananda outlines the discussion which has been carried on in the various schools of Hindu philosophy on the criteria of valid knowledge. He is right in pointing out that this discussion has much in

---

[107] Satprakashananda, p. 66.
[108] *Ibid*, p. 135; cf. Staal, pp. 120, 123 f.
[109] Satprakashananda, pp. 138 ff.
[110] *Ibid*, p. 140.
[111] *Ibid*, p. 140.
[112] *Ibid*, pp. 96 f.
[113] *Ibid*, p. 136.
[114] *Ibid*, p. 127.
[115] *Ibid*, p. 112.

common with what Western philosophy has brought up in this connection. The theme of the *Nyāya-Vaiśeshika* School is that the validity of knowledge consists in correspondehce between cognition and its object.[116] The *Kumarila* School, one of the schools of the *Mīmāṃsā*, has an additional measure based on the effect of knowledge in practice, and, furthermore, demands coherence with other facts. Some other schools also point to the necessity of practical assessment — even though this demand was and is disputed.[117] Satprakashananda, as mentioned, requires that statements be consistent and clear, and that knowledge not conflict with other known truths. Knowledge must form a coherent whole, or at the very least, it must not be contradictory. Thus, the principle of *non-contradiction* is recognized. Indirect knowledge accepted on the authority of the divines of the Vedic Scriptures may be regarded as true and certain, unless it is in conflict with knowledge gained by virtue of another competence. The possibility that the knowledge which one owes to the Vedic Scriptures be contradicted by the rest of knowledge is then excluded, as we have already indicated: the *śruti* speaks of higher truths which are unattainable for common experience. Satprakashananda regards the *principium non contradictionis* (*satyatvam badharahityam*) as crucial for the Vedānta.[118] It replaces the principle of correspondence, which, as Satprakashananda remarks, can never be proven.[119] Such, in sum, is Satprakashananda's account of knowledge of the truth concerning the relative world.

e) Self-realization

Seen from the point of view of the absolute, the world does not exist. It is illusory. Its substratum is real, however; the One and the Absolute *is* in the many phenomena of this world. Yet, one breaks through to higher truth when one realizes that the Self is not his body or mind.[120] Accepting as true the knowledge of this state of affairs is not sufficient, however. Ignorance has taken root very deeply, and egoism is the result. Egoism has fundamental significance here. It is not merely reckoning things in terms of oneself and putting oneself in the foreground; it is attachment to everything other than Brahman. Realizing oneself thus means becoming Brahman and giving up the private, fragmentary 'self' that one is. In this way the self also advances beyond the subject-object distinction which imprisons thought in the world of illusion. The true 'knowledge' which one pursues is thus not knowledge in the common sense of the word, for God cannot be objectified. As long as there is an object in cognition there is also a subject, and one is then not participating completely in

---

[116] *Ibid*, p. 115.
[117] Cf. Satprakashananda, p. 117f; the validity of this text has been contested by T. P. Ramachandran, *Dvaita Vedānta* (New Delhi 1976), p. 45.
[118] Satprakashananda, pp. 116f.
[119] *Ibid*, pp. 116f.
[120] Cf. Devaraja, pp. 72ff.

Brahman. Knowing God, says Satprakashananda, means either knowing that one is essentially one with Him, or realizing union with Him. These are in fact the two steps of *samādhi* (concentration). On the first and lowest step the notion of God as the other still remains; on the second step, the awareness of the distinction between knowing and Known disappears.[121]

Much is required before one advances that far. Śaṅkara summed up four conditions which every seeker of *mokṣa* must meet:

(1) One must learn to distinguish between eternal and non-eternal.
(2) One must learn to be indifferent to whether one does or does not enjoy the fruits of one's labours.
(3) One must acquire peace and self-control.
(4) One must yearn for final liberation.[122]

Mokṣa is thus attained only after a process of purification and deepening of insight. Satprakashananda himself —leaving aside the question of the relationship between his insights and those of Śaṅkara— characterizes the way as threefold; hearing, reflection, and meditation.[123] He points out the necessity of a pure way of life, of spiritual guidance, and the importance of monasteries.[124] Those who travel this road —it is given to but few— will find the highest form of *samādhi*; they abide in Brahman and thus find liberation (*mokṣa*).[125] Such liberation is final, since union with Brahman has been realized.[126] *Karma* has been broken. Upon death, these souls are not reincarnated, but remain in union with Brahman. Only Brahman shines then. They dwell in the light, without awareness of individuality, their unification with Brahman complete. The distinction between subject and object is completely obliterated in such non-dual experience.

The way to the highest *samādhi* experience is not the destiny of everyone in this life. Satprakashananda outlines various ways which people can take, adapted to the level on which one finds oneself.[127] It is the task of the guru to determine how far along someone is and to give him the right assignments. Moral virtues are even more important for attaining knowledge of the self than intellectual capacity.[128] For the less advanced, faith (*śraddhā*) is more important than rational analysis.[129] For yet others, more room is allotted to *bhakti*.[130] They are advised to imagine God as a person, as *saguṇa Brahman* (as opposed to true, impersonal

---

[121] Satprakashananda, pp. 276.
[122] *Ibid*, pp. 262f.; cf. Śaṅkara, *Sourcebook*, p. 510 (I. i. 1); Satprakashananda gives an elaboration of Śaṅkara's thoughts.
[123] Satprakashananda, pp. 256ff.
[124] *Ibid*, pp. 263ff.
[125] *Ibid*, p. 258.
[126] *Ibid*, pp. 278f.
[127] *Ibid*, pp. 290ff.
[128] *Ibid*, pp. 266ff. This understanding is widely accepted in Hinduism; cf. also Śaṅkara himself, *Sourcebook*, p. 540 (III. iv. 51); cf. Kranenborg, p. 304.
[129] Satprakashananda, p. 290.
[130] *Ibid*, p. 298.

nirguṇa Brahman).[131] One may also worship an aspect of Brahman in the form of the religion of Viṣṇu, Śiva, Śakti, or Kṛṣṇa. Whatever the case, self-control, compassion, and a loving disposition towards all other people always belong those qualities which one must realize.[132]

f) Dual and non-dual *samādhi*

There are then two forms of *samādhi*. The higher, final liberation means a definitive absorption in Brahman.[133] This experience is non-dual, the distinction between subject and object having been overcome.[134] Absorption in Brahman is such a magnificent experience that those whom it befalls are ipso facto convinced of its truth and bliss. In fact, words fail altogether — and one does well to bear this in mind when giving a description of non-dual experience with words! The liberated do not experience the truth about *samādhi*, but Truth; the dissolution of the distinction between subject and object; non-relational Awareness; Absolute Oneness.[135]

Nirguṇa Brahman is Awareness, but it is an awareness without distinction. *Saguṇa Brahman* is to be imagined as a link between *nirguṇa Brahman* and the world. In *saguṇa Brahman* distinction is present; He is a Person, distinguishing himself from what He is not.

Those who have realized final *samādhi* can continue living for a time.[136] They then see the all-pervasive presence of Brahman in the relative world; they are no longer taken prisoner by illusion. Only such a person has true knowledge of the universe and of the Highest Lord. Such a person will never again lose the vision of non-dual Awareness.[137] His perception of reality is non-dual, although his presentation of it will of necessity still be dual.[138]

In summary we can say that the concept of truth in the epistemology of Satprakashananda's interpretation of the Advaita Vedānta functions at three levels: (1) Brahman is (non-dual) truth. (2) The holy person, who has realized Brahman, sees the world as it really is, as being one with Brahman — this view of the world is present in consciousness. (3) For those who live in the world without having appropriated this experience of the 'world,' true knowledge consists of the presence within consciousness of the (separate) things which one knows. Finally: true knowledge is ipso facto certain.

---

[131] *Ibid*, pp. 297 f.
[132] *Ibid*, p. 299.
[133] *Ibid*, pp. 277 ff. He terms it *nirvikalpa samādhi*.
[134] *Ibid*, pp. 248 ff.; cf. Śaṅkara, in *Sourcebook*, pp. 519 f. (I. iv. 22).
[135] Satprakashananda, p. 212.
[136] *Ibid*, pp. 254 f.
[137] *Ibid*, p. 254, with reference to the *Bhagavadgītā*, VI. 31 f.
[138] Satprakashananda, p. 256.

3.3 Theistic Vedānta (Rāmānuja)

a) General remarks

Śaṅkara's analysis of non-dual truth was not shared by all Vedantins. One of the most prominent spokesman from another current was Rāmānuja (11th century). Rāmānuja is considered to be the father of the *Sri Vaiṣṇava Sampradāya*, a sect in the southern part of India which worshipped Viṣṇu (and his wife). In worshipping Viṣṇu, one seeks to approach him as the Highest God. This current believes in a personal God. God has properties. As with some other currents of the Vedānta school, they reject speaking about an impersonal Brahman which is reputedly higher than *saguṇa Brahman*.[139] They do no believe that dual knowledge can be transcended in non-dual knowledge. God-in-himself remains unknowable for man. But how can we then know about God and what is the nature of religious knowledge according to Rāmānuja? In our exposition we will follow John Carman's study on Rāmānuja.

The incisiveness of Rāmānuja's thought has been awarded different estimations. Carman cites an Indian, Christian scholar who finds in him the "loftiest philosophical expression" of Indian theism.[140] Carman regards Rāmānuja as representative of much thought within the various theistic schools in India. One of the points on which Rāmānuja diverges from the Advaita Vedānta is his belief that the root of misery is not only ignorance or egoism, but also the underlying power of *karma*. This power must be broken, but this is not possible simply by acquiring knowledge. Rāmānuja contends that one must ultimately make an appeal to God's generosity in one's *bhakti* of the divinity.[141]

Rāmānuja is an orthodox thinker. Along with the Vedānta, he acknowledges the authority of the *śruti*. He contends that the Advaitins do not do full justice to the Vedic Scriptures. Sometimes they speak of the unity of the self with Brahman, but sometimes a distinction continues to exist alongside this unity. Rāmānuja gives a different interpretation of the well-known word, *Tat tvam asi* (Thou are That) than does Śaṅkara. He does not want to appeal to disconnected scripture passages, pointing out the importance of good hermeneutics which allow all facets of the scriptures to come into their own.[142] Rāmānuja also shares with other orthodox thinkers what Carman calls his fideism: knowledge of God is only possible on the basis of Scripture, for proofs for God are not stringent.[143]

---

[139] Carman, p. 105.
[140] Carman, pp. 24, 263. He deems Rāmānuja to be representative for theistic thought in India.
[141] *Ibid*, pp. 87, 55 f.
[142] *Ibid*, pp. 202 ff.; cf. pp. 51, 124, 109.
[143] *Ibid*, pp. 259, 270, cf. pp. 261 ff. (with notes).

Although Rāmānuja's conception is representative for many orthodox Hindu thinkers, and although *bhakti* receives an important position in his thought, it of course remains different from the popular religion. Since the worship of Viṣṇu, his consort, and their son occupies an important place in Rāmānuja's thought, this form of piety occupies a position between that of the polytheism of common Hindu religion and the monotheism of explicitly sectarian theologians.[144]

The central idea in Rāmānuja's doctrine of God is that the divine permeates all of finite, limited existence.[145] Brahman is both the material and the efficient cause of the universe, which is animated by Him as the inner Self of the universe.[146] This position is characteristic of Rāmānuja, who thereby attempts to choose a middle way between those thinkers who deny (from an absolute point of view) that God and the world are different, and those who declare, on the contrary, that a fundamental difference does exist. Rāmānuja affirms that one must do justice both to the unity as well as to the difference between God and the world.

b)   The world, man, and God

God created the world.[147] Earthly reality is no illusion; the cosmos is God's body.[148] People have a finite self which can know God.[149] The two-ness in the oneness is never overcome. The Self need not be transcended, as in the Advaita Vedānta, but it must be directed towards God. The soul of man is his self, which is beyond the world, an essentially unfettered consciousness.[150] The soul is congealed and contracted into a separate, individual soul by the *karma* of a person. The actual soul of a person must thus be viewed from two angles. (1) The essential nature of the finite self is the self which is animated and infused by God.[151] (2) In the state of ignorance (caused by *karma*),[152] there is a finite, individual self.[153]

God is the animator of created reality, since the world is the incarnation of Brahman. God imparts existence to created reality.[154] Rāmānuja insists on the perfection of God in his doctrine; God is far from the

---

[144] *Ibid*, p. 262.

[145] *Ibid*, p. 247.

[146] *Ibid*, p. 51.

[147] *Ibid*, pp. 114 ff.

[148] *Ibid*, pp. 108, 263; cf. also V. R. S. Chakravarti, *The Philosophy of Sri Rāmānuja (Viśiṣṭadvaita)* (Madras 1974), pp. 136 ff., 129 f.

[149] Carman, p. 108.

[150] Chakravarti, p. 10; cf. pp. 11 ff., where the soul, *cit* or *ātman*, is distinguished from body and spirit; *cit* is imperishable and unchangeable, 'the abode of *jñāna* or consciousness.'

[151] Carman, p. 152.

[152] Chakravarti, p. 120.

[153] Carman, p. 152.

[154] *Ibid*, pp. 124 f., 101.

imperfections of this world.[155] This insistence makes it possible to understand Rāmānuja's distinction between God-in-se and God in his relationship to people.[156] The distinction is not completely clear in Rāmānuja's work, according to Carman. It has been explained in the manner which we have presented: God's immutable, essential nature exists next to his changeable nature. The essential nature of God is untouched by modifications, and is free of material blemishes. In himself, God is pure knowledge and blessedness.[157] But God the Creator also exists in relation to mankind. He enables people to know Him.[158] The anthropomorphic elements of Viṣṇu play a role in God's condescension. God's properties are distinguished in two groups. (1) In relation to the world, God is merciful and full of compassion. He descends to the world in commiseration. He lovingly forgives and protects. (2) Essential properties of God are *satya*, knowledge, strength, sovereignty, immutability, creative power and magnificence, purity, and infinity.[159]

c) Knowledge of the world, man, and God

People can acquire reliable knowledge of the world, of themselves and of God, since He has made the world and has given mankind the possibility of knowing the world. People acquire knowledge through perception and through conclusions based on perception.[160]

As far as knowledge of their true self goes, people are faced with great difficulties. Their true self is withdrawn from view by the confining power of *karma* and the restrictions of material reality.[161] Still, it remains possible for man to learn to know himself. As in other Vedānta schools, the concern in this Vedānta school is not simply with knowledge concerning the deepest nature of human-being, but with the realization of the union of the Self with the highest Self — even though the distinction between God and man is never abrogated. This knowledge is a gift of God. Man cannot break the power of his *karma*; for this he is dependent on God.[162] God can intervene in the course of *karma* and liberate the soul from the chain of *saṃsāra* (the chain of reincarnation).

Knowledge of the true self is related, naturally, to knowledge of God, which can be gleaned from the Vedic Scriptures. Purely external knowledge of Vedic doctrine and reasonable understanding alone are insufficient to

---

[155] *Ibid*, pp. 108 ff., 132.
[156] *Ibid*, pp. 90 f.; see also pp. 78 ff.
[157] *Ibid*, p. 72.
[158] *Ibid*, p. 79.
[159] *Ibid*, p. 79, cf. pp. 93, 124 (*sat*).
[160] *Ibid*, pp. 108, 263. Chakravarti, states that the Vedānta School acknowledges as valid means of knowledge 'perception/inference,' *jñāna* or *śruti*, and *smṛti*— other means of cognition being reduced to these three. Sense perception is valid only with respect to those things which can be known through sense perception, pp. 6 f.
[161] Carman, p. 94.
[162] *Ibid*, p. 177.

overcome ignorance.[163] Deeper knowledge is required, involving greater personal commitment. This knowledge is to be obtained in devotion and meditation. One of Rāmānuja's central tenets is that the highest to which people can and must aspire is that form of knowledge which emerges through *bhakti*.[164] Sacrifices and other religious customs are the means, in the spiritual life, for the realization of such knowledge through religious commitment to Brahman. Analytical knowledge is not enough, although it is also not unimportant.[165]

d) Truth

Knowledge (*jñāna*) and truth or Reality (*satya*) are two of the properties of God's essential nature.[166] What Rāmānuja means by the property of 'being true' (*satya*) is that the Being of Brahman is not conditioned, and God's being is thus distinct from non-intelligent matter, which is subject to change, as well as from intelligent beings in the world, who are confined by changeable matter.[167] The word 'knowledge' or 'awareness' (*jñāna*) indicates a state of permanently uncontracted knowledge.[168] Brahman differs in this regard from the enlightened souls who have known a period of discursive consciousness. Brahman is infinite, while created souls are not. But the finite selves, in contradistinction to material elements, are true or real (*satya*) in the sense that their essential nature is unchangeable.[169] The Highest Person is the reality (*satya*) of these souls, who are themselves unmoved by the determinations to which they are subject in accordance with their *karma*. God is therefore their *satya,* being more real than they are, or at least thus Thibaut's translation of Rāmānuja.[170] We run across a notion in Rāmānuja at this point which we shall encounter again in other doctrines of God as well — God in himself is or has unlimited non-discursive knowledge. Human thought is always determined and limited. People cannot imagine God's thought, for God is pure thought. Brahman is knowledge, yet at the same time He is the subject of this knowledge, and blessedness.[171]

How can a person then realize knowledge of God? One obtains knowledge concerning God and one's self (*jñāna*) from the Vedic Scriptures and one must do his duty in the world (*karma yoga*). These are preparatory

---

[163] *Ibid*, pp. 55 f.
[164] *Ibid*, p. 51.
[165] *Ibid*, pp. 55 f.; cf. Chakravarti, § Existence of God cannot be proved by inference, pp. 201 ff.
[166] Carman, p. 90 ff.
[167] Rāmānuja, in *The Vedānta-sūtras, with Commentary by Rāmānuja*, tr. Thibaut, Sacred Books of the East Series 48 (Oxford 1904; rpt. Delhi 1984), p. 129, 23; in Carman, p. 102.
[168] Carman: 'state of permanently uncontracted knowledge,' p. 102.
[169] *Ibid*, p. 103.
[170] *Ibid*, p. 103.
[171] *Ibid*, pp. 111 f.

steps on the path to insight. Though they result in contemplation of *ātman* (the self), they do not yet effect deep knowledge of God.[172] If a person pleases God through his works and through *bhakti*, His displeasure in sin will be dissolved; He will then lift the ignorance of the soul concerning one's own nature and Himself,[173] thereby freeing the road towards realizing knowledge of one's nature and of God. Such deeper knowledge consists in achieving communion with Brahman; one is then liberated from *saṁsāra*.[174]

If we perceive it aright, Rāmānuja has a twofold answer to Śaṅkara's doctrine of supreme, non-dual knowledge and *nirguṇa Brahman*. In the first place, the relation to God consists in deep knowledge through personal relationship to God, in which the bonds of *karma* have been overcome. Second, he advances the doctrine of God's essential properties, which on the one hand makes allowance for the Advaita distinction between *nirguṇa* and *saguṇa Brahman*, but on the other hand, evokes the question as to the relation between God's essential and his relative properties. Carman repeatedly points to this problem.[175]

In what does truth consist? Rāmānuja in fact distinguishes various levels of knowledge. In his translations, Carman often notes that Rāmānuja regards certain revealed, theoretical insights as true.[176] At the level of daily life, truth refers to the cognition by which one knows things as they are.[177] Apart from knowledge of the divine, however, one does not see that 'ordinary' things are less real than that which exists entirely in God. God alone is wholly *sat*, eternal, real, and true.[178]

Human knowledge meets its boundary at knowledge of the divine. It is stated with emphasis that God's essential nature cannot be known or understood by man; it is beyond the reach of language and thought.[179] He can be known only in *bhakti*, as He reveals himself in relation to the soul. One experiences his presence in the union of the Soul with God. Truth is realized in the mystical communion of the soul with God, in which God and the soul are one, yet remain distinct.[180] This informs the specific position of Rāmānuja — union which preserves distinctness.

---

[172] *Ibid*, p. 61; see J. A. van Buitenen, *Rāmānuja on the Bhagavadgītā* (Den Haag 1953), pp. 85 f., 100.

[173] Carman, p. 177.

[174] *Ibid*, p. 177.

[175] Carman has some critical questions on the issue, p. 264; cf. p. 92.

[176] *Ibid*, pp. 132, 167.

[177] Chakravarti, p. 157, "By *prakasa* is meant true knowledge of things as they are."

[178] Carman, p. 169.

[179] In Carman, p. 183.

[180] On the relation of God and souls, also Chakravarti, pp. 103-19. Carman cites Rāmānuja, "All this means that the person who has Brahman as the object of his knowledge becomes happy," p. 152.

3.4 Sarvepalli Radhakrishnan

a) Self, God, and the Absolute

In Radhakrishnan's thought (1888–1969), we find a modern interpretation of Advaita Vedānta doctrine. Radhakrishnan has enunciated his ideas in several series of lectures which he gave in England in the twenties.[181] He is familiar with Western philosophy and develops his religious philosophy with reference to many Western thinkers.[182] He accepts the Vedic Scriptures because they articulate the experiences of inspired people.[183] Their experiences refer to the unutterable.[184] The Vedic Scriptures owe their authority to their description of the (spiritual) facts.[185]

What are the spiritual experiences which are described in the *śruti*, and which Radhakrishnan in his studies in the philosophy of religion tries to indicate on behalf of others? It is the experience of the unity of all things, deep in the self.[186] The Highest is the ground for the individual self: *Tat tvam asi* (Thou art That).[187] God is thus immanent, the source of the Being of the world, yet he is not entirely co-extensive with this. God is not wholly immanent, nor is He wholly transcendent.[188] Both aspects of God belong together. Viewed from his immanence in the world, the divinity is called 'God'; viewed from his loftiness above all finitude, he is called the Absolute.[189] As total representation of a divine Person, the word 'God' is a symbol in which religion recognizes the Absolute.[190] Religion venerates the Absolute in the form of personal gods, hence salvation is to be found in *bhakti*, in faith, and in religious commitment.[191] God is the creator of the world. In his lofty play (*līlā*), He fashions one world after the next. But this God is not simply the Absolute, without further qualification. Here, in Radhakrishnan's case, we are confronted by the same twofold division between *saguna* and *nirguṇa Brahman*, which we have already encountered in our exposition of the Advaita Vedānta. God the Creator is lower than

---

181   Sarvepalli Radhakrishnan, *An Idealist View of Life* (1932; rpt. London 1980), based on lectures in Manchester and London in 1929 and 1930; Radhakrishnan, *The Hindu View of Life* (London ²1928).

182   For his philosophy of religion, see Radhakrishnan, *Idealist View*, pp. 66 ff., and others. P. T. Raju, *Idealistic Thought of India* (Cambridge, Mass. 1953), states that Radhakrishnan has been influenced strongly by Western idealism, p. 342.

183   Radhakrishnan, pp. 70, 147 f.

184   In his opinion this is true of great seers all over the world, p. 93.

185   *Ibid*, pp. 70 f.

186   Cf. *Ibid*, p. 80, "The true and ultimate condition of the human being is the divine status. The essence of life is the movement of the universal being; the essence of emotion is the play of the self-existent delight in being; the essence of thought is the inspiration of the all-pervading truth; the essence of activity is the progressive realization of a universal and self-effecting good."

187   *Ibid*, p. 81.

188   *Ibid*, p. 83.

189   *Ibid*, pp. 84 f.

190   *Ibid*, p. 86.

191   *Ibid*, p. 270.

the Absolute. God the Creator, Sustainer, and Judge of this world is the Absolute approached in human terms. The Absolute Itself, however, is perfect, and therefore immutable and blessed. It is a continual 'I am,' the immutable centre which mysteriously lies at the basis of changeable reality.[192]

b) Intuitive knowledge

The Absolute cannot be known discursively. All the forms in which people, by necessity, think, are contaminated by untruth,[193] yet without language, myths, and metaphors, no knowledge could be passed on. The aim of all philosophical religious knowledge is to motivate people to seek such truth as can only be realized in awareness. True knowledge transcends thought. It is an immediate experience; one is conscious of it, but not via the categories of one's understanding.[194]

A precondition for attaining this knowledge is that one purifies one's life from all factors which bar self-realization. Depth and power are lacking in the ordinary life of this world of ignorance. One must change oneself — history is directed toward development for the good.[195] One must learn to discriminate what matters from what does not. The concern is not so much sharpening one's understanding, but purity of the mind. One must become familiar with the deepest reality.[196] Not until one is free of the superficial motives which normally govern human existence, is one capable of intuitively experiencing the Absolute.[197]

Not all people are capable of this. People need a series of lives in order to so perfect themselves that they can be absorbed into the Absolute.[198] For this reason, those who have realized truth must try to explain to others what the reality of this world is like. In such explanations, they may proceed from general human experience. Most people must ultimately simply trust that what the wise say is true.[199] What we should demand of such explanations is that the intuitive certainty of God be consistent with the visible universe as it appears to all of us.[200] Radhakrishnan therefore attempts to demonstrate that his view is congruent with all kinds of other insights which people have reached scientifically.

---

[192] *Ibid*, p. 273.
[193] *Ibid*, p. 76.
[194] *Ibid*, p. 77.
[195] On progress in history, *Ibid*, p. 242.
[196] *Ibid*, p. 167.
[197] *Ibid*, p. 169.
[198] *Ibid*, pp. 231f., 239.
[199] *Ibid*, pp. 174f.
[200] *Ibid*, pp. 174f., 176.

c) Truth

Hindu philosophy has a great respect for the facts. The world is no illusion; it really exists, at least at the level of earthly experience. For Radhakrishnan, truth at this level of being and knowing is knowledge of things as we see them when we isolate certain facets of experience from the whole.[201]

Knowledge serves as preparation for intuitive insight. Articulations of deep, intuitive experience must of necessity resort to the use of concepts. Deep philosophical truth are not proven, however, but are realized in awareness.[202] Discursive knowledge is transcended in intuitive, all-embracing knowledge. Discursive knowledge is necessarily untrue inasmuch as reality itself is one. The abundance of myths, metaphors, and concepts is incapable of properly expressing that unity.[203] "Strictly speaking, logical knowledge is non-knowledge, *avidyā*, valid only until intuition arises."[204] Doctrine is untrue, strictly speaking. Philosophy can attempt to demonstrate this insight. Sometimes Radhakrishnan also speaks of the "truth of the nature of things (*tattvajñāna*)."[205] In this 'relative' sense, Hindu doctrine is *true*, because it sees the nature of things. It prepares people for truly deep insight.

Real knowledge of the truth is the result of growing in truth. Here, knowing and being coincide, and, consequently, there can be no correspondence of an idea to something beyond that idea.[206] Since the cognitive subject realizes himself and experiences the unity of all things in so-doing, the distinction between subject and object dissolves. The truth which is realized and experienced intuitively is non-dual and immediate.[207] This enables Radhakrishnan to say that the Absolute is not true: "The Supreme is real, not true, perfect, not good."[208] He expresses in this way that the real truth is not discursive *satya*, but a real *sat*, reality. When linking up with Western terminology, he also speaks of truth. Mankind wants to know the truth in things themselves, as the truth is, independent of time and differentiation.[209] That truth is the Absolute, "the abiding 'I am.' "[210]

In terms of this view of an Absolute Truth which must be realized, and of philosophical truths which merely point to the Absolute, Radhakrishnan does have an appreciation for the manifoldness of philosophical conceptions. Since the Absolute is inexpressible, Hindu thinkers permit

---

[201] *Ibid*, pp. 176 ff.
[202] *Ibid*, p. 120; cf. also D. M. Datta, *The Chief Currents of Contemporary Philosophy* (1950; rpt. Calcutta ²1961), p. 146.
[203] Esp. Radhakrishnan, pp. 75 f.
[204] *Ibid*, p. 115.
[205] *Ibid*, p. 242.
[206] *Ibid*, p. 114.
[207] *Ibid*, pp. 114 f., 72, 87, 108 f., 77 f., 239.
[208] *Ibid*, p. 81.
[209] *Ibid*, p. 271.
[210] *Ibid*, p. 273.

themselves a range of interpretations, varying from the most impersonal to the most personal.[211] People in themselves, in their individuality, are 'masks'; they participate in life and see the world in terms of their own, individual point of view.[212] Philosophy shares this limitation of earthly life. The thinker has insight (*darśana*) into the whole of experience,[213] but all expression of it is plural.[214] Hindu tradition encompasses many currents: " . . . truth wears vestures of many colours and speaks in strange tongues."[215] Persecution of heretics is unknown to Hinduism. There was once a worshipper of Visṇu who was holding something against someone who worshipped Śiva. One day, as he was bowing before the statue of Visṇu, the statue split in two, Śiva appearing on the one side and Visṇu on the other; both together smiling downward on their worshipper as one face. This incident illustrates in the form of a story the tolerance which one ought to have with respect to other ways to God.[216] What is the Absolute really like? Although it is possible to say something about the Absolute, always, again and again, throughout all of India, the *'neti,' 'neti'* resounds: 'not thus, not so.'[217] Against this backdrop, Radhakrishnan does appreciate other religious traditions as ways to God.[218] He regards claims to exclusive truth as foolishness, however, for strictly speaking, all doctrine is untrue.[219] Other religions would do well to learn from the tolerance of Hinduism, in his view.[220]

3.5 Mahatma Gandhi

a) General remarks

Gandhi led India to liberation from British domination. He also strove to improve the lot of the pariahs. His political activity was an expression of his choice for the way of *karma yoga*, which can be characterized by two concepts: truth (*satya*) and non-violent love (*ahiṃsā*). Gandhi himself never devoted a systematic study to the theme of religion and truth, but he did make many remarks on the subject. His ideas were pronounced and his thought appealed to and influenced many. Others have summed up his ideas.[221] Against the backdrop of the whole of our exposition in this

---

[211] *Ibid*, p. 79.
[212] *Ibid*, p. 213.
[213] *Ibid*, pp. 143, 100.
[214] *Ibid*, p. 95; see also *Hindu View*, pp. 28 ff.
[215] Radhakrishnan, *Hindu View*, p. 36.
[216] *Ibid*, p. 37.
[217] *Ibid*, p. 26.
[218] *Ibid*, pp. 23 f.
[219] See *Ibid*, p. 25.
[220] *Ibid*, pp. 51 f.
[221] D. H. Datta, *M. Gandhi*; B. H. Wilson, "Ultimacy as Unifier in Gandhi," in *Religion in Modern India*, ed. R. D. Baird (New Delhi 1981), pp. 227-46; Richards, *Gandhi* (London ²1983); cf. also Raju, pp. 292-99.

chapter, it will suffice here to describe the peculiar accents which Gandhi places. Gandhi himself has put forth the main issues of his view in a collection of essays edited by Radhakrishnan and Muirhead, in which a large number of Hindu thinkers briefly summarized their view. Gandhi found one page of text adequate:

> I have been asked by Sir S. Radhakrishnan to answer the following three questions:
> (1) What is your religion?
> (2) How are you led to it?
> (3) What is its bearing on social life?
> My religion is Hinduism, which, for me, is the religion of humanity and includes the best of all religions known to me.
> I take it that the present tense in the second question has been purposely used instead of the past. I am being led to my religion through Truth and Non-violence, i.e., love in the broadest sense. I often describe my religion as Religion of Truth. Of late, instead of saying God is Truth I have been saying Truth is God, in order more fully to define my religion. I used, at one time, to know by heart the thousand names of God which a booklet in Hinduism gives in verse form and which perhaps tens of thousands recite every morning. But nowadays nothing so completely describes my God as Truth. Denial of God we have known. Denial of Truth we have not known. The most ignorant among mankind have some truth in them. We are all sparks of Truth. The sum total of these sparks is indescribable, as-yet-Unknown-Truth, which is God. I am being daily led nearer to it by constant prayer.
> The bearing of this religion on social life is, or has to be, seen in one's daily social contact. To be true to such religion one has to lose oneself in continuous and continuing service of all life. Realisation of Truth is impossible without a complete merging of oneself in, and identification with, this limitless ocean of life. Hence, for me, there is no escape from social service, there is no happiness on earth beyond or apart from it. Social service here must be taken to include every department of life. In this scheme there is nothing low, nothing high. For all is one, though we seem to be many.[222]

b) Truth

Truth for Gandhi is the Highest, as we see in his answer to the query regarding his religion. An atheist too recognizes Truth.[223] The Truth is thus not a theory to Gandhi, but Truth is what really exists, the source of all things.[224] 'Satya' is 'sat,' the True is Being, according to Gandhi:

> The word Satya (Truth) is derived from Sat, which means 'being.' Nothing is or exists in reality except Truth. That is why Sat or Truth is perhaps the most important name of God. It is actually more correct to say that

---

[222] In Contemporary Indian Philosophy, eds. Radhakrishnan and J. H. Muirhead (1936; rpt. London [4]1966), p. 21; likewise in Gandhi, In Search, II, 265 f.
[223] Richards, p. 77; Datta, p. 39.
[224] Wilson, p. 236.

Truth is God, than to say that God is Truth.... *Sat* or *Satya* is the only correct and fully significant name for God.[225]

The True, Real permeates all that exists, even though one cannot simply gather this from things in the world. All things are one, even though they appear to be many — that is how the fragment which we have employed ends. The Self in mankind is related to the Self of the other; it is the Self that gives all things their existence.[226] The 'true, Real' is a more inclusive term for the Highest than 'God.'[227] Gandhi has no objection to worshipping God; he himself imagines God in the *avatāra* Rama, but at the same time, he emphasizes God's transcendence.[228] God is impersonal, omniscient, omnipotent. Every limitation is foreign to Him. Although Gandhi allows that religious worship has a place, the Highest ultimately transcends every concept and representation.[229] For Gandhi, the concept of Truth expresses this transcendence better than the concept of God. In this sense, the concept of Truth expresses God better than the 1000 names by which Hindus denote God. "*Sat* or Truth is perhaps the most important name for God." Where there is truth, there is knowledge (*cit*). Where there is knowledge, there is blessedness (*ananda*): God unifies *sat*, *cit*, and *ananda*.[230]

Whether Gandhi takes an *Advaitin* or a *Vishishta-vedantin* position is a question which can be disputed.[231] He stresses the relativity of speaking about God: the manifold approaches via representations of the divine are transcended by the one Truth. In this, his position bears some resemblance to the Advaita School, although it is pointed out that Gandhi does not use the pertinent philosophical terms in their exact meaning.[232] In his view, the truth is not realized non-dually; rather, people are sparks of the truth and they see flashes of the truth. In this sense, his approach resembles more closely that of Rāmānuja and his School — the so-called 'qualified Advaita' tradition.[233] *Bhakti yoga* also receives a place, not so much as prayer, but as meditation and serenity. This form of communion with the Truth is the essence of religion for Gandhi, and the cornerstone on which life itself rests.[234]

---

[225] In Wilson, p. 236; Gandhi, II, 10.

[226] Richards, pp. 32f.

[227] *Ibid*, p. 2; Datta, pp. 35ff.; Wilson, p. 229.

[228] Datta, pp. 23, 28.

[229] Richards, p. 22; M. Gandhi, *The Voice of Truth*, ed. S. Narayan (Ahmedabad 1969), p. 100.

[230] Richards, p. 1; Gandhi, *Truth*, pp. 96ff.

[231] See Richards, p. 3; Datta, pp. 24, 63; see also G. Richards, "Gandhi's Concept of Truth and the *Advaita* Tradition," *Religious Studies* 22 (1986): 1-14, where he compares Gandhi's view with Śaṅkara's, and shows that Gandhi's view resembles most the position of the Neo-Vedantins.

[232] Richards, pp. 32f.; Datta, p. 25.

[233] Datta, p. 24, cf. p. 7.

[234] Richards, p. 12.

Such a relationship to the truth has consequences for ordinary life. Invoking the *Bhagavadgītā*, Gandhi advocates *karma yoga*, a life in harmony with the cosmic order (*ṛta*).[235] The essential unity of all things results in universal love for all of reality. This love finds its expression in the attitude of *ahiṃsā*, beneficence towards everything and everyone, without violence.[236] In order fully to achieve non-violence in practice it is needful that one be free of worry, as Jesus also taught, and free of fear — for one is living in the Truth. In the Truth, one has steadfastness, as expressed by the term *satyāgraha*.[237]

c) Religion and truth

The truth of religion lies in the first place in the participation of people in the truth, that is, in a way of life in which one realizes *ahiṃsā*.[238] *Ahiṃsā* forms the heart of the doctrine of the great religions.

This deeper view of truth is of course accompanied by the demand that one keeps to the facts. Before rendering a judgment on a certain matter, one must know the facts. Knowledge of complicated situations of a social or political nature, however, requires purification of the heart and mind. One must conquer the six mortal enemies: lust, anger, avarice, blindness, arrogance, and untruthfulness; only then does one achieve insight into the truth.[239] One must, as it were, become truthful before one can see the truth.

Gandhi examined the Bible in depth. He also acquainted himself with writings from other religious tradition.[240] It was his firm conviction that a common ethical basis lies at the bottom of all religions — a universal religion.[241] This religion is a faith in the moral order of the universe. "This religion transcends Hinduism, Islam, Christianity, etc. It does not supersede them. It harmonizes them and gives them reality."[242] Gandhi seems to place even the Hindu approach in a relative position. Hinduism is one way among the many ways which lead to the one goal —the truth.[243] All religions have their own symbols, and that is good. Religion is a personal matter; everyone must travel the way which suits his aptitude and circumstances.[244] In this sense all religions are 'true' to him.[245] But they all contain errors as well, because all human approximations of the Highest are necessarily deficient. Human language is too limited to put the One

---

[235] *Ibid*, pp. 1, 157; Datta, p. 44.
[236] Richards, pp. 31 f.; Wilson, pp. 229, 237; Datta, p. 76.
[237] Richards, pp. 48 ff.; Wilson, p. 242.
[238] Richards, pp. 9 f., cf. pp. 17, 32 f.; Gandhi, *In Search*, II, 25 f.
[239] Datta, p. 95.
[240] *Ibid*, pp. 10 f.
[241] *Ibid*, p. 49.
[242] Gandhi, in Datta, p. 49; cf. Richards, p. 17.
[243] Richards, p. 20; cf. Gandhi, *In Search*, III (Ahmadabad 1962), pp. 3 f.
[244] Richards, p. 20.
[245] Datta, p. 45; Gandhi, *In Search*, III, 3.

Truth into words.[246] What people say of the Truth are human constructions.[247] Therefore no one religion is superior to the others. Gandhi rejected the exclusive claims which some religions make. He contends that Jesus is not literally the only begotten son of God. God is not exclusively the father of Jesus. Jesus is just as divine as Kriṣṇa, or Rama, or Mohammed, or Zoroaster.[248] Gandhi found the acknowledgment of the value of other religions to be lacking in the exclusive religions, something one does encounter in the *Bhagavadgītā*.[249] It was precisely this sweeping inclusiveness of Hinduism that enabled Gandhi to remain a Hindu and still do justice to what is of value in other religious approaches to the one Truth.[250] In that sense, Hinduism is the best religion to Gandhi, even though he takes the liberty of explaining the Hindu tradition in his own manner.[251]

In Gandhi's attitude towards other religions, the typically neo-Hindu approach can again be discerned. Since the One, True, transcendent is in principle beyond the reach of human naming, many names *must* be given. Since it is Sublime, many ways *must* be travelled. There must be an abundance of religious expressions to allow the exaltation of the Ultimate to be brought out, for God is immanent and transcendent, creative and non-creative.[252] Human approaches are often contradictory. Thus Gandhi explains the contradictions in the human approximations of the Unutterable in terms of the Sublimity of the one Truth.[253]

§ 4 Truth, plurality, and contradictions

4.1 Truth

The Hindu thinkers discussed equate truth with God. *Truth is what is real.* In all that exists, the divine is the ground of being, the real.[254] God is the Truth. For thinkers of the Advaita tradition the highest Truth (*nirguṇa Brahman*) is higher than the personal God (*saguṇa Brahman*). For Gandhi too, the Highest, the Truth, is 'higher' than God; to put it differently, the reality of the truly transcendent and foundational is better denoted by 'truth' than by ('personal') 'God.'

At the highest level, according to what the Advaita School purports to know of it, knowing and being coincide. Since the distinction between

---

[246] Richards, pp. 19f., 24.
[247] *Ibid*, p. 18; Datta, p. 49.
[248] Gandhi, in Richards, p. 25; Gandhi, *In Search*, III, 17.
[249] Datta, pp. 47f.
[250] Datta, p. 48; Richards, pp. 14f.
[251] Wilson, "Ultimacy as Unifier...," pp. 237f., cf. p. 229; Datta, p. 45; cf. Gandhi, "All-Inclusive Hinduism," in *In Search*, III, 9.
[252] Richards, pp. 17f., 20, 27.
[253] Datta, pp. 28f.
[254] Cf. Bowes, p. 153, and others.

subject and object dissolves, no 'true' formulated knowledge is possible. But at the lower level of human discursive knowledge, what is meant by non-dual cognition must be explained, for better or worse. For the thinkers of other traditions as well, knowledge lies at the level of doctrine and stories, where reference is made to the reality of God. Since God surpasses our knowledge, there can be no possibility of a correspondence between knowledge and God. Knowledge is limited; speaking refers to God, but God is beyond all concepts and images. At this level of discourse we encounter the thesis that there are many approaches to the divine being.

4.2 Plurality

The thesis of the legitimate and necessary plurality of theological-philosophical concepts and cultic approaches to the Divine is based on several insights which are anchored deeply in the Hindu view of reality. We wish to point out *three premises* in the Hindu view.

(1) The Hindu view of knowledge concerning the Divine is correlated to their view of the nature of divine Reality. The divine permeates all of existence. It does not coincide with it, but is present everywhere.[255] P. Bowes, himself no follower of Śaṅkara, states that the immanence of the ground of existence has as consequence that the whole of reality is, in a certain sense, an expression of divine reality, the transcendent immanent ground of everything.[256] Since all things are related to the Divine, one can regard any single thing as a symbol for the whole.[257] For this reason, the tree and the river can be holy. The divine is worshipped in parts of nature and in many images. Diane Eck remarks that even the least educated Hindus will obligingly explain that in worshipping the diverse gods in and around the temple, they are of course focussing on the one Divine Reality.[258] The One suffuses the many. All things are connected to it. Hindu epistemology does not attempt to delineate things and classes of objects by means of sharp definitions but tries to describe them in the concrete relations in which they stand.[259] A fragment which occurs in one of the *Upaniṣads* is apt to be cited in this context: The seeker (i.e., of wisdom) Vidagha Shakalya poses a question of the wise Yājñavalkya: "How many Gods are there, Yājñavalkya?" His answer:

> "Three thousand three hundred six," he replied.
> "Yes," said he, "but just how many gods are there, Yājñavalkya?"
> "Thirty three."

[255] *Ibid*, p. 137.
[256] *Ibid*, p. 81.
[257] *Ibid*, p. 262.
[258] Eck, *Darśan*, p. 20.
[259] B. Heiman, "Indische Logik und Erkenntnistheorie," in Heiman, *Studien zur Eigenart Indischen Denkens* (Tübingen 1930), pp. 213, 209.

"Yes," said he, "but just how many gods are there, Yājñavalkya?"
"Six."
"Yes," said he, "but just how many gods are there, Yājñavalkya?"
"Three."
"Yes," said he, "but just how many gods are there, Yājñavalkya?"
"Two."
"Yes," said he, "but just how many gods are there, Yājñavalkya?"
"One and a half."
"Yes," said he, "but just how many gods are there, Yājñavalkya?"
"One."[260]

There is one divine Reality which permeates all things, but remains transcendent nevertheless. Since the divine is present everywhere, the whole of life is marked by religion, and the many are intrinsically related to the One.[261]

(2) The second premise concerns the epistemology which is correlated to this ontology. Since the One has many aspects, it can be approached in more than one manner. One can make a statue of the divinity, install it, and worship it. This image is then the Divinity in a certain sense. One can also speak about the divine. *OM,* the sound which sums up all sounds, is in a certain sense the divine.[262] The teaching of the philosophers is also an approach. There are many ways, but their goal is one — the Divine. An abundance of approaches is not only permissible but even necessary. The Divine is the many; justice can be done to this multiplicity only by a whole gamut of approaches. Reality is far too complex to be presented in one theory.[263]

(3) The third premise is that one's faith justifiedly agrees with one's nature. A person is as is his faith. This doctrine from the *Bhagavadgītā* is to be found in the cult as well as in modern authors.[264] One selects a certain cult because one feels a special attraction to a god. One adopts convictions which agree with one's character and which pertain to the circumstances in which one finds oneself.[265]

The differences between people necessitate the existence of more than one religious current. Bowes mentions that Ramakrishna used to say that a wise mother prepares the fish differently for each of her children, in the manner in which each child can eat the fish and enjoy it; religion must likewise be adapted to the taste of the believer.[266] For he or she must experience the Divine him(her)self! The value of a religious current or a philosophical approach therefore depends on the person. The approaches

---

[260] Eck, *Darśan,* p. 20; *Bṛhadāraṇyaka-Upaniṣad* 3. 9. 1. Cf. *The Upaniṣads,* II, tr. F. M. Müller, The Sacred Books of the East, 15 (1879; rpt. New York 1962), pp. 139 f.
[261] Bowes, pp. 130, 18.
[262] Cf. R. Fernhout, *Woord en Naam in de Religies* (Kampen 1979), pp. 178, 195.
[263] Bowes, pp. 274 ff.
[264] Cf. *Bhagavadgītā,* XVII. 3.
[265] Bowes, pp. 78 f.; 86 f.; 287.
[266] Bowes, p. 290.

are of equal value in this sense, although they are not all alike or
equally valuable to every person.[267] The background of this view is the
doctrine of reincarnation; not all people have travelled equally far on
their life's journey. What is good for one, might not (yet) be good for
another.

4.3 Contradictions?

Diverse conceptions co-exist peacefully within Hindu philosophy. They
represent *darsanas* — points of view which are linked to the perspective
in which one perceives reality. We have already encountered this view
several times. We will now pursue it somewhat more elaborately. Bowes
links this view to the Jain religion's doctrine of *syādvāda* — the 'maybe
it is' doctrine, which entails the notion that two propositions do not
contradict each other if they are proposed from a different standpoint.[268]
Stated in modern terms, the contextuality of knowledge makes plurality
inevitable; at the same time, it makes it difficult to establish precisely
where two conceptions impinge on or contradict one another.[269] Bowes
illumines his view in four points:

(1) No proposition represents reality as it is itself, because all
   propositions are made from a certain position.
(2) Apparently contradictory propositions are not really contradictory if they are made in terms of different standpoints.
(3) A true proposition may be untrue from another standpoint.
(4) There are many points of view from which one can look at
   the same matter.

Bowes considers this Jain doctrine to be illuminating for the Hindu
conception of the 'many truths.'[270]

Bowes' approach seems typical of currents in Hinduism which dissent
from the Advaita philosophy, which tries to overcome plurality in a non-
dual mystical experience. The many exist in the One, but the One cannot
be known except in the many. A great variation in points of view is
possible on the basis of this doctrine of God. Differences in approach are
not excluded because the Divine Himself permeates reality in all its
bounty and sometimes painful abundance. One seeks the all-encompassing,
the relationship of things; then points of view are sooner seen as being

---

[267] Cf. Satprakashananda, *Hinduism and Christianity: Jesus Christ and His Teaching in
the Light of Vedānta* (St. Louis: Vedānta Society of St. Louis, 1975), pp. 17, 74 f., 53 ff.;
A. Sharma, "All Religions are — Equal? One? True? Same?: A Critical Examination
of some Formulations of the Neo-Hindu Position," *Philosophy East and
West* 29 (1979): 59-72.

[268] Bowes, pp. 276 f.

[269] Compare to my analysis in *De Schrift Alleen?* (Kampen ²1979), pp. 242 ff.

[270] Bowes, p. 277. It is of interest to note that a Buddhist author like Jayatilleke
criticizes this theory, *Early Buddhist Theory of Knowledge* (London 1963), pp. 347 f.

complementary than contradictory. This approach itself, however, is based on a particular view of the Divine.[271]

The modern Advaita position, at least in our understanding, goes one step further. The manifoldness of religious conceptions is here approached in terms of the third premise mentioned: the idea that one's religion and philosophy have to do with one's character and situation, which are in turn determined by *karma*. The degree of insight of which one is capable depends on the extent to which one has advanced on the whole of one's life journey. There are more mature positions and approaches, as well as less advanced ones for those who have travelled less far. The worship of divine images and the religion of God as a Person attest to a less advanced stage on the way to blessedness, which is the non-dual experience or realization of *nirguṇa Brahman*. As Satprakashananda quotes Śaṅkara:

> ...true knowledge must be unvaried, being in conformity with Reality. That is Reality which is invariable.... the difference of views in the case of true knowledge is absurd. But the conclusions reached by reasoning, being mutually contradictory, are well-known to be divergent.[272]

The typically Hindu view is that all religions are paths to the one Reality. The abundance of views represents a multiplicity of ways to the truth, not an array of equally valid positions.[273]

Still, in our opinion, there is a cleft within the Vedānta School between the Advaita position of Satprakashananda and the qualified position of Rāmānuja. One party asserts that the experience of the Absolute surpasses all devotion to a personal God in non-dual transcendence; the other denies non-duality. The first party then counters that non-dual experience of blissful union with Brahman carries the proof of its reality in itself, and that the other has not yet advanced far enough on the way of purification to be able to attain awareness of it.[274] There is a conflict here between the two currents in this philosophy which cannot be reduced to a difference in points of view, according to 'non-Advaitins.' Bowes and Chaudhuri are rather noticeably not enamoured with Śaṅkara's doctrine.[275] Another difference in 'doctrine' lies in the extent to which one can and must conquer one's *karma*, and whether one must rely on grace to do so. There are at least differences in accent present here, and perhaps even contradictions.

The opposition between the various schools is relative because of the common recognition that reflections about knowledge are serviceable to the aspiration of purifying one's self and the achievement of true insight

---

[271] O'Flaherty, p. 46, cf. pp. 2 f.; Streng, *Emptiness*, pp. 122 ff.

[272] In Satprakashananda, p. 197.

[273] Sharma, p. 63.

[274] Satprakashananda, for instance, p. 258.

[275] Bowes, pp. 138 ff.; Chaudhuri, pp. 149, 322. Also compare the differences between the Dvaita Vedānta of Madva and the other Vedānta Schools; see Ramachandran, *Dvaita Vedānta*, passim.

and liberation. It is not difficult to see when the limits of the Hindu view of life have been exceeded. We have considered the premises on which it is based.

4.4   The neo-Hindu approach to other religions

The Hindu tradition's approach to internal differences in perception has been expanded in our time to accommodate other religions as well. On the basis of the Hindu view of the relationship between the Divine and the whole of reality, nothing impedes the acknowledgement that those outside of India have experienced something of the Highest Reality. Exclusive representations such as those held in connection with the Torah, Jesus, and the Koran, are judged naive by Hindu standards. Denials of the existence of a highest reality or a Soul, such as Buddhists allege, are considered erroneous. Hindu appreciativeness of other religions therefore refers to aspects of those religions which can be appreciated in terms of the Hindu view. From the standpoint of the Hindu religion, one can expansively point to the eminent significance of these religions.[276] One must conclude on the basis of our exposition, however, that this appreciation is based on the three premises mentioned at the beginning of this section (§ 4). The aim of religion is to join oneself to the divine reality, Bowes says.[277] For Radhakrishnan as well, religion is the bond with the Divine. It is therefore incorrect to think that all religions are of equal value in the Hindu view. To use an image: They are all paths to the top of the mountain, but they do not all have the same height — that is how one could express it in this image.[278] The parable of the elephant is well-known: Blind men gropingly feel parts of the animal; they cannot perceive the whole and thus interpret wrongly; the one who feels the leg thinks it is a pillar, the ear is mistaken for a strange kind of blanket, another thinks the trunk to be a snake, etc. This fable has been used since ancient times to express the notion that everyone has some experience of the whole, yet without knowing the complete truth. Recall that the Hindu has cause to be aware of such limitations in everyday religious life. Religions in which people believe they know the exclusive truth are off the mark, according to the Hindu view, inasmuch as such religion fails to see this limitation (and possibly refuses to learn from others). The Hindu view of the Divine Reality therefore implies a certain view of other religions. As we have seen, some Hindus voice the hope that the other religious traditions will also adopt this tolerant view.

The neo-Hindu approach to other religious traditions and the characterization of the Hindu tradition as tolerant, has not gone uncontradicted.

---

[276] Satptrakashananda, for instance, *Hinduism and Christianity*, esp. Chapter III.

[277] Bowes, p. 286.

[278] See for instance a quotation from Vivekananda in Satprakashananda, *Methods*, pp. 206 f., about the unique content of the Veda.

P. Hacker points out —and rightly so— that tolerant legislation and tolerant behaviour with respect to those who think differently must be distinguished from 'dogmatic tolerance,' that is to say, acceptance of the proposition that the doctrines of two or more religious currents are at the same time in conflict and of equal value. He offers examples throughout the centuries of practical tolerance, but also points out intolerant practices, particularly in connection with caste regulations. Dogmatic tolerance is a different matter. Thinkers of the various traditions disagreed with one another, and they did not in the least consider their positions to be 'of equal value,' says Hacker. "All theological and philosophical teachers in Hinduism have been fundamentally and dogmatically intolerant."[279]

Even where the relative value of other systems was acknowledged, people held fast to the superiority of their own religious insights. The term tolerance is not properly applicable here. Hacker would rather speak of *inclusivism*; an assessment is given of the relative merit and truth of other religious traditions in terms of one's own religious perceptions.[280] This approach announces itself in the *Bhagavadgītā* text which we have already quoted (IX. 23). This text is truly characteristic of the neo-Hindu approach, which Hacker considers to be present in exemplary fashion in Radha-krishnan.[281] Hacker's view thus supports the conclusion of our exposition that many conflicting opinions existed and that not all dissenting conceptions were regarded as 'equally true.' It must be interposed here that the seriousness of conflicting views within a tradition depends on the value which is ascribed to articulated doctrine. If the formulations are less important that the *religio* (worship) and the experience of union with the divine, then the controversies will receive a different place within the whole of the tradition. Within that context, those who point to the relatively 'tolerant' attitude within the Hindu tradition regarding conflicting views in the matter of doctrine are right. We will again examine the role of doctrine in religious traditions in the ensuing chapters, and will return to this issue in more detail in the analytical part of this study.

---

279 P. Hacker, "Zur Geschichte und Beurteilung des Hinduismus: Kritik einiger verbreiteter Ansichten" (1964), in Hacker, *Kleine Schriften* (Wiesbaden 1978), p. 480; and his "Religiöse Toleranz und Intoleranz im Hinduismus," (1957), in Hacker, *Kleine Schriften*, p. 384.
280 Hacker, pp. 480, 386.
281 Hacker, "Aspects of Neo-Hinduism as Contrasted with Surviving Traditional Hinduism," (1970), in Hacker, *Kleine Schriften*, p. 608.

Chapter IV

The Concept of Truth in Buddhist Tradition

§ 1 Introduction

1.1 Preamble

The Buddha was born about 563 years before the common era[1] and preached in northern India. Buddhism has since then spread over the whole of India, and from there, to Sri Lanka. Since the 2nd century C.E. it has been preached in China, in Tibet, and later in Japan, and has spread as far as Indonesia. In India itself, Buddhism died out around 1200 C.E.

Buddhism underwent enormous developments during the 2500 years of its existence. Although it was originally a skeptical, reserved, and empirically oriented movement among monks (according to some authors), its later forms display all the abundance which popular religion can produce. Some currents of Buddhism have undergone such extensive development that they differ just as much from original Buddhism as Christianity does from Judaism.[2] Before we set about our proper task —a description of the concept of truth in the Buddhist tradition— we will begin by outlining the contours of the Buddhist tradition. We will subsequently sketch several of the main lines in Buddhist thought; later folk religion will be left out of consideration in so doing. After that, the concept of truth will be discussed. We will pay particular attention to the classical exponent of the *Mahāyāna* tradition, Nāgārjuna and to the ideas of the modern Japanese philosopher, Nishitani.

---

[1] See J. Fischer-Schreiber, *s.v.* 'Buddha,' *Lexikon der östlichen Weisheitslehren* (Bern 1986), p. 52.

[2] E. Conze, *Buddhist Thought in India* (London 1962), p. 203, see pp. 159 f.

1.2 Developments in the Buddhist tradition

Traditionally the following story is told: Prince Gautama was startled out of his privileged existence when trips outside of his palace abruptly confronted him with the old age, sickness, and death of mankind.[3] These experiences formed such a contrast to the life to which he was accustomed that they precipitated an about-face in his existence. He forsook the parental palace, his wife, and his little son to lead a wandering existence, in search of imperishable truth and deliverance from an existence inevitably saturated by profound and never ending suffering. After years of roaming Gautama finally attained insight into the nature of suffering and how to overcome it. All speculation concerning matters which one cannot experience was foreign to him. The cause of an existence attended by much suffering, begun anew again and again (in a series of lives, *samsāra*), is people's thirst for life — their attachment to it. This thirst makes people vulnerable to the inevitable vicissitudes which their life brings them. People in effect themselves incur their own misery. The Buddha recommended a way of life, called the eightfold path, aimed at extinguishing this 'thirst.' The attachment to things also has harmful effects on the operation of human thought. The representations which are held of things do not spring from objective reality. They are the result of previous thought. They have been produced by thought itself, as the beginning of an old Buddhist writing, the *Dhammapadda* (the Path of Truth) says.[4] People think wrongly. If someone speaks or acts with wrong thoughts, sorrow follows him as cart wheels follow the legs of the ox which pulls it.

At a certain stage of development, it was said that the cause of suffering lay in ignorance and attachment. In order to overcome suffering, one would have to overcome both attachment and ignorance. Meditation and concentration are the path along which one can attain insight and liberation. The problem is that both factors occur together. If there were only ignorance regarding the nature of existence, then it would in principle be possible to explain the truth to people. But since attachment also plays a role, people are incapable of seeing things as they are. Such attachment and thirst must therefore be conquered. Buddhist teaching is therefore not so much a description of reality, but more an indication of the path which the seeker must travel in order to continuously acquire more insight into existence, and to stand increasingly free in relation to people, things, and himself. The teaching is like a raft for crossing the river; once there, there is no longer need for it.

---

[3] See some introductory works for what follows, e.g., R. H. Drummond, *Gautama: the Buddha* (Grand Rapids 1974); H. Beckh, *Boeddha en zijn Leer*, (1916) Dutch tr. M. B. A. Laffrée; rev. edn. J. C. Ebbinge Wubben (1916; Rotterdam ²1979); also, *Het Leven van de Boeddha* [Life of Buddha], translated into Dutch from the earliest Chinese tradition by E. Zürcher (Amsterdam 1978).

[4] *A Sourcebook in Indian Philosophy*, eds. S. Radhakrishnan and Ch. A. Moore (Princeton ⁵1973), pp. 292 ff.

Many differences between the various Buddhist schools can be traced back to the emphasis which they place on either meditation or intellectual analysis as the method for achieving insight. Just as was the case in Hinduism, this means that the various schools do not always contradict one another; the difference primarily concerns what the attention is focussed on. Of course, this does not serve to exclude differences of opinion in the least. The centuries of analyzing reality, cognition, and the way of meditation, brought forth many schools. Vetter describes how after a certain time *discriminating insight* was accepted by Buddhism as a vehicle for liberation.[5] Vetter endeavours to plot out the development of early Buddhism in which the theoretical element was sometimes accentuated at the cost of the Buddha's meditative 'middle way' of the Buddha, *dhyāna* (meditation).[6] Later schools attempted to correct this shift.

Yet another circumstance which influenced the later development of Buddhism was that Buddhism was originally a movement of roaming mendicant monks. Whoever begs is dependent on the generosity of others, obliged to eat anything that is put into his bowl. That is why lay sympathizers play such an important role.[7] An attempt was made in the later history of Buddhism to make salvation more accessible to ordinary people with their day to day cares and chores. This extension on behalf of lay people signified an enormous shift. In some currents, it was taken so far that wisdom, detachment, and meditation came to have secondary standing; one school even taught that it was sufficient to invoke the name of *Amida Buddha* to obtain salvation.[8] A reforming element was present in *Zen* Buddhism, however, with its emphasis on direct perception; it turned against intellectualism and systematization, and all the emphasis was put on *dhyāna* (meditation).[9]

Edward Conze divides the history of Buddhism into four periods; three periods of 500 years, and a fourth starting from the year 1000 C.E.[10]
(1) The reconstruction of the first period is uncertain. The doctrine of the Buddha was transmitted orally within circles of monks and nuns for centuries.[11] There was much mutual contact, because they roamed continually. Since no highest authority was instituted after the departure of the Buddha, differences of interpretation could be settled only by consensus or the formation of schools. An important source for the knowledge of ancient Buddhism is the *Pali* canon, a series of writings in which the

---

[5] T. Vetter, *The Ideas and Meditative Practices of Early Buddhism* (Brill: Leiden 1988), p. *xxiii*, pp. 35 ff.

[6] *Ibid*, p. *xxxv*.

[7] Conze, *Short History of Buddhism* (Bombay 1960), pp. 25 f., (rpt. London 1980), p. 41.

[8] Conze, pp. 73 ff.; cf. also his *Het Boeddhisme*, tr. C. T. van Boetzelaer and van de Klashorst (Oxford ³1957; Utrecht 1970), p. 216; *Lexikon, s.v.* 'Amidismus' and 'Amitabha.'

[9] Conze, *Short History*, pp. 73, 99; *Lexikon, s.v.* 'zen.'

[10] Conze, *Short History*, the book's scheme.

[11] *Ibid*, p. 16.

received doctrine was recorded in the Pali language in Sri Lanka. These form the canonical texts of *Theravāda* Buddhism.[12]

Just as in other religions, many writings of a later date have been imputed to ancient authorities. Many dialogues were attributed to the Buddha. What genuinely belonged to the Buddha's original teaching is a matter of uncertain reconstruction. One must realize that the issue of historical reconstruction is of less gravity in Buddhism than in a religion like Christianity in which historical events occupy an important position within the beliefs.[13]

A first schism took place within the Buddhist movement around 340 B.C.E. concerning the question of who was holy. The monks who had attained Enlightenment, *Arhats,* were less perfect than was sometimes thought — so it was said.[14] Despite the semblance of saintliness, they showed signs of being ordinary human beings. It was possible to create more room for the lay adherents of the Buddha by detracting from the saintliness of the Enlightened. Two of the insights of this school, the *Mahāsānghikas* (*mahā*: great; *sāngha*: community), were to retain great influence on later forms of Mahāyāna Buddhism: (1) Human thought is pure and transparent; the impurities are accidental and incidental. (2) The value of conceptual knowledge is greeted with skepticism. Some taught that the objects of one's knowledge are not real, but exist only in the imagination.[15]

This current opposed the adherents of the monastic tradition, known as the *Staviras.* Starting around 200 C.E. the *Abhidharma* writings emerged among the various directions which this monastic movement took.[16] Despite significant differences between the various schools, similar subjects are dealt with in these writings, such as the analysis of the elementary events which constitute experience, their concurrence, interdependency, etc. Theravāda Buddhism, which exists to the present day in Sri Lanka, Thailand, and Burma, emerged within this tradition of *Hīnayāna* Buddhism.[17] Mahāyāna Buddhism ultimately left its imprint on the remaining segments of the Buddhist world.

(2) The second period of Buddhist history distinguished by Conze, from 1 to 500 C.E., was characterized by the propagation of Mahāyāna Buddhism.[18] *Mahāyāna* literally means 'the great vehicle.' The expression is linked to the aspiration of making salvation possible for more people, particularly lay people. The term *mahāyāna* was used initially for the acceptance of the path of a 'great spirit,' who does not have his own salvation foremost

---

[12] *Ibid*, p. 27; *Lexikon, s.v.* 'Pali.'
[13] Conze, *Short History*, p. 2; see also by Conze, *Boeddhisme*, p. 158.
[14] *Ibid*, pp. 17f.
[15] *Ibid*, p. 19.
[16] Conze, *Short History*, p. 21; see also by Conze, *Buddhist Thought*, pp. 120ff.; 178ff.
[17] Conze, *Short History*, pp. 91f.; *Boeddhisme*, p. 123.
[18] Conze, *Short History*, pp. 28ff.

in mind but rather the achievement of Buddha-hood, in order to thus be able to help other creatures.[19] The expression Mahāyāna Buddhism later came to refer to a movement, the 'Great Vehicle,' by which many can obtain salvation.[20]

The historical significance of the Buddha is minimized within Mahāyāna Buddhism. The historical Buddha is seen as an embodiment of the *dharma*. As such, the Buddha is the embodiment of the eternal Truth. Coupled with this was the idea that all new insights were therefore in effect the Buddha's understanding as well, and that other embodiments of the Truth are thus quite possible.[21] The Mahāyāna trend assigned a more important place to *faith*, and introduced a new pantheon.[22] The idea of a heavenly world inhabited by many gods has presumably played a role in Buddhism since ancient times. It is important in this context to remember that the gods are equally subject to the exigencies of cosmic existence as are people.[23] Philosophically speaking, it is above all the teaching of emptiness which is of significance. Two schools emerged within Mahāyāna Buddhism after 150 C.E., the *Mādhyamikas* and the *Yogācārins*.[24] The Mādhyamika School was founded by Nāgārjuna (circa 150 C.E.). This school flourished for centuries and witnessed a continuation in China and Tibet. The emphasis lay on a certain form of skeptical, reasonable analysis of existence which could bring a person closer to the ineffable truth. We will return to this later.

The school of the Yogācārins stressed the actualization of liberation through yoga and meditation.[25] In later times, they taught that consciousness alone truly exists. Liberation is achieved in non-dual experience when the subject succeeds in transcending the subject-object distinction in pure consciousness.[26]

After the start of the common era, Buddhism spread to China and elsewhere.[27] During the first four centuries, a great many works were translated into Chinese. Buddhist leaders sought a certain link with the spiritual inheritance of the native religions, Taoism and Confucianism. The *bodhisattvas* exercised an appeal on the masses. *Bodhisattva* refers to someone who, having attained *enlightenment*, helps others to reach *nirvāṇa*. The Buddhist pantheon affords a handle to common piety, as well

---

[19] D. T. Suzuki, *Outlines of Mahāyāna Buddhism* (1907; rpt. New York 1963), pp. 7f., who records that the term originally meant the Highest Reality itself.

[20] See Conze, *Boeddhisme*, p. 126.

[21] Conze, *Short History*, p. 29.

[22] *Ibid*, p. 30.

[23] Conze, *Boeddhisme*, pp. 53f.

[24] Conze, *Short History*, p. 35; see also *Buddhist Thought*, pp. 238ff.; 250ff.; see T. R. V. Murti, *The Central Philosophy of Buddhism: A Study of the Mahāyāna System* (1955; rpt. Londen ³1970), pp. 104f.

[25] Conze, *Short History*, p. 35.

[26] *Ibid*, p. 35.

[27] *Ibid*, pp. 44ff.

as support and encouragement for those who are struggling to prepare themselves for Enlightenment by concentration.

(3) The period from 500 to 1000 C.E. witnessed the upsurge of *Tantra* in India.[28] The endeavour was made to transcend the intellectualism of the Buddhism of the day. We will mention two of the many currents from this period. First, the Chinese and Japanese Buddhism of the Pure Land tradition, or Amida Buddhism.[29] Amida Buddha was a saint who had promised, already aeons ago, that all who invoked his name would be saved. They would find salvation in the Western Paradise. Amida Buddhism has also made its way to contemporary Japan as popular religion.

The second current from this period to which we want to draw attention is the *Ch'an* School. Conze mentions this current after the Abhidharma, Mahāyāna, and Tantra School as the fourth and last great reform of the Buddha's thought.[30] The Ch'an School pointed out the necessity of a practical realization of the Truth. They contended that amidst the panoply of means of salvation which were developed in later Buddhism, such as *sūtras*, commentaries, statues, and rites, the original aim was being lost to sight. They relegated all the rest to a subordinate position in order to concentrate fully on the path to enlightenment. In response to the question, "What is the Buddha?," a Ch'an master could answer: "What is not the Buddha? I never knew him." By means of such unexpected answers the Rinzai School did, and still does attempt to transcend thought itself to achieve enlightenment — *woe* (Chinese), or *satori* (Japanese).[31]

(4) The fourth period (1000–) offers little that is new, according to Conze. In India, Buddhism disappeared. Hinduism reasserted its ancient rights. In China it continued to live for centuries until great damage was inflicted on it by Christians (1850/1865), and later by the communists.[32] In Japan, Amida Buddhism (*Jōdō*) and Zen Buddhism, which originated from one of the schools of Ch'an Buddhism, exist up to the present. The Zen master Dogen (1200–1233) restored to Buddhism the search for the Highest Truth as its true aim.[33] As opposed to intellectualism, he emphasized the need for the proper posture — *zazen* (meditation in the cross-legged position). We will presently deal with the nature of enlightenment in the contemporary Buddhism of the Kyoto School. These notes about a few of the many developments which Buddhism underwent must suffice here.

---

[28] *Ibid*, pp. 57f.; see also *Boeddhisme*, pp. 183ff.
[29] Conze, *Short History*, pp. 72f., 96ff.
[30] For what follows, see Conze, *Short History*, pp. 73ff.
[31] Conze, *Short History*, pp. 76f.; *Lexikon*, s.v. 'Rinzai-Schule.'
[32] Conze, *Short History*, p. 95.
[33] *Ibid*, pp. 96f.

§ 2 Central insights

2.1 The Four Noble Truths

Buddhist teaching is summarized in four doctrines. According to received tradition, the Buddha preached the substance of the Four Noble Truths to his first followers after he had achieved enlightenment. These Four Truths are as follows:

(1) The Noble Truth of suffering.
(2) The Noble Truth of the origin of suffering.
(3) The Noble Truth of the cessation of suffering.
(4) The Noble Truth of the path which leads to the cessation of suffering.

We will present them briefly and then deal somewhat more extensively with their elaboration in the teachings.

The Noble Truth of suffering is clarified in an ancient *sutta* as follows: "Birth is anguish and aging is anguish and dying is anguish; and grief, sorrow, suffering, misery, and despair are anguish. And not getting what one desires, that too is anguish."[34] Pain is ineluctably bound up with life; no one can evade suffering or shield himself from extreme situations. One must therefore attempt to free oneself from the cycle of rebirths.

The second Noble Truth is illumined in the same *sutta* as follows: 'It is this thirst which leads to rebirth, bound up with pleasure and desire, finding pleasure here and there.' Man is attached to pleasure in what is good and pleasant. Desire and attachment to life are thus indicated as the cause of suffering.

The cessation of suffering, in the third place, lies in overcoming this thirst, in being without attachment: 'It is stopping this thirst through being perfectly unattached, giving it up [the thirst], rejecting it, letting go of truth, not holding on to it [this thirst].'

The path which leads to the cessation of suffering is identical to the Noble Eightfold Path: ' [It is] identical to the Noble Eightfold Path.' We will return to this presently. By following this path one can attain *samādhi* (concentration).

This 'doctrine of the Four Noble Truths' has undergone much elaboration in the course of history and has been subject to various interpretations. Perhaps the Buddha himself already provided a further analysis of the 'thirst.' Existence is traditionally characterized as *dukkha* (suffering, or better, unsatisfying), as *anitya* (transience, perishable) and as *anātman*

---

[34] T. Vetter, *Early Buddhism*, p. 14. For an exposition of the four Noble Truths, see also Conze, *Boeddhisme*, pp. 45 ff.; Drummond, *Gautama*, pp. 85 ff.; *Het Leven van de Boeddha*, p. 116; an old survey by G. Grimm, *Die Lehre des Buddha* (Munich, 6ᵉ-8ᵉ Aufl., 1920). See *The Middle Length Sayings* (Majjhima Nikāya), III, tr. I. B. Horner (1959; rpt. London 1967), p. 296. See D. J. Kalupahana, *Buddhist Philosophy: A Historical Analysis* (Honolulu ³1982), pp. 36 ff.

(not-self). At a somewhat later time, the Noble Truth of the cause of suffering was related to the 'chain of dependent origination.' The doctrine provided the occasion for reflection; analysis itself was utilized to conquer attachment. In what ensues, we will provide a brief outline of the Buddhist 'doctrine,' thereby remaining aware of the fact that the various currents placed divergent accents and arrived at different interpretations. The first two characteristics of existence are discussed here; the third will be treated in § 2.2.

(1) All things in life are impermanent (*anitya*). Nothing of good or evil endures. Today the trees flourish, tomorrow the wind blows the blossoms hence. The fruit of this world fall away when they are ripened. There are beautiful and ugly things. Buddhism continually insists on the transience of existence. All things pass away. This perception has been consistently elaborated to mean that all things change from moment to moment, without anything remaining the same, without there being any 'essence' to things. What there 'is' are all momentary things which one perceives moment by moment.

Subsequently, existence is unsatisfying (*dukkha*) because beauty is necessarily related to suffering. Often *dukkha* is translated as suffering; the import is actually more *dread* and *dissatisfaction*. What is beautiful is genuinely beautiful, but everything good and worthwhile carries decay within itself. The bud falls off, birth leads to death, and the day to night. People must realize the perpetual presence of painfulness and dread in our experience of reality.

Whoever has only a superficial acquaintance with these insights will not understand them deeply. To really acquire insight into the unsatisfying quality of existence, one must travel a long road. The initial insight must be deepened; one must make it one's own. For that reason we must include a caveat in our exposition. According to Buddhist standards, our awareness is superficial and ineffective. Perhaps we have seen, and what is more, tasted something of suffering; perhaps we have discovered something of the ambiguity of human existence — nevertheless, the profound insight indicated by the words *dukkha* and *anitya* has not yet come about so long as we feel no inner distance growing between ourselves and the 'ordinary' world. Only the saint who has achieved perfection, according to Conze, can fully comprehend the first truth.[35]

(2) The Second Noble Truth, as we have seen, concerns the origin of suffering. If one knows the cause of suffering, one can do something about it. After a time, greater emphasis was put on overcoming lack of insight. Not-knowing was seen as the cause of all misery. This idea was expressed in the *twelvefold chain of dependent origination*. This chain of

---

[35] Conze, *Boeddhisme*, p. 47; see Beckh, pp. 205 ff.; K. K. Inada, "Some Basic Misconceptions of Buddhism," *International Philosophical Quarterly* 9 (1969): 102.

causality has become the traditional form in which the perception of the origin of suffering has been articulated.[36] The 'chain' is explained differently by various currents. The principle has been transmitted in a variety of forms. One of the most current forms is the following:

> When this is present, that comes to be; on the arising of this, that arises. When this is absent, that does not come to be; on the cessation of this, that ceases. That is to say, on ignorance depend dispositions; on dispositions depends consciousness; on consciousness depends psychophysical personality; on the psychophysical personality depend the six 'gateways' [of sense perception]; on the six 'gateways' depends contact; on contact depends feeling; on feeling depends craving; on craving depends grasping; on grasping depends becoming; on becoming depends birth; on birth depend aging and death, sorrow and lamentation, suffering, dejection and vexation. In this manner there arises this mass of suffering.[37]

Ignorance (*avidyā*) stands at the beginning of the sequence in which one thing evokes and conditions the next. Ignorance is a complex phenomenon; it is more than merely not being cognizant of Buddhist doctrine. It is more a question of indistinctness — turning away from the world as it really is, and attachment to the world as people normally experience and interpret it. Ignorance is thus tied to attachment. A mere exposition of the doctrine (Pali: *Dhamma*; Sanskrit: *Dharma*) cannot abolish ignorance. Although knowledge and analysis do play a prominent role in Buddhism, *avidyā* is related to human disposition. *Avidyā* is like a king who is never without an entourage, always accompanied by desire, hate, etc.[38] Since ignorance has entered into an unholy accord with avidity and attachment, it is difficult to remedy the fault. If one wishes to attain salvation one must break through the attachment. The intertwining of both factors, ignorance and attachment, hold man captive in the ordinary world. The various divisions of Buddhism have emphases. Vetter shows how after a time the accent was placed on *analytical understanding*, which made the need for the meditative path of *dhyāna* (meditation/the middle way) less strongly felt.[39] Within the context of our study, it is permissible to pass over the discussion about the exact meaning of the 'chain of dependent origination.' The teaching of causality, which joins with one another in a comprehensive causal chain not only the being of things but also human

---

[36] Beckh, pp. 212f.; Drummond, pp. 102f.; Kalupahana, pp. 31f. Vetter thinks that the formula does not stem from the Buddha himself because it exhibits a somewhat later stage of Buddhist reflection —as does so much of Buddhist doctrine. See Vetter, *Early Buddhism*, pp. 45ff.

[37] See Kalupahana, p. 31. *The Book of the Kindred Sayings* (Samyutta Nikāya), II, tr. Mrs. Rhys Davids (London 1922; rpt. 1952), pp. 23f.; for the other way around, see II, 21; also Vetter, *Early Buddhism*, p. 46.

[38] H. de Wit, "Samsara en het Pad van Meditatie," *Saddharma* 17 (1985): 26; see Conze, *Buddhist Thought*, p. 55; Inada, p. 105.

[39] Vetter, *Early Buddhism*, pp. 13, 43, notes that *dhyāna*-meditation is frequently no longer valued as highly at a later time because discriminating insight (*prajñā*) received greater accentuation. Analysis was sometimes able to achieve a more independent standing.

attachment to things, ignorance, birth, and death, has preoccupied Buddhist thinkers throughout the ages.

(3) The Third Noble Truth, the truth of the cessation of suffering, entails the notion that suffering can be terminated by conquering attachment and ignorance. One must learn to be neither attached to things nor to one's self. Then one becomes free from everything — free too, to totally embrace the truth. The purpose of the rules for the life of the monks is to make their lives as free of attachment as possible. Received traditions narrate how the monks in the Buddha's time led a wandering existence; on their way they were not to look up or back. They had to hold up their bowl and eat what was put into it. Only in the rainy season did they come together at a fixed place. All of life was aimed at conquering attachment and ignorance, and so it still is even now among those who earnestly pursue enlightenment. There are many striking legends which testify to the difficulties which people must surmount on the way to liberation, and many examples of the high degree of detachment and purity which were achieved.

(4) The Fourth Noble Truth signals the path which leads to the cessation of suffering. It is the Noble Eightfold Path, which consists of right view, right aim, right speech, right action, right living, right effort, right mindfulness, and right concentration (*samādhi*).[40] Here we encounter references to a good disposition in life. Attachment and lust must be vanquished. One needs the right conviction, i.e., faith in the Buddha's teaching and trust in the way to salvation which he proclaimed. Vetter says that in the earliest Buddhism all emphasis lay on the Eightfold Path and on *dhyāna* (meditation); in meditatively inclined Buddhist currents this still holds true.[41] The search for insight is a means to conquering attachment.

The relation between the two human deficiencies, ignorance and attachment, is a point of dispute. Accordingly, it has been pointed out that two different ways of salvation are indicated in the directives for meditation in the Theravāda tradition: one aimed at being without attachment, and a second aimed at obtaining insight.[42] In the mainstream of Mahāyāna Buddhism the one is not separate from the other. One acquires

---

[40] E.g., Vetter, *Early Buddhism*, pp. 11 ff.; Drummond, pp. 89 f. "It is this Eightfold Way itself, that is to say: right view, right aspiration, right speech, right action, right mode of livelihood, right endeavour, right mindfulness, right concentration," *Majjhima Nikāya*, III, 298.

[41] See Vetter, *Early Buddhism*, pp. *xxi* ff.; for a more popular contemporary Buddhist exposition concerning the two veils (wrong opinions, contradictory emotions) that should both be removed, cf. H. de Wit, "Vrijheid en Individualiteit in Boeddhistisch Perpektief," *Saddharma* 18 (1986): 4.

[42] See P. Griffiths, "Concentration or Insight: The Problematic of Theravada Buddist Meditation-Theory," *Journal of the American Academy of Religion* 49 (1981): 605-24. Griffiths mentions passages where dissolution of perception is reached by meditation, and where meditation leads to insight and thus to pure 'awareness,' pp. 610, 614.

deep understanding only when one reforms one's life according to the initial knowledge which one has acquired.[43] The teachings and the pursuit of being without attachment are equal resources on the way to liberation. We have seen in the historical overview that the different schools placed divergent accents. The possibility of putting first either the path of being without attachment and concentration or that of reflection and analysis has led to differences between the various currents. Reform movements attempted to counter-balance what they regarded as a blurring of the insight of original Buddhism. Mahāyāna Buddhism heavily stresses the deficiency of cognition. Murti, as well as Conze, regarded the Mādhya-mika, which brings the view of Mahāyāna Buddhism to expression, as the Buddhist current which possibly stands nearest to the notions of the historical Buddha — with all the qualification due such a historical assertion.[44] Already in the period prior to the Mādhyamika, scholastic systems were developed in the already mentioned Abhidharma writings. This resulted in the mitigation of the importance of the original meditative path to liberation. The Mādhyamika, with its strong anti-scholastic slant, formed a counterbalance to this.

2.2   The *anātman* teaching

It may well be that the world is full of appearances and temptations by which it binds man to itself, yet the source of deception and false sentiment lies above all in the human experience of reality.[45] People think they have or are a 'self,' while in reality there is no continuous self lying at the basis of phenomena. This is the *anātman* doctrine, which —although of a somewhat later origin— is very much essential to the Buddhist tradition. The *Prajñā* tradition distinguishes various components of human existence (*skandhas*) which together form a human being. Five are mentioned: form (*rūpa*), that is, the material, physical side to human existence; feelings (*vedanā*); perceptions and representation (*saṃjñā*); mental formations (*saṃskāra*), be they conscious or unconscious; and awareness or conscious perception (*vijñāna*). A human being is a relation between these components. His existence is determined by them. Man himself is not removed from the chain of dependent origination. It is therefore possible to dissect human existence in a manner not dissimilar to that of a *behaviourist* psychologist such as Skinner in the 20th century. The comparison of man with a wagon is familiar:

---

[43] See D. K. Swearer, "Two Types of Saving Knowledge in the Pali Suttas," *Philosophy East and West* 22 (1972): 364. Swearer sees no contradiction in the Pali Suttas between meditation and insight, pp. 369 f.

[44] Conze, *Buddhist Thought*, p. 10; Murti, *The Central Philosophy of Buddhism*, note the title.

[45] For what follows, see Kalupahana, pp. 36 ff.; also, Lynn A. de Silva, *The Problem of the Self in Buddhism and Christianity* (London 1979), pp. 17 ff.

For, just as when the parts are rightly set
The word 'chariot' ariseth (in our minds),
So doth our usage covenant say:
'A being' when the aggregates are there.[46]

In didactic dialogues the comparison is elaborated. Is the wheel the wagon? Or the goat? The wagon is a relation between wheels, axles, and benches. In like manner, man is relation between *skandhas*. And the soul then? Do not believe what the Brahmans say! There is no eternal, immortal, and immutable self, hidden behind the flux of things. Each person has his own life, conditioned by many factors. Pointing out a soul amidst the causal nexus, which is supposedly free from and beyond that causality, is unnecessary and without basis. On the contrary, the notion that man possesses something precious and imperishable amidst a world which is *dukkha* and *anitya*, produces great harm. The experience of reality in terms of one's 'self' is a source of attachment, because it effects a deterioration to egocentrism and egoism. Not just the world, but also human existence itself is included in the stream of things. People are conditioned by many factors. Experiences are stored up, as it were, to yield their result in a subsequent life. Everything is included in the conditioning processes of life; one has no *ātman* which is stands untouched by it.

This is —in brief— the *anātman* doctrine which fundamentally distinguishes Buddhism from Hinduism. It is not difficult to see why, at a later time, the question arose as to wherein the identity of a person consisted in the cycle of rebirths. Around 300 B.C.E., a single current accepted, in this connection, the existence of a kind of identity core in man (*pudgala*), which was supposed to be imperishable and would therefore stand to benefit from the way of salvation.[47] This notion was repudiated by other schools because a free self, independent from suffering, is in effect introduced in this way. Vetter opines that the resistance to the idea (inconsistent with the rest of the doctrine) of a *pudgala* presumably formed the occasion for the denial of the existence of a self, since the collection of *sūtras* in the Pali canon is still incognizant of it.[48] The *anātman* doctrine is accepted by the mainstream of Buddhism. It is related to the Buddhist aspiration of overcoming attachment and the *ego*; in the words of Atisha: "The purpose of all Dharma is contained in one point," viz. the pursuit of conquering attachment to the *ego*.[49]

---

[46] In Kalupahana, p. 39.

[47] Conze, *Buddhist Thought*, pp. 122ff.; *Short History*, pp. 17f. D. Dunkel, *Stufen der Wahrheit: Der erkenntnismetafysische, ontologische und theologische Wahrheitsrelativismus bei indischen und christlichen Mystikern*, thesis with G. Mensching (Munich 1963), p. 2.

[48] Vetter, *Early Buddhism*, pp. 42ff.

[49] Atisha, "The Seven Points of Mind Training," with commentary by 'Jam-mGon Kong-sPrul the Great in *A Direct Path to Enlightenment*, ed. Ken McLeod

2.3 Empiricism and anti-metaphysics

The Buddha resisted the speculations of the Brahmans. He patiently eluded the metaphysical questions which were presented to him. Asked: "Will the Buddha be, after his departure?," he answered: "I would not say: The Buddha is, after his departure." "Will the Buddha not be, after his departure?," he answered: "I would not say: The Buddha will not be, after his departure." Question: "Will the Buddha both be and not-be, after his departure?" Answer: "I would not say: the Buddha will both be and not-be, after his departure." Question: "Will the Buddha neither be nor not-be, after his departure?" Answer: "I would not say: the Buddha will neither be nor not-be, after his departure."[50] On another occasion, the Buddha was asked whence he would go at his passing away (his *parnirvāna*, in which *nirvāna* becomes definite). When the flame is extinguished, asked the Buddha, does the flame go somewhere? Thus shall the Buddha be extinguished. For the rest, one must remain silent.[51]

Even though speculation can secure but little hold on this empirical line in Buddhist thought, heavens and gods, netherworlds and spirits, are spoken of freely. Yet notwithstanding their ethereal provenance, these belong to the reality in which one lives. Sometimes these creatures are (re)interpreted as dispositions of people.[52] People can be reincarnated as (mortal) gods or as demons, according to the *karma* which they have accumulated.[53] This entire cosmos is determined by the chain of causality. It is understandable that in certain currents of Buddhism the pantheon was able to obtain an important position, and the lay people aimed above all at a good rebirth in a subsequent life, while in other currents the stories about gods and demons played a less prominent role, and people strove to achieve salvation itself.[54]

Some firmly maintain that the Buddha himself was averse to all speculation. In his extensive work, *Early Buddhist Theory of Knowledge*, Jayatilleke, of Theravāda Buddhist extraction, defended the proposition that in many respects the original Buddhism showed similarity to the empirical disposition of Wittgenstein, and his silence about that which cannot be said. Jayatilleke himself contends that *nirvāna 'is'*, in some sense of the word, even though nothing can be said about it.[55] His pupil Kalupahana, however, goes beyond this and discards this notion.[56] The Buddha was an empiricist in his view: All things are determined by a

---

(Vancouver n.d.), p. 12, see commentary, p. 43.
[50] *Majjhima Nikāya*, II, 163, 159 ff., and Kalupahana, pp. 22 ff., 153-161; see K. N. Jayatilleke, (London 1963), p. 476, see also pp. 433, 452, 464.
[51] Jayatilleke, pp. 289-91; Kalupahana, p. 80.
[52] H. de Wit, pp. 9 ff.
[53] On karma and rebirth, Kalupahana, pp. 44 ff.
[54] See Conze, *Boeddhisme*, pp. 82 f.
[55] Jayatilleke, p. 476; cf. Wittgenstein, above Ch. II § 1.
[56] Kalupahana, pp. 80, 87.

myriad of causes, "and that is it." We will see that the founder of the Mādhyamika School, Nāgārjuna is sometimes presented in similar fashion. The problem of whether Buddhism acknowledges transcendent being in *nirvāṇa*, is a matter of debate, as we shall see (§ 3.3).

One does well to bear in mind, in connection with the alleged 'empirical' interpretation of Buddhism by such thinkers as Jayatilleke and Kalupahana, exponents of the tradition of Theravāda Buddhism, that the concepts 'empirical' and 'experience' can accommodate different contents. Whoever pauses to recall the struggle of Logical Positivism to demonstrate how *all* valid knowledge arises from sense perception, does well to realize that early Buddhism, according to Kalupahana, accommodates extrasensory perception: psychokinesis, clairaudience, telepathy, retrocognition, clair-voyance, and knowledge of the path by which one can conquer bad impulses.[57] The insights of Buddhism, in this view, are based in large measure on these 'extraordinary' experiences.[58] If one is unprepared to accept on the authority of others that man is *anātman*, that the world is *essentially dukkha* and *anitya*, and that deliverance from this world is possible, then one must attain insight through meditation, moderate asceticism, and concentration. Only then is one capable of verifying the 'chain of dependent origination' himself. Since attention will be paid in detail to views within Mahāyāna Buddhism in what ensues, we will suffice with the consideration given, which, as regards § 2.3, has been borrowed heavily from authors in the Theravāda tradition.

§ 3 Truth

3.1 Knowledge is subjective

Since ancient times, Indian philosophy has insisted on the personal commitment in cognition of the person doing the knowing, and on liberation as the (religious) aim of knowledge.[59] The subject forms knowledge. Religious knowledge is no aloof cognition. In analyzing the religious understanding, as we have already seen, the person of the man himself is at issue. In the East, philosophical or religious teaching, which in the West sometimes seems to live a life of its own, free of the thinkers' personal commitment, is (ideally) always tied in with the quest for salvation. 'Knowledge for the sake of knowledge' is not sought; one

---

[57] Kalupahana, pp. 21f.; see Jayatilleke, pp. 457, 459, 463. Swearer states in p. 356, that Jayatilleke is not very far removed from Buddhism as it is described in Guenther's works (n. 93). Also F. J. Hoffman, "The Buddhist Empiricist Thesis," *Religious Studies* 18 (1982): 151-58.

[58] For the role of extraordinary means of knowledge, Jayatilleke, pp. 418-23, 426f., compare pp. 467f., 438ff., 457.

[59] E. A. Burtt, "What can Western Philosophy Learn from India?" *Philosophy East and West* 5 (1955): 203f.; Conze, *Buddhist Thought*, pp. 214, 108ff.

attempts to obtain insight into the *condition humaine* in order to improve
life or to find deliverance from this blighted world.

Knowledge arises from the person. Knowledge of things is based on
the activity and the attachment of the subject. Cognition is thoroughly
subjective. Whoever wants to change reality must therefore work on man.
If people change their representations, reality itself changes. The normal
situation in the world wherein people generally and commonly dwell is
that they do not know things as they are.[60] They themselves create a
certain outlook on things.

Corresponding insights are to be found in Western philosophy. Jacobson
has pointed to kindred thoughts in Hume: in his view, the idea of causality
arises from the human experience of things and not from the things
themselves. There is, in reality, merely the succession of moments. People
gain impressions from moment to moment. They connect the perceptions
by the idea of causality.[61] Kant has also been alluded to frequently. 'Things
in themselves' cannot be known, Kant has stated. What people know are
things as they are perceived by people by virtue of the principles which
govern human perception and the human cognitive faculties. These ideas
have been developed further in subsequent philosophical phenomenology.
Human thought is thoroughly determined by one's representation of
matters, which is imbibed via the spirit of the times, upbringing, culture
and religious tradition. It is in this context that frame of reference and
horizon of understanding are spoken of. Heidegger spoke of '*Bewandtnis-
ganzheit*' (totality of involvements) to make plain just how closely human
thought and experience are bound up with life as a whole.[62] Wittgenstein
connected people's understanding to 'forms of life' and to human action.
In modern Western philosophy, attention is likewise demanded for the
subjective aspect of knowledge for countless reasons.

The understanding arrived at within Buddhism is that the ordinary
forms of perception and representation of matters are based on error. It
is a collective, conventional error. From a higher standpoint one is capable
of unmasking this reality as incorrect and as no more than convention. The
illusions with which and in which people live are superficial and incidental.
What we call reality does not truly exist. Things are not as we think to
know them nor are they commensurate with the part they play in our
actions. We perceive the components of the wagon as the wagon and the
components of man as the man, though the structuring of experience
actually arises from man.

Within the various currents in Buddhism radical differences exist with
regard to the nature and the status of what is perceived. The *Staviras*

---

[60] M. Heidegger, *Sein und Zeit*, pp. 166f., 130.

[61] See N. P. Jacobson, *Buddhism: The Religion of Analysis* (London 1966), pp. 162ff.;
D. Hume, *An Enquiry Concerning Human Understanding*, ed. E. Steinberg (Indiana-
polis 1977), pp. 15ff., 49ff.

[62] Heidegger, pp. 83f.

(within the old Hīnayāna Buddhism) taught that the indivisible instants in which reality consists from moment to moment are not fictitious. They ascribed reality to the elements (*dharma*) out of which the forms of apparition which one observes are composed.[63] But if reality possesses no permanence at all, it is impossible to acquire reliable knowledge. At a later time, people sought to indicate a certain permanence which bridged the discrete moments. The solutions which were proffered from this side were unconvincing to the thinkers in the tradition of Mahāyāna Buddhism.[64] This movement denied not only the reality of things, but also the value of discriminating, conceptual thought. Every form of conceptual discrimination leads to untrue views. This deeper, more radical concept of the 'ignorance' of everyday man leaves far behind what is regarded by the Staviras as wisdom. Even the *dharmas* of the Staviras do not exist.[65] They are no more than conventional modes of expression used to identify things. They have a certain amount of reality, but one cannot say that they really *are*.[66] What truly exists, according to later Mahāyāna Buddhism, is the Absolute, in which the conceptual distinction between existence and non-existence is overcome, since everything is one. For the Yogācārins, the One is the Absolute. No distinction any longer exists therein. The distinction between subject and object too is effaced. The pupil must learn through meditation to recognize that such objects do not exist in reality. Then he must discover that the subject as well has no proper being. The ultimate fact for the Yogācārins is pure thought, pure mind.[67] In the Mādhyamika School, matters lie somewhat differently. For Nāgārjuna thought ultimately does not touch on anything. In this sense, experience is void of what we think about it and thought is void of experience. This void-ness is denoted by the term *śūnyatā*.

It is evident from this short exposition of Buddhist epistemology how closely its ontology and anthropology are related to epistemology. No treatment of its epistemology can be given whereby the subject remains beyond consideration.[68] Everyday things exist only within the illusory, estranged reality of the perceiving individual.[69] They have a certain real-ness; their true being, however, can only be discovered from a higher perspective. In order to attain that perspective, it is needful for a person

[63] Conze, *Buddhist Thought*, pp. 134 ff.

[64] *Ibid*, pp. 204 f.

[65] *Ibid*, p. 210.

[66] See *The Awakening of Faith*, tr. Yoshito S. Hakeda (London 1967), pp. 73 ff.; Conze, *Buddhist Thought*, pp. 221 ff.

[67] Suzuki, "Introduction" to the *Laṅkāvatāra Sūtra*, ed. & tr. D. T. Suzuki (1932; rpt. London 1956), pp. *xxviii* (ff.); compare with Kalupahana, p. 122, and Conze, *Buddhist Thought*, p. 252.

[68] Conze, *Buddhist Thought*, p. 113.

[69] Lily de Silva, "Man and Nature in a Mutual Causal Relationship," in *Man in Nature: Guest or Engineer?* eds. S. J. Samartha and Lynn A. de Silva (Colombo 1979), pp. 10 f.

to free himself from the bonds which confine him to his estranged, seemingly normal, human existence.

3.2 Conventional and Absolute Truth

One frequently encounters the word 'truth' in the literature about and from the Buddhist tradition as a translation of *Dhamma* (Pali) or *Dharma* (Sanskrit). What is then intended is true doctrine.[70] Buddha's followers took a vow which concerned the acceptance of the Buddha, the *Dharma,* and the *Sangha* (the community of the monks). The *Dharma* is the truth; the Four Noble Truths (*satya*) are true. We must presently pursue in which sense such true doctrine is true. We shall see to what extent this line of questioning is characteristic for Buddhist thinkers themselves.

Satya is truth. At a later date, two kinds of truth are distinguished: the truth in and of this world, the conventional truth (*saṃvṛti satya*); and the real, deeper truth (*paramārtha satya*), the understanding of those who are initiated and enlightened.

The stock expression frequently used as an equivalent of *satya* is *yathābhūtam,* consistently translated 'as it is' or 'as things are.' These English expressions suggest a correspondence theory of truth.[71] Making *yathābhūtam* and the correspondence theory of truth equivalent is a dangerous simplification, however. For what does 'as it is' mean? The expression is itself no more than a paraphrase of the concept of truth. It therefore cannot do service as an explanation. What one actually means to say is, 'as things are in reality.' As soon as we distinguish between appearance and reality we abandon the field of naive realism and common sense. Siderits says that early Buddhism seems to have entertained a naive realism and a naive correspondence theory of truth. The aim, however, is always liberation from 'suffering,' and enlightenment. Pragmatic considerations accordingly entered into the appraisal of such conceptions.[72]

In Mahāyāna Buddhism the term 'suchness' (*tathatā*) was used for non-discursive 'knowledge' of things. This concept expresses the thought that one is aware of things as they really are, and not as they are seen within the field of conventional reality. According to Barclay, the intent in using the term is to avoid ascribing substance to things or awakening any suggestion that *things* are being described.[73] It is clear that Buddhism has undergone developments with regard to the concept of truth, and that

[70] For other meanings of *dharma,* Conze, *Short History,* pp. 12f.

[71] Jayatilleke's suggestion, p. 352; compare Kalupahana, pp. 18, 134; Kalupahana refers to *Dīgha Nikāya,* I, 17 (*Dialogues of the Buddha,* tr. from Pali by T. W. Rhys Davids, I [1899; rpt. London 1969], Sacred Books of the Buddhists, ed. F. M. Müller, II, 29.)

[72] M. Siderits, "A Note on the Early Buddhist Theory of Truth," *Philosophy East and West* 29 (1979): 432, 437f.

[73] W. F. Barclay, "On Words and Meaning: The Attitude toward Discourse in the *Laṅkāvatāra-sūtra,*" *Numen* 22 (1975): 70-79, esp. 75: "Suchness (*tathatā*) is a term which attempts to avoid positing any substance to ultimate reality or provide any description. It asserts that reality simply is such as it is." See Suzuki, *Outlines,* Chapter 5.

there are differences between the various Buddhist currents. Also, we must conclude that expressions such as 'as it is' or 'suchness' are not very helpful for analysis of the concept of truth. 'As it is' is a common sense expression whereas 'suchness' applies to non-discursive truth.

The *twofold division of the truth* in Buddhism is a sequel to the distinction between two sorts of dialogues by the Buddha. The Buddha's concern is to awaken people for a deeper understanding. He therefore does not expound the doctrine in conversations with the ignorant, but tries to move his discussion partner so far along that he starts to see what is truly of concern, in reality. Such *suttas* are called *neyyattha suttas (suttas* with an indirect meaning). In other discussions with his closest pupils, the Buddha speaks directly in terms of the *Dharma*. These discussions with a direct meaning are called *nītattha suttas*. Jayatilleke mentions a few passages in the Pali Canon where this distinction is already made. He regards this distinction as meaningful and correct; it makes clear that the Buddha adopted two different postures, depending on the degree to which his discussion partners had achieved understanding.[74]

Later commentators on the writings in the Pali Canon make a similar distinction, indicated by the terms 'conventional' and 'absolute truth' *samvṛti satya* and *paramārtha satya*.[75] Jayatilleke explains the double truth of the Pali Canon commentaries as follows. Both sorts of truth are true. The conventional way of speaking is suitable for one person, the absolute for another. From the standpoint of the absolute truth, the conventional truth is not untrue, but it is truth only at a lower level of understanding. This distinction thus arises from the distinction between two sorts of dialogues in the Pali Canon and, according to Jayatilleke, pretty much coincides with it.[76]

The interpretation of the two truths is disputed. This issue shall continue to occupy our thoughts in what ensues in this section. First we will present the empirical interpretation by Jayatilleke and Kalupahana. We will subsequently mention the other interpretation.

(1) In connection with relative or conventional truth, frequent mention is made of the significance of the familiar parable of the elephant. A number of blind people feel sundry parts of an elephant; each arrives at certain conclusions regarding the nature of the reality which he experiences. The perceptions thus obtained contradict one another. According to many, the parable wishes to make apparent that people approach reality from many

---

[74] Jayatilleke, pp. 361 ff.; see Dunkel, pp. 3 f.

[75] Jayatilleke, p. 364; see Murti, pp. 251 ff.; also Swearer, pp. 355, 370, for other distinctions.

[76] Jayatilleke, p. 365. Dunkel, p. 11, sketches a further development of this distinction; in a certain early phase, *samvṛtisatya* is synonymous with the Hīnayāna canon; *paramārthasatya* refers to the (newer) Mahāyāna teachings; cf. further developments as described by Dunkel.

sides, but, since each sees merely their own piece of it, contradictory conceptions ensue. Such contradiction arises from deficiencies in human cognition. The parable is used in Hindu thought to characterize the relationship between religions (Ch. III § 4.d). Jayatilleke points out that despite everything, the truth in this parable is still one. There *is* an elephant and not a pillar, a curved weapon, or a snake. The teaching of the individual or partial truth does not deny the truth of this knowledge; neither does it deny the existence of the reality experienced, but it says only that contradictory theories stem from limited human experiences. The unity of the truth remains presents, according to Jayatilleke.[77]

Thus the empirical interpretation which Jayatilleke gives to Buddhist doctrine. He believes that at a later time, the doctrine of the twofold truth grew in the direction of opposition between conventional relative truth and the absolute truth. Seen from a higher standpoint, the relative truth is then merely relative, and in that sense, untrue. We find this conception —many purport— in Nāgārjuna's thought. Jayatilleke, however, regards the Mahāyāna view as incorrect and not the original Buddhist position. In his view, the Buddha wanted to stick to the facts. His skepticism concerned those things about which people talked but could not say anything sensible. Jayatilleke points to an affinity between what the Buddha wanted and what impelled Wittgenstein. A certain correspondence between the Buddha and Wittgenstein has been pointed out more frequently: whereof one cannot speak, one must remain silent. But even though Jayatilleke sat at Wittgenstein's feet, it is disputable whether the Buddha wanted no more than Wittgenstein. The Buddha's concern was to guide people to an experience of well-being, enlightenment, and salvation — and, in our opinion, this sufficiently counters any purely empiricist interpretation of Buddhism.[78]

(2) The doctrine of the two truths is the basis of epistemology in the Mahāyāna tradition. The following words by Nāgārjuna the classical Mādhyamika teaching master, are to be encountered many times:

> The Buddha's explication is based on two truths, on the concealed truth of ordinary life (*laukika-saṃvṛtisatya*), and on the truthful truth (*para-mārthasatya*).
> Whoever does not acknowledge the distinction between these truths, does not acknowledge the profound truth (*tattva*) in the Buddha's teaching. Independently of the ordinary (Truth) (*vyavahāra*), the truthful cannot be learnt; independent of the truthful, *nirvāṇa* cannot be attained.[79]

---

[77] Jayatilleke, pp. 354 ff. The point of the story in *Udāna* (68 f.) corroborates this, in *The Minor Antologies of the Pali Canon*, II, tr. F. L. Woodward (London 1948), pp. 82 f.

[78] See Hoffman, p. 156.

[79] *Mādhyamika-Kārikās* 24:8-10; German translation by Dunkel, pp. 23 f. The doctrine of the two truths is fundamental in Mādhyamika thought, see Murti, p. 243; Suzuki, *Outlines*, p. 95. Compare with the translation by A. Wayman, "Contributions to the Mādhyamika School of Buddhism," *Journal of the American Oriental Society* 89 (1969): 148, *vyavahāra* — 'manner of speech.'

Non-Buddhist scholars such as Murti and Conze, but others too, surmise that the Mādhyamika tradition has understood and elaborated the Buddha's central intentions better than other currents.[80] The relative truth remains significant merely at the level of ordinary life; it is a practical truth which provides no real understanding of the nature of things.[81] What then is the exact reason *saṃvṛti satya* falls short? The reason, say thinkers from the Mādhyamika tradition, lies in thought itself. Thought entails distinguishing between things. It isolates the one thing which is thought from the rest. It distinguishes not only between things which are known but also between the object known and the subject who is doing the knowing. Such distinction between things as well as between subject and object is the flaw of cognition. The highest truth is free of such distinctions. This implies that ordinary thought is necessarily imperfect. It is limited by nature, and not discerning this limitation is a serious illness. The word *saṃvṛti* in *saṃvṛti satya* is derived from *sam* (together--with) and *vṛ* (cover over): the true nature of things is covered over by conventional conceptuality.[82] In order to know truly, one must abandon the domain of logic and consistency in favour of a spiritual life. The highest truth is —within this tradition— not just the result of philosophical analysis, but of a centuries long meditation.[83]

The next problem which announces itself, of course, is how people can advance far enough to practise an open-minded, non-conceptual experience of mental and sensory reality as it is? Ordinary mortals need some bolstering in this regard. They cannot discover it for themselves, as the Buddha did once, but must be told when they are ripe.[84] Thus, at this point we encounter the Buddhist doctrine as an explication of the understanding which the enlightened can attain. Such an explication is naturally conceptual. The Buddhist teaching itself thus belongs —so it is consistently stated— to the province of conventional truth, the *saṃvṛti satya*. It is understandable that after this had been established in later times, an inclination emerged to introduce nuances into the category of *saṃvṛti satya*. Further subdivisions were made of which we will mention the division by which Norbu sums up the higher Mādhyamika view; this agrees to a large extent with the division Suzuki presented as the view of the Yogācārin School.[85] Norbu introduces a threefold division; this can

---

[80] See *n.* 44.

[81] See Murti, p. 245.

[82] Kalupahana, pp. 134f.

[83] Conze, *Buddhist Thought*, pp. 211, 244.

[84] It should be evident from this that in principle the Buddha had great authority. Esteem for the Bhuddha's authority changed in later Buddhism. For a discussion of the Buddha's authority, faith in doctrine, and trusting one's own insight, Conze, *Buddhist Thought*, pp. 26 ff.; Jayatilleke, pp. 169-204; 369-415.

[85] See Dunkel, pp. 35 f.; Thinley Norbu, *The Small Golden Key to the Treasures of the Various Essential Necessities of General and Extraordinary Buddhist Dharma*

be reduced to a twofold division between relative and absolute truth, with
which we have already made acquaintance, as follows. The relative truth
is now distinguished as twofold: 'inverted' relative truth and 'actual'
relative truth. We describe the divisions as follows:

(1) *Parikalpita* (illusion; 'inverted' relative truth). Illusory perceptions
    such as the bending of a half submerged stick are reckoned to this
    category, but so are world views based purely on illusions. All
    knowledge produced by attachment and egoism, and which is not
    subservient to the abandonment of *samsāra* and the attaining of
    nirvāṇa belongs to this category.

(2) *Paratantra-lakṣaṇa* ('actual' relative knowledge). Knowledge in which
    one realizes the relativity of 'ordinary reality' and sees through
    'illusion.'[86]

(3) *Paranispañña-lakṣaṇa*, literally, 'a world view founded on perfect
    knowledge.' One attains such knowledge when the mind is free of
    illusion and prejudice. This is the realization of non-duality. One
    ought to recall that this *insight* is not an insight into something
    other than what one knows in ordinary, alienated experience, but an
    understanding of that which is not distorted and covered by one's
    own fixations, projections, and conceptions. Norbu points out that
    from this standpoint of real understanding there is ultimately only
    one truth: "Where there is no dualistic mind, there are no two
    truths."[87]

We thus see that the Buddhist *Dharma* is 'true' at the level of relative
knowledge. The ultimate truth lies not at the level of relative knowledge,
however, but is an absolute insight which is not conceptual and therefore
cannot be articulated in words — in that sense 'doctrine' does not qualify
as (real) truth (*paramārtha satya*). However, doctrine can count as 'truth'
within the totality of conventional truth;[88] viewed from a higher standpoint, the teachings too lie at a lower level and are no higher than
conventional truth. Expressions like higher and lower are themselves
constituents of relative knowledge, which is transcended in absolute
knowledge.[89] We will now deal with the *paramārtha satya* in somewhat more
detail; we will subsequently again raise the relationship between the two
levels of knowledge.

First a word regarding *paramārtha satya* then: What cannot be
understood by discriminating knowledge nor conveyed by words can be
experienced in enlightenment. Liberated from the attachment to worldly

---

(New York ²1985), Chapter 8, pp. 38-44; Suzuki, *Outlines*, pp. 88-98.
[86] Suzuki, pp. 88 f.
[87] Norbu, p. 44; see Dunkel, pp. 35 ff.
[88] Dunkel, p. 35, notes *yogisaṃvṛtisatya* as the term by which the Yogācāra refers to
     such intermediating teaching. See Murti, p. 246.
[89] See Wayman, p. 149.

things and ways of knowing, the saint is able to perceive the world as it really is.[90] It is difficult to put this experience into words — that much has become evident by now. The very word 'perceive' already summons confusion. Our habit is to think of a perceiver to go with 'perceiving.' The very distinction between perceiving subject and perceived object, however, is a form of distinction and cognition at the level of *saṃvṛti satya*. It is surpassed in enlightenment. The words from the *Laṅkāvatāra Sūtra* (Yogācārin School), for instance, are used to articulate something which cannot be expressed by words.[91] Words represent the truth wrongly. The *doctrine* concerning the deepest and highest truth is not itself the truth *Description* of the highest knowledge lies at the level of *saṃvṛti satya*. Our terms are therefore misleading. In order to truly grasp what the Buddhist thinker and monk mean by *paramārtha satya*, one must free oneself of attachment and discriminating thought. One must oneself be aware of what can only be experienced immediately.[92] Then one attains the highest knowledge, the deepest understanding. Such insight is designated as transrational, intuitive, synthetic, all-encompassing, non-transient, and free. It is knowledge of ultimate reality, direct insight into the nature of things as they really are.[93] Knowledge of the absolute is therefore accompanied by being without attachment and by liberation from the burden of discriminating cognition. Whoever is so enlightened is also liberated from the burden of transience — there is no more perishable *ego*. What is it that is experienced in this fashion? This non-conceptual knowledge, or better, pure awareness, is designated as *śūnyatā*, emptiness — provided one thinks of this as something positive.[94] This knowledge is 'empirical' and immediate. It is not influenced or deformed by tradition and human habits of thought. Buddhist tradition points the way to this knowledge; it helps people to raise themselves to this experience. The experience itself amounts to standing eye to eye with the Absolute.[95] All expressions used to describe this experience fall short, including the expression standing eye to eye. It is a supra-sensory experience;[96] there is no longer any distinction between subject and object. One experiences oneness — the absolute.[97]

---

[90] Murti, p. 25; concerning the Yogācārins, Conze, *Buddhist Thought*, pp. 256f.
[91] Barclay, p. 74; see the *Laṅkāvatāra-sūtra*, p. 240.
[92] See Conze, *Buddhist Thought*, p. 243; Suzuki, *Outlines*, pp. 99ff.
[93] Swearer, pp. 365f.; see *The Awakening of Faith*, pp. 34, 100ff.; H. V. Guenther, "The Levels of Understanding in Buddhism," *Journal of the American Oriental Society* 78 (1958): 20, 23.
[94] See Wayman, pp. 146ff.; Conze, p. 243 ('emptiness' as ladder); Swearer, p. 368, writes, "not mere emptiness, but as that ultimately real, which gives meaning to the world of multiplicity."
[95] Swearer writes, " ... *paññā* is able to perceive the ultimately real 'face-to-face,' just as *vijñāna* is able to perceive the phenomenal world as it really is," p. 366.
[96] Compare, Wayman, p. 149, for example; see also *The Awakening of Faith*, p. 33.
[97] Murti, p. 236.

From the *paramārtha satya*, one can return to the level of the relative knowledge of daily life, the *saṃvṛti satya*, which then appears as *paratantra*, and no longer as *parikalpita*. The illusion has now been penetrated, the attachment broken. Such immediate experience leaves 'behind' an impression which fundamentally cannot be described, but which nevertheless can be more or less explained to others, thus giving rise to the *dharma*. Much needs to be explained about the world, about man, and about the path to the Truth, even though real, ultimate understanding cannot itself be transmitted.[98] Not all knowledge at the level of *saṃvṛti satya* is swept into one great undifferentiated heap; nuances are introduced. In the end, with great exertion, one ought to transcend the category of conceptual knowledge.

The next problem which we will raise concerns the *mutual relationship between the two levels* of knowledge and understanding. The *paramārtha satya* is not concerned with another reality.[99] There is only one reality; it is either experienced inadequately and conventionally, or adequately, non-conceptually, and as freely. *Saṃvṛti satya* is *allegedly* true knowledge, but ultimately untrue, because it is fettered to ignorance, attachment, and conceptuality. In the experience of enlightenment, one experiences things freely and openly, without making a distinction between what is experienced and oneself. The absolute, that is to say, the reality which is experienced then as absolute, is known in a non-dual intuition. "It is that Intuition itself," says Murti.[100] What kind of reality one may ascribe to that which is experienced in this intuition is disputed. Kalupahana believes that the Buddha did not teach that *nirvāṇa* is 'something.' F. Streng, with the support of others, contends that by the introduction of *śūnyatā* at the end of all analysis, Nāgārjuna introduces —and not in a furtive manner— a kind of Absolute in the sense of Brahman after all.[101] If one were to ask: What then is the nature of the reality which is experienced in enlightenment?, the answer would be thus: This experience extends beyond the opposition between being and non-being. It is an experience of liberation which is also designated as salvation, as Vetter emphasizes.[102] Those who want to know how it really is, however, must travel down the path themselves many years, and not just read of it in books or listen to

---

[98] See Guenther, pp. 21, 27f.; Swearer, pp. 362ff.
[99] Murti, p. 251.
[100] *Ibid*, p. 236, see also pp. 250f., 228; on the difference with the Vedānta, pp. 236f.; on the similarities and the differences between both traditions, T. V. R. Murti, "Saṃvṛti and Paramārtha in Mādhyamika and Advaita Vedānta," in *The Problem of Two Truths in Buddhism and Vedānta*, ed. M. Sprung (Dordrecht 1973), pp. 9-27.
[101] Fred. J. Streng, *Emptiness: A Study in Religious Meaning*, with a translation of the *Mūla-Mādhyamika-Kārikās* (Nashville 1967), p. 75; Kalupahana, p. 133.
[102] T. Vetter, "Die Lehre Nāgārjunas in den *Mūla-Mādhyamika-Kārikās*," in *Epiphanie des Heils: Zur Heilsgegenwart in Indischer und Christlicher Religion*, ed. G. Oberhammer (Vienna 1982), pp. 91f., 107.

stories about it. After now having introduced the teaching of two levels of knowledge, we will deal in somewhat more detail with several individual thinkers: first, the classical philosopher Nāgārjuna, then Jñānagarbha, an exponent of one of the schools within (Nāgārjuna's) Mādhyamikas, and finally, a modern Japanese exponent of the Zen tradition. In so doing, we will limit ourselves to deliberation within the Mahāyāna tradition.

3.3 Nāgārjuna

It is assumed that Nāgārjuna lived in the 2nd century C.E. He is the father of the Mādhyamika School. In the lines already quoted, Nāgārjuna has given a classical formulation of the doctrine of the two truths. He gives a very consistent refutation of every reification: no thing 'is' (i.e., as a permanent thing). This criticism also holds true of propositions. There are no propositions which are true in the strict sense. There is nevertheless a guiding towards the truth. Critics reproached Nāgārjuna for inconsistency: he asserts that assertions cannot be true, but that too is an assertion.[103] Nāgārjuna himself deals with this criticism. In later times, two schools arose among his pupils, the one accentuating the impossibility of articulated truth, the other acknowledging the utility and validity of logical analysis, provided it is wielded with a certain goal.[104] Jñānagarbha belongs to this last school.[105] The goal which is served by doctrine must now first be explained. The concern is, briefly and properly, the realization of *Emptiness*. Buddhist philosophy is a doctrine of salvation. The aim is the transformation of a person and not ascertaining what is true doctrine. The liberation of man from the confining bonds caused by an existence full of suffering lies in the realization that in the light of further analysis the bonds do not exist but arise from human cognition; they are 'empty'; everything is *śūnyatā* (emptiness).[106]

Nāgārjuna analyzes all the important concepts of the philosophy of his day, and proves that these concepts are untenable. They have no demarcated meaning. He continually shows how all things stand in causal relations; yet they do not therefore exist in themselves. They are connected. The being of one being is conditioned by other beings. A separate being does not 'exist' independently. Therefore it cannot, says Nāgārjuna be the cause of something else. With his critical analysis he aims to demonstrate the untenability of any thought of something that exists in and by itself. He opposes what he regards as wrong interpretations of the Buddha's teaching, for example, the doctrine of the ('existing') moments, the

---

[103] Nāgārjuna, "The Arguments of the Opponents," in *Averting the Arguments*, Part I, tr. Streng, in Streng, *Emptiness*, pp. 221 ff. (I, no. 2; II, no. 29).
[104] Streng, pp. 35, 96 ff.
[105] M. D. Eckel, *Jñānagarbha's Commentary on the Distinction Between the Two Truths* (Albany 1987), p. 5.
[106] Nāgārjuna, *Averting the Arguments*, Part II; see also Streng, passim.

dharmas, as advanced by the *Abhidharma* Schools.[107] They tried to achieve detachment by denying the permanence of things; with respect to the perpetual change of all things, they arrived at the conception that only a certain state of affairs exists, each for but a short moment, which subsequently makes way for another moment. Nāgārjuna had no peace with this conception. The moments (*dharmas*) also have no independent existence. Everything is included in the conditioned *flux* cf things. Not a single thing rates an independent significance. There is no substance that supports phenomenal reality. All experience and conceptuality are based on custom and attachment. Nāgārjuna is thus far more critical than Kant would later be in the West: even the 'things in themselves' and the categories of the understanding do not exist. What *is* there then in reality? *Śūnyatā* (Emptiness).

The term *śūnyatā* thus applies to what one observes without those things having any being. One must learn to view them accordingly, as phenomena without foundation. Things do not exist, but are construed by the human mind. The reality which forms the object of religious understanding is therefore the same reality which one apprehends in daily experience. There is no other reality. In his study, *Emptiness,* Streng never tires of stressing that *nirvāṇa* for Nāgārjuna is not in any sense a higher or another, 'objective' reality.[108] It is this empirical reality, only experienced in a totally different way.[109] He who has reached enlightenment, continues to deal with things as before in the practice of daily life.[110] The difference is that he sees through the *appearance*; all of conditioned reality is fabricated by man. The same is true even of the *Dharma.* Even the 'chain of dependent origination' is an idea which people have imposed on reality. Just as the Hindus sought a fixed point in human existence, in *ātman,* so the Buddhist tradition has designated a principle which is basic to reality, that of 'dependent co-origination.'[111] Taken precisely however, the chain of dependent origination 'is' not. Causal relationship too is a human idea which man imposes on things in his attached, ignorant state.[112]

True insight into things has a liberating effect. This witnesses to Nāgārjuna's religious motivation. When people see that nothing exists in reality they will be without attachment. If things are not real, suffering too is unreal.[113] Deep understanding is therefore a liberation.

Since things have no being and all of phenomenal reality is given and experienced within a human fancy, nothing can be said about it, speaking strictly from the higher standpoint at which one understands this. The

[107] See Nāgārjuna, *Mūla-Mādhyamika-Kārikās*, esp. VII. 29 ff., and see Streng's explanation, p. 53.
[108] Streng, pp. 146, 83, 86, 89.
[109] *Ibid*, p. 69.
[110] *Ibid*, p. 52; see p. 95, 'valid when correctly applied.'
[111] *Ibid*, p. 58.
[112] *Ibid*, pp. 52, 55.
[113] *Ibid*, p. 92.

experience of *śūnyatā* does not permit verbal expression. The problem in this is of course that something must be said if others' eyes are to be opened.[114] True doctrine —if we may introduce this term for a moment in order presently to make qualifications— is not a doctrine about an object. Understanding has no object for Nāgārjuna, Streng comments.[115] Strictly speaking, Nāgārjuna confirms no propositions about anything. No claim is made to truth in the sense of a number of true assertions. The doctrine's function is to invite the hearer to view things in a certain manner. It is thus inaccurate to speak of a true doctrine. Profound wisdom does not consist of conceptual knowledge, therefore all terms fall short in expressing the truth. Concepts themselves belong to the order of this world and participate in its emptiness. The concept of true doctrine too, or that of absolute truth, is and remains a non-absolute, worldly concept.[116]

Nāgārjuna analyzes many of the central tenets of Buddhism and demonstrates that they are untenable, as we have already noted.[117] Streng calls his way of operating *negative dialectic*. In a scrupulous weighing of pros and cons, Nāgārjuna displays the vacuity of presumed truths with an iron logic.[118] He demonstrates the untenability of all understanding, but does not defend a new theory.[119] With this negative dialectic, he wants to help people change their 'outlook' and to start seeing things as *śūnyatā*.[120]

The doctrine concerning *śūnyatā* is not just explicated. In order to advance sufficiently to one see things as they really are (i.e., as empty), one must practise being without attachment in the conduct of one's life. The ultimate truth cannot be taught apart from practical action.[121] In a final liberation, one is at last aware of things as they really are. The notion 'as they really are' recurs many times in Streng's presentation of Nāgārjuna when he defines true understanding — leaving aside whether the expression concerned occurs in Nāgārjuna's work.[122] The things that one perceives as they are, are the same things that are experienced in ordinary experience, but in a different manner, viz. in attachment and by discrimination. Buddhist doctrine aims to alter one's way of perceiving reality. By educating people in a different pattern of experience, they can learn to understand reality and at the same time be liberated from the burden of

---

[114] *Ibid*, pp. 92 f., 72, 74 f.
[115] *Ibid*, pp. 82 ff.
[116] *Ibid*, p. 84.
[117] *Ibid*, p. 93; see Nāgārjuna's text.
[118] *Ibid*, p. 148; Dunkel, p. 15.
[119] Nāgārjuna himself, *Averting the Arguments*; in Streng, p. 224 vs. 29; see also Streng, pp. 89, 91, 163.
[120] Streng, pp. 96, 163; "The Significance of Pratītyasamutpāda for Understanding the Relationship between Samvṛti and Paramārthasatya in Nāgārjuna," in *The Problem of Two Truths in Buddhism and Vedānta*, ed. M. Sprung (Dordrecht 1973), p. 33.
[121] *Ibid*, pp. 145, 96, 156.
[122] *Ibid*, pp. 96, 98, 161, see p. 84.

their existence.[123] The negative dialectic shows that the Absolute does not exist, and that phenomena are not real. Opportunity is thus created for the absolute experience of emptiness. *Saṁsāra,* interpreted by Nāgārjuna as the process of conditioned existence, does not differ from *nirvāna.*[124] For Nāgārjuna there is no higher absolute being, a *nirvāna* which (in whatever sense of the term) 'is', according to Streng. Once aware of the vacuity of all human representations regarding phenomenal reality, one is indifferent to truth claims which people make at the level of common worldly reality.[125] How does one know that one has experienced this lofty truth? If one does indeed have this understanding, one knows that one sees things as they are, non-dually and directly.[126]

We will conclude our presentation of Streng's interpretation of Nāgārjuna's negative dialectic here. We have seen how radically he recapitulates the contours of Buddhist philosophy. The highest truth, *paramārtha,* is fundamentally unstatable.[127] Now another aspect of Nāgārjuna's thought must be raised. It is the presupposition on which he bases his negative dialectic. No thing has existence, as we saw, because all things are related in a chain of conditioning. Nāgārjuna's self-evident point of departure is that all that which is conditioned does not exist independently. This thought recurs many times in the *Mūla-Mādhyamika-kārikās.* We already encounter it in the first chapter: "Since existing things which have no self-existence are not real . . . "[128]

On the basis of this presupposition, the chain of determinations entails that all things are empty, *śūnya*: "The 'originating dependently' we call 'emptiness.' "[129] Since all that exists is conditioned, things do not exist and *nirvāna* is not an existing something.[130] The question ought to be posed, in our view, whether perhaps Nāgārjuna does not defend a position after all: the position that only that which has no cause truly exists. Since no true existence is awarded to things which exist within the chain of dependent origination, they are void. The Highest Truth presupposes that one has realized that all is conditioned. One learns to see things just as they are, a constant stream of changing things which cannot be named. Even the categories of existence and non-existence are no longer applicable.

---

[123] *Ibid,* p. 158.
[124] Nāgārjuna, *Mūla-Mādhyamika-Kārikās,* XXV. 19.
[125] Streng, p. 166, "Truth, then, is not a statement which claims validity because of its intrinsic relation to an actually real entity, but it is an indifference to every such claim."
[126] *Ibid,* p. 173.
[127] *Ibid,* p. 94.
[128] Nāgārjuna, *Mūla-Mādhyamika-Kārikās,* I. 10; XV. 2, 4, 10; XXVII. 22; XXII. 9; XXIV. 33, vgl. VIII. 2; XX. 17; XXI. 17; cf. Murti, "Samvṛti and Paramārtha . . . ," pp. 15 f. Dunkel, p. 18, mentions another presupposition, the later so-called *satkaryavada,* the belief that cause and effect must be substantially identical.
[129] Nāgārjuna, *Mūla-Mādhyamika-Kārikās,* XXIV. 18.
[130] Nāgārjuna, XXV. 4.

We have allowed Streng's interpretation to guide us in our presentation of Nāgārjuna since this is the customary interpretation among Buddhologists and Buddhist scholars.[131] T. Vetter, however, does not concur with Streng's interpretation of Nāgārjuna on all points. Vetter believes that the customary interpretation of the twofold truth in Nāgārjuna does not do justice to the text. In reality, there are three levels: the practical truth of worldly knowledge, the higher truth, and *nirvāṇa*.[132] Vetter conceives of *paramārtha satya* as the Buddhist 'doctrine,' or better, as Nāgārjuna's denial of the applicability of normal concepts. In this Vetter bases himself on the propositions which we already cited in the previous section, in which Nāgārjuna says that without the twofold truth *nirvāṇa* cannot be reached; one must also relinquish conceptual denial (*paramārtha satya*):

> Supported by the truth valid in practical life (*vyavahāra*), the highest truth (*paramārtha*) is learnt. Without the highest truth *nirvāṇa* cannot be attained.[133]

Vetter equates Nāgārjuna's view as stated with *paramārtha satya*. It is, to be precise, a truth which characterizes *nirvāṇa* as indescribable. Vetter points out the objective of this truth: the realization of salvation.[134] He describes the salvific experience as follows:

> One does not remain there [i.e., in the doctrine], but reaches *nirvāṇa* from there, which is not something in the Beyond, but is that which until now was the world but now has lost its determined and conditioned character in such a way —and not just as a matter of reasoning either— that nothing concrete is perceived and represented any longer.[135]

Non-dual experience 'of the world' is thus (if it be permitted that one speaks indicatively) the experience to which the doctrine summons people. Vetter calls this experience a 'mystical experience of transcendence.'[136] He is thus diametrically opposed to Streng on this point, who excludes a mystical experience of transcendence.[137] Streng leaves unexplained why one should go to all that trouble to attain the experience of *śūnyatā*, according to Vetter. It must be an extraordinary, salutary experience, and not the simple realization that this world does not truly 'exist.'[138] After the denials, there is apparently an extraordinary experience of transcendence

---

131 According to D. Eckel (in a conversation, spring 1983) and H. de Wit.
132 Vetter, p. 106 *n.* 37.
133 Vetter, p. 106; *Mūla-Mādhyamika-Kārikās*, XXIV. 10; see the translation by Dunkel, (already cited in the text). Streng, gives a somewhat different translation, "The highest sense (of the truth) is not taught apart from practical behaviour. And without having understood the highest sense one cannot understand *nirvāṇa*."
134 Vetter, p. 107 *n.* 37.
135 *Ibid*, p. 107, see pp. 92f.
136 *Ibid*, p. 92.
137 *Ibid*, p. 90.
138 *Ibid*, p. 91.

(of which one cannot say that it is beyond this world).[139] As we have seen in the quotation, Vetter believes that Nāgārjuna himself conceives of his *'negative dialectic'* as *paramārtha satya*, while in the (later) tradition, this term always means the unutterable, final understanding. Streng identifies *paramārtha satya* with non-discursive understanding.[140] Whatever the case may be, Nāgārjuna's negative dialectic forms a bridgehead to an experience of *śūnyatā*. In that sense it is 'true': it shows things in their emptiness and points the way to the realization of *śūnyatā*. Even though Nāgārjuna attempts not to prove any positive proposition as 'true,' he does endeavour to display that other philosophical conceptions are unsound; he wants to thus lead people to the experience of the Highest Truth, *śūnyatā*.

3.4 Jñānagarbha

Jñānagarbha (8th century) ends his short but basic treatise, *Satyadvaya-vibhaṅgakārikās* (*The Verses on the Distinction between the Two Truths*), with the following words:

> May the merit I have gained by distinguishing the two truths cause the whole to develop the seed of understanding.[141]

The work stands within a Mādhyamika tradition strongly influenced by Bhavaviveka.[142] Just as was the case with Nāgārjuna, the founder of the Mādhyamika School, the question arises here as to how one can assume a certain position in a world of *emptiness*. We have seen that Nāgārjuna assumes the value of the Buddhist doctrine, but also that he subsequently casts aspersions on it with the aid of his dialectical method, and that he finally defends the notion that he actually assumes no position. For the sake of people's salvation, the truth must be preached, but so long as people are unenlightened, they cannot properly understand it, and certainly cannot corroborate it. Now Jñānagarbha, in his treatise on the twofold truth, gives very generous treatment to this problem. M. D. Eckel, who has translated the text and provided an introduction, points out that the typically Mahāyāna position consists in looking for a balance between two different perspectives with regard to reality.[143] Seen from one position, reality is different than seen from the other. Since he continually changes his perspective, Jñānagarbha is able to accommodate his discussion partners and clearly explicate the typically Mahāyāna stance. In respect

---

[139] For reference, see above, *n.* 135.
[140] Translation by Streng,; see *n.* 133; also pp. 94 ff.
[141] See the translation by Eckel, in *Jñānagarbha's Commentary*, p. 103. An interesting treatise on the doctrine of the two truths by Atiśa († 1056 C.E.), can be found in Chr. Lindtner, "Atisa's Introduction to the Two Truths and its Sources," *Journal of Indian Philosophy* 9 (1981): 161-214.
[142] Eckel, p. 15.
[143] *Ibid*, pp. 35 ff., 43 ff.

of knowledge, he makes distinctions which he designates as distinctions in the truth. He gives both a positive and a negative approach to the ultimate truth, which is 'expressible' and 'inexpressible.' The distinctions made can be schematized as follows:

I. *conventional truth*, 'what corresponds to appearances' (*yathādarśana*):

    A. relative knowledge:
        1. correct relative knowledge, *tathya-saṃvṛti satya*
           (test: proper behaviour/effective action, *arthakriyā*)
        2. incorrect convention, *mithyā-saṃvṛti satya*.
    B. rational analysis of the world
        ('the expressible ultimate' *saparyāya-paramārtha*).

II. *unutterable truth*: 'the inexpressible ultimate,' *aparyāya-paramārtha*.[144]

With respect to the level of daily life (I. A), the following can be said: Reality appears to man as it, for whatever reasons, appears to him. There is no point to analysis of this reality: "It is just that one thing appears to be caused by another. What more is there to say?" (vs. 22). At this level, the test for settling what is and what is not valid knowledge lies in the results of knowledge for action. To state the matter in more contemporary terms, actual practice is the criterion of the truth. The criterion for determining what is right action is determined by Buddhist philosophers in relationship to the proper objectives (*artha*) of human existence, as Nagatomi shows. What right action is, is determined in relationship to the regularities of the empirical world.[145]

One can infer from the scheme cited that *paramārtha satya* can be viewed in two perspectives: as true doctrine and as fundamentally inarticulate understanding. At the level of reasonableness, the true doctrine has value; it is *paramārtha satya*; but viewed from the higher point of view (II), the doctrine is no more than conventional. Eckel describes the contradictory but nonetheless complementary perspectives as follows:

> From one perspective the two truths are distinct and have to be kept apart for the system to function, but from another perspective the two reinforce and complement each other. Someone who understands the system can hold the two perspectives together and not be confused by their apparent contradictions.[146]

One cannot surmount this dialectic in a separate, third position. Eckel points out the affinity of Jñānagarbha's line of thought with that of

---

[144] *Ibid*, pp. 38 ff., 70 ff., 76, 87. The term *aparyāya-paramārtha* occurs on p. 112.
[145] M. Nagatomi, "Arthakriyā," *Dr. V. Raghavan Felicitation Volume*, Vols. 31-32 of The Adyar Library Bulletin, 1967–68; see pp. 56, 62, 72 concerning *Dharmakīrti*. For a critical analysis of praxis as a criterion for the evaluation of world-views, see H. M. Vroom, *De Schrift Alleen?* pp. 168-81.
[146] Eckel, p. 41.

Nishitani, to whom we will devote the next section.[147] Seen from the truly highest point of view, rational analysis such as given in the great example of the Mādhyamika's, Nāgārjuna's *Mūla-Mādhyamika-kārikās,* is also ultimately conventional. At the conventional level, however, the 'negative dialectic' is the highest possibility for reason. Buddhist doctrine is 'true'; at the level of conventional existence it is *paramārtha satya*; but viewed from enlightenment, true doctrine is nevertheless no more than conventional.

In Jñānagarbha's treatise on the two truths, we see reflected the Buddhist struggle to say something about what fundamentally cannot be articulated. Eckel stresses that in the tradition to which Jñānagarbha belongs there is ultimately no difference between the conventionally true and the ultimate truth. The 'dialectical approach' is not surpassed in an independent synthesis. " ... the distinctions with which he began can only be affirmed if he can also affirm that there are no distinctions. Distinctions can apply only if they are relative, not ultimate."[148] Ultimate insight cannot be articulated, because distinctions are not valid. Reason, which necessarily operates by discrimination and synthesis, appears to be conventional. The unity of relative and absolute truth can only be approximated dialectically, or perhaps better said, paradoxically, or, as Eckel puts it, ironically; it can never be expressed.

3.5 Keiji Nishitani

Nishitani is one of the most prominent spokesman of the *Kyoto School,* which arose from within Zen Buddhism and has also been influenced by other currents in the Mahāyāna tradition. The Kyoto School was founded by Nishida († 1945) and Tanabe († 1962). The school has its roots in Zen and Hua-Yen, Vetter states.[149] Nishitani presents the world of Buddhist thought in dialogue with Western philosophy. He describes the phenomenon of religion as he himself has learnt to see it. He claims that his arguments are universally valid. At the same time, he describes how an ultimately true and saving understanding can be realized in *śūnyatā,* emptiness. One may view what he writes as an attempt to describe reality as he experiences it in terms of his experience of *śūnyatā.*

Vetter shows how Nishitani uses his dialectical reasoning in an attempt to bring the reader to a positive experience. In his dialectical manner of reasoning, Nishitani wants, in Vetter's words, to:

> ... designate, with the aid of contradictory formulations, the properly inexpressible result of decidedly negative —but positively intended (the

---

[147] *Ibid*, pp. 46 ff.

[148] *Ibid*, p. 46.

[149] T. Vetter, "Buddhismus und Christentum: Zum buddhistischen Hintergrund von K. Nishitanis Dialektik (I) und zu F. Buris Vorschlag zum christlich-buddhistischen Dialog (II)," *Zeitschrift für Miss. Rel. Wiss.* 7 (1987): 1.

true destiny of man)— procedures of thought and experience; this may be regarded as necessary for the orientation of man —of those who desire to accustom themselves to such a practice of denial— and for the indication of an ethic related to the result.[150]

What is involved, he says in a closer description of the dialectical movement, is the denial of current views which want not only to deny, but also want to say something positive, even though one cannot express this in generally accessible concepts. For a receptive hearer, this is a meaningful way of speaking about what cannot be said. The dialectic of Nishitani continues beyond this; by heading straight through contradictions —which are manifested in such expression as *saṁsāra is nirvāṇa* and 'the not-self is the true self'— the Buddhist thinker attempts to bring the reader to another, purer experience of reality. The dialectical statements do not present the truth, to be sure, but do more justice to the matter of concern than straightforward pronouncements.[151]

With this it is already clear that Nishitani stands in the oldest line of the Buddhist tradition in which *samādhi* is considered to be a non-discursive precipitate, even though his way of arguing is less ancient.[152] For Nishitani, genuine reality is seen only from a 'place' where the level of intellectual knowledge has been breached; the deepest understanding is therefore non-intellectual.[153] One must transcend cognition and reason; at the same time, the ground of one's own existence lies here. Nishitani designates this experience as " 'ecstatic' self-awareness (*Gewahrnis*) of existence."[154]

In order to attain to genuine and penetrating insight into reality, the customary anthropocentric habits of thought must be fractured.[155] Nishitani indicates the 'place' where this reality is seen (or better said, realized) in more than one way in his book. He analyzes the problems of death and finitude, the status of reality (i.e., the lack thereof, emptiness), and he gives an analysis of defectiveness, of evil, and of sin. Along these three routes he points to the 'place' where understanding can be attained.[156] Thus Nishitani too attempts to say what cannot be said — a desire which according to Vetter arises from the 'ethics of compassion,' which induce the more advanced person to articulate his insights as *true teaching.*[157]

---

[150] *Ibid*, p. 19.
[151] *Ibid*, p. 10.
[152] *Ibid*, p. 8.
[153] Keiji Nishitani, *Was ist Religion?* authorized version, tr. Dora Fischer-Barnicol (Frankfurt 1982), p. 272 (Am. tr., *Religion and Nothingness* [New York 1982]).
[154] *Ibid*, p. 269.
[155] *Ibid*, p. 271.
[156] Vetter, pp. 12f.
[157] T. Vetter, *Der Buddha und seine Lehre in* Dharmakīrtis Pramāṇavārttika, an Introduction and German tr. (Vienna 1984), p. 18.

The goal of such analysis [and the transformation of the person] is to see things as they are. Nishitani explicates his view many times, with reference to Kant as well. The Copernican twist which Kant gave to epistemology must as yet be enacted in a revolutionary manner, he says.[158] Kant taught that one knew things according to the a priori forms and categories of human perception and understanding. This relation must now be inverted again so that, in a certain sense, a relationship to things again comes about in which we allow things to guide and direct us, and in which our knowledge *consists of correspondence to things*. The Buddhist philosopher can apparently agree with Kant in saying that man himself constitutes knowledge — in an even far more radical sense than Kant had in mind. The gist is that one must rid oneself of this 'projection' of the knowledge of things by taking a non-anthropocentric standpoint. One must transcend the *ego* in the Western *ego cogito* ... to a genuinely ec-static 'place.'[159] Nishitani —paradoxically enough— goes so far as to designate the new knowledge gained from the standpoint of such an (indescribable) 'abode' with a term from classical Western epistemology: *correspondence to 'things.'* What one knows is not Kant's *Ding-an-sich* (thing-in-itself), as distinct from the phenomenal object, but the 'thing-itself, as it appears without a fore and a back side.'[160] There is then an agreement, a correspondence, an identity between subject and object. This identity must be thought of far more strictly, according to Nishitani, than in the Western philosophical tradition, where a fundamental demarcation between subject and object remains. This separation is precisely what must be overcome. This can be accomplished only by transcending the province of reason in an experience of union.[161] One then attains the 'place' where each thing appears in its true reality, in its own proper being-thus (suchness).[162] Only when all thoughts of substantiality have been overcome, both with respect to what is perceived as well as to the perceiver, is there *śūnyatā* (emptiness), in which the principle of *equality* has been realized and in which no distinction endures.[163] To put it in our own words: If one manages to liberate oneself from all the representations and all the structures which one willy-nilly introduces into experience, then one is aware of the things themselves. This holds equally true for the 'outside' of perception as for the 'inside.' A continuous field of awareness is experienced in which the inside and the outside of experience have been unified. Nishitani speaks of this experience as 'self-realization of reality,' of which he says: "The self-realization of reality occurs only in such a

---

[158] Nishitani, p. 227.
[159] See Nishitani, pp. 55 f.
[160] *Ibid*, p. 226.
[161] *Ibid*, pp. 192 f.
[162] *Ibid*, p. 182.
[163] *Ibid*, p. 177.

way, that it produces a *true* becoming-real of our existence."[164] The personal involvement of the subject in this cognitive process is apparent here. People are attached to their thoughts, themselves, and their possessions. Modern technological society with its advertising machinery nourishes greed and teaches people to understand themselves in terms of the possessions with which they surround themselves. People are egoistic but one can only attain true insight and achieve liberation if one conquers one's *ego*. One must *realize* that one's ego is *śūnyatā* (emptiness). If one does —with great difficulty— realize this, then one realizes his true non-ego.[165] In the experience of enlightenment, two things are involved according to Nishitani: a psychological and an ontological event. We can understand this in the following way. *Samādhi* apparently has a psychological side; it concerns the transformation of an attached, alienated personality into a 'true person,' *ego/non-ego,* no longer alienated and egocentric. *Samādhi* is ontological in the sense that in *samādhi,* one 'is' at one with reality.[166] If one succeeds in both thought and experience in relinquishing all and any substantiality in things and in one's own mind, then a continuous field of reality remains with which one is uninterruptedly at one. This experience rises beyond the classical opposition between idealism and realism as they are known in Western philosophy. Taken strictly, things are neither idea nor thing. In non-dual experience this opposition is surmounted.

In this experience, the hold of suffering has been broken. In effect, the course of *saṁsāra* (rebirth) has been abolished. *Saṁsāra* itself may not be ascribed any substantiality either. Nishitani can, on this account, give a non-mythological, Buddhist interpretation of the 'myth' of rebirth, adding a reference to the Christian theologian Bultmann.[167]

Nishitani heavily emphasizes, as does Nishida, the 'place' where one gains this experience. It is an 'abode' which one must reach.[168] This is the 'place' (one could say, 'a no-place/place'), where reality appears as it *is.* Here, in the *field of emptiness,* things are truly the things themselves. Everything together is nothing or (*sive*) being.[169] Here there is identity between contraries, and so between being and non-being, between being and knowing.[170]

As for the concept of truth, we can ascertain that Nishitani speaks in a very qualified manner of the correspondence between thought and

---

[164] *Ibid,* p. 45.
[165] *Ibid,* pp. 74, 378; see Vetter, "Buddhismus und Christentum," p. 14.
[166] Nishitani, p. 260. Dunkel, mentions an early commentary on Nāgārjuna, which uses *satya* in an epistemological and in an ontological sense; afterwards *satya* has both meanings (knowledge/being), p. 25.
[167] Nishitani, pp. 271 ff.
[168] H. Waldenfels, *Absolute Nothingness: Foundations for a Buddhist–Christian Dialogue,* tr. J. W. Heisig (New York 1980), p. 42.
[169] Nishitani, pp. 259, 236.
[170] *Ibid,* p. 257.

being, and even of the identity of 'thought' and 'being.' Waldenfels uses the common sense expression 'as it is' many times for 'truth.'[171] What this actually signifies with respect to Nishitani is the *absolute truth,* and not *true doctrine.* This absolute truth is not a theory, but an open-minded awareness of reality with which one is at one. Things are then no longer objects; the ground of all things is experienced.[172]

Vetter believes that the identification of things, including the *skandhas,* with *śūnyatā,* an identification also found in Nishitani's work, stems from the *Hṛdaya Sūtra,* an Indian text, perhaps from the 3rd century C.E., which became very popular in China and Japan. Matter is equated with emptiness in this *sūtra.* Vetter remarks that one might read this text with Nāgārjuna's distinction between the two truths as backdrop. With the denial of truth at the first level of the human mind, Nāgārjuna meant to lead people towards the second level.[173] In the course of history, the distinction between the two truths continually provided cause for estimating the lower truth very lowly. The value of the lower truth, however, is that it leads to the higher, absolute truth, the experience of things as *emptiness.* What is involved is another kind of experience of ordinary reality, and not a mere relinquishing of this reality. Nishitani expresses this with his dialectical terminology of self/not-self and *saṁsāra sive nirvāṇa.* Nishitani's exposition can be understood as an attempt to show people ensnared by attachment the path to attain deep insight into reality as *śūnyatā,* and thus to liberation from attachment and suffering.

§ 4 The Path and the Truth: other religions

With this section we will close our discussion of the Buddhist view of truth and religion. First we will draw some conclusions from the reflections presented and we will briefly examine the tolerant attitude of Buddhism. Then we will summarily present Nishitani's and Abe's view of Christianity. Here again it becomes apparent that the appraisal which one religion has of the other springs from the content of belief.

Three mutually related notions are of fundamental significance for the Buddhist attitude towards those of other faiths:

(1) The doctrine of the two truths (which includes the resistance to reification).
(2) The idea that every human being must achieve liberation through personal transformation.
(3) the idea of rebirth.

---

[171] Waldenfels, pp. 43, 99, 139, 142.
[172] Nishitani, pp. 258, 186.
[173] Vetter, "Buddhismus und Christentum," p. 3; see also Dunkel, p. 24.

(1) The doctrine of the two truths makes all doctrine a relative matter. Even though the Buddhist *dharma* is *true* in a certain sense at the level of the relative world, seen from an absolute point of view, the relative truth is only an attempt to point out another perspective on reality. The *dharma* is therefore not a doctrinal whole which must be forcefully maintained to the exclusion of all other insights. On the contrary, it is possible to be appreciative of insights from other traditions which lead towards the alteration in perspective which Buddhists favour, or which at any rate imply a critique of the customary, estranged way of thought. It is quite possible to say of others that they have seen something of the true nature of the world, or that they, having learnt from experience, are on the way to discerning that the world is *dukkha* and *anitya*. We saw how Suzuki could appreciate certain currents in Western thought because of their skepticism; Nishitani believes that Nietzsche and Heidegger had deep understanding.[174] By making the doctrinal beliefs relative, there is room for regarding highly the value of other insights. However, no matter what value may be ascribed to certain insights from outside the Buddhist tradition, the value of someone's understanding ultimately depends on the degree in which it helps someone to tread the spiritual path. The mere acceptance of doctrine is criticized. The truth is likelier a way or a path than a description of worldly reality. Many Buddhist masters therefore do not attach much importance to the theoretical presentation of doctrine, and focus entirely on meditation and personal transformation. The nature of the *dharma's* truth (in the sense of relative truth) is not so much that it describes the world as it is (no matter how often this expression might crop up), but far more that it offers people handles for attaining a different view of reality. The doctrines offer some central insights which are fundamental in terms of the Buddhist perspective for discovering the misleading character of the ordinary experience of reality. If someone becomes somewhat aware of it, one will be prepared to tread the spiritual path.[175] With regard to other religious beliefs, this means that inasmuch as they tend towards the alteration in perspective known as *śūnyatā*, they will be positively appraised, but that, on the other side, they must be criticized since doctrine is merely relatively true (and many religious currents are not even aware of this relativity).

(2) In their evaluation of other religions, the emphasis on *personal* transformation thus plays an important role. This second factor determining the attitude to those who think differently is closely related to the first

---

174 Nishitani, pp. 110 f., 169.
175 On the role of *śraddhā* (faith) at the beginning of the spiritual path, Beckh, pp. 151 ff., compare pp. 206 ff.; Jayatilleke, pp. 383-99; Conze, pp. 47 ff.; on authority, Jayatilleke, pp. 376, 169-204, and pp. 416 ff., 467; see W. C. Smith, *Faith and Belief*, pp. 20 ff.

point. Buddhism does not strive for worldly power.[176] It has no strong national or international organizations.[177] There is no desire to impose doctrine on others, only the desire to help them liberate themselves from the wrong way of experiencing reality. The concern is strictly *liberation*, which is liberation from *karma*, from the chain of dependent origination which sustains projected reality. The aim is not compulsion of others, but their liberation. The emphasis on the *path* which everyone (in this life or the next) must travel implies that one person has progressed further in this life than another. The people with more understanding have learnt to regard others in terms of how far along they are. The desire is not to enlist others for certain beliefs, but to teach or tell them those things which can aid them in advancing further along at their own stage of development. *Compassion* is the word by which this benevolent disposition towards others is designated. The term 'neighbourly love' can still be conceived of in such a manner that the person who loves another likewise expects love from the other; as the saying goes, 'love is a two-way street.' Compassion, however, can come from one side. From a recognition that one has seen something of the truth, one can feel compassion for those who are not as far and thus trap themselves in what is unprofitable. This disposition on the part of the more advanced does not mean that one allows oneself to be commended for his deeper insight; on the contrary, having partially realized detachment and non-ego implies that there is no longer a self to be proud of, or to esteem as more important than others. What matters in Buddhism is *kindness, clarity, and insight*.[178]

(3) The third factor is closely related to this last point: the doctrine of rebirth. The content of belief is determinative for how one views others. If one believes that people must deplete their *karma* through a long cycle of lives, then one will not begrudge them time to attain more understanding. By way of comparison, think of the conceivable notion that all who do not adhere to the true faith are in effect disobedient and worthy of doom; that notion will lead to a different approach to one's fellow man, regardless of good or bad intentions.

An obliging and tolerant attitude towards those who think differently allows, accordingly, of explanation. This does not mean that the substance of all belief is regarded as equally good. Examples of controversies are easy to find. The purpose of the *anātman* doctrine is —within the current relations— to undermine the Hindu idea of the self. There is also objection,

---

[176] Buddhism was protected in India by Aśoka (about 250 B.C.E.), see Conze, *Buddhist Thought*, pp. 89 ff. In Tibetan Buddhism as well, the Dalai Lama had worldly authority, which was primarily conceived of as spiritual leadership.

[177] See M. Palihawadana, "A Buddhist Response: Religion beyond Ideology and Power," in *Christian Faith in a Religiously Plural World*, eds. D. G. Dawe and J. B. Carman (Maryknoll 1978), pp. 39 ff.

[178] Compare the title of the volume of lectures of the fourteenth Dalai Lama, *Kindness, Clarity, and Insight* (Ithaca 1985).

as we shall see later, to the notion of god. Conflicts of view with respect to other traditions also exist in the area of the relative or conventional truth. Buddhism too is familiar with *internal* differences. We have already mentioned in passing the disagreements about the core of human identity, and about the doctrine of the *moments* in early Buddhism.[179] Kamstra describes the tolerance of Buddhism in India; this toleration and openness is probably accountable for the disappearance of Buddhism in India.[180] Buddhism absorbed all kinds of Hindu elements. The emphasis on the path of salvation and the exercise of concentration provided occasion for the acceptance of the co-existence of various forms of Buddhism. Buddhism in India was tolerant. In China, Buddhism underwent an identity crisis in the 4th century C.E.[181] These circumstances gave rise to "formulations of belief which clearly indicated who belonged and who didn't," says Kamstra.[182] From the moment that Mahāyāna Buddhism came into conflict with other religions, the excellence of its own tradition above that of all other religions was stressed.[183] Formulations were later developed in China and Japan whereby others' purity of doctrine could be tested.[184] Next to forms of syncretism and great tolerance towards popular religion, there were conflicts among the Buddhist 'experts' and the 'real' adherents concerning what was true — although most of the time it was not denied that the contrary party might attain salvation.[185] We have already seen that Nāgārjuna opposed the teaching of the factors of existence (*dharma*); in many other writings one encounters the combatting of other views.[186] Apparently not all relative truth is equally good. The fundamental Buddhist perceptions can —to a certain degree— be put into words. Although the formulations are relative truth, they apparently have enough value to matter, and therefore do, to a certain extent, permit discussion. As the core of an *insight* is approached, the conflicting views are apparently felt more strongly as opposition than simply as the other party valuing in a 'different way.' For debate, generally accepted ways of reasoning are recognized. The dialectic of Nāgārjuna as well as the *kōan* (cryptic saying) can only produce their effect when the validity of elementary logic is assumed at the level of day to day knowledge. In order to reach the highest level of understanding this lower level of knowledge must, to be sure, be transcended, but the truth is apparently also at stake at this level of relative truth.

---

[179] Conze, pp. 122-34, 105, 140 ff., 196.
[180] J. H. Kamstra, "Tolerant en Intolerant Boeddhisme," *Nederlands Theologisch Tijdschrift* 32 (1978): 92.
[181] *Ibid*, p. 90.
[182] *Ibid*, pp. 91 f.
[183] *Ibid*, p. 90.
[184] *Ibid*, pp. 104 ff.
[185] *Ibid*, p. 105.
[186] See Nāgārjuna, *Mūla-Mādhyamika-Kārikās*, Chapter 17; compare to the rejection of Hīnayāna ideas in (among others) *The Awakening of Faith*, p. 101.

An example of this attitude towards those who think differently is to be encountered with Abe and Keiji Nishitani. After a presentation of the Christian doctrine of God, Abe remarks that from a Buddhist perspective this concept of God is ultimately inadequate.[187] The experience that all things are *anitya* is inevitably connected to the chain of dependent origination. Nothing falls outside of that. The belief in a God who exists independently of things beyond causality is therefore unacceptable. Nishitani points out that the idea of God, human identity, and an enduring afterlife bespeak human attachment.[188] The Christian view on the deficiency of mankind does not extend far enough from the Zen point of view. Abe acknowledges that Buddhists and Christians agree on some of the aspects of human finitude; further evaluation of this and of the context in which it is interpreted quickly bring differences to light, however.[189] Human finitude is designated as sinfulness in Christianity. The nature of brokenness is seen differently than in Buddhism. Faith in salvation from destruction through Jesus Christ does not extend far enough either; it does not penetrate to 'ultimate reality.'[190] Abe has appreciation for Christianity, however, insofar as faith in God leads to an experience of reality in which justice and responsibility are central.[191] For this reason he believes that religions can learn from each other.[192] Nishitani challenges Christian theologians to analyze the concept of God further. Behind the notion of God's personality lies the un- or trans-personality of transcendence, in his estimation.[193] From this short exposition one can see how these Buddhist views of Christianity are related to the basic ideas of Zen.

---

[187] Abe, Masao, "Zen as Self-Wakening," in *Japanese Religion* 8, no. 3 (1975): 29.

[188] Nishitani, pp. 181, 328, 353, 123; see H. M. Vroom, "Aan het Nihilisme voorbij: de Godsdienstfilosofie van Nishitani" *Nederlands Theologisch Tijdschrift* 40 (1986): 147, esp. *n.* 26. Several more essays by Abe and Nishitani have been edited in *The Buddha Eye*, ed. Fred. Franck (New York 1982); as is Suzuki, the thinkers of the Kyoto School are highly appreciative of the *theologia negativa* of Meister Eckhardt.

[189] Masao Abe, "Man and Nature in Christianity and Buddhism," *Japanese Religion* 7, no. 1 (1971): 7ff.

[190] Abe, "Zen as Self-Awakening," p. 30.

[191] *Ibid*, pp. 33f.

[192] *Ibid*, pp. 34f., 25f.

[193] Nishitani, pp. 118, 129. For Nishitani's ideas about Christianity, see also his article "Ontology and Utterance," *Philosophy East and West* 31 (1981): 29-43; cf. Vetter, "Buddhismus und Christentum," pp. 23f., *n.* 22.

Chapter V

The Concept of Truth in Jewish Tradition

§ 1 Introduction

1.1 Preamble

In our presentation of the Jewish tradition's outlook on truth, we will follow the same outline as in the other chapters in the second Part of our enquiry. In the introductory sections we will sketch some of the main ideas in Judaism; we will thereupon give a concise sketch of historical developments within Judaism. In the second section (§ 2) we will examine in more detail some of the central ideas of Jewish thought. Occasionally the thesis has been defended that the 'biblical' 'concept of truth' has a colour all of its own, and that its meaning is the opposite of the so-called Greek concept of truth. The same holds true of the notion that Judaism has no dogmatics of its own, as does Christianity. The exposition in the second section is important in this regard; it can help us to discern the meaning and role of doctrine in the Jewish tradition. After such preliminary orientation, we will return to the concept of truth in the third section. Since a great deal has been written within Christian theology on the Biblical or Jewish concept of truth, it is somewhat surprising that it has been given comparatively little deliberate attention in Jewish thought. Our enquiry will therefore be directed to the nature and the value of doctrine in the context of Jewish tradition, for the question of the nature of doctrine is closely related to questions regarding the concept of truth. In the third section, after an exposition on *ĕmet̲* in the Bible, we will therefore delve into doctrine in classical rabbinic literature; we will then consider the thought of Maimonides, the great classical Jewish thinker, and the writings of two modern Jewish thinkers, Heschel and Fackenheim. To round out our discussion, we will return to the question of conflicting views within Jewish tradition with respect to doctrine and life, the appraisal of other religions, and we will consider what all of this teaches us about the concept of truth within Judaism.

1.2 Jewishness

The most characteristic and distinctive feature of the Jewish tradition among the major religious traditions is that Jewishness is determined by parentage. Expressed pointedly, one does not hold the Jewish faith, but one *is* a Jew. Jews are therefore liable to ask themselves different questions about their faith than adherents of other traditions. Others can ask what *Islam*, Christian faith, a Buddhist view, or the Hindu philosophy of life involves, or whether they want to remain Hindu, etc.? A Jew, however, is de facto confronted with the question of what his Jewishness means. He can try to avoid the question, he can live a secular life, or he can observe all of the orthodox regulations — yet he *is* and remains Jewish by birth. He is a member of a people which has been sustained and formed by a certain tradition and which has often been persecuted for that tradition.

Many Jews are secularized nowadays, and in that sense are not religious. Philosophies have sprung from circles of secularized Jews, in which a certain role and mission is assigned to the Jewish people in this world. We will not occupy ourselves with such thinkers. Our enquiry is focussed on religion and thus principally on believing Jews. In the third section we will be presenting Fackenheim's thought. He believes that even the existence of non-believing Jews also has religious significance. Being Jewish in the present world has intrinsic religious significance even apart from explicit belief in God. Be that as it may, it remains a fact that Jewish faith is connected with belonging to a people. Proselytes are incorporated into Israel if such is their desire, so that they and their descendants will henceforth belong to the Jewish people as well.

Perceptions of a more doctrinal nature which will demand our attention in the second section all stand within the context of this Jewishness. This people has been called by God; God has chosen it; it has taken on a special mission at Sinai. This people shall not, as other peoples, serve idols and live amidst injustice. This people shall serve only God, the Creator of heaven and earth, and obey His will. For orthodox Jews, being Jewish means living according to the regulations which God has given. These injunctions are to be found in the Jewish Bible (i.e., in what Christians call the Old Testament); their explanation is determined extensively by the *Talmud*. Both together count as God's revelation to Israel. If Israel performs God's will, He will be with Israel in a special way. God has accordingly found in Israel a partner who has assumed responsibility for helping along God's plan for the world. Given the age-old persecution of the Jews, especially by Christians, the Jewish tradition has been accompanied through the ages by many questions as to the content of God's calling, God's presence, and the meaning or meaninglessness of suffering.

1.3 Developments in Jewish tradition

In this sketch of the development of Judaism, we will follow the exposition by Robert Seltzer.[1] Seltzer distinguishes four periods in Jewish history: (1) the period in Israel and the environment of Babylon, up until the beginning of the Common Era; (2) the period up until late antiquity, classical rabbinic Judaism; (3) the Middle Ages and early modern times; (4) the modern era.

(1) According to the narrative of Genesis, the first book of the Bible, God created the world and mankind. After Adam and Eve had sinned, they were expelled from Paradise. Upon the degeneration of the human race, God caused mankind to perish in the deluge, save for Noah's family with whom He had made covenant. In later centuries, God called Abraham out of Mesopotamia, and eventually brought him to Israel, the promised land. Drought drove his grandson Jacob to Egypt, where the Israelites remained as slaves for centuries. Under Moses' command, they fled Egypt and wandered through the desert until they finally settled in Israel. In the desert God gave Israel the law as a sign of His covenant. Israel's share in the covenant was that the people would keep the commandments and thus serve God. According to the book of Joshua, the Jews first purified the land of Canaan of its original inhabitants, because they served idols and Israel was to live monotheistically. For several centuries, the Jews lived in a kind of federal association of twelve tribes until the time that they chose a king, King Saul. The second king, David, captured Jerusalem from the Jebusites and made Jerusalem the capital. During David's reign, the Jewish kingdom achieved its widest boundaries.

Traditions up until the time of David are known to us from the biblical writings. Scholars generally assume that these traditions underwent quite a long history of composition, and that the final written form was not fixed until during or after the Exile.[2] Scholars sometimes point out the literary nature of all the historical narratives up to the time of the kings. Many Canaanite tribes would by then have been absorbed, in effect, into the Jewish people, and this implies that not all of the forefathers of the Jews had stood at the foot of Mount Sinai. The historical account of the period of the later kings is considered to be more reliable, but here too it is pointed out that the historical authors wrote in terms of religious points of view, or, perhaps all too humanly,

---

[1] R. M. Seltzer, *Jewish People, Jewish Thought: The Jewish Experience in History* (New York 1980).

[2] See C. Houtman, *Inleiding in de Pentateuch* (Kampen 1980), esp. pp. 251 ff.; also H. Jagersma, *Geschiedenis van Israël in het Oudtestamentisch Tijdvak* (Kampen 1979), e.g., pp. 263 ff.

were swayed considerably by the outlook of the group to which they belonged.[3]

Shortly after the reign of David and his son Solomon, the kingdom broke up into two smaller kingdoms. The Northern Kingdom was subjugated by Assyria in 732 B.C.E. The Southern Kingdom was crushed in 587, and Jerusalem was demolished by Nebuchednezzar, ruining the first temple, which had been built by Solomon. A portion of the Southern Kingdom's people were carried into Exile in Babylon. The major biblical writings were collected and edited during and after the Exile, including the *Torah*, a large historical work (Joshua-Judges-Samuel-Kings), as well as prophetic traditions from before the Exile (Isaiah, Jeremiah, Ezekiel). Many Jews returned from Babylon after about half a century; they were permitted to rebuild the temple (starting in 538 B.C.E.), so that the temple cult prescribed in the Torah could be resumed. Several more prophecies stem from the period after the return; no prophets arose in Israel thereafter. A tradition of wisdom teachers flourished and several biblical writings had their source here. Israel later came into the Hasmonian sphere of influence, one of the royal houses which arose after the disintegration of Alexander the Great's empire. Under the leadership of the Maccabees, the Jews resisted the conversion of the temple into a heathen cultic site. Although the influence of Hellenistic culture made itself felt, the Jews sought to integrate this into their own religious tradition. The belief in a resurrection of the dead at the end of time arose in this period, and was later to play an important part in Christianity and Islam.

(2) Jewish communities were established throughout the Hellenistic world during the period of classical antiquity, and later in Rome too. The Roman occupation provoked a new insurrection, the Jewish war (66–70 C.E.), resulting in the destruction of the second temple. Of the various religious groups, the Pharisees obtained the greatest influence. Out of their circles came the rabbis, religious leaders who earned their own living, but who used their remaining time for the study of the Bible and the leading of the Jewish communities. Most Jews lived in Israel, but since the Exile many Jews also lived in Babylon. The life of the Jews under the rule of heathen sovereigns required enormous adjustments of the Jewish tradition to the altered circumstances. The *hermeneusis* of the biblical commandments was authorized with an appeal to the oral tradition which God had given next to the written Torah.[4] This tradition had reached the rabbis orally. It was both possible and proper, in accordance with a number of hermeneutical rules, to adapt the Jewish tradition recurrently to altered circumstances.

---

[3] This is the accentuation given by the so-called materialistic reading of Scripture, which distinguishes between the texts of oppressors and the texts of the oppressed; e.g., M. Clévenot, *Een Materialistische Benadering van de Bijbel* (French edn. 1976; Baarn 1979).

[4] See also E. Fackenheim, *To Mend the World* (New York 1982), pp. 322f.; J. L. Palache, *Inleiding in de Talmoed* (Amsterdam ³1980), pp. 30ff.

This process of reinterpretation mainly concerned regulations for the life of the Jewish communities (*halakah*), but also included considerations and views regarding the content of faith (*haggadah*). The interpretations given by various rabbis formed part of the oral tradition from then on. In the course of time, many written collections arose, called the *Midrashim*. The most important compilations of traditional material, primarily *halakah*, but also *haggadah*, are the two *Talmudim*, the one from Palestine and the other of Babylonian provenance. Characteristic for both the *halakah* as well as the *haggadah* is the rabbinic insistence on founding their opinions on concrete biblical texts. Much *haggadah* consists of sermons or fragments of sermons, but stories (*haggadah* literally means 'telling') and speculations about God and His intentions have also found a home here. All these collections of *haggadah* and *halakah* together are called rabbinic literature. The Babylonian *Talmud* is the most significant compilation next to the countless *Midrash* collections. They cover the period from the beginning of the 1st century of the Common Era to the 5th/6th century (Babylonian *Talmud*), with an extension of several centuries for the later *Midrashim*. The *halakah* material from the early period is recapitulated in the *Mishnah*; this contains large complexes of laws and regulations in thematically ordered form, without the customary references to biblical texts. The Palestinian (or Jerusalem) *Talmud* and the Babylonian *Talmud* arose thereafter from commentaries and additions to the *Mishnah*. Together with the biblical writings, the *Talmud* belong to the authoritative books of Judaism.[5]

(3) The Jews in the area of the Euphrates and the Tigris came under the sway of Arabic domination during the middles ages. The Muslims regarded the Jews as 'people of the book.' The Jews retained their social status, in the sense that Jewish communities could lead their own life. In Spain especially, Judaism experienced a period of flowering. Jews lived in Christian countries as well, where they suffered persecution at times.[6] In the Arabic countries, the first Jewish philosophies evolved. Familiarity with the thinkers of Greek antiquity was gained via Muslim theology. Moses ben Maimon (1135–1204 C.E.) was the greatest Jewish philosopher of his time (and perhaps the greatest ever). Maimonides presented a Jewish philosophical theology, *The Guide for the Perplexed*. He was strongly influenced by Aristotle in his philosophical thinking.

The Middle Ages are also the time in which Jewish mysticism blossomed, marked by the writing of the great works of the Cabbala. The Jewish population of Germany expanded into Poland and Lithuania.[7] In times when they suffered less from discrimination and persecution, they could manage to live a properly Jewish life according to the guiding rules of the rabbis.

---

[5] Seltzer, p. 269. From Prof. dr. A. van der Heide I received very valuable suggestions concerning the issue which is dealt with in the text.

[6] *Ibid*, pp. 360ff., 371.

[7] *Ibid*, pp. 454ff.

From about the 15th century they frequently lived in ghettoes, being obliged to do so by sovereigns and city governments.[8]

(4) The inception of the modern period did not begin at the same time for all Jews. By developing his own thought, Spinoza found himself excluded from the Jewish community. At a later time, prosperous Jews like Mendelssohn in Germany were in touch with the Enlightenment.[9] The French Revolution entailed an immense change for the Jewish community.[10] People were seen increasingly as individuals and less as members of certain groups. For the Jews this meant that they were no longer regarded as one nation which had a certain, albeit insecure, position in various countries. Instead, their religious community was seen as one religion among others, while the area of the state became neutral in more and more countries. Thus faith became a matter of private conviction on the part of the citizens. The authority of the rabbis changed due to this; they were no longer judges possessing a certain official competence within the Jewish community, but simply the spiritual leaders of the Jewish religious community.

In intercourse with European culture and Western philosophy, a number of new currents presented themselves within Judaism, as elsewhere.[11] A Reform movement arose as well as neo-orthodoxy. In the spirit of Romanticism, some began to reflect on the distinctive nature of the Jewish religion, on its 'essence.' In addition, people of Jewish extraction sometimes disengaged themselves from Judaism. Some had themselves baptized in the Christian church, either due to conviction or as an admission ticket to Western culture. Others, such as Karl Marx, turned against religion in general, and sometimes against Judaism in particular.

Just as many Jews were starting to find recognition as citizens, a new wave of anti-Semitism arose. Reference was made to the exclusivism of early Judaism and the part which Jews had played (albeit by force of circumstances) in society. One of the Jewish responses to this emerging anti-Semitism was the Zionist movement. It was initially sustained mainly by secularized Jews, since they had to find a solution to their Jewishness more urgently than to the question of faith.

The events of the thirties and forties in Germany are, sad though they be, familiar enough. The holocaust of the European Jews by the Nazis —unchecked by the population of other European countries for various reasons— made its mark on post-war Judaism. Many Jews from Eastern Europe have since reinforced the Jewish community in North America, which had its origin in 1654 and which has been augmented by

---

[8] J. Katz, *Exclusiveness and Tolerance* (1961; rpt. Westport, Conn. 1980), pp. 131 ff.

[9] *Ibid*, pp. 169 ff.; see Seltzer, pp. 557 f.

[10] Katz, pp. 182 ff., 188; Seltzer, pp. 521 ff.; this is a recurring theme in Fackenheim: Jews are accepted; not as Jews, however, but as 'men'; Judaism is thus conceived of as a religion (not as a 'nation'), analogous to other 'religions.'

[11] Seltzer, pp. 580 ff.

large numbers of Jewish immigrants since the previous turn of the century. Many Jews also migrated to Israel, which acquired independence in 1948. The state of Israel occupies an important place in contemporary Jewish thought. According to Eugene Borowitz, a substantial development has taken place in the large Jewish community in the United States since the Six Day War of 1967, for it represented the threat of a second holocaust.[12] The loss of the 'homeland' was threatening to the Jews in the *Gālût* (diaspora/Exile), and many secularized Jews again became aware of their Jewishness, Borowitz maintains.

Contemporary Judaism contains many currents. There are orthodox, Chassidic, Reform, liberal, and secularized Jews in Israel as well as in the United States and many other countries —altogether about 15 million.[13] The degree of adaption to Western culture plays a role in the distinctions between the groups, but so do differences in spirituality (e.g., between the orthodox and the Chassidim). One of the most important aspects in which the various currents distinguish themselves from each other is the degree to which they feel obliged to the traditional regulations.

§ 2 Central Insights

2.1 Life

The most notable feature of Jewish doctrine is that it is entirely rooted in life. In Hellenistic Judaism, faith acquired a more intellectual tone; it then started to mean belief in one God.[14] In the (Jewish) Bible, faith is the response of mankind to God's promises and to His manifestation and acts. Faith is trust in the existence of divine providence, according to Urbach's characterization of Jewish faith during the period of the rabbis.[15]

Faith is thus faithful life in obedience to God's commandments and prohibitions. This way of experiencing faith is determinative for whether a doctrine has a relatively central or peripheral position. By *central,* we understand that certain *perceptions* belong to the deposit of Jewish faith in such a way that they cannot be separated or surrendered, and that the rabbis generally agree about them, while their contradiction is understood as unbelief.[16] Such substantial beliefs are the belief in the oneness of God, the election of Israel and the gift of the Torah, the resurrection of

---

[12] E. Borowitz, *Choices in Modern Jewish Thought* (New York 1983), pp. 13 f.

[13] 0.4% of the world's population, according to a publication by the WCC, *My Neighbour's Faith — and Mine* (Geneve 1986), p. 53; see *Lexikon der Religionen*, ed. F. König and H. Waldenfels (Freiburg 1987), p. 556.

[14] E. E. Urbach, *The Sages: Their Concepts and Beliefs*, tr. I. Abrahams (Jerusalem-²1979), I, 32 f.

[15] Urbach, pp. 34, 36.

[16] See M. Kadushin, *The Rabbinic Mind* (New York ³1972), pp. 347 ff.; cf. § 3.2.

the dead, and the coming of the Messiah. There is great freedom of belief surrounding this core with respect to numerous problems of faith, such as the relation between God and suffering, and, therefore, between the election and obedience of Israel and its often sorrowful lot throughout the ages. In addition, systematic reflection on faith such as Christian and Hindu theology has hardly occured until the time of the philosophizing Jewish thinkers of the Middle Ages. Despite the great authority acquired by Maimonides in particular, the fragmentary approach to the great problems of faith remained characteristic of Judaism; it was not suppressed by scholastic thought. We will return to these matters in the third section (§ 3). In this section we will direct our attention to the doctrine of the rabbis from the first four centuries C.E., called the 'wise,' whose thoughts were collected in the *Mishnah, Talmud,* and *Midrashim.* Urbach has written a standard work in which he has summarized rabbinical thought, primarily on the basis of the *haggadic* portions of the rabbinic literature.[17] He makes quite plain that he can do no more than attempt to show the unity of very scattered remarks and to offer some insight into the discussions which were carried on in rabbinical circles for generations. The work of Urbach can be regarded as representative of orthodox Jewish thought up until our time.

2.2   Election and covenant

From among the people of the earth, God, the creator of heaven and earth, has chosen Israel to be His people. God called Abraham. He later gave His people Israel the law, or Torah.[18] The rabbis tell the story that God offered the law to the seventy peoples of the earth, but that only Israel wanted to accept the Torah. The election of Israel involves a mission. The Jews have assumed the obligation to keep the 613 laws; God has assumed the obligation of being near to His people.

Authors from outside of Judaism have sometimes remarked that the Jews esteem themselves because of God's preference for their people. The election of Israel is understood as a kind of boasting about a special closeness and love of God of which other peoples are deprived. This interpretation of Israel's election is obviously incorrect. The doctrine of the election and of the covenant between God and Israel is exclusive to be sure; according to this belief, the position of the people of Israel differs from that of all the other peoples of the earth. But the mission which Israel has assumed within the covenant is extraordinarily difficult;

---

[17] Urbach, pp. 1 ff., 17 f.; see also *The Mishnah: Oral Traditions of Judaism,* selected and translated by E. J. Lipman (New York 1970); S. Schechter, *Aspects of Rabbinic Theology: Major Concepts of the Talmud.* (1909; rpt. New York 1961); and Palache, *Inleiding.*

[18] Urbach, pp. 315 ff., 400 ff.

the fate of the Jews is sometimes harsh. The election has frequently brought more suffering and poverty than prosperity.[19]

2.3 The revelation

The Jewish Bible (Old Testament), is the revelation of God. Since Israel was established by the covenant at Sinai in which God gave Israel the law, the Torah is the heart of the revelation. To be more exact, the commandments and prohibitions in the Bible are the revealed will of God. The rest is the history which God has traveled together with His people, the prophets' summons, and the songs of the temple cult. All of these together shaped an outlook on life in which one aims to perform the will of God.

The Torah has to be adapted to altered circumstances. During the centuries before the Exile, prophets made the will of God known. Prophecy ended after Haggai, Zechariah, and Malachi. A tradition of teachers who explained and applied the law took over the task of the prophets. Their understanding of the Torah is of course not exclusively determined by the written Torah. A written and an oral Torah were distinguished.[20] In addition to the written Torah (i.e., the law in the sense of the books of Moses, or sometimes in the sense of the whole Bible), there was the oral Torah, which, in the opinion of the rabbis, had been given to Moses by God along with the written one at Sinai. The oral Torah was transmitted orally for centuries. Afterwards it found a written deposit in the rabbinic literature, particularly in the *Talmud*. What has been decided and accepted by the majority of 'the wise' counts as oral Torah and thus belongs to the revelation. These traditions are believed to descend directly from the giving of the law at Sinai. All that has obtained general consensus, possibly after tough discussions, is authoritative revelation.[21] Anomalous and individual opinions do not have that status, yet they are not eliminated; they endure as witnesses of the process of the truth's unfolding. The rabbis taught that the oral Torah is the authoritative interpretation of the written Torah. *Haggadah* and *halakah* elaborate on the laws and stories from the Bible, but they can never fundamentally contradict what is written, or maintain something absolutely new. It is more a matter of discerning the right behaviour for situations which did not yet apply in earlier days, concrete applications, and deeper reflections on the substance of faith.

The division between Scripture and tradition, the clearly defined written Torah and the continually unfolding oral Torah, is extremely important to the Jewish concept of revelation. Even today, all the details

---

[19] *Ibid*, p. 525, on explanations of the conflict between the humble position of Israel in the world and its election.

[20] *Ibid*, pp. 286 ff.; Kadushin, p. 353.

[21] Urbach, pp. 292 ff.; W. Zuidema, *Gods Partner* (Baarn ³1979), pp. 29 ff.

of the *halakah,* as parts of the oral Torah, are divine revelation for
orthodox Jews. Whether or not one heeds them is not a matter of rational
insight, but of straightforward obedience. Deliberation concerning application
of the Torah gives rise to discussion of the reasons why certain commandments are observed. The reason one observes them, however, is not that
one discerns the reasons for such commandments, but because those
commandments come from God. There is joy in performing the law.[22]

2.4 Monotheism

The decalogue occupies a central position among the commandments and
prohibitions in the Bible. Israel must serve God and not worship any
idols, as the first commandment says. This does not merely mean that
Jews ought to be of the opinion that there is one God and must deny
that other Gods exist. Serving God is a way of life. This service is
expressed in keeping God's commandments. Sinning against one of the
other commandments is an implicit denial of the first commandment in
the sense that one does not take God's commandment or existence to
heart in one's life.[23]

The chief Jewish creed concerns the uniqueness and exaltedness of
God. The *Shema* is a central part of the Jewish liturgy: "Hear, O Israel, the
Lord is our God, the Lord is one" (Deuteronomy 6:5). Whoever denies the
confession of the one God is called *kōp̄er bā-'Iqqār* (he who denies the
chief principle of faith).[24]

God is designated by various names. The expression *Šĕḵînāh* connotes
His presence in the world. God is also called the Omnipresent One,
Almighty, and Holy. The divine name itself, the *tetragrammaton JHWH,* is
never pronounced; in more mystical currents, the attempt has been made
to penetrate the secret of the divine names.[25] Urbach points out, as do
others, that all reflection on the divine qualities or other matters of
faith does not serve any systematic or speculative purpose, but always
bespeaks a quest for God's presence and intentions in the midst of the
life which one leads.[26]

2.5 Humankind

Mankind is the image of God.[27] The whole of man is in the image of
God. The distinction between matter and idea made in the Platonic
tradition is rejected by the rabbis. Existence in the world is valued

---

[22] Urbach, pp. 392f.; Zuidema, pp. 24, 159.
[23] Urbach, p. 27.
[24] *Ibid,* p. 26.
[25] See Seltzer, pp. 429ff.
[26] Urbach, p. 65.
[27] *Ibid,* pp. 217ff.

positively as such, no matter how intensely one lives in anticipation of the coming age.

Faith in God's providence does not erase man's own responsibility. The question of how God's omnipotence and providence are related to mankind's freedom has of course been asked. Regardless of how this relationship was seen, the covenant and Israel's task in it always remained central.[28]

2.6 People, land, suffering

The land of Canaan was the promised land to which Moses brought the people from Egypt and which they conquered under Joshua's leadership. The land of Israel played a role in the covenant: Israel was allowed to live and be happy in the land as long as it served God. In actual fact, however, the temple was destroyed twice and the people were expelled from Canaan, first to Babylon, and later to the diaspora.

Orthodox Jews saw and see the *Gālût* (diaspora) as a punishment for the unrighteousness of the Jews. Many Jews, however, believe that the suffering inflicted on the Jews in the course of centuries goes beyond a just punishment. They do not know why suffering has overcome so many Jews and question where God is.[29] Believing Jews hold fast all the same to the mission which they have received from God.

The return of the Jews to the land of Israel is viewed by many Jews in relation to God's grace. The Jews are now in a position to build up a Jewish culture in their own land which accords with the laws which God has instituted. Orthodox Jews sometimes object to this viewpoint. There is a current which believes that Jews in the *Gālût* are in a much better position to exemplify the true religion of the one God for the benefit of the heathen. Sometimes secularized Zionist Jews do not ascribe any religious significance at all to the promised land. They believe that the Jews in Israel have the opportunity of becoming a country like any other nation.[30] Others, such as Fackenheim, then again point out a religious moment within secularized Zionism. This will be brought up in more detail in the next section.

2.7 Reward and punishment

Keeping God's law is rewarded by prosperity or in the hereafter. In like manner, punishment is the consequence of disobedience. The rabbis are capable of viewing these things with various shadings and nuances and also discern the problematical sides to it. But they insist on the fact that it is of great consequence whether the believer obeys or not, for his

---

[28] *Ibid*, pp. 255 ff.; 284 ff.

[29] *Ibid*, pp. 525 ff.; 420 ff.

[30] Cf. Seltzer, pp. 696 ff.; see also E. Schweid, "The Rejection of the Diaspora in Zionist Thought: Two Approaches," *Studies in Zionism* 5 (1984), esp. pp. 53 f.

own sake as well. Connected with this is the anticipation of the future,
both for the people as a whole as well as for the individual. The end of
the Exile, the coming of the Messiah and his kingdom, and the establishment
of a world which conforms to the will of God form the substance of such
future expectations.[31]

§ 3   Truth

In this section we will examine the concept of truth more closely. As
indicated earlier, the concept of truth is in fact at issue when we deal
with the role of doctrine in the *haggadah* and in the Jewish tradition. We
will first consider the so-called biblical concept of truth. We will then
examine the nature of doctrine in rabbinic literature. We will subsequently
deal with Maimonides. After that we will focus on two modern Jewish
thinkers, Heschel and Fackenheim. Finally, in § 4 we will examine Judaism's
relationship to other religions.

3.1   The biblical concept of truth

The Hebrew word *ĕmet,* usually translated 'truth,' has a broad
meaning. The rootedness of Jewish thought in Jewish life again becomes
apparent here. The concept of *ĕmet,* according to Van Dorssen, in his
philological study on the root *āman,* primarily means firmness. From this
primary meaning the word has received many different shades of meaning.
In considerations of the meaning of *ĕmet* in the Bible it is pointed out that
'truth' is always connected with interpersonal relations.[32] *Ĕmet* is an
ethical, and not purely theoretical concept. Since *theoria* was not the way
to ultimate understanding for the Jews —their ideal lay more in living
according to the way of God— true understanding is always connected to
the good Jewish life. The truth cannot, therefore, be separated from the
total context of life. According to Van Dorssen, *ĕmet* is always bound to
concrete situations and mutual intercourse in which concrete interests
play a part. The truth here is not concerned with statements which can
be disconnected from the rest of life. "The disposition as well as the
action proceeding from it are implicit in *ĕmet. Ĕmet* is accordingly not
only thought or said, but is also done, as is apparent from the expression
'doing the truth.' "[33]

The Hebrew concept of truth applies in the first place to the life
which people lead, that is to say, the life of the Jewish people within the
covenant with God. This can be detected in the usage of the word *ĕmet*

---

[31] Urbach, pp. 439f.; 657, 690.

[32] J. C. C. van Dorssen, *De Derivata van de Stam* āman *in het Hebreeuwsch van het
      Oude Testament* (Amsterdam 1951), p. 112.

[33] *Ibid*, p. 113.

which is much broader than in large segments of modern philosophical thought, where the concept of truth is related entirely to statements. In his enquiry into the meaning of *ĕmet* and its derivatives in the Bible, Van Dorssen summarizes the variations in the meaning of *ĕmet* as follows:

(1) permanence
(2) immutability
(3) genuineness, truthfulness (e.g., Jeremiah 10:10, "but JHWH is the truthful God")
(4) trustworthiness (Exodus 18:21, "trustworthy men")
(5) uprightness, truthfulness
(6) justice, righteousness (Zechariah 7:9, "render true judgments")
(7) faith, as an attribute of God or of people
(8) truth:
   (a) of certain words of people (Deuteronomy 13:14, "and behold, if it be true and certain"),
   (b) of prophetic utterances,
   (c) of words or promises of God,
   (d) speaking the truth in general,
   (e) as the truth revealed by God or the true religion (Daniel 11:2, "and now I will show you the truth");
   (f) as true wisdom for life;
   (g) as reality (Jeremiah 28:9, "that JHWH has truly sent him").[34]

From his broad study, Van Dorssen himself draws the conclusion that *ĕmet* never refers to an abstract theory which is 'true' apart from concrete life.[35] *Ĕmet* always applies to lived reality. It is said of statements, actions, and people, and of God too — the *ĕmet* God (Jer. 10:10). What is true is what is reliable, and that is what is established within the community of God and His people.[36]

In studying the Hebrew concept of truth one sometimes meets up with authors who point out the tremendous disparity with the 'Greek concept of truth' (by which people have in mind the notion of truth as knowledge in the sense of correspondence to reality). Some discern a conflict between the Hebrew and the Greek concept of truth. Two remarks are in order here. In the first place, one ought to bear in mind that a 'concept of truth' is a theoretical construction. A philologist such as Van Dorssen does not construct a concept of truth, but sums up shades in its meaning; indicating a primary meaning is sufficient for him, e.g., firmness. It is uncertain to what extent the primary meaning of *ĕmet* would have reverberated for the first listeners in all its gradations or

---

[34] *Ibid*, pp. 44, 76.
[35] *Ibid*, p. 112; see J. H. Vrielink, *Het Waarheidsbegrip: Een Theologisch Onderzoek* (Nijkerk 1956), p. 64.
[36] Van Dorssen, pp. 113f.; see also Vrielink, pp. 63ff.; G. Quell, *s.v.* '*alètheia*,' in *Theologisch Wörterbuch zum Neuen Testament*, I (Stuttgart 1933), pp. 233-37.

with the connotations given it by such situations as it was used in. In the second place, people often construct an erroneous opposition between the Hebrew and Greek concept of truth, in our opinion. To use an example from modern common sense philosophy, 'the cat is on the mat' is also true for Jews if and only if 'the cat *is* on the mat.' A Jew also naturally demanded that what was told him match reality. The point at issue is that the Jews had another view of reality than did 'the Greeks.' For the Jews, the reality within which statements, actions, and people could be 'true' or 'untrue' was the reality of God's covenant with His people. Doctrine did not stand free of life, but was tied up with it in an immediate way. That is the source of expressions such as 'doing the truth'; for the truth 'is' the law of God which leads unto life. This differs with the truth of propositions not in that what is said is 'untrue,' but in that what is said is not separated from the action of man among his people, in relationship to God.

The religious truth of Judaism is never separate from ordinary life. Religious truth does not allow of reduction to a doctrine which one could consider apart from Jewish life. The truth of living faith (that is, trusting in God) is always connected with life. The truth of this faith and of this life appears from the security which it provides. Just compare with the classical text in which the verb *āman* (from which *ĕmet* is derived) occurs in two senses: If you will not believe (*ta'ămînû*), surely you shall not be established (*tĕ'āmēnû*; Isaiah 7:9). This establishing occurs in life itself; it is not the legitimation of an abstract theory.

3.2   The nature of doctrine in rabbinic literature

Judaism has no well defined doctrine. It is frequently said that it has no dogmatics. But there is still reflection, of course. The rabbis deliberated concerning conflicting conceptions.[37] They reflected on the relationship between God's qualities, the fact that He is both good and just.[38] There is apparently a search for a coherent understanding of faith. And yet a clear system of confessional statements which one is required to believe is lacking. The first systematic confession is of late date, from Maimonides, and thus springs from the spirit of the Medieval thinkers.[39] The rabbis' typical 'form of thought' is fragmentary; one clarifies by narrating stories and does not attempt to give a logically constructed derivation of the doctrine from fundamental principles.[40] Characteristic of many of the stories is that they make one stop and think, and do not offer watertight answers to the questions of believers and of the rabbis themselves.

---

[37] Urbach, p. 186.
[38] *Ibid*, pp. 454ff.
[39] See Seltzer, pp. 395f.; J. Guttmann, *Philosophies of Judaism* (1964, from the German; rpt. New York 1973), pp. 176, 202f.
[40] See Urbach, p. 4; also Kadushin, *Rabbinic Mind*, pp. 5f.

It is not true, without further qualification, that Judaism has no doctrine. All Jews ought (properly) to believe in the one God, Creator of heaven and earth; the exodus from Egypt; the gift of the Torah at Mt. Sinai; the Torah as the revelation of God; and the resurrection of the dead.[41] Whoever cast doubts on these truths of faith was banned from the synagogue. But even though one can indicate some generally accepted beliefs, the binding tie lies not in believing *that*, but in living according to the Torah; in other words, in deliberate Jewishness. The *halakah* is more central than the *haggadah*. The purity and holiness of Israel is more dependent on the keeping of the Torah than on conscious agreement with a creed. It must not be forgotten that people belong to this tradition by birth and upbringing, and only exceptionally by choice at a later age. Jewish life is the binding element, or at least was until a few centuries ago. Still, a certain religious content remains in the background. One cannot celebrate the *Pesach* liturgy without answering the question: In what does this night differ from all other nights?[42] One must then believe that the events which are commemorated occurred in one way or another, and that the night of commemoration itself is also special, and thus different from all other nights. There is then some religious content. What is the nature of the doctrine which sustains living in accordance with the Torah?

The nature of doctrine has been analyzed profoundly by Max Kadushin.[43] He attempts to describe the peculiarity of rabbinical thought. He calls terms with religious content *value-concepts* as distinct from cognitive terms. (Cognitive) terms which aid people in describing and knowing things label things by isolating them from the context in which they stand. Discriminating thought breaks situations up and represents objects and their qualities as accurately as possible.[44] Value-concepts do the opposite. They connect things; they integrate experience in a comprehensive situation.[45] They indicate the relationships in which life transpires. They do not accomplish this in the manner of speculative theology or philosophy, however, which endeavour to give a logical analysis — consequently displacing value-concepts by cognitive concepts. But since cognitive concepts disintegrate situations, this is inadmissable. Moreover, one cannot, starting from piecemeal experiences, arrive at an understanding of the whole.

The totality of value-concepts which form part of the Jewish tradition have been transmitted since days of old.[46] They are of an entirely different

---

[41] Kadushin, pp. 340, 367.
[42] See Zuidema, *Gods Partner*, pp. 133ff.; S. Ph. de Vries, *Jüdische Riten und Symbole* (Dutch 1968; German tr. Wiesbaden ²1982), p. 124.
[43] Kadushin, *Rabbinic Mind* and *Organic Thinking* (New York 1938).
[44] Kadushin, *Rabbinic Mind*, p. 68, see p. 50.
[45] *Ibid*, pp. 69ff.
[46] See Kadushin, p. 49.

nature than cognitive concepts, according to Kadushin. Their significance is not fixed; Kadushin calls them indeterminate.[47] They have the capability of integrating disparate experiences into larger contexts. Their fluidity affords one room to interpret one's situation within the context of one's faith. To give an example, in the case of certain events one speaks of the closeness of God; in others, of His holiness and exaltedness. The concepts by which God's otherness and His closeness are indicated cannot be flawlessly combined in a theoretical system.[48] The tradition itself, however, gives indications as to what sort of situations should be connected with the one and which circumstances should be connected with the other. The tradition helps to interpret life; conversely, the occurrence of various kinds of situations makes application of the tradition possible and thus in turn interprets the tradition. The tradition remains an organic, living whole in this way. The understanding of the tradition is related to the understanding of the situation in which one finds oneself.[49] The tradition does not pass on a rabbinic system of thought, but the rabbinic experience of the world itself. Kadushin goes so far as to say that the terms of the rabbis themselves must be used in presenting their thought, otherwise their experience of the world will be omitted.[50] Kadushin also indicates the coherence in Jewish thought. A foursome of concepts is fundamental: God's righteousness (*Middat Hā-Dīn*), God's love and mercy (*Middat Raḥămīm*), Torah, and Israel.[51] Other concepts are subordinate to these four value-concepts. Some concepts are related because they are opposites. It is not possible, however, to bring all concepts into a hierarchical system.[52]

Thus we see that the Jewish tradition cannot be fixed in a dogmatic system according to Kadushin. The reason is not that the rabbis could not think accurately; their oftentimes acute analyses of *halakah* problems proves the opposite. No, the nature of reality itself, with which faith is concerned, resists systematic treatment. The experience of God in the midst of life can only be put into words metaphorically.[53] Kadushin speaks of a mystical awareness; he calls it 'normal mysticism' to indicate that it does not imply remoteness from the world. God is experienced in the context of normal life.[54]

It is precisely the relationship of the experience of the divine to ordinary life which carries with it the notion that everyone experiences

---

[47] *Ibid*, pp. 131 f.
[48] *Ibid*, pp. 324, 303.
[49] *Ibid*, pp. 30 f.
[50] *Ibid*, pp. 58 f.
[51] *Ibid*, p. 15, see also pp. 57 f.
[52] *Ibid*, p. 70.
[53] *Ibid*, p. 271.
[54] *Ibid*, p. 257, et passim.

faith in his own manner, and appropriates the tradition personally.[55] The diverse religious situations of the rabbis and their personal concerns are also the cause of the fact that the talmudic tradition itself is not a uniform whole. Many of the rabbis' conflicting opinions have been passed on in the *Talmud*, without any comment or attempt at resolution. As far as the *haggadah* is concerned, there is a large measure of freedom for opinion forming. One can find one's own way in the rich inheritance of the *haggadah* traditions.

We may conclude, if we have understood Kadushin well, that doctrine offers us understanding of the conditions for the Jewish life. The tradition informs us about Israel, about God and His will, His mercy and righteousness. Insight into the tradition is always related to personal experience. Only those who hold the tradition to be true will choose the *halakah* as the guiding light for their conduct.[56]

The doctrinal freedom in Judaism is great, and there is hardly any accumulation of dogma. Religious reflection is less deeply determined by Aristotelian thought than in the Christian tradition. The rabbis, who earned their own living, focussed less on speculative understanding and stringent dogmatic reasoning than on articulating the religious aspect of the situations in which they and their people found themselves.[57] The sermon and the poignant story have been far more characteristic of Judaism through the centuries than the philosophical tradition, as in Maimonides' case. The truth of doctrine hardly dissociates itself from the experience of life. On the one hand, the content of faith is a condition for the Jewish life; on the other hand, it is always understood in the context of Jewish life. True life is more than true doctrine, although it presupposes the truth of certain perceptions. Such an interpretation seems justified, when we bear in mind the meanings of *ĕmet* in the Bible. It is, we might add, also Kittel's contention that the rabbis' concept of truth does not diverge from the 'biblical concept of truth.'[58]

3.3 Maimonides

Moses ben Maimon (1135–1204) is the most influential medieval Jewish thinker. Originally from Cordoba, he settled in North-Africa. Maimonides lived in Cairo from 1165 until his death. He achieved renown as doctor, as *Talmud* scholar, and as Jewish philosopher. Among his works is the *Mishneh Torah*, the classical systematic recapitulation of the Jewish law. In it, and elsewhere, he gives a summary of the articles of faith. This summary is regarded as a deviation from the rabbinical tradition because

---

[55] See Kadushin, p. 272.
[56] See Seltzer, p. 262.
[57] See Urbach, pp. 4, 608 f.
[58] R. Kittel, "*ĕmet* im rabbinischen Judentum," *s.v. 'alètheia*,' in *Theol. Wörterbuch zum N. T.*, I, 237 ff.

the cognitive aspect of faith receives a different position than it had up to that point in the Jewish tradition.[59] The most important philosophical work of Maimonides is *The Guide for the Perplexed* (1190).[60] In it, Maimonides describes the view he had reached of God, of revelation, of the world, and of science. He indicates how a Jew formed by philosophy and science might understand his faith and interpret Scripture. Maimonides thus poses the problem which has not left the Jewish tradition since that time: the question as to the relationship between philosophy and faith, and the significance of both for the content of religious faith.[61]

Maimonides came into contact with Aristotelian philosophy through Arabic scholars (such as Al-Fārābī, Avicenna, and others). For Maimonides, the expression 'the philosopher says' means 'Aristotle says.' Maimonides is aware of the radical difference between Aristotelian philosophy and the Jewish tradition, but was also deeply struck by the many similarities. Religion and philosophy point to the same truth.[62] Maimonides is, all in all, the most important Medieval Jewish thinker.[63]

In the exposition which now follows, we will focus on the *Guide*. The work was written as an aid for educated persons who felt confused by the conflicting statements in Scripture and philosophy. He wants to demonstrate how one can believe in what the Torah says in a responsible manner.[64] At the same time, he wants to clarify a number of Scripture passages and expressions which are obscure to reason. Maimonides wrote for an intellectual elite. The bulk of the populace is incapable of comprehending the hidden meaning of Holy Scripture. Maimonides therefore deliberately wrote in such a way that only philosophically schooled people would be able to follow.

Maimonides gives *thought* a more prominent position than is customary in Judaism. The knowledge of God's acts and commandments was directly tied in with life, as we have seen; it is knowledge of Scripture and tradition. Maimonides first adds to this theoretical knowledge, that is, knowledge of the philosophy and science of his day. But, second, this new knowledge brings drastic changes in its wake. It pervades the knowledge related to faithful living. The nature of the knowledge which is transmitted within the Jewish tradition is modified, even though the relationship to that life remains. We will begin by examining what Maimonides says about knowledge in general. Knowledge concerning God and God's knowledge will subsequently be brought up.

---

[59] Guttmann, p. 203.

[60] The Arabic Title is *Dalālat al-Ḥaʾirīn* (1190); in Hebrew it is *Mōreh Nebukīm;* see Guttmann, p. 175.

[61] See Seltzer, p. 407.

[62] *Ibid,* p. 395; Guttmann, pp. 175 ff.

[63] See Guttmann, p. 173.

[64] M. Maimonides, *The Guide for the Perplexed*, tr. M. Friedländer (²1904; rpt. New York 1956), p. 2.

Typical for the significance which Maimonides ascribes to knowledge is what he writes concerning the perfection of man. Maimonides mentions two perfections of man. Besides the healthiest material condition, Maimonides counts as a second perfection that man become an actually apprehending being, knowing everything which a perfectly educated person can know about all that exists.[65] Whoever has aptitude for this perfection ought to take care that he apprehend such as there is to know. Knowledge itself is a value.

Maimonides points out that not all objects can be known by man in the same manner. Some objects which we perceive lie within the scope of the human mind, some do not, and yet others again only partially. Thought is not much different than sense perception in this regard. Just as the one has greater powers of observation than another, so the one understands by himself what another can never comprehend. Yet all knowledge has a limit. Certain things lie entirely beyond human conceptual faculties; we cannot determine exactly the number of stars or animals. Concerning some other things, people will never be able to finish thinking or speaking. Maimonides sums up four things which prevent people from discovering the exact truth: (1) arrogance; (2) the depth and difficulty of a subject; (3) incompetence and inability to understand what is capable of being understood as such; (4) prejudice and habituation to misrepresentations.[66]

We can detect the reason why Maimonides ascribes so much weight to knowledge when we examine his explanation of how cognition works.[67] Maimonides follows the Aristotelian tradition here. Before someone actually apprehends something, he must have a *potential* understanding of it. If someone understands, for example, a tree, then he apprehends the *form* of the tree. That is to say, one does not apprehend the tree in all the details of its unique manifestation, but in the not directly visible qualities which give a specific tree the form which it has as, for example, a cedar. If one abstracts and apprehends this form of the tree from its unique manifestation, then the abstracted form of the tree is in the human mind.[68] This means that the tree which is apprehended is not a non-mental object: "For in such a case the intellect is not a thing distinct from the thing apprehended."[69] What one apprehends is at the same time the abstract form of the tree and the acting intellect. In actuality, the intellect and the abstract object are one and the same, since the intellect is identical with its action, and the true nature and essence of intellect is apprehension. The intellect does not stand behind such comprehension, but is the apprehension itself. Intellect is active; the *intellectum* is thus

---

[65] *Ibid*, p. 313.
[66] *Ibid*, p. 41.
[67] *Ibid*, pp. 100f.
[68] *Ibid*, p. 100.
[69] *Ibid*, p. 100.

itself *intelligens*. Since the *intelligens* consists in the form (of the tree, for example), the intellect *is* the form. That is why Maimonides concludes that where the intellect acts, the intellect and that which is apprehended are one and the same thing. Whereas there are three things before the act of apprehension, i.e., man, the power of comprehension, and the abstract form (of the tree), in apprehending the tree there is only one thing.

This view of cognition embraces several aspects which are of importance in relation to knowledge concerning God. In the first place, knowing itself is a relation between subject and object, or better yet, a unity. In the second place, something happens to things in their objective existence in the cognitive process: 'the tree is changed into an abstract idea.' When we deal with the understanding of the images used by the language of Scripture concerning God, we will again encounter this idea of the transformation of what is known in its manifestation into an abstract idea which is apprehended.

Man cannot apprehend everything; as we have seen, some things are inaccessible to man. Maimonides has in mind here such things as the createdness of the world. He considers the proofs for God's existence in Aristotelian Islamic philosophy to be valid, but contends that rational thought cannot yield conclusive knowledge on the question of whether the earth was created or is eternal.[70] Man is dependent on revelation for certain insights.

Knowledge concerning God is partly gained through speculation. The existence of God and a number of God's attributes have been proven by the philosophers apart from any revelation. Thus reason supports what revelation says; philosophical reflection removes some doubts which can be held with respect to Scripture.[71] The attributes of God which can be apprehended by reason are the simplicity of God, His omniscience, omnipotence, and such like. What does not permit of demonstration by reason is —as we have already mentioned— the eternity of the world and the creation. Maimonides contends that speculation can yield no conclusion here; he refutes the Aristotelian arguments for the eternity of the world, then gives reasons for accepting creation, and in the end establishes that the issue remains undecided for reason.[72] Maimonides thus accepts the creation on the authority of the prophets. Prophecy teaches things which fall beyond the scope of philosophical speculation. One must be content with what can be known rationally; for what lies beyond, one must look to the Mosaic revelation.[73] All the same, Maimonides esteems the powers of reason highly. It is unacceptable to him that revelation and reason could lead to

---

[70] *Ibid*, p. 178. The Arab philosophers dealt with the same issue.
[71] *Ibid*, p. 155.
[72] *Ibid*, pp. 178 ff.
[73] *Ibid*, p. 198.

conflicting results.[74] If Aristotle had given conclusive proofs that the world had not been created, then the doctrine of creation would have to be rejected and Scripture interpreted differently.[75] No more accessible to reason in their entirety are the Commandments. The first two of the Ten Commandments are reasonably accessible, but not the rest.[76] The reasons for the Commandments have not all been given; some commandments have no reason save to exercise people in the service of God.[77]

Scripture imparts knowledge of God to those people who are incapable of philosophical speculation. That is why the Torah speaks the language of the people; in this way she is comprehensible to youth, women (!), and the common man. They do not understand the true meaning of the words in Scripture, but do perceive the necessary truths and ideals.[78] Maimonides sums up five reasons why the populace must be satisfied with the knowledge concerning God which the Scriptures impart and why they cannot be educated in pure metaphysics: (1) the subject is too difficult; (2) they have insufficient intelligence; (3) the preparatory study of logic, mathematics, physics, and metaphysics takes a long time; (4) a prerequisite for intellectual progress is behaviour of high moral standing; (5) people are compelled to squander much of their time to fill material needs.[79] It is therefore good that prophecy tells what many would otherwise never come to know before dying. All the same, Scripture only teaches the main points of the true understanding which leads man to true perfection. Scripture teaches the existence, omniscience, omnipotence, the will, and the eternity of God, Maimonides notes.[80] In addition, Scripture demands our belief in a number of truths which are indispensable for the regulation of our social relations, such as the belief that God is angry with those who disobey Him.[81] In summary, most people know God only on the basis of Scripture. Some, however, know God better. They not only believe that what Scripture says is true, but also *comprehend* the true meaning of Scripture — which is not always what is literally written.

Real knowledge of God is obtained by reflecting on what man can know by reason and from Scripture about God. Maimonides describes in detail the images with which Holy Scripture speaks of God's deeds. He constantly points out that words employed in reference to God are homonyms.[82] They mean something else in relation to God than they do in relation to people. For example, the line, "the heavens are my throne and

---

[74] Seltzer, pp. 395, 407; Guttmann, pp. 175 ff.
[75] Maimonides, p. 200.
[76] *Ibid*, pp. 221 f.
[77] See Maimonides, p. 311.
[78] *Ibid*, p. 44; see A. van der Heide, "De Grote Adelaar: Momenten uit het Werk van Mozes Maimonides," *Ter Herkenning* 13 (1985): 148 ff.
[79] Maimonides, pp. 44-49.
[80] *Ibid*, p. 313.
[81] *Ibid*, p. 314.
[82] *Ibid*, pp. 52 ff., 21 ff.

the earth a stool for my feet," means to say that heaven and earth testify to the existence and omnipotence of God.[83] The metaphorical language from Scripture is thus reduced to the terminology of philosophical knowledge about God. By such means, knowledge concerning God is improved. For it is an insult to God, according to Maimonides, to avow an erroneous conception concerning Him.[84] Philosophical apprehension of God is therefore important. One's knowledge of God must be purified. One ought not to ascribe any imperfection to God, nor any other qualities which might be quite good qualities for people to have, but not for God.[85] God is of such perfection that it cannot be expressed by human language. This perfection can be indicated by negative attributes, whereby it is made plain that one is aware of the fact that the terms which man employs are not really applicable to God. Only such usage of terms does justice to God's simplicity. Were one to impute positive attributes to God, one would violate the simplicity of His being.[86] The highest knowledge to which man can attain is that God exists, that He is a being to whom no creature is equal, and to whom it bears no resemblance.[87] This is the highest knowledge about God. Instead of speaking about God's body, one can learn to speak of God's incorporeity; instead of imputing positive attributes to Him, one can learn to ascribe attributes to Him only negatively. This is progress in the knowledge about God:

> every time you establish by proof the negation of a thing in reference to God, you become more perfect, while with every additive positive assertion you follow your imagination and recede from the true knowledge of God.[88]

Silence is praise of God.[89] The tetragrammaton (JHWH) is the only true divine name.[90] God is one, without attributes such as oneness, greatness, etc.[91] Philosophical reflection thus helps to purify our knowledge concerning God. A condition for such an exaltation of man to the deepest knowledge of God is that a man purify himself by conquering his desires. If one allows himself to be guided by his desires, one will merely come to accept a theory which agrees (all too) much with human inclinations. As long as bodily pleasure is regarded as an aim in itself, one dissipates his intellectual energy and degenerates to lust, hate, and war.[92] True knowledge of God is profoundly related to life. It is attained only by those who free themselves from their desires. Moreover, the knowledge of God itself is by no means simply theoretical. True knowledge of God is accompanied by

---

[83] *Ibid*, p. 21.
[84] *Ibid*, p. 52.
[85] *Ibid*, pp. 84, 35.
[86] *Ibid*, pp. 81 f.
[87] *Ibid*, p. 87.
[88] *Ibid*, p. 84.
[89] *Ibid*, pp. 85 f.
[90] *Ibid*, pp. 89 f.
[91] *Ibid*, p. 97.
[92] *Ibid*, pp. 327, 195, see pp. 312 f.

love for God. It is a precondition of love for God to know the true nature of things and discern the divine wisdom in them.[93] When he states that the true and highest perfection of man is possession of the highest intellectual faculties, Maimonides' concern is not with the intellectual alone. The highest which a human being can achieve is the knowledge and the love of God, *ḥokmāh*, wisdom. It is this wisdom which induces man to follow the path which God has charged him to follow, the path of love and justice.[94] The knowledge of God is always a relationship with God. For such a person who rejoices in the knowledge of God and frees his thoughts of worldly affairs, it is impossible that any evil befall him, since he is with God and God with him.[95] Knowledge for Maimonides is a relation of the person who knows to what (whom) he knows!

Not everyone can appropriate such philosophical understanding, though. For the majority of people it is sufficient to accept the central truths of faith and to keep the commandments in order to obtain life in the coming age.[96] Maimonides has summarized these beliefs in other works. He considered the following principles of faith to be essential: that God exists; that He is one, incorporeal, and eternal; that idolatry is absolutely forbidden; that there are true prophets, among whom Moses is unique; that the oral as well as the written Torah are divine and immutable; that God is omniscient; that God rewards and punishes; that the Messiah shall surely come and raise up the dead.[97] Faith encompasses not only these beliefs, but also the conviction that the object of faith is as we perceive it and know it in our soul.[98]

In this view of knowledge concerning God, Maimonides joins Aristotelian and Neo-Platonic elements, not entirely without inner tension.[99] The idea

---

[93] *Ibid*, p. 314.

[94] *Ibid*, p. 397; Guttmann, pp. 199 f.

[95] Maimonides, p. 389; on the relation of love to God, D. Hartman, *Maimonides: Torah and Philosophical Quest* (Philadelphia ²5738/1977), pp. 76 ff.; A. van der Heide, p. 155, points to the contemplative dimension of Maimonides' thought.

[96] Guttmann, p. 199, says that for Maimonides knowledge is a condition for the soul to obtain immortality. He tries to escape the conclusion that only thinkers will live in eternity (Guttmann, p. 202). Guttmann refers to the *Guide*, I, 70 and III, 27 (in our edition p. 106 and p. 313). On these pages Maimonides does not say that actual, developed knowledge of God is a source of eternal life, but that the Law seeks to train people in faith and to impart true and correct opinions when the intellect is sufficiently developed (p. 313). In my opinion it does not follow that only people who reach actual knowledge of God can or will inherit eternal life. Compare with how Maimonides elsewhere stresses that the Law of Moses should be acknowledged, not on the grounds of reason, but on account of Moses' teaching. See L. Jacobs, *A Jewish Theology* (London 1973), p. 290. See also Maimonides, p. 384: Men without religion are not human beings.

[97] Seltzer, p. 395; Guttmann, p. 202. See Maimonides' 13 principles of faith in the commentary on the tenth chapter of the *Tractate Sanhedrin*, cited in *The Commandments: Sefer ha-Mitzvoth*, by Maimonides, tr. C. B. Chatel (London 1967), I, Appendix, IV, pp. 272-80.

[98] Maimonides, *Guide*, p. 67.

[99] See Guttmann, pp. 197 ff.

that one can at bottom say nothing about God conflicts, to our mind, with belief in prophecy and revelation. It is permissible to ascribe attributes to God on the basis of God's deeds (grace, mercy, etc.), but this does not mean to say that God really 'has' these qualities which have been derived from the human world of intercourse.[100] The deepest knowledge about God is awareness of the incomprehensibility of God. Even though this knowledge remains immediately bound up with life for Maimonides, true knowledge of God for him is more theoretical and elitist in nature than it is within rabbinical Judaism.[101]

The tension between the Jewish inheritance and the philosophical teaching about God also attains prominence in Maimonides' view of God's knowledge. Maimonides insists on the unity of God. What we wrote earlier about Maimonides' view of knowledge was derived from a passage in which he speaks of *God's knowledge*. The intellect coincides with the (abstract) form of its object. The same holds true of God. The *intellectus, intelligens,* and the *intelligibile* are one in God.[102] For if there were a distinction between subject (*intellectus*), cognition (*intelligens*), and object (*intelligibile*) in the knowledge which God has, then God would no longer be one. God is perfect, so there can be no increase of knowledge in Him; He knows all things. *Intellectus* and *intelligens* are therefore one. But the object of knowledge is also one with the intellect in action. Accordingly, we can understand how Maimonides was able to state that, "He and the things apprehended are one and the same thing, that is to say, His essence."[103] Sometimes the inference is made that God knows only His own essence.[104] Maimonides rejects this idea. God's knowledge is then thought of as being too similar to human knowledge, even though the term knowledge too is used as a homonym in relation to God. In this way Maimonides wants to accommodate God's knowledge of things in their specificity, and not just in their abstract forms. God's knowledge of many things does not imply plurality; how God's unity can be possible even though He knows all things remains incomprehensible for human beings.[105]

We encounter no explicit treatment of the *concept of truth* in the *Guide*. On the basis of the above and on the basis of the passages in the *Guide* where the English translation uses the word *truth*, we can, however, say something about it:

(1) The word is often used in relation to *true statements* or *true doctrine*.[106] Knowledge is correct when one comprehends the *true knowledge*

---

[100] Maimonides, p. 76.
[101] See Hartmann, pp. 204 ff.; Seltzer, pp. 404 ff.
[102] Maimonides, p. 101.
[103] *Ibid*, p. 101.
[104] *Ibid*, p. 293.
[105] *Ibid*, p. 294.
[106] *Ibid*, e.g., pp. 18, 296, 395.

of things.[107] Things are apprehended by means of the intellect. That is how man distinguishes between what is true and false (*ĕmeṯ* and *šeqer*).[108]

(2) Maimonides speaks of the hidden meaning of texts and the real truth with regard to knowledge concerning God. The real truth concerning God lies in the *theologia negativa*. The negations do not convey a true idea of God; consequently, our knowledge of God consists in the circumstance that we know that we are incapable of truly apprehending Him.[109] As we have seen, Maimonides regards this as a better knowledge of God than that possessed by people who take metaphors literally. From his own level of knowledge, Maimonides must in effect cast doubts on the amount of truth in the religious beliefs with which the majority of the population must make do. It is safe to say that Maimonides approaches the doctrine of the double truth here, for statements about God in which attributes are mentioned are untrue in the strict sense, but for the majority of people they are 'true' enough to inherit eternal life.

With Maimonides, philosophical systematic reflection received a more conspicuous position than was customary in the Jewish tradition. One can no longer think about religious traditions in the modern period without being aware of the confrontation between 'theology' and 'philosophy.' Thought and reflection stand in the foreground in the *Guide*. The knowledge of God nevertheless has immediate ethical significance for Maimonides. God's acts are merciful, considered, and just — that is why a person who knows God will also want to live according to such values.[110] Knowledge of God results in love for God and is, strictly speaking, a condition for it. The give and take between the Jewish tradition and philosophy which permeates Maimonides' thought makes it fascinating at times and unclear at others.

3.4 Two modern thinkers: Heschel and Fackenheim

Finally, we will focus on two modern Jewish thinkers: Heschel and Fackenheim. The selection of these two authors came about as follows. Heschel is one of the most influential thinkers in American Judaism. He has been influenced strongly by Chassidism. Fackenheim ascribes a religious significance to Jewishness as such. Since what is specifically Jewish about the Jewish tradition lies in the fact that one *is* Jewish in the first place, it is of importance in the context of this study to examine how Fackenheim couples the Jewish religion's 'being true' to a possibly secular Jewishness.

---

[107] *Ibid*, p. 277.
[108] *Ibid*, p. 15.
[109] *Ibid*, p. 85.
[110] *Ibid*, p. 397.

a) Abraham Joshua Heschel

Heschel (1907–1972) originally came from Poland. He was a descendant of two important Chassidic families.[111] After his Jewish upbringing, he studied at the university of Berlin. In 1937 he succeeded Martin Buber at the *Jüdisches Lehrhaus* in Frankfurt; he fled to the United States in 1940 where he became one of the most prominent exponents of Judaism through his prolific writing. According to Seltzer's judgment, the Chassidic tradition has found an authentic modern interpretation in him. Just as is the case with Buber, a certain affinity with the phenomenological and existentialist philosophical tradition can be detected in Heschel, as appears from what he has written about Kierkegaard, for example. In Heschel's thought we encounter a modern orthodox view originating from Chassidic circles. We treat in sequence his view of knowledge, the importance he attaches to action, and finally his concept of truth.

In a number of his works, Heschel tries to point out openings in modern secularized Western life in which an experience of the divine is possible. To this end, he points to the many experiences over which people have no control and which they cannot comprehend. He also points to the limitations of the most conspicuous Western means of cognition in this context; that of sensory perception and the sciences. In the area in which it is valid, scientific thought has its use and value. Knowledge arises on the basis of sensory perception and the labeling of things. It is man, however, who names the things, one by one. In terms of his philosophical epistemology, Heschel stands in the tradition of philosophical phenomenology, pointing out the active role which the subject has in cognition.[112] Man constructs a view of reality via labeling and induction. One strives for knowledge which is *clare et distincte*. One seeks to describe things. This knowledge has its right, but also its limitations. Whoever does not perceive these limitations is liable to attempt using methods suitable to descriptive knowledge for obtaining knowledge about God as well. Heschel contends that one comes to unreal and impertinent knowledge about God via that route, because ultimately God cannot be known descriptively. He rejects proofs for God, because they reason in terms of human problematics towards a possible God, instead of proceeding from the overwhelming and awesome experience of God's reality.[113] His objection to the argument from design, the teleological proof of God, is that it proceeds from the notion that a person experiences the world as ordered and as something we can take for granted, while the world is actually unfathomable and baffling.[114]

---

[111] Seltzer, pp. 752ff., see also A. J. Heschel, *A Passion for Truth* (New York ³1977), "Introduction."

[112] A. J. Heschel, *Man Is Not Alone* (1951; rpt. New York ¹⁰1982), pp. 11f.

[113] Heschel, pp. 81ff.; A. J. Heschel, *God in Search of Man: A Philosophy of Judaism* (New York ³1978), pp. 110f, 140ff.

[114] *Ibid*, pp. 109f.

Next to descriptive knowledge, there is intuitive 'knowledge by appreciation,' the 'understanding.'[115] In ordinary cognition one labels pieces of reality. One cannot, therefore, know reality as a whole. The mystery which lies at the basis of reality and which impinges upon each human being is experienced in a different kind of cognitive act, which is intuitive and has immediate certainty. Knowledge of the mystery is not descriptive, for by its very nature, the mystery can only be suggested and alluded to, and the terms used are metaphors. This intuition arises from marveling at the groundlessness of the world and the unfathomableness of the human 'I'. Heschel calls these experiences pre-cognitive, since they precede any labeling. They must be verbalized to explain them to others and to alert others to the reality which is being experienced, but of themselves they are not susceptible of exact description and comprehension. According to Heschel there is nonetheless a definite knowing of something real involved. God is not a human fancy, but is reality. God is the reality which man cannot think, since He is implicated in thought itself as a total act of man; knowledge about God does not flow from natural phenomena because God is implicated in nature as such.[116]

When we refer to 'God,' we must acknowledge, if we know no more than is plain to people in general, that we do not truly know what is experienced. One experiences the mysterious, but the experience itself remains inexpressible. The whole of Heschel's conception of God is pervaded by the *ineffable*.[117] Even if something can be said about God on the basis of special deeds of the Living One, God remains the Other, whose being-other cannot be revealed to people. In Himself, He remains the *ineffabile*.[118]

The human response to the experience of the reality of God is faith. Faith is a disposition in life, not a persuasion at the level of normal human knowing. It reaches far deeper than that and encompasses the whole human person. Faith is a certain sensitivity for the mysterious; it is insight into the true dimensions of the world; it is involvement and commitment.[119] If one has experienced the mystery, says Heschel, one feels responsible in life. One seeks a different orientation; one sees reality in a different light.

We have spoken in general religious terms until now, since Heschel continually points to experiences which every person has. At a certain point, however, Judaism crops up, for God is the Living One. People cannot of themselves denote the ineffable in words, but God Himself can reveal to people what He wants to make known. The mystery does not

---

[115] Heschel, *Man Is Not Alone*, pp. 35 ff.; *God in Search*, p. 131.

[116] Heschel, *God in Search*, p. 102.

[117] *Ibid*, pp. 61 ff.

[118] Heschel, *Man Is Not Alone*, pp. 97 ff.; not a self-revelation of God, but a revelation of His way, *God in Search*, p. 261.

[119] Heschel, *God in Search*, p. 154.

always elude people; in exceptional moments it entrusts itself to people who have been chosen. People cannot bring God to expression, and yet God articulates His will for people.[120] People do not possess a definition of God; they merely have experiences of the Wonderful. Since God Himself makes His will known, something can be said about it. We should take notice of the fact that Heschel does not mention God's self-revelation in relation to revelation, but only the revelation of God's will. He repudiates the notion of self-revelation: God is and remains ineffable; God's essence is entirely hidden from people. Heschel sometimes makes pantheistic statements: 'God' means to say, "the togetherness of all beings in holy otherness," experiencing all people in one person, and the whole world in a grain of sand.[121] But if our understanding is correct, the accent in what he wants to say lies not in a philosophical conception which could be labeled as pantheism, but in the mystery which is hidden in and behind all things — thus pointing towards God.

Heschel makes the importance of knowledge about God and His deeds extremely relative. All the emphasis comes to rest on pious observance. Words are unnecessary, he says, because the ineffable in man —who himself is also unfathomable— communicates with the Ineffable.[122] For Heschel, one could say, this immersed knowledge would be quite sufficient. The biblical revelation does not report any information about God; the Bible tells us nothing about God as such; everything that is narrated refers to His relations with mankind.[123] The core of the revelation is God's will for mankind. The will of God, which He made known to the Jewish people, was so drastic that they were never the same after Mt. Sinai.[124] The Torah is of such importance that one could say that Judaism cannot, as can other religions, be described as a relationship between man and God, but as a relationship of man with the Torah and God.[125] Thus, Judaism is completely entwined with the giving of the law. Judaism is a way of thinking and living.[126]

Since this way of living is tied to a people, faith is not an individual affair. Remembrance of what has befallen the Jewish people plays an important part in Judaism.[127] Believing is commemorating, but it is also more than "dwelling in the shadow of old ideas."[128] Heschel certainly does not want to deny that knowledge of the traditions stands at the basis of Jewish life, with the consequence that articulated knowledge belongs to the Jewish tradition. But he regards dogmas alone as insufficient. "Dogmas

---

[120] Heschel, *Man Is Not Alone*, p. 99.
[121] See Seltzer, p. 754; Heschel, *Man Is Not Alone*, p. 109.
[122] Heschel, p. 131.
[123] *Ibid*, p. 143.
[124] Heschel, *God in Search*, pp. 167f.
[125] *Ibid*, p. 167.
[126] *Ibid*, p. 197.
[127] *Ibid*, p. 164.
[128] Heschel, *Man Is Not Alone*, p. 164, see also p. 161.

are the poor mind's share in the divine. A creed is almost all that the poor have."[129] Are dogmas not necessary then? "We cannot be in rapport with the reality of the divine except for rare, fugitive moments."[130] Doctrine is not the point. But still, even though the tradition is not always a living one for the believer, one cannot do without it. For faith must be passed on. Heschel continually insists on the experience of what one believes, however. This brings him to the following formulation by which he indicates the balance between faith (religious trust) and belief (creed): "A minimum of creed and a maximum of faith is the ideal synthesis."[131] Belief is secondary in his view; he calls belief an 'afterthought.' One attempts to capture an 'overpowering reality' in words.[132] Since what one wishes to represent exceeds the possibilities of human understanding, more than one formulation is necessary. Heschel relates this idea to the role of the *haggadah*. There are undoubtedly 'truths' in Judaism, but they stand in relationship to the whole of life.[133] The *haggadah* makes apparent the disposition with which we should comply to the *halakah*.[134] Due to the fact that the priority lies not with the creed, but in faithful living, there is leeway for differences in understanding. Heschel mentions as examples of the doctrinal differences within the Jewish tradition the dispute between the Sadducees and the Pharisees around the beginning of the Common Era over the resurrection of the dead and the relationship between Scripture and tradition; the conflicts over Maimonides' doctrine concerning the role of the *halakah* and his view of angels, prophets, miracles, resurrection, and creation; and, Gaon of Vilna's opposition to the Chassidim.[135]

In summary we can state that though doctrine and tradition play a large part in Judaism, Heschel puts that role in relative terms as much as possible in order to fully emphasize the experience of faith itself. This is narrowly related to the observance of the law in which one experiences the nearness of God. The relative character of religious knowledge within Judaism arises from the ineffability of God's nature, so that one can say nothing about God save for what has regard to God's relation to people. God reveals not Himself but His law.

Heschel opposes people who regard all religion, including Judaism, as merely a product of the human mind, and who thus explain all religion symbolically. He marshals against them the fact that Judaism wants to be

---

129 *Ibid*, p. 169.
130 *Ibid*, p. 169.
131 *Ibid*, p. 170.
132 *Ibid*, p. 84.
133 Heschel, *God in search*, p. 330.
134 *Ibid*, p. 338.
135 *Ibid*, p. 332.

taken literally.[136] The *halakah* wants to shape *true* life, as God wants it. Yet knowledge of God is symbolically true.[137] The symbolical designation arises from his resistance to any objective way of speaking about God; the cognitive mode of faith is different than that of tangible sensory reality, as we have seen already.

The parallel position of the two ways of knowing implies that faith and reason cannot come into conflict with each other. Since God is the Creator of the world, no contradiction can exist between revelation and what is known on the basis of rational enquiry from the creation, as the medieval Jewish thinkers wrote earlier.[138] Heschel joins them in this conception. Faith can therefore never compel someone to accept something that is contrary to reason. Neither reason nor faith is sufficient for life if isolated: faith without reason is dumb; reason without faith is deaf.[139] Some Jewish beliefs cannot be entirely justified rationally: the creation of man after the image of God, their view of God, and their view of history.[140]

We wish to add to this consideration of knowledge a brief note about action. The core of Jewish religion is awareness of God's interest in people — awareness of the Covenant, according to Heschel.[141] God wants a just people. This people is not a nation of definers but of witnesses.[142] Their testimony lies in their way of life. This way of life must be brought into accordance with sensitivity for the ineffable.[143] That is where the joy in performing the law comes in. If one fulfills the commandments, the *miṣwôt*, one fulfills God's purpose for our life, and senses His presence.[144] Operating as he does in terms of this emphasis on the close relationship between inner experience and outward behaviour, Heschel rejects the interpretation of Judaism as a legalistic religion and opposes the (Christian) narrowing of faith to the acceptance of grace alone.[145]

In Heschel's remarks concerning *truth*, the accents mentioned recur. He acknowledges, first, that Judaism holds certain facts to be true.[146] He speaks of the 'verities' of Judaism.[147] What one says must have some *rapport* with reality. This truth, second, can be superficial and external. The

---

[136] Heschel, *Man's Quest for God: Studies in Prayer and Symbolism* (New York 1954), pp. 132 ff.

[137] See also Heschel, pp. 127 ff; on the value of the *haggadah*, *God in Search*, pp. 324 f.

[138] Heschel, *Man Is Not Alone*, p. 172.

[139] *Ibid*, p. 173.

[140] Heschel, *God in Search*, p. 349.

[141] Heschel, *Man Is Not Alone*, p. 241.

[142] Heschel, *God in Search*, p. 140.

[143] *Ibid*, p. 350.

[144] *Ibid*, p. 355.

[145] *Ibid*, pp. 293 ff., 320 ff., 330.

[146] Heschel lays all the accent on the commitment of faith, but he assumes that faith has to do with a state of affairs; in his opinion the factual, ascertaining, and logical way of reasoning is only an 'afterthought,' *Man Is Not Alone*, pp. 84 ff.

[147] Heschel, *God in Search*, p. 330.

appropriation of religious truth is not self-evident: "the power of religious truth is a moment of insight, and its content is oneness or love. Source and content may be conveyed in one word: *transcendence.*"[148] The truth is connected to the awareness of the ineffable here. The words employed in the tradition are transcended in the experience of God's presence. The concept of truth receives a third dimension when it is finally related to life itself:

> ... truth is not timeless and detached from the world but a way of living and involved in all acts of God and man. The word of God is not an object of contemplation. The word of God must become history.[149]

A way is cleared in this manner for speaking about *being truth.*[150]

Thus we recognize in Heschel's concept of truth what was said earlier about (1) the relative character of doctrine, (2) 'knowledge by appreciation' and ineffability, and (3) the importance of living observance.

b) Emil L. Fackenheim

Fackenheim (born 1916) is characterized by Seltzer as a liberal, existentialist theologian.[151] Fackenheim was professor of philosophy in Toronto, but settled in Jerusalem after his emeritation. The land of Israel plays an important role in his thought. In his philosophy of Judaism, the emphasis lies on *being* Jewish. That is why his thought is of importance in the context of our enquiry. We have seen constantly in this chapter how the Jewish religion is entwined with Jewish life.

In the modern period, there is an increasing number of Jews who no longer regard themselves as 'religious.'[152] The term 'religious,' is readily conceived of as an orientation to the transcendent alongside of ordinary life. For Judaism acquired a status similar to the other religions in Europe after the French Revolution, even though this was predicated on the condition that the Jews behave religiously in the same way as the others. Their faith was to stand next to their existence as Frenchman, German, or whatever.[153] It can be understood that many Jews nowadays do not consider themselves to be religious against the backdrop of this conception of religion — as one human faculty among others. They remain Jews all the same. Kaplan has made an attempt to interpret Judaism more or less sociologically.[154] Religion then plays a role in determining group identity. His view is not important in the context of our study.

---

[148] *Ibid*, p. 162.

[149] *Ibid*, pp. 196 f.

[150] Heschel, *Passion for Truth*, pp. 163 ff.

[151] Seltzer, p. 762.

[152] See E. Fackenheim, *Encounters between Judaism and Modern Philosophy* (New York 1973), p. 167.

[153] E. Fackenheim, *The Jewish Return into History* (New York 1978), pp. 149 ff.; see also above, the text at *n.* 10.

[154] Borowitz, *Choices*, pp. 98 ff.

Fackenheim, on the contrary, interprets Jewishness itself as religious. The Jewishness of secularized Jews also obtains a religious dimension in his thought. Fackenheim relates his thoughts about the significance of being Jewish to surviving the holocaust and continuing to exist afterwards. The extermination of the majority of the European Jews, altogether a third of the total number of Jews at the time of the second world war, forms Fackenheim's central theme, and not only must Judaism come to a modus vivendi with this, but all of philosophy. Contrary to orthodox Jews, Fackenheim does not believe that Judaism can no longer be shocked again after the giving of the law at Mt. Sinai. He reminds us that the intention of the Nazis was to exterminate the Jews.[155]

Judaism was produced by 'root experiences,' Fackenheim declares.[156] The classical experiences which produced and marked Judaism are the exodus from Egypt and the making of the covenant at Sinai.[157] Later Judaism also received the imprint of two other epoch making events of destiny, the destruction of the second temple and the diaspora. The rabbis found a response to the new situation which shaped Judaism up until the 20th century.[158] The fourth great collective event which shaped Judaism is now the holocaust.[159] Amidst the vast amount of injustice in the world the holocaust occupies a unique position.[160] Usually the injustice inflicted on people serves some objective, no matter how reprehensible. In the case of the holocaust there was no other objective save the senseless destruction of the Jews. The destruction had become an end in itself, for which Hitler and the likes shunted pressing military interests. It was 'evil for evil's sake.'[161] This evil affects Christianity and philosophy. It affects humanity as a whole. All thought in the Hegelian tradition has become impossible in the sense that history does not appear to be an ascending line and that evil cannot be overcome (aufgehoben) by some higher good. What has been struck by this exceptional evil for the sake of evil is the belief in human nature. Human nature after Auschwitz is not what it was before.[162] The holocaust means 'a deep rupture' in the Jewish tradition, yea, in the history of humanity as a whole. The problem which Judaism now faces is how this 'epoch making event' is to be assimilated in an authentically Jewish way into further Jewish tradition.

---

[155] Esp. the volume mentioned in n. 153; also in To Mend the World: Foundations of Future Jewish Thought (New York 1982) pp. 13, 301, 308.

[156] Fackenheim, God's Presence in History (1970; rpt. New York 1972), pp. 8 f.; see R. Munk, "Authentiek Denken vanuit de Openbaring: Een Introductie tot het Denken van Emil L. Fackenheim," in H. J. Heering et al., Vier Joodse Denkers in de Twintigste Eeuw (Kampen 1987), pp. 76f.

[157] Fackenheim, To Mend the World, p. 16; God's Presence, pp. 8 , 14 ff.

[158] Fackenheim, To Mend the World, p. 17.

[159] Ibid, pp. 18, 13.

[160] Fackenheim, Jewish Return, p. 47.

[161] Ibid, pp. 27, 108.

[162] Fackenheim, To Mend the World, p. 99.

The covenant between God and His people stands central in the Jewish tradition.[163] God needs humanity. The idea of the partnership of God and Israel is a classical Jewish thought, as we have seen; Fackenheim fastens on this. Judaism is God's ally, making it plain to this world that God is *different*.[164] Judaism does not have to be so afraid of secularization and demythologization of idols since it has been demythologizing the idols since olden days.[165] Fackenheim calls attention to the depth of *haggadic* thought. Thinking in fragments, in short, deep thoughts and symbols, extends farther than systematic speculative thought.[166] History continues onward, however. In the modern period an appeal to a revelation given once and for all is no longer adequate.[167] New events have significance for thinking about God, man, and the world. After the immense debacle of the holocaust, the traditional observance is no longer an adequate response for Judaism to give. Fackenheim does not write the Torah off, but he does want to search in another direction for the answer.[168] He finds elements in the Cabbalistic tradition which help him in interpreting the holocaust. Where the *Midrashim* speak only symbolically about God, and do not always assume that their symbols correspond literally to the reality of God, Cabbalistic thought goes further. It says that in the symbols of language, reality itself becomes transparent. For when one says that "the *Šĕkînāh* has gone into exile," then one means that something has truly happened with God because of the destruction of the second temple.[169] Historical events have cosmic significance. Fackenheim's point is that Cabbalistic thought assigns to human beings a share in the mending of the rupture in history. A genuine response was possible to the rupture which the destruction of the second temple effected in Jewish history. Fackenheim is looking for the possibility of a new restoration after the new rupture in (Jewish) history. Furthermore, if the rupture is also a 'rupture' in God Himself, then man as covenant partner can help Him heal the rupture. Corresponding to the cosmic significance of the holocaust is the cosmic significance of a possible mending of the damages of this evil. If humanity is thus capable of coming to God's aid, that is due to the help of God Himself.[170]

Fackenheim is thus looking for the circumstances which could make the world better. He owes the title of a book to this quest: *To Mend the World*.[171] He points to the Jewish resistance to the murder of the Jews and a few signs of Christian solidarity with the Jews as precursors of such an

---

[163] Fackenheim, *Encounters*, pp. 118, 152f.
[164] *Ibid*, pp. 151f.
[165] Fackenheim, *Jewish Return*, p. 12; see *Encounters*, pp. 184ff.
[166] Fackenheim, *God's presence*, p. 20.
[167] Fackenheim, *To Mend the World*, pp. 4, 16.
[168] *Ibid*, p. 327.
[169] *Ibid*, p. 253.
[170] *Ibid*, pp. 253ff.
[171] On the Cabbala, Seltzer, pp. 443f.

improvement.[172] The resistance of the victims to the executioner could in
no way check the holocaust. It was a sign of humanity in the midst of
inhumanity. It was a testimony to the value of mankind and at the same
time an allusion to the mission of the Jewish people. That mission is to
testify among the nations that man was created after the image of God.[173]
Without God everything appears to be possible and permissible.[174] Such
reference to God and to the value of mankind is thus a genuine improvement
of the world. Such an improvement was the effect of Jewish resistance to
the massacre of their people. Such resistance can provide a basis for the
hope that the world is not irredeemably lost.

The holocaust has significance for Judaism. The holocaust sounds the
imperative: Be Jewish and remain Jewish! If the Jews do not remain Jews,
but start to blend in with other peoples, Hitler will have his way after
all. The Voice which speaks to the Jewish people in the holocaust is not
a saving Voice, but only a commanding Voice as yet.[175] The mission
given to the Jewish people is to survive as Jewish people.[176] The command
to honour Life, *qidduš ha-ḥayyîm*, now stands at the same level as the
command to honour the holy Name once did: *qidduš ha-šēm*.[177] Judaism must
survive. The election of Israel obtains new content in this way. The
existence of the Jews as Jews is a sign to the world that the power of
evil has not gone uncontradicted. The bare existence of Jews is already
an improvement of the world in that sense. That is why the existence of
Jews has religious significance, secularized or not. In his book, Fackenheim
is looking for a *religio-secular truth*.[178] The religious is intertwined with
the worldly in Judaism.

Finally, Fackenheim connects these ideas to the state of Israel. The
Jewish state guarantees Jewish life. He refers to Cabbalistic ideas in
which God, the Torah, and Israel are identified. Fackenheim applies these
notions to the state (and not just the people) of Israel. There is a
mystical union between God and the people of Israel.[179] In the existence
of the state of Israel, resurrected after the holocaust, God is present in
some way. That is why *tikkun*, improvement of the world, lies in the
continued existence of the Jewish state.[180] God is affected in his existence
by the service of His people which exists after the holocaust, through
continued existence of Israel. Fackenheim quotes a cherished *Midrash*:
"You are My witnesses, says the Lord — that is to say, if you are My

[172] Fackenheim, *To Mend the World*, pp. 321f., 289f., see also pp. 201ff.
[173] Fackenheim, *Jewish Return*, p. 111.
[174] *Ibid*, p. 108.
[175] Fackenheim, *God's Presence*, p. 88, *To Mend the World*, p. 299.
[176] For the so-called 614th commandment, Fackenheim, *Jewish Return*, pp. 22f.; *To Mend the World*, p. 300.
[177] Fackenheim, p. 223.
[178] *Ibid*, p. 22.
[179] *Ibid*, pp. 327, 329ff.
[180] *Ibid*, pp. 312; see Munk, pp. 83f.

witnesses, then I am God, and if you are not My witnesses, then I am, as it were, not God."[181]

Fackenheim claims that he has not explicitly described the transcendent dimension in his book, *To Mend the World*. He has merely attempted to demonstrate how the simple fact of the existence of Jews after the holocaust is not something to be taken for granted, but implies a reference to the transcendent and, as such, is service to God and improvement of the world. Thus Judaism's being true lies, we might add at this juncture, in its *being*-Jewish. The truth of Judaism is not an unutterable mystical union with God; it is a truth lived in relationship to God, whether conscious or not. In that truth, in the existence of that people, the reports about the history and fate of the Jews play a role. New awesome events can impinge on the tradition's course.

§ 4 Truth and other religious traditions

To round out the discussion, we will begin by looking at the attitude of Jews towards followers of other faiths in actual practice. The practical arrangements of the life of the Jews who lived amid the heathen in the diaspora is so important because the practical regulations were not there to protect the Jewish beliefs, but to protect their *Jewishness,* and the observance of the Torah. The purpose of the traditional rabbinic legislation was to keep Jewish existence free of foreign contamination, particularly of all traces of paganism. Innumerable rules in the *Talmud* make plain in what way Jews are allowed, for example, to conduct business with heathens. They shall not accept oaths, shall not conduct trade on Jewish holidays, and in general, have no intimate dealings with the heathen. Jacob Katz describes how European Jews in the Middle Ages learnt to interpret the regulations in a manner required by new situations, under the pressure of circumstances. In new situations it was difficult to maintain regulations which stemmed from a time in which there were many Jews living in the same vicinity. It was forbidden, for example, to buy wine from pagans. One was not permitted to sleep with them under one roof. How were these and other rules to be applied in the dispersion in Europe? They learnt, little by little, not to see Christians as ordinary heathen.[182] The doctrine of the trinity and the worship of Jesus as the Son of God were rejected, but it was acknowledged that Christians were not common heathens with countless idols.[183] Still, the relationship between Jews and Christians remained tense. Christians regarded themselves as the true heirs of Israel, so that in theory they had to assume a repudiatory

---

[181] Fackenheim, p. 331.
[182] Katz, *Exclusiveness and Tolerance*, pp. 114 ff.
[183] *Ibid*, pp. 18, 23; see also Jacobs, pp. 286 f.

position vis à vis the continued existence of Judaism after Jesus of Nazareth; sadly enough, things went beyond a dismissal at the level of doctrine. Conversely, Jews were convinced of the truth of Judaism; if they died for it, they died as witnesses to this truth.[184] During the time of the Enlightenment, a different relation between Christians and Jews came about, as Katz shows. Moses Mendelssohn takes the posture of a *human being* within the thought of his time rather than any particular posture as a Jew; in like fashion, he approaches others as human beings rather than particularly as Christians. The common denominator then becomes universal, reasonable human nature.[185] The optimism of the Enlightenment echoes here, which could not sense how irrational the relation between Christians and Jews in particular could become.

The covenant with Noah is central to Judaism's view of other nations. The covenant which God made with Noah holds for all people. The commandments given by God in it are obligatory for all. If heathens keep the seven commandments which God gave at the time of Noah, then they will inherit salvation. Uriël Simon briefly describes the current conception.[186] He himself distinguishes between the presence of salvation ('Heil') and the presence of truth. Just people from the nations also possess the prospect of eternal salvation. They do not possess the truth as the Jews know it, however.[187] Since Judaism is the religion of a nation, it is a particularistic and exclusivist religion. Proselytes can become members of the Jewish people, but Judaism remains a 'national religion,' as opposed to Buddhism, Christianity, Islam, and even Hinduism.[188] This election is no easy privilege for the Jews, however. They bear the 'yoke of the kingdom,' while the just from other nations can inherit salvation more easily by heeding far simpler commandments — seven as compared to the Jews' six hundred and thirteen.[189]

It seems obvious that the attitude of Judaism with regard to other religions is determined by its own beliefs.[190] The election of Israel implies

---

[184] Katz, pp. 81, 92.

[185] *Ibid*, pp. 170ff.

[186] U. Simon, "De Uitverkiezing en de Roeping van Israel," *Ter Herkennning* 12 (1984): 16-23.

[187] *Ibid*, p. 17.

[188] *Ibid*, p. 21.

[189] The total number of commandments in the Torah is 613. The seven Noachite commandments are: (1) not to worship idols, (2) not to commit murder, (3) not to commit adultery and incest, (4) not to eat a limb torn from a living animal, (5) not to blaspheme, (6) not to steal, (7) to have an adequate system of law and justice; Jacobs, p. 285; Jacobs wants to broaden the concept of the 'good man' among the nations to all people who lead a good ethical life; he creates room for a positive evaluation of other monotheistic (or, at least, non-polytheistic) religions, pp. 290f.

[190] See Jacobs, p. 289. He writes, "The position one ought to adopt is that there is *more* truth in Judaism than in other religions." Notwithstanding, Jacobs rejects the faiths of India and East Asia as polytheistic or atheistic; he judges the Christian concept of God to be false, viewed from a Jewish standpoint; he does not allow that Mohammed received a revelation from God, making him the last of the prophets,

that other nations are not chosen in the same sense and therefore do not have the same special mission which God has given to Israel. We have seen that there is a certain margin for valuing differently religious currents which display more similarity with the faith of Israel than religious traditions whose customs and beliefs are at odds with what is central for Israel — service to the One God.

We have seen in this chapter to what degree Judaism is a way of being. One *is* a Jew by birth. One can cease observing the Torah, but one does not cease being Jewish. This fact defines the specific cast of the Jewish religion. Being Jewish does not concern just some facets of life; no, it marks the whole of life. We have seen that within orthodox Judaism, prominence is given to the observance of the Torah. It was equally apparent that the observation of the *halakah* was sustained by certain religious ideas, in particular faith in the double revelation on Mt. Sinai. The *halakah* is the revealed will of God. The often heard assertion that Judaism has no 'doctrine' is therefore not entirely true. It is possible to state that there is great doctrinal freedom in Judaism; great tolerance exists with regard to discussion of the *haggadah,* and in the *halakah* as well, deviating opinions are not suppressed; there is less tolerance vis à vis deviant behaviour. It is apparent that no believing Jew can avoid believing that God is implicated in Israel's existence. The problems concerning the relation between God and suffering also presuppose God's involvement with His people. To summarize, doctrine exists, albeit less elaborate and less systematically described than in Christianity, for example.

When it is said that the concept of *ĕmet* concerns life as a whole, and not just doctrines, that is true to an extent: being Jewish itself has religious significance, and the observance of the Torah is a form of communion with God for the orthodox Jew. This does not mean, however, that Jews do not hold their beliefs to be true. What they say about God furnishes reliable information concerning God and His deeds in history, even though there is an awareness of the inadequacy of human language for describing the reality of God. Always we encounter qualification with respect to religious language usage. The *Talmud* regularly uses the following formula: "Were it not for what is written ... it would be impossible to say ... " This is then followed by something which does not directly describe the reality of God, but which reveals something of that reality nevertheless.[191] Maimonides viewed a large number of important biblical terms as mere metaphors and comparisons, images and allegories; he described the homonymity of human concepts when applied to God. Heschel wrote concerning the symbolical meaning of the religious use of language. One encounters everywhere qualifications such as metaphorical,

---

the Koran rather than the Torah being final. However, it does not follow for him that God did not make Himself known to other peoples than the Jews, nor that there is no truth in other traditions.

[191] Kadushin, *Rabbinic Mind*, p. 276.

analogical, and symbolical. Nonetheless, what is thus known is the history of God with the people of His covenant. The focus of attention is not God in Himself, but God in His relation to Israel. It is believed that true statements can be made about this, even though some matters seem more apparent than others.

Although the emphasis therefore rests on lived truth, and, after taking into account the nuances and subtleties which we have described, we must still conclude that there is true doctrine in Judaism. One ought to appropriate this true doctrine personally, however, so that it starts to govern the whole of life. What is the nature of the truth of this true doctrine and tradition? We have discovered no elaborate technical treatment of this. The claim is clear however: one way or the other, the stories told describe what has really come to pass. Since the *doctrine* is centered strongly on the many-faceted history of God with people, especially His people, the doctrinal tradition is not seen as a systematic whole or as a doctrinal system.

Chapter VI

The Concept of Truth in Christian Tradition

§ 1 Introduction

1.1 Preamble

In this chapter some important conceptions regarding truth in the Christian religion will be presented. Christianity is the largest of the world religions, with adherents on all continents. This sweeping breadth of Christianity is a phenomenon of the past few centuries. It was for centuries concentrated in Western Asia, the countries around the Mediterranean Sea, and in the rest of Europe. With the expansion of Western civilization, Christianity also expanded, especially to America and Australia. Since the Roman Catholic Church has its centre in Rome and central doctrinal authority fundamentally establishes what Catholics may (and must) believe, a certain degree of unanimity exists within the Roman Catholic Church. In the Protestant churches, similarly, creeds guarantee a certain coherence and correspondence of ideas. We therefore consider it possible to sketch a rough portrait of some of the main lines of Christian doctrine in § 2, just as we did for the other traditions. To counter speaking about 'Christianity' too monolithically, we will also outline a few of the developments which have taken place, making the Christian tradition as variegated as the others. We will for the most part pass over developments in the Eastern Church; the most important doctrines of the Christian church were formulated before the schism between the Eastern and the Western Church. In § 3, we will examine the concept of truth in more detail. We will then discuss first of all the concept of truth in the New Testament, then the influential views of the church father Augustine, of the Medieval theologian Thomas Aquinas, and of John Calvin, the reformer. For the modern period, we will give consideration to Karl Barth and Karl Rahner because of their enormous influence in the Protestant and the Roman Catholic traditions respectively on how the relation between Christianity and other religions is conceived. In § 4, we will briefly present the positions with regard to other religions developed by special commissions convened by the Vatican and the World Council of Churches for this very issue.

1.2   Christian faith

Characteristic for Christian faith is its focus on the person of Jesus Christ and the relationship with him. Christianity arose out of Judaism. It was believed that the personal presence of God Himself was experienced in Jesus Christ. The message of Jesus was no longer directed only to the Jewish people, but —so it was believed— had universal significance. People from all nations could join the church. In principle, the proclamation of the Christian Church is therefore directed to all people. It is always proclamation of God's salvation, no matter how divergent the interpretations by theologians from various currents within Christianity might be.

The reference to Jesus is one of the reasons why doctrine occupies a rather important position in Christianity. The Revelation of God is not only tied to the history of the people of Israel, but to the person of Christ as well. The revelation is for Christianity not in the first place the revelation of God's will (as in Judaism), but the revelation of God's unconditional love and of His offer of forgiveness. The reference to the historical events surrounding Christ and the belief that Christ *is* God in a certain sense, while God is at the same time completely different from human beings, is determinative for the content of Christian belief. The ensuing reflection on the difficulties which were thereby raised formed the environment in which the formulation of Christian doctrine took place. Since Jesus occupies a central place, the first centuries already saw a detailed reflection on the nature of God's presence in Jesus. This reflection resulted in the dogmas of the ancient church about God and Christ.

Christian doctrine refers to events. The nature of these events is disputed in modern Christian theology, to be sure, but the fact is that the reference to Jesus of Nazareth is a defining characteristic of Christianity. This has consequences for the concept of truth within the Christian tradition. The doctrines refer to those events, so the doctrines must in some way be 'true' in referring to what has happened. This referring to the historical basis of Christian faith has been the object of much continuing reflection. We have already adumbrated several moments from that discussion in Ch. II.

1.3   Developments in the Christian tradition

(1) Jesus of Nazareth, son of a carpenter and acting as rabbi, marks the beginning of the Christian calendar reckoning. His position within the Jewish currents of his own day is disputed. In any case, it has been

possible to establish close affinity with the Pharisaical tradition.[1] The history of Jesus and his followers is described in the four gospels, which, together with some other writings, form the *New Testament*, a term which thereby contains a reference to the Jewish Bible, which is designated the Old Testament in Christianity, and which also belongs to Holy Scripture. According to the Gospels, Jesus became involved in a clash with the leaders of the Jewish people partly because His interpretation of the law conflicted with theirs, and partly because of His claim that the Kingdom of God was near. This conflict led to his crucifixion. According to the New Testament, Jesus arose from death after three days and ascended to God.

The young church originated from a group of followers and spread over a large part of the Roman Empire in a relatively short time.[2] At first, the Christians lived under the legal protection of Judaism, which had a certain freedom in the Roman Empire. Christianity later freed itself from Judaism almost entirely and oftentimes endured severe persecution. Christian belief was recapitulated in creeds in the first centuries already. Reflection on the substance of Christianity also arose, and Christianity was defended against polemic attacks by exponents of paganism. Christianity slowly gained in strength, culminating in the emperor Constantine the Great's conversion to Christianity in 313 C.E. The Roman Empire was slowly Christianized in the ensuing centuries; the power of Rome waned during the same period.

The expansion of Christianity in the Hellenistic and Roman worlds had a major effect on the further development of Christianity. It was deeply influenced by the Platonism which it encountered in Greek culture. The Jewish focus on earthly life was largely subordinated to Platonist, dualistic thought in which the spiritual stood next to and above the material. Within Latin culture, Christianity came into contact with a more structured organization. Given the fact that Rome was the capital of the empire, the bishop of Rome obtained a pre-eminent position among the bishops as 'successor to Peter.' In the Latin church, the doctrine of the atonement came to occupy a central position, partially on the basis of interpretation of a rather legal character given it by the church father Tertullian.

On the outskirts of the ecclesiastical mainstream, groups of enthusiasts formed who stressed a spontaneous and free spiritual experience under the influence of the Holy Spirit. Such groups have accompanied the

---

[1] In the Gospels, the differences between Jesus and the Pharisees seem to be sketched more sharply than they actually could have been. Expositions of early Rabbinic thought show that the differences between Jesus' teachings and the Pharisees' could not have been as great as portrayed by the New Testament; cf. the exposition of Judaism given in Ch. V. For a treatment of the so-called anti-Judaizing passages in the New Testament, S. Sandmel, *Anti-Semitism in the New Testament?* (Philadelphia 1978).

[2] For what follows, K. Heussi, *Kompendium der Kirchengeschichte* (Tübingen [12]1960).

church during the entire course of her history. Movements of monks also arose, who tried to lead their lives as free of sin as is humanly possible through renunciation and by leading an existence distant from ordinary life, looking ahead to the life hereafter, and frequently also living in service to their fellow man.

(2) The large scale development of doctrine follows in the period after 313. Christian doctrine was explicated and pondered in confrontation with philosophical traditions. Initially, many questions arose in this process, especially with respect to the relationships between God and Jesus and the Spirit of God. The doctrine of the Trinity, and somewhat later, that of the two natures, were formulated in these early centuries. A number of Greek language church fathers played an important role in the fourth century. The influence of the Latin *patres* gradually became more important, starting the middle of the third century. The thought of Augustine († 430) in particular left its imprint on Western Christian theology far into the Middle Ages, and also on a great deal of later Protestant theology via Luther and Calvin. The Christianization of Europe lasted up until the 10th century. A so-called Christian culture emerged meantime from the remnants of the Roman Empire in Europe, known as the *corpus Christianum*, which exhibited a great degree of entwinement between spiritual and worldly power. Sometimes the bishops possessed worldly power, and they were not infrequently involved in wars. The concern for earthly life which we mentioned in our discussion of Judaism took on forms all of its own.

(3) After the disintegration of the Roman Empire into an Eastern and a Western part, the two parts of the church led a life of their own, to a certain degree. This culminated in a schism between the Eastern Orthodox and the Western Church in 1054. In the orthodox Church, to put matters very succinctly, Easter occupies a central position in the liturgy, and also in theological reflection. The emphasis falls on liberation from the powers of sin and death through the resurrection of Christ. In the Western Church, salvation is traditionally viewed more in terms of the reconciliation between God and man through Christ's death.

(4) The entwinement of church and state after the Reformation in 1517 and led to the emergence of national Protestant churches. The Reformation was, as the very word indicates, a movement of reform. The Reformers thought it incumbent upon themselves to point out the abuses in the Medieval church. Perhaps most notable for the development of the Christian tradition as a religious movement was the opposition to the authority of the pope. What stood most central theologically was the ambition to recognize only the Bible as authoritative, and the accent given to human-kind's incapacity to help in obtaining salvation, so that man was completely reliant on the grace of God. These Reformation principles are known as *sola scriptura* and *sola gratia*. The Reformational movement, which

rejected the central authority of Rome, had no new central leadership of its own. Various currents exist within the movement, of which the Lutherans were strongly determined by the influence of Martin Luther (1483–1546), and the Calvinists by that of Calvin (1509–1564). The English Church carried out an independent Reformation which retained the office of bishop; the English Church has afterwards been known abroad as the *Episcopal Church*. The Methodists in the 18th century stem from the Anglican Church. The spread of Western culture over the entire world via colonialism also transposed these European denominations to other continents.

(5) While Christianity obtained many adherents on other than the European and West Asian continents, in the Western world itself secularization has increased strongly since the beginning of the 20th century and has accelerated even more since the sixties.

The larger Protestant churches work together in the World Council of Churches. About half the members of the churches affiliated with the World Council of Churches live in non-Western countries. The tendency to combine Christian faith with one's own cultural inheritance is becoming more pronounced, so that in future, Christianity will possibly become even more variegated than it has been so far.

§ 2 Central Insights

2.1 God: Creator and Saviour

The fountainhead of Judaism lies in the covenant between God and His people; Christianity's lies in creation and salvation. God is the Creator of heaven and earth, a belief which Christians share with Jews and Muslims. Monotheism is common to these three religions, if we allow for the fact that according to Jews and Muslims, the doctrine of the Trinity compromises this.

The classical threesome of Christian dogmatics is creation, fall into sin, and redemption. Within more modern theology, discussion has arisen as to whether one first knows God as Creator and can only then recognize Him as Redeemer, or whether one first learns to know Him from redemption and the revelation in Christ, and afterwards comes to believe in the creation on the basis of that knowledge.[3] One's perspective on this issue influences one's view of other religions. In any event, it is believed that the God whom Jesus confessed as His Father is also the Creator and the Perfecter of the world.

---

[3] See G. von Rad, *Theologie des Alten Testaments*, I (Munich [5]1966), pp. 149 ff.; K. H. Miskotte, "Zur biblischen Hermeneutik," in Miskotte, *Geloof en Kennis* (Haarlem 1966), pp. 200-229, esp. pp. 213 ff.

Referring to the creation as an intentional act by God is fundamental to the Christian view of the world. The world, inasmuch as it was created by God, is good. The lesson of the story of the fall into sin and of the Christian doctrine of sin is that the corruption of the world does not come from God. In the meantime, however, mankind has become thoroughly corrupt and is no longer capable of obtaining salvation on his own.

To what extent salvation can be thought of as 'earthly' within Christianity is a point of debate. People can participate in salvation during their lives to a certain degree; this is generally viewed in terms of peace with God (and one's fellow man), a "peace which passes all under-standing," and which cannot be directly inferred from a person's material circumstances. Salvation is usually related to an eschatological expectation: a new heaven and a new earth, without tears, in which God will be all in all. This anticipation of salvation did not entail a turning away from this world, at least not insofar as the Christian tradition has always had an eye for the needs of the poor, to which the *diaconate* ministered. Nowadays there is a sizeable current within Christian thought which emphasizes the rights of the poor and the destitute; it is pointed out that eschatological expectation must not be permitted to obscure the Old Testament ideal of justice.

God is not only the Creator but also the Redeemer of mankind. Through the election of Israel, He redeems people from the situation in which they have ended up due to the fall into sin, full of injustice, lovelessness, and lawlessness, in order to offer them the prospect of salvation. Israel did not listen however; they strayed time after time. After having sent prophet upon prophet, God finally sent His own son, Jesus Christ. God thereby also achieved his purpose of enabling people other than just the Jews to obtain salvation. The place of the people of Israel is under discussion within the churches. As is familiar, the Jews in 'Christian countries' have generally had to live with the reproach that they have 'rejected the messiah.'

2.2 Jesus Christ

God's salvation has become accessible to all people through the mediation of Jesus Christ, according to the Christian interpretation of the New Testament. That salvation is not only for Israel is also true within Judaism to a certain extent (see Ch. V § 4). But according to Christian tradition, God's saving purpose is revealed more plainly in Jesus and in the global proclamation of the Gospel than by the mere existence of the people of Israel.

Where Judaism emphasized the proximity and the holiness of God, Christianity holds the belief that whoever knows Jesus, knows God: "He who has seen me has seen the Father."[4] In that sense, Jesus is the revelation of God. The relationship between God and Jesus as His revelation is so close that, as the Gospel of John puts it, Jesus is the *Logos,* the Word by which and with which God made all things in the beginning. Many similarities to Greek philosophical thought can be pointed out in the later *logos* doctrine, which profoundly determined the ecclesiastical interpretation of the Gospel for centuries.[5] However it has been further elaborated and understood, the claim of Christianity remains that Jesus is God and that Jesus reveals God's will. A lengthy discussion has even taken place about whether Jesus would have come without the fall into sin, not to redeem but just to reveal.

The emphasis in the Eastern Orthodox Church is on the redemption of mankind through the mediation of Jesus Christ. By dying as a sinless man, He has released sinful people from their guilt and from the power of death and corruption. The resurrection of Jesus from the grave is the central redemptive event, particularly in the orthodox liturgy. One obtains a share in this salvation through baptism.[6] In the Western Church, the emphasis has most frequently been on the reconciliation which Jesus effected. The whole of humankind has fallen into sin and is eternally doomed because of Adam and Eve's fall into sin.[7] Since Jesus died without sin on the cross, and so took on the sin of humanity, God, who is not only merciful but also just, can now accept mankind and promises those who have been incorporated into Jesus by faith and baptism a heavenly future (or, a new earth). The followers of Jesus are called 'a new creation,' in the sense that the human nature corrupted by sin is replaced by a restored one; this often was the explanation given for the phrase that believers 'are in Christ.'

Jesus not only revealed God, but also made plain what God expects of people. There is discussion within Christianity about whether (and to what degree) the moral rules of Christianity are specific to itself, or whether they are also known outside of this religious tradition. What is especially pointed out nowadays is the fact that much of what is said in the New Testament was also commended in the Judaism of that day by many rabbis. In any event, for centuries it was believed within the Christian tradition that the sermon on the mount was peculiar to Christianity and to Jesus' ideas, even though people usually did not believe that the intended purpose of the sermon was literal observance. *Conformity* to these injunctions is considered to be the task of Christians. They ought to live according to the example of their Lord. The ideal of neighbourly love (put on par with the commandment to love God), the call to commiserate with and to support the weak and the poor, and the call to

---

[4] John 14:9.
[5] See A. Adam, *Lehrbuch des Dogmengeschichte,* I (Gütersloh 1965), pp. 184f.
[6] See Adam, pp. 343ff.
[7] Thus Augustine, see Adam, p. 268.

righteousness all belong to the heart of Christian ethics.[8] Believers ought to 'sanctify' themselves, which means that they should learn to live according to the will of God and the example of Christ. Such sanctification is the expression of a living relationship between God and man. Faith is living in trust of God.

2.3   The Doctrines of the Trinity and the two natures

Christianity speaks not only of God and Jesus, but also of the Holy Spirit, who was given to the first Christian community at Pentecost, and who since then leads the church in an invisible manner. Christ is present in the church through the Spirit. This speaking of the Father, the Son and the Holy Spirit goes back to the New Testament.[9] Subsequent generations attempted to comprehend and to explain how Jesus and the Spirit were related to God, and such attempts proved the occasion for the origin of the doctrines of the Trinity and of the two natures.[10] The doctrine of the two natures of Jesus expresses the fact that Jesus is both God and man. He has a divine and a human nature. Sometimes this was conceived of as meaning that Jesus was the restored, general human nature, the *anima generalis,* so that whoever shares in that nature is a renewed human being. The belief that Jesus was born of the virgin Mary points to his divine origin. To express that He was also God, they declared that He also possessed the divine nature. Both these natures coalesced into a unity, although some writings ascribe some of Jesus' words and deeds to either the divine or the human nature. The classical formulation of this doctrine was molded at the Council of Chalcedon (451): the two natures are undivided and inseparable, without confusion or change. Thus the incomprehensible was stressed: the unity of the person of Christ, and at the same time, the reality of his humanity and divinity.

The doctrine of the Trinity expresses the unity of God as Father, Son, and Holy Spirit. It was formulated in such a way that there is an underlying, *hypostatic,* unity in God, while God at the same time exists in these three persons in His outward manifestation. Within Christianity this manner of viewing the matter is considered to be monotheistic, even though the objection that this damages the unity of God has been raised both on the part of Judaism and Islam.

Lying at the heart of Christianity is the relationship of Jesus and the Spirit to the one God, and the presence of God in Christ — disclosing a mystery which, as is generally affirmed, cannot be fathomed rationally. The many debates about arguments for the existence of God and the possibility of rational 'proof' for it leave unaffected the mystery which

---

[8] See Matthew 5-7; Acts 2:41-47.

[9] Matthew 28:19; see also I John 5:7.

[10] For what follows, and for studies in Christian dogmatics on Christology and the doctrine of God, Adam, pp. 115 ff., 305 ff.

Christian tradition holds to be attached to the person and the work of Christ, a mystery inaccessible to reason. Reasoning can do service in making people ripe to discover the ultimate truth; it cannot prove the divine presence in Christ. To accept this mystery, people must learn to see it through the enlightenment of the Holy Spirit, and they must be prepared to consider themselves as sinners, reliant upon grace to obtain more insight. Christianity thus contains a certain amount of doctrine not wholly transparent to reason.

2.4 Holy Scripture and doctrinal authority

Many of the events upon which Christian faith is based have taken place before human gaze. In order to perceive the import of these events, enlightenment by the Spirit of God is necessary. The biblical writings contain messages by people inspired by the Spirit. Their insight —through faith— into the things which they had experienced, enabled them to communicate to later generations what had happened and what significance it has. It is widely accepted in Christian theology that the biblical writings contain not only the 'facts,' but in addition, always present the theological reflection of the first Christian community on what happened.[11]

No other access exists to the events of salvation than through Holy Scripture, according to Christian conviction. Within the Christian tradition, the Bible plays a decisive role in knowledge concerning God.[12]

Since the Bible contains a myriad of practical rules of life, Scripture must be continually explained anew. How could the Bible preserve its authority and yet be interpreted in the light of new circumstances? After some centuries, a transition was made to expressing the consensus of the church in councils of all the bishops, or at least as many as possible. Certain conceptions were rejected outright as heresy. An attempt was made to articulate what was properly Christian. The bishop of Rome obtained an increasingly stronger position within the church organization, which was later to become more rigid. He was asked for advice in difficult issues or pressed to take certain steps. Whatever the process, a certain authority attaching to the bishop of Rome developed in the early Middle Ages, who was seen then as primate of the church. Within the context of our enquiry, the relationship between the pope and ecclesiastical doctrine is of significance. In Christianity —since the schism of 1054 one should say, within the Roman Catholic Church— an authority has grown which watches overdoctrinal rectitude and doctrinal development. This doctrinal authority resides with the bishops communally. The growing power of the pope implied that the pope obtained increasing say in

---

11 E.g., D. Nineham, *The Use and Abuse of the Bible* (London ²1978), esp. pp. 174-97; C. W. Mönnich and H. J. L. van Luijk, "Het Christendom," in *Antwoord*, ed. J. Sperna Weiland (Amsterdam ²1982), pp. 140f.

12 Consult the sections on Calvin and Barth below.

doctrinal issues, a development which ultimately —in 1870, after many centuries— led to the dogma of the infallibility of the pope's doctrinal authority in what he officially proclaims to be doctrine. Within the Roman Catholic Church then, there is a doctrine of which one must (in principle) approve, or at least be prepared to accept.[13]

Matters lie somewhat differently within the Protestant churches. Confessional statements emerged in the 1st century after the Reformation which summarized the doctrines and which articulated Christian faith. No doctrinal authority such as was present in the Roman Catholic Church was ascribed to the synods which had approved the confessions; on the contrary, the *sola Scriptura* was expressly professed. Actually, however, the confessions explain how the Bible is understood by the Protestant Churches.[14] Since the Reformed Churches have no strict organizational unity, a central doctrinal authority with the competence for ruling on what one ought to believe or not is lacking. Within the World Council of Churches, the attempt is made to arrive at common convictions on important items through mutual deliberation. For what remains, it is up to the churches of the various countries to make pronouncements about their teachings themselves. Generally speaking, the larger churches have much freedom of doctrine and the smaller churches less so.

The background for developments within the ecclesiastical tradition is formed by the Christian belief that the Holy Spirit leads the church in truth. Sometimes this faith is related to beliefs, sometimes to ethical and practical matters.

§ 3 Truth

3.1 In the New Testament

With respect to the concept of truth within the New Testament, the same can be said, in part, as was said regarding the Old Testament. The Greek word *alètheia* is used with more than one shade of meaning. Within theological investigation in the first half of the 20th century, it became customary to look for the *essence* of truth, and thus also for the *essence* of the Old and the New Testament, or sometimes also the 'biblical,' concept of truth. The thought of the early phenomenological tradition was present in the background, believing it possible to perceive the *essence* of

---

[13] See G. C. Berkouwer, *Vaticaans Concilie en Nieuwe Theologie* (Kampen 1964), pp. 105-76; Berkouwer, *Nabetrachting op het Concilie* (Kampen 1968), pp. 112-40; compare with the declarations in H. Denzinger and I. B. Umberg (eds.), *Enchiridion Symbolorum Definitionum et Declarationum de Rebus Fidei et Morum* (Freiburg i. Br.).

[14] An edition of the confessions of the Reformed churches is W. Niesel, *Das Evangelium und die Kirchen: Ein Lehrbuch der Symbolik* (Neukirchen ²1960).

things in the multitude of phenomena.[15] According to this conception, the biblical concept of truth is then not concerned with doctrinal truth but with 'truth as reliability.' People sought to distance themselves from the widespread notion of truth as 'true doctrine.' Nowadays many people tend to dismiss such attempts at finding the 'essence' of the biblical concept of truth. The search for the essential meaning of a word in its many usages has given way to an insistence on the context within which a word tends to be used. This development was fostered by later phenomeno-logical philosophy, also known as hermeneutical philosophy, and by the opposition of the later Wittgenstein to any such pursuit of unity, and his thesis that words only possess their meaning within 'language-games' and 'life forms.' More emphasis is thus to be seen in contemporary theological investigation for the various shades of meaning of the word *alètheia* running through the various New Testament writings. The relation between the 'biblical' and the 'Greek' concept of truth is now also assessed with somewhat more subtlety.

It is thus pointed out that the content of the Christian proclamation in the New Testament is sometimes called the 'truth.' In a certain sense, it is the Christian *doctrine* which is then being referred to, although not in such an elaborated form as we will encounter later.[16] Central to Christianity, as we have seen, is that God has revealed Himself in Christ; therefore convictions with respect to God and Jesus do play a role in Christian faith. Beliefs are present, and one presumes them to be true. This truth, in the sense of right doctrine, is what is preached.

The environment in which such beliefs exist is of course conditioned by those religious beliefs themselves. The Christian proclamation speaks about sin and grace, about the work of the Holy Spirit and the necessity to sanctify one's life. Doctrine thus stands within a broader context. Just as Judaism placed religious ideas within the context of God's covenant with His people, so too Christianity places doctrine within the context of the communion between God and those who believe in Him, a communion made possible by Christ and which, according to Christian conviction, is realized 'in Christ.'[17] The truth of doctrine is thus imbedded in —to put it in words— the truth of life. Connotations of trustworthiness and steadfastness, so characteristic of the Hebrew word ĕmet, are often also attached to the Greek word *alètheia* in the New Testament. The expression 'the truth of God' can thus amount to an indication of God's faithfulness.[18] 'Truth' stands for what is abiding and for that upon which one can rely

---

[15] See K. H. Miskotte, "De Opdracht der Exegese," in Miskotte, *Om het Levende Woord* (Kampen ²1973), pp. 51 ff.

[16] See J. H. Vrielink, *Het Waarheidsbegrip: Een Theologisch Onderzoek* (Nijkerk 1956), pp. 76 f. (e.g., II Corinthians 4:2; Colossians 1:5.)

[17] *Ibid*, pp. 79 f.

[18] *Ibid*, pp. 73 ff.; Romans 3:7.

on. Since Christian truth stands in the context of life lived in communion
with God, there is a relationship between religious belief and life.

An opposition between the Hebrew, or, more broadly, the biblical, and
the Greek concept of truth has occasionally been concluded. In his
investigation of the concept of truth, Vrielink has shown that the Greek
notion of 'unrevealed reality' has been incorporated in the New Testament
'concept of truth.'[19] The concept of truth has obtained a shade all its own
in one of the four Gospels, that of John. Mentioned in the Gospel and in
the epistles of John is the phrase 'being in the truth.'[20] The intent of this
term is a life in love, knowledge, and insight. The knowledge concerned
is therefore not a purely theoretical knowledge, but knowledge of the
heart — experiential, personal, and trusted knowledge, to put it in a way
which makes use of a number of expressions widespread in the Christian
tradition. In fact, one might say that the truth here means the communion
of God and man; the believer *is* in that communion.[21] Whoever *is* in that
communion has passed from the kingdom of darkness and lying into the
kingdom of light and truth. This is what enables Christians to say, "The
truth shall set you free."[22] The truth is not thought of —and certainly not
in the Johannine writings— as a theoretical insight which one must
obtain in order subsequently to act on one's own, but as active insight,
religious belief, and communion with God in Christ — all in one.[23]

We also encounter this combination of knowledge and reality in the
prologue of the Gospel of John, which states that all things were created
by the Word (i.e., Christ). The Word is here the creating Word of God; it
is the same Word which became human in Christ; and that is again
identical, or at least closely related, to the proclaimed Word of God. No
matter how this has been elaborated in the dogmatic tradition, the truth
here has a reality side and a cognitive side. The knowledge concerned is
'relational'; it consists in a living relationship between the believer and
God. This relationship exists; one is aware of it; and the latter represents
the cognitive aspect within that relationship.[24]

Since Christ is the ground of what has been created as well as the
content of the Gospel, one can understand why He Himself is called the
truth in the Gospel of John: "I am the truth, the way, and the life"
(John 14:6). In Him both the reality of the world as well as the reality of
God are revealed. Communion with God embraces life, and therefore the
conduct (the way) and the knowledge of this life. If it is said that it is

---

[19] *Ibid*, p. 75.

[20] *Ibid*, pp. 81ff.; see also L. Goppelt, "Wahrheit als Befreiung: Das Neutestamentliche
Zeugnis von der Wahrheit nach dem Johannes-Evangelium" in *Was ist Wahrheit?* ed.
H. -R. Müller-Schwefe (Göttingen 1965), pp. 80-93.

[21] See also R. Bultman, *s.v.* '*alètheia*,' in *Theol. Wörterbuch zum N. T.*, I, ed. G. Kittel
(Stuttgart 1933), pp. 246f.

[22] John 8:32.

[23] See also Vrielink, pp. 94ff.

[24] *Ibid*, p. 101.

determinative for the Christian concept of truth that Christ is the truth, this may be so understood, in our opinion, that, on the one hand, Jesus Christ reveals God, and on the other, he reconciles and joins God and man as humanity's Redeemer. That is why the proclamation of the Gospel in the New Testament is always accompanied by the call to conversion and the offer of forgiveness. One often reads nowadays that 'Christian truth' is not a theory, but trust in a person, that is, Christ. It seems to us that according to the biblical representation of matters, knowing God through the mediation of Christ is not a purely intellectual knowing, but an experiential knowing which comprises a Christian disposition and religious experience. The corollary of this is that the concept of truth stands in the context of life. One could say that in Christian faith, it is the truth of life itself which is at issue, including knowing. This comes to the foreground most clearly in the notion of 'doing the truth' and 'being in the truth' in the Johannine writings, which, it is commonly supposed, were written a few decennia later than the letters of Paul and the other three Gospels. People warn us nowadays against 'reading' the thought pattern of one Bible book into other Bible books. Also with respect to the 'concept of truth' in the New Testament, one must take into account that the various meanings which the word *alètheia* acquires exhibit family resemblances, without, however, it being possible to speak of the *essence* of the biblical concept of truth. Given the fact that the word *alètheia* in the New Testament appears in various contexts and accordingly shows various shades of meaning, it is understandable that divergent accents were laid in later Christian tradition. It is nevertheless defensible, in our opinion, to state that truth in the New Testament concerns experiential insight in personal commitment to God and His Kingdom. A certain relation between Christian faith and specific historical events is of course presupposed here.

3.2 Augustine

Augustine (354–430) already exercised an enormous influence on the Christian church in his own time but afterwards as well. His thought made its impress on a large segment of the Western Church in the Middle Ages. Augustine was born in Thagaste, North Africa; he was familiar with the Christian church since boyhood, but during his education in rhetoric in Carthage, he succumbed to the influence of Manicheism, a dualist philosophy of life, which assumed two mutually antagonistic forces, both conceived of materialistically.[25] By way of skeptical philosophy, Augustine came to *Platonism,* which seemed to him an antechamber to a deeper, non-materialistic understanding of the Bible. While in contact with St. Ambrose in Milan, Augustine came to believe; upon his return to North

---

[25] For what follows, A. Sizoo, *Augustinus: Leven en Werken* (Kampen 1957).

Africa, he became bishop in Hippo Regius, where he dictated most of his works. He points to deep similarities between Platonism and Christianity, as well as differences.

The New Testament view of truth, as we have encountered it in John, lies at the heart of Augustine's thought. As the Word through which God created all things and through which God has communicated Himself, Christ is the truth. The only begotten Word of God is the immutable truth. But the doctrine is also 'truth' (*veritas*). God is also the truth (*ubi enim inveni veritatem, ibi inveni deum meum, ipsam veritatem*).[26] Another point on which Augustine insisted is that although the truth is near to man, yet as a result of sin, man does not take hold of it. The doctrine of sin obtained an emphatic form in Augustine.[27] The impediments to knowing the truth are raised many times.

a) Epistemology

The truth is near to man. Man '*is*', because he receives his existence from God. As a creature, man is limited and changeable, and thus imperfect and not self-sufficient.[28] Man can only achieve the fulfillment of his existence in relationship to God. This is expressed by Augustine with the famous words, *inquietum est cor nostrum, donec requiescat in te.* (Our heart is restless until it finds rest in Thee.)[29] Mankind has become estranged from God by the fall into sin, and has deteriorated to that which pleases the eye and is pleasant to the stomach, to *concupiscentia* (lust).[30] Sin can be forgiven, because Christ is the mediator between God and man, having atoned for sin. In order to truly know God, the relationship between God and man must be restored, and one must learn to conquer one's sinful impulses.[31] We will now describe some of the basic tenets in Augustine's epistemology. Augustine ascends to the existence of God from an analysis of doubt and cognition.

In answer to the reproach by the skeptics that one cannot know anything with certainty, Augustine gives an analysis of doubt in which he establishes the possibility of certain knowledge. Whoever errs, exists (*si enim fallor, sum*).[32] One can thus be certain that one '*is*'. Augustine contends that *reason* is the highest in man. He derives this from an

---

[26] Augustine, *Confessions*, X, XXIV; ("...where I found the truth, there I found my God, Truth itself"); see P. Böhner and E. Gilson, *Christliche Philosophie von ihren Anfängen bis Nikolaus von Cues* (Paderborn ³1954), pp. 185 f.

[27] See Adam, pp. 264 ff.; concerning the influence of Augustine's thought in theology, see O. Weber, *Grundlagen der Dogmatik*, I (Neukirchen ⁴1972), pp. 662 ff.

[28] See Böhner–Gilson, pp. 205 ff., 210 f.

[29] Augustine, *Confessions*, I, 1.

[30] See Adam, p. 267 f.

[31] See G. Groenewoud, "*In tam Excellenti Luce:* Saint Augustine on Faith and Understanding," in *Geloven en Denken*, ed. A. Th. Brüggeman-Kruijff (Amsterdam 1982), pp. 47, 49.

[32] In Böhner–Gilson, p. 172.

analysis of sensory cognition. The senses play a role in knowing things; still, it is not the ear or the eye that knows, because one knows by combining observations. Knowledge therefore lies in an inner sense (*sensus interior*).[33] Reason decides on the correctness of what one thinks to observe. Reason itself must also acknowledge a norm: above reason stands the truth, which sits in judgment on reason. The truth is universally valid; people arrive at the same perceptions. How is that possible? The truth, so runs the answer, is given to people; the eternal truths are transcendent and transsubjective. In its analysis of reason, reason itself thus finds something in consciousness which is beyond itself, an absolute — eternal and immutable.[34] Thus we see how Augustine considers the eternal, conceived of as the immutable, to be the only true being. Plurality and complexity imply mutability. The transcendent must therefore be one, indivisible and immutable. Augustine is thus brought to call the absolute, which is discovered by an analysis of knowledge, God. The Highest is God; He judges all things. Augustine, for the first time in the history of Western philosophy, according to Böhner-Gilson, thus gives a proof for God in terms of the cognitive subject.[35]

We will briefly return to the knowledge of composite things. Knowledge of things as such arises not from hearing or from the eye, as we have already heard. Man consists of a body and a soul. The apprehension of things as things belongs to the soul. How does the soul attain knowledge? Augustine distinguishes a double light by aid of which we perceive, to wit, a bodily light which is observed by our eyes, and a light by aid of which our eyes can perceive what is corporeal. There is an object which one sees, and a cognitive means (the light) by aid of which one sees. The cognitive faculty is based on a purely spiritual light which springs from the soul. With its aid one can learn to discern composite matters, such as a poem.[36]

Augustine distinguishes between the *ratio inferior* and the *ratio superior* (lower and higher reason). The *ratio inferior* knows the corporeal images which are present to the mind. The *ratio superior* stands in relation to eternal reason, and is thus capable of making judgments regarding things which come to the mind through the senses, as well as discerning the reasons by aid of which the mind pronounces judgments.[37]

The above is valid for knowledge in general. But it is not possible to acquire knowledge of all things by means of sensory perception. One can come to know a great deal of reality in this fashion, but not all of it. Consideration of what one perceives affords no knowledge of history or of the resurrection of the body, for example. It is a privilege of the

---

[33] *Ibid*, p. 177.
[34] *Ibid*, pp. 178f.
[35] *Ibid*, p. 176.
[36] *Ibid*, pp. 181ff.; on the doctrine of enlightenment, *ibid*, pp. 186f.; Groenewoud, pp. 58f.
[37] Böhner–Gilson, pp. 192f.

angels to have insight into such matters, and of certain people, who, enlightened by the Holy Spirit, are able to discern what will come to pass.[38]

On the basis of these considerations, Augustine grants legitimacy to knowledge based on *authority*. A reliable witness is a source of valid knowledge.[39] An extension of this reasoning, of course, lies in the fact that Augustine regards Holy Scripture as the source from which one receives knowledge regarding such matters as the resurrection, Christ, and the justification of mankind. Given the importance of the knowledge which can be procured from the Scriptures, Augustine considers knowledge based on Scripture of great significance.[40]

According to Augustine, it is possible not only to believe but also to comprehend what Scripture says by means of rational reflection. The acceptance of the Gospel precedes understanding (*credo ut intelligam*: I believe in order to understand).[41] True understanding is possible only for those who keep God's commandments and who have a pure heart.[42] Groenewoud points out that the chief question for Augustine after his conversion is no longer whether knowledge of God is possible, but why, as a matter of fact, the Truth is not discovered.[43] Just as in other religious epistemologies, we find a strong accent here on the obstacles which impede people from discovering (and seeking) the truth. One must not conceive of this emphasis on knowledge intellectualistically. Since thought abides by the norm of the truth, thinking is related to God. A close, immediate relationship exists between cognition and God. If one achieves conscious knowledge of God, then one lives in relationship to God. Groenewoud notes that for Augustine, knowing God means being in touch with the Truth; it means meeting God.[44]

b) Truth

After an explication of what deceiving is, Augustine arrives at the following definition of truth in *De vera religione*: 'Once we have accepted as evident that deceptiveness is that by which non-being is held to be something that is, then we understand that *the truth is that by which being is made manifest.*'[45] In what follows, we will explain this definition of truth.

---

[38] Groenewoud, p. 69.
[39] *Ibid*, pp. 68f.
[40] *Ibid*, p. 70.
[41] *Ibid*, p. 42, see pp. 49ff.
[42] *Ibid*, p. 49.
[43] *Ibid*, p. 43.
[44] *Ibid*, p. 59, see p. 65.
[45] Augustine, *De Vera Religione*, § 66; the definition is *eas esse veritatem, quae ostendit id quod est*, Augustine, *Opera*, XXXII (Turnhout 1962).

For an understanding of Augustine's concept of truth, it is necessary to bear in mind that he connects ontology and epistemology. In Augustine, as in Platonic philosophy, the Highest is the One; it is true Being. To his mind, Truth is One. We can comprehend the relation between Truth, Being, and Oneness as follows: All things are subject to mutation, Augustine writes; they consist of parts, each with its own function. If one thinks that one perceives a thing, one does not, strictly speaking, see a unitary thing, but one receives a number of impressions which one understands as a unity, as a single thing.[46] Unity is therefore seen with the mind.[47] Actually, no perceptible body achieves that unity completely. Even the most beautiful body cannot fully realize the unity striven after, because it has parts which inevitably occupy more than one point in space. Whoever knows an object as a unity judges that his perception is in accordance with the *concept* of unity. One 'sees' the unity with one's mind. But where do we see the unity, Augustine asks? As to its spatial location, it is nowhere; as to its power, it is everywhere.[48] Because and inasmuch as things possess something of that Unity, they refer to that which has and is the highest Oneness.[49] They partly participate in the being of that Oneness, and to that extent, they truly '*are*'. Augustine relates unity, being, and truth; truth is the standard of thought; the truth is the One by which everything that '*is*', exists.

One must try to know the Truth, which is that according to which all things are judged, the Highest Oneness, surpassing all things in simplicity.[50] This Highest therefore does not lie in composite things. One cannot 'ex-plain' by verbal articulation since this would be composite. Human 'truth' is referential by nature for that very reason. Augustine thus arrives at a definition of *truth* as *that by which being is made manifest*.[51] What allows being, real Being, to be manifest? In the first place, Christ; in a second, derivative sense, things and words. Christ 'so resembles the only Oneness, the source and the origin of all existing unity, that He realizes it perfectly and is the Same. This is the Truth, the Word, which was in the beginning, the Word which is with God.'[52] Christ is the Truth, Being, equal to the Father, the Oneness in Whom all things were created, in Whom all things have their being, in Whom they are known well.[53]

Since all things have their existence —their true being— in Christ, they can be *true* to a certain extent. 'All things can be called similar to

---

[46] Augustine, *De Vera Religione*, § 55 ff.
[47] *Ibid*, § 60.
[48] *Ibid*, § 60.
[49] *Ibid*, at the end of § 63.
[50] *Ibid*, § 65.
[51] *Ibid*, § 66; see also "nam verum mihi videtur esse id quod est," *Soliloquia*, II, *c.* 5; see J. Aertsen, *Middeleeuwse Beschouwingen over Waarheid* (Amsterdam 1984), p. 7, n. 16, where truth is conceived of in a Platonic fashion as the truth of being.
[52] *Ibid*, *s.v. De Vera Religione*, § 66.
[53] Augustine, *De Civitate Dei*, XI, 29.

that Oneness insofar as they are, because to the same degree they are also true.'[54] God is immutable being. His name is *ego sum qui sum* (I am who I am).[55] Christ is the truth about God, in which God has expressed Himself.[56]

God *is*. People exist, but the degree in which people really truly 'are' depends on the degree to which they are with God. Whoever is with God has obtained insight into God's law, in accordance with which all things must be judged.[57] 'One is with God when one has a purged understanding and also loves with a wholesale love that which one understands.'[58] The pure in soul can acquire knowledge of the eternal law and they see things as they are.[59]

Augustine speaks about Jesus Christ as the Truth in Whom God is known. He speaks of people who participate in the truth of Christ. In addition, he of course treats of true statements, such as this *confession*: 'For it is true, Lord, that You have made heaven and earth.'[60] This statement is true in the sense that it 'allows being to be manifest.' But this statement is not unqualifiedly accessible. Understanding of 'the truth' requires moral growth and faith in Christ. For Augustine —as one might put it— the truth of propositions refers to the Truth itself, Christ, Who allows He Who fully '*is*' to be manifest.

We have also seen that in all cognition of things whatsoever, mankind must rely on the light of the truth. For the knowledge of Christ as the Truth, one is dependent on the Holy Scriptures. This knowledge can be appropriated only if one repents and turns to God, who forgives sins, and if one lives as God wants. The deepest truth of faith is always accompanied by love for God.

3.3 Thomas Aquinas

Thomas Aquinas (1224–1274) has permanently influenced the history of the Western Church. Of noble Italian ancestry, he worked in Paris and Rome. He was acquainted with the writings of Aristotle.[61] While Platonism was of great influence on Augustine and Augustinian theology, Thomas joins this line of thought to the Aristotelian approach to reality.[62] Perhaps on account of a less eventful life, Böhner and Gilson note, Thomas's

---

54 Augustine, *De Vera Religione*, § 66.
55 Augustine, *De Civitate Dei*, XII, 2; Groenewoud, p. 34; Exodus 3:14.
56 See also Groenewoud, p. 36.
57 Augustine, *De Vera Religione*, § 58, see § 66.
58 *Ibid*, § 58.
59 *Ibid*, § 58.
60 Augustine, *Confessions*, XII, 28; cf. ff.
61 Böhner–Gilson, p. 512.
62 See J. A. Aertsen, *Natura en Creatura: De denkweg van Thomas van Aquino* (Amsterdam 1982), I, 8; Aertsen, *Waarheid* (Amsterdam 1984), p. 7.

outlook on life was more optimistic, and he had a higher estimation of mankind's intellectual powers than Augustine.[63]

One must distinguish between 'the real Thomas,' as he is seen in modern interpretations, and Thomas as the Christian tradition has read him for centuries. The most influential Thomas interpreter, Cajetanus (1469–1534), so say contemporary interpreters, left the Platonic element in Thomas's thought underexposed, that is, the thought that all being *'is'* by participation in the Being which God gives (and is). The emphasis lay on the power of human reason to obtain rational understanding of God's existence and also of the createdness of the world by analysis of the causal relations in nature. Creation in *time* —as with Maimonides— is an article of faith.[64]

A two part division in the knowledge of God is often considered to be the most characteristic feature of Thomist philosophy. (1) By means of rational analysis, proceeding from the world of sense perception, one can infer the existence of God as Creator. (2) For knowledge of God as Father, Son, and Holy Spirit, and thus for knowledge concerning Jesus, His crucifixion, and His resurrection, we must rely on Holy Scripture. We shall see shortly that Thomas distinguishes a third form of the knowledge of God; for the moment, however, we will leave things be in terms of this twofold division. This twofold path to the whole knowledge of God corresponds to a —disputed— 'duplex ordo' in his anthropology. In Thomist thought, as it has been influenced by Cajetanus, the natural and the supernatural in man are to be distinguished.[65] According to Thomas, all things find their fulfillment in reaching the end to which they are predisposed. In Cajetanus' interpretation, the natural end of man is the knowledge of God which can be obtained from created things.[66] Only if God, in His grace, supplies an additional supernatural faculty to man, is the end of man —then attainable— the beatific *visio Dei* (contemplation of God).

According to the Thomist scholastic theology and philosophy, there are thus two kinds of knowledge of God, natural and supernatural: knowledge of God on the basis of reason, and knowledge of God on the basis of revelation and grace. A tendency to relate the 'natural' and 'supernatural' in man more closely to each other can be observed in the 20th century. This tendency is related to renewed study of Thomas himself, which detects a closer relationship between man and the *visio Dei beatifica* than was supposed by scholastic philosophy. It is believed that the inter-relationships in the thought of Thomas are more complicated

[63] Böhner–Gilson, pp. 512, 542.
[64] *Ibid*, pp. 528f.
[65] Aertsen, *Natura*, p. 358.
[66] *Ibid*, p. 358; compare Böhner–Gilson on the doctrine of analogies which plays a role here, pp. 53ff.

than it has been customary to think for many centuries.[67] Thomas believes that the ultimate happiness of man after the fall into sin, the *visio Dei*, can not be attained in a straightforward manner. After the fall into sin, mankind still remained human; Thomas speaks of human nature in this connection. Of this natural man, it must be said that he has the propensity for an end (the knowledge of God).[68] The natural longing of man for the fulfillment of this end is no idle desire; the existence of God can in principle be understood by the intellect.[69] The *visio Dei* remains unattainable for the natural man, however, and is therefore a *supernatural* happiness in which man not only knows that God exists but also knows what He is *in se* (in Himself). Ultimately beatific knowledge therefore lies outside of the scope of 'natural' reason. For deeper, true knowledge of God, grace and revelation are needful. We will now inquire in somewhat more depth into Thomas's epistemology and subsequently into his concept of truth.

In the acquisition of knowledge man searches for the permanent, necessary order of things; it involves knowledge of the reasons for that which is perceived by the senses (*rationes eorum quae videntur secundum sensum*).[70] All that can be known is based on necessity (*omne scibile est ex necessitate*).[71] Thomas is a pupil of the Greek philosophers in this regard; only the permanent and the necessary is the real. Knowledge is therefore not knowledge of the many phenomena in their particulars, but is knowledge of structures and *causes*. As opposed to Platonism, Thomas —along with Aristotle— looks for what is permanent not in the *ideas*, ideal beings which substand visible reality, but in the necessary order of things. Investigation of things must penetrate to the causes —ultimately to the First Cause— in order to comprehend becoming, moving, and being moved.[72] Rational investigation thus leads to knowledge of nature as creation. Thomas indicates five ways, or *viae*, which compel reason to conclude that God exists. These *viae* reason to God's existence in different ways; by motion, by efficient cause, by possibility and necessity, and by teleology (governance). In addition, one of the proofs is based on the different degrees of perfection in created reality which point towards God's perfection.[73] This last proof is more closely related to the participation doctrine of the Platonic tradition than the Aristotelian analysis of

---

[67] Cf. Aertsen, pp. 359 f.; see also below, our exposition of Rahner, § 3.6.

[68] *Ibid*, p. 361.

[69] See also B. Delfgaauw, *Thomas van Aquino: Een Kritische Benadering van zijn Filosofie* (Bussum 1980), p. 38. One does well to recall in this connection that the knowledge of God remains limited. "For we cannot grasp what God is, but only what He is not and how other things are related to Him . . . ," Thomas, *Summa Contra Gentiles*, Chapter 30, conclusion.

[70] Aertsen, *Natura*, p. 244.

[71] *Ibid*, p. 244.

[72] *Ibid*, p. 245; cf. the 1st and 2nd Chapters.

[73] Böhner–Gilson, pp. 518 ff.; cf. Aertsen, *Natura*, p. 151.

causes.[74] Man can rationally infer the existence of God along these 'ways.' Thomas proceeds in terms of a harmony between reason and faith. He therefore relates universal human rational analysis of things as they appear to reason to what revelation says about the creation. In all of his thought, Thomas relates the consideration of things as nature to the consideration of things as *creatum*, Aertsen remarks in his study on Thomas.[75]

Knowledge occupies a prominent place for Thomas. For knowledge implies a relation to its object; knowing things produces a change in the understanding due to the influence of what is apprehended.[76] The understanding is not just another function of man — it is his essence. 'That by which man is, is his intellect.'[77] The human soul, itself indeterminate, strives by nature for *habitus scientia* (actualized knowledge) as its perfection. Knowledge is a good as such; it is the fulfillment of human propensities. This quest for knowledge of causes, and ultimately of the First Cause, is conditioned by the philosophical context of the ancient *theoria* (contemplative) ideal in which the aim is always the contemplation of what things are *in themselves*.[78] The understanding molds itself to things; it is receptive to the order of things. 'The perfection which man desires, is that the order of causes is inscribed in his soul. This perfection can also be characterized as *scientie veritatis* [knowledge of truth] ... ' Aertsen comments.[79] Man attains the fulfillment of his existence in this knowledge. This is particularly true of knowledge of God.

Man's reason leads him to God along five 'ways,' as we have seen. By knowing God, man knows Him who is both the Source and the End of all things.[80] God Himself also knows, in His own way, for God does not have, but *is* perfect knowledge; He is the truth.[81] His knowledge is the *logos,* or Christ. In human cognition, the subject participates in the Truth. Perfect knowledge is the end towards which man is predisposed. That is why the Truth is the ultimate end of the universe.[82] As such, knowledge of God as the Truth, as the end towards which man is predisposed, is bliss; for in knowing, the subject is related to its Object.[83] We will now pursue more closely Thomas's concept of truth.

---

[74] F. Sassen, *Thomas van Aquino* (Den Haag ²1961) pp. 112f.; cf. also Delfgaauw, pp. 60, 126.

[75] Aertsen, *Natura*, p. 120.

[76] Böhner–Gilson, p. 542, "Der Mensch bleibt wesentlich passiv im Erkennen"; cf. Sassen, pp. 98ff.; Aertsen, *Waarheid*, p. 17: this change is an assimilation.

[77] In Aertsen, *Natura*, p. 40.

[78] *Ibid*, p. 51; see also Delfgaauw, p. 136.

[79] *Ibid*, p. 135; see also *Waarheid*, pp. 14f.

[80] Thomas, *Summa Contra Gentiles*, I, 91f., 246; see also Aertsen, p. 151.

[81] *Ibid*, I, Chapter 60f.; see also Chapter 45. 7.

[82] *Ibid*, I. 1. (2); see also Aertsen, *Natura*, p. 136.

[83] Delfgaauw, p. 136; see also Aertsen, *Waarheid*, p. 17: identity of the knowing mind and the known.

The familiar definition which Thomas gave for truth is as follows: *adequatio rei et intellectus* (correspondence of subject-matter to the mind).[84] In cognition, one knows the object; the concept of truth adds something to the object, viz. the relation of corresponence (*adequatio* or *conformitas,* or *convenientia*). Truth is always a relation between thought and reality.[85] This relation exists in the fact that an interiorization of the thing occurs, that is, as an object of cognition.[86] Being is manifest in judgment. The *home* of truth is the word, foremost the inner word.[87] The object of cognition has an existence of its own outside of the subject and his knowledge, and it remains unaffected by cognition.[88] Knowledge is based on reality and on the apprehensiblity of its object.[89] Knowledge stands in relation to the object of cognition; the object does not stand in relation to cognition. The truth of things only becomes manifest in human knowledge, however.[90] Things can only be apprehended if they are *apprehensible,* which they can be only if their *form* is conformable to the intellect.[91] If the *form* of the object is realized in the actual object of cognition, then it is apprehensible; Aertsen calls this the cognitive 'unconcealed-ness' of the thing.[92] The possibility of human knowledge is contingent upon the prime forms and principles of the things one knows.

The idea of a form waiting to be realized points towards God. One cannot view things in isolation. In themselves, things have no being. The constant aspiration of the Franciscans in their use of Augustinian theology in the Middle Ages was to point out the imprint of the Creator on the world. Aertsen points out that a similar train of thought is to be found here in Thomas's case.[93] Considered in themselves, without a ground, things are non-being, darkness, and without truth (*si consideretur sine hoc quod ab alio habet, est nihil et tenebra et falsitas*).[94] Their truth is created (*veritas rei est aliquid creatum*).[95] Things have being because they are known by God. They are apprehensible to human beings thanks to their conformity to their Principle. The truth of things therefore ultimately lies in God's ideas, just as the 'knowing' of an artist is the standard which

---

[84] Thomas, I. 59. (2); see also *De Veritate,* German tr. E. Stein, *Des Heiligen Thomas von Aquino: Untersuchungen über die Wahrheit* (Leuven 1952), art. 1 (p. 11).

[85] Aertsen, *Natura,* p. 137; *Waarheid,* pp. 16ff.

[86] B. Rioux, *L'être et la Vérité chez Heidegger et Saint Thomas d'Aquin* (Montréal and Paris 1963), p. 236, "nous avons conscience que notre intelligence devient l'être tel qu'il est en lui-même," cf. pp. 180ff., 188f.; Aertsen, *Waarheid,* p. 18.

[87] Aertsen, *Waarheid,* p. 19.

[88] See also Rioux, p. 238.

[89] Aertsen, *Natura,* pp. 145f.

[90] Rioux, p. 185, "la vérité n'est manifestée qu'en nous."

[91] In Aertsen, *Natura,* p. 143.

[92] *Ibid,* p. 144; see also Rioux, p. 180, "le vrai ne dit formellement que l'être manifesté." See also p. 238.

[93] Aertsen, *Natura,* p. 148.

[94] In Aertsen, p. 148.

[95] *Ibid,* p. 148.

the objects he makes must meet.[96] The truth of things is thus derived from the *veritas mensurans* (the measurement giving Truth), which is to say, the source of all that *is* true, or God.[97] The relationship of God to things is essential for their truth. The true exists by participation in God's original truth. Truth and being therefore have the same origin, namely God, who is Truth and Being.[98]

God is the ultimate end towards which all that is creaturely moves.[99] Therefore for man, as a cognitive being, says Aertsen, 'only the contemplation of God, who is the truth *per essentiam* . . . [can] make him completely happy.'[100] The perfection of man, to which he aspires, is being assimilated to God through essential knowledge of God.[101]

The relation between God and man also has an ethical significance. The divine majesty evokes fear of God; one is brought to works of gratitude; the knowledge that God leads all things for good summons us to patience in adversity; the knowledge of God's purpose obliges us to a responsible dealings with what is created; understanding of the dignity of man arises from the knowledge that God has made all things for the sake of man.[102]

Not all things can be plain to reason. The believer knows from revelation that the world was created by God in *time*, knowledge which one cannot find in Greek philosophy; such knowledge would be impossible without revelation.[103] Because of the revelation, knowledge of God is also accessible for those not capable of rational analysis. Aertsen cites the following phrase of Thomas: 'Before the coming of Christ, not a single philosopher, despite all his exertions, could know as much about God and the things necessary for eternal life as an old woman can know by faith since the coming of Christ'![104]

Human knowledge of the divine is actually threefold.[105]

    (1) By rational analysis of what is created, man can attain to knowledge of God.

    (2) God, in His goodness, has revealed the divine truth which surpasses the human intellect. Theology reflects on this truth.

    (3) If the human mind is elevated to an understanding of what

---

[96] *Ibid*, p. 155; see also Delfgaauw, p. 59.

[97] Aertsen, *Natura*, pp. 150f.; *Waarheid*, p. 20.

[98] Aertsen, *Natura*, p. 151; *Waarheid*, pp. 21f. As the Word of God then, Christ is the Truth.

[99] Aertsen, *Natura*, p. 352.

[100] *Ibid*, p. 352.

[101] *Ibid*, p. 373.

[102] *Ibid*, p. 188.

[103] *Ibid*, pp. 188ff.

[104] In Aertsen, *Natura*, p. 188; see also Gilson-Böhner, p. 516; compare with the reasons Maimonides gives for why most people are totally dependent on revelation.

[105] Aertsen, *Natura*, pp. 196f.

has been revealed, then the first truth is *known* not as something which is believed but as something which is seen.[106] Thus reasonable knowledge and faith are joined by Thomas. Thomas sees the beatific *visio Dei* primarily as contemplation of the divine essence, a *visio Dei per essentiam*.[107] The emphasis which Thomas placed on thought and on theoretical knowledge has been of great influence in the entire Western Church, both in the Middle Ages as well as in later Protestantism, and especially in the Neo-Thomist resurgence at the end of the 19th and the beginning of the 20th century.

In summary, we can state that the core of Thomas's concept of truth insofar as it concerns human, and particularly religious, knowledge, is:

(1) That in true knowledge there is a complete correspondence between knowledge and what is known.

(2) That a relationship arises between subject and object through cognition.

(3) This relationship ultimately results in a participation in God, the *visio beatifica Dei*, inasmuch as the knowledge of God is concerned.

This also makes clear that for Thomas (just as for Maimonides), intellectual knowledge is essential to man.

3.4 John Calvin

John Calvin (1509–1564), born in northern France, was one of the leaders of the Reformation.[108] He worked chiefly in Geneva. Calvin has for centuries inspired a large part of Reformed theology with his *Christianae Religionis Institutio* (1536), which he expanded greatly in the course of his life up until the last edition of *The Insitutes of the Christian Religion* in 1559, and which became the founding work of the Reformed and Presbyterian Churches. In addition, the biblical commentaries by Calvin have had great influence.

The Reformation began in 1517 with Luther's actions in Wittenberg, by which he wanted to publicly challenge some of the customs and conceptions of the Catholic Church of his day. Luther's action found an echo in the response of others; it led to a confrontation with papal authority, and ultimately to a major secession from the Roman Catholic Church. Protestantism itself encompasses many movements, such as Lutheranism, Baptists, Calvinism, and Anglicanism. The 'Reformed family,' with about 70 million members, currently forms the largest among the traditions which sprang from the Reformation. That forms a second reason, next to

---

[106] See F. Diekamp, *Katholische Dogmatik nach den Grundsätzen des heiligen Thomas*, I (Münster [11]1949), pp. 6 f., 'überdiskursiv.'

[107] Aertsen, *Natura*, p. 202.

[108] For what follows, C. Augustijn, *Calvijn* (Den Haag 1966).

Calvin's systematic exposition of religious doctrine, to devote a section to him within the context of this enquiry.

The Reformation advocated concentrating on the message of the Bible. They wanted a purification of the late Medieval church, both with respect to doctrine and to ecclesiastical custom and structures. The Catholic Church ascribed an authoritative position to the ecclesiastical tradition in the interpretation of the Bible and in the government of the church. This ultimately resulted in a number of conceptions which did not square with the content of the Bible, in the eyes of the Reformers. They tried to develop doctrines and a church organization themselves which were in agreement with the Bible.[109] All valid knowledge about God and created reality ought to be derived from Holy Scripture, in their judgment. The formal criterion of Reformational theology was thus the *sola scriptura* (Scripture alone).[110] They wanted to keep to what was written, without subtractions or additions. The core of the Reformational confession was substantially the *solus Christus* (Christ alone): both salvation as well as the knowledge of God are in fact acquired exclusively on the basis of God's revelation in Jesus Christ.[111]

Calvin recognizes two fundamental forms of revelation: Firstly, a general human revelation and, secondly, a special, Christian revelation.[112] According to Calvin, all people have a *sensus divinitatis,* which is an awareness that there is a God.[113] This awareness is universally human. It is a feature of being human. Corresponding to this is the fact that created reality as such testifies that the world is *opus Dei* (the work of God).[114] Creation and the course of things testify to the existence and the guidance of God. However, although they actually do testify, this is not always effective. Because of the fall into sin, the significance which can be gleaned from the facts is not seen unless people have first come to know God from the other form of revelation, the Holy Scriptures.[115]

The special revelation is Jesus Christ, in whom God has made Himself known to humanity and in whom He has reconciled humanity to Himself.[116] To make Himself known to humanity, God acted in Israel's history, and more particularly, in Jesus Christ. The Bible gives God's faithful and true announcement of these things. That is why knowledge of God is to be

---

[109] E.g., J. van Genderen, "Calvijns Dogmatisch Werk," in J. van Genderen et al., *Zicht op Calvijn* (Amsterdam 1965), pp. 28 ff.

[110] See T. H. L. Parker, *Calvin's Doctrine of the Knowledge of God* (1952; rpt. Edinburgh 1969), p. 75; also H. Liebling, "Sola scriptura: Die reformatorische Antwort auf das Problem der Tradition," in *Sola Scriptura?* (Marburg 1977), pp. 81-95.

[111] Liebling, p. 91; see also Parker, pp. 101 f.; John Calvin, *Institutes of the Christian Religion,* 2 vols., Library of Christian Classics, ed. John T. McNeill, tr. Ford Lewis Battles (Philadelphia: Westminster Press: [7]1975), IV. viii. 7.

[112] Calvin, I, 1 ff.

[113] Parker, pp. 32 ff.; Calvin, I. iii.

[114] Calvin, I. v; Parker, pp. 36 ff.

[115] Calvin, I. v. (8); Parker, pp. 48.

[116] Parker, pp. 102; Calvin, II. xvi.

found in the Bible.[117] Holy Scripture, as was mentioned, is therefore the norm and criterion for all religious knowledge.[118] This knowledge concerns God. Calvin sharply resists all philosophical speculation about the essence of God on this point.[119]

The knowledge of God which really matters is no speculative knowledge of God's essence. Such knowledge is unattainable for man, because his reason is inadequate — and the pursuit of such knowledge is irreverent; man should be content with what it has pleased God to reveal. What God has made known in Scripture concerns God in relation to people. The knowledge of God is always knowledge of the Creator and the Redeemer. This knowledge of God immediately refers back to man.[120] Calvin begins the *Institutes* with the following words: "Nearly all the wisdom we possess, that is to say, true and sound wisdom, consists of two parts: the knowledge of God and of ourselves."[121] Knowledge of God as Creator and Redeemer correlates to knowledge of man's sin and pardon. Knowledge of God as Creator and governor of all things has profound significance for man. Calvin writes, " . . . you will easily perceive that ignorance of providence is the ultimate of all miseries; the highest blessedness lies in the knowledge of it."[122]

For Calvin, faith is the knowledge of what God says in Scripture, which —through the mediation of the Holy Spirit— one has appropriated.[123] The relationship between faith and knowledge in the history of the church has often been determined in terms of the Augustinian *credo ut intelligam* (I believe in order to understand); knowledge was usually esteemed as the highest. Calvin stands in this tradition; he insists on the fact that the initial knowledge ought to convey a person to faith-knowledge.[124] Calvin's concern is living knowledge of God, as again appears from his definition of faith: "We call it a firm and certain knowledge of God's benevolence towards us, founded upon the truth of the freely given promise in Christ, both revealed to our minds and sealed upon our hearts through the Holy Spirit."[125]

Faith is therefore based on a state of affairs, on God's revelation and promise. Calvin therefore regards healthy doctrine as being of great importance.[126] Purely theoretical knowledge is not sufficient however; if knowledge of God remains 'doctrine,' then it appears that one actually

---

[117] Calvin, I. vi. (2).
[118] *Ibid*, IV. viii. (8, 9); I. xiii. (21).
[119] *Ibid*, I. xvii. (1); I. ii. (12f.); see also L. Nixon, *John Calvin's Teaching on Human Reason* (New York 1963), pp. 112f.
[120] Calvin, I. ii.
[121] Calvin, I. i. 1.
[122] Calvin, I. xvii. 11.
[123] *Ibid*, III. ii. 33f.
[124] Parker, pp. 131f.
[125] Calvin, III. ii. 7.
[126] "But the basis of [faith] is a preconceived conviction of God's truth," *Ibid*, III. ii. 6.

does not know who God is. Calvin states that it is impossible to know God without trusting in Him. For Calvin, knowing is an activity of one's whole being; that is why it is not purely intellectual and is always linked to trust, love, and reverence.[127]

Although Calvin does not, to our knowledge, deal specifically with the concept of truth in the *Institutes*, we can infer that for Calvin, true knowledge of God is knowledge with personal commitment which both assumes and encourages the sanctification of life.[128] One attains God-fearing knowledge by the grace of God, by the working of His Spirit via Holy Scripture, and by the church's preaching.[129] Knowing God means living in relation to God. Just as God both reveals Himself and reconciles man to Himself in Christ, so too knowledge and salvation are interwoven in human knowledge.

Even though the *semen religionis* (seed of religion), or *sensus divinitatis* (sense of divinity), may be universally human according to Calvin, one is led to true knowledge of God only by grace and by the revelation in Christ. To Calvin, the manifold religious currents display to what extent people suppress the truth in unrighteousness.[130] They are not other forms of (good) knowledge of the divine; they represent erroneous and corrupted knowledge of God. The truth is distorted. Man's intellect itself has become corrupt as a result of the fall into sin. Only if the intellect is restored by grace is a person capable of applying his intellect to good end — at least if one keeps to that which is written. Calvin ascribes the fact that people who do not believe in God, or at any rate, do not know Him aright, can still do good deeds and attain generally correct insights to the merciful operation of God's Spirit on humankind.[131]

3.5 Karl Barth

The Swiss Reformed theologian Karl Barth (1886–1968) has exercised a great influence, particularly in Reformed theology, through his many publications. The theme of the *Church Dogmatics* is the priority of God's Word and God's Grace above human initiatives.[132] Barth elaborates this thought in an exceedingly consistent manner. During his study and the early years of his charge as preacher, Barth was influenced by liberal theology. The awareness slowly ripened in him that this form of Christian thought is incapable of truly preaching the radical Word of God. The

---

127 *Ibid*, I. ii. 1; v. 9; x. 2.
128 *Ibid*, III. ii. 8, "For even assent rests upon such pious inclination ... without a doubt, no one can duly know him without at the same time apprehending the sanctification of the Spirit," p. 552.
129 *Ibid*, III. ii. 34.
130 *Ibid*, I. iv; see Parker, Chapter II, 'Vanitas Mentis.'
131 Calvin, II. ii. 15. According to Parker's interpretation, Calvin ascribes no value to other religious traditions with respect to the worship of God, pp. 52 ff.
132 K. Barth, *Die Kirchliche Dogmatik*. For our exposition, see Part I, *Die Lehre vom Wort Gottes*, I/1 (Munich 1932), I/2 (Zürich 1938).

advances of liberal theology are subject to perpetual criticism by Barth, who spurns as uncritical the importance which is attached to historical-critical investigation for understanding the Word of God, as well as the efforts to legitimate faith in universal human terms.[133] Barth's work in the thirties must be understood in terms of his resistance to national socialism. He was one of the driving forces behind the *Barmen Declaration,* a statement by a minority group in the *Evangelical Churches,* which thereby adopted a critical posture with regard to the collaboration by the church leadership with national socialism.[134] From this one can understand that Barth vehemently opposed all attempts to relate certain aspects of human existence or certain historical figures or movements with God's work in the world. The 'German Christians' too easily pointed to the hand of God in the history of Germany. Barth was afraid that in seeking certain points of contact for revelation in human experience, certain experiences would be declared sacred, as it were, so that these elements of experience would start to determine what one wished to believe or not believe.[135] It was Barth's aspiration to dislodge any and all certainty in man, until he should stand empty-handed before the face of God and listen only to the Word of God. This aspiration can be recognized in Barth's considerations of *doctrine* and *religion.*

Barth's criticism also has bearing on the church itself. He criticizes not only the life philosophy of those who believe they can become good and happy on their own, but also movements in the church which believe that they can possess certain fundamental truths. Barth repudiates every theology which believes it possesses the truth in the form of correct articles of belief.[136] The truth for him is not true doctrine, as we shall see upon closer consideration. We shall also see that Barth speaks out against all religiosity with acerbity. But his criticism is directed most emphatically against Christianity as religion.[137] He opposes not only liberal theology, but orthodox theology as well, and Barth's thought is sometimes branded as neo-orthodox for that reason. He points to the priority of the revelation with all the insistence possible, yet without wholly subscribing to the doctrinal and orthodox character of conservative Reformed theology. Barth obtained great influence in Protestant circles in post-World War II theology. His thought about truth and religion cannot, however, be called representative for Protestantism. Since Barth can well be considered the greatest non-Roman Catholic theologian of the 20th century, his thought deserves a place in our overview.

---

[133] *Ibid,* I/2, 546.; I/1, 130 ff.

[134] See *Bekenntnisschriften und Kirchenordnungen der nach Gottes Wort reformierten Kirche,* ed. W. Niesel, pp. 333 ff. Note Barth's opposition to the 'Deutsche Christen,' *K. D.,* I/2, 318.

[135] Barth, *K. D.,* I/1, 134 f.

[136] *Ibid,* I/2, 967 f.

[137] *Ibid,* I/2, 358.

Barth's view of religion arises from his consideration of human dependence on God's Word. Central to the *Church Dogmatics,* which in its first part contains his most well-known consideration of *religion,* is the fact that man, seen by himself without God, is incapable of anything good, as well as the fact that God is forgiving and merciful, as we know from the life and work of Jesus Christ, the living Word of God.[138] Theology for Barth is theology of the Word of God. The term, Word of God, refers to: (1) Jesus Christ, in whom He lived among humankind and reconciled Himself with humanity; (2) the Bible as the book in which Jesus Christ encounters the church; (3) the proclamation of the church.[139] It is clear from this threesome that Barth's ultimate concern is that the Word of God is proclaimed as a concrete Word which confronts people personally in the situation in which they find themselves. Through the enlightenment of the Holy Spirit, it can transpire that a certain passage of Scripture is used by God and thus becomes the Word which He speaks to a certain person. The Word of God, when it is heard, is always a *verbum concretissimum* (concrete words).[140] Any human being who is confronted by that Word knows himself to be a sinner and realizes that he stands before the face of God empty-handed. On the basis of the Word of God, which the sinner accepts, and which forgives his sins and justifies him, the person makes a start at living in conformity to the Gospel. The sanctification of life is of course very important, but here too, according to Barth, it remains true that a person can never acquire merits through his works. If someone does what is good, then it is by the grace of God. Barth thus consistently insists on the constant priority of grace. God has created the world, the light, and life, out of darkness and 'nothingness.' He is true to His creation and gives it daily existence (*creatio continua*). In the same manner, He remains with the people whom He has elected to accept his mercy and listen to his Word — *electio continua* (continual election) or better, God's faithfulness and patience.[141]

God's Word confronts sinners. It comes *senkrecht von oben* (straight down from on high), as a new sound, as a new force in life which man does not anticipate in any way whatsoever.[142] Jesus was born without the virgin Mary having undertaken any action. People do not prepare a place for the Word of God to fill. God Himself creates an opening in which He makes Himself known and where His Word is heard. People must live from the hearing of forgiveness. Sanctification of life does not, therefore,

---

[138] *Ibid,* I/1, 208, 258; see H. M. Vroom, *De Schrift Alleen?* pp. 90 f.
[139] Barth, *K. D.,* I/1, 89 ff.; see Barth, *Einführung in die evangelische Theologie* (Zürich ²1963), pp. 23-33; see *De Schrift Alleen?* pp. 9 f., 88 f.
[140] Barth, *K. D.,* I/1, 141.
[141] *Ibid,* I/2, 383.
[142] Barth uses the expression in other passages as well; cf. the image of the angel who moves the water in the bath at Siloam, I/1, 114; I/2, 589.

entail a certain preparation for salvation. Salvation exists purely and only in living from forgiveness and grace.[143]

In later portions of the *Church Dogmatics,* Barth sometimes speaks of 'lights' which flash in certain spots in this dark world.[144] He then seems to allow for a more positive appraisal for certain persons, perceptions, and events. Barth's 'light doctrine' is mentioned in this spirit. Recall, however, that these nuances have exercised less influence than the 'radical Barth' of the first parts of the *Church Dogmatics.* In relation to the thematics which occupy us in this enquiry, it is especially important to indicate the influence which Barth's thought obtained in the Protestant churches' thought on missions. The line running from Barth's work to Christian missions run particularly via Hendrik Kraemer's study, *The Christian Message in a Non-Christian World* (1938).[145] Kraemer gives a more or less Barthian approach to other religions in this work, and he describes the task which the Christian church has, in his opinion, in the proclamation of the Word of God among the adherents of other religions. Kraemer has added precision and introduced nuance to his view in later works, but his first great study still remains an example of a Barthian approach to other religions from Christianity.[146]

What position did Barth ascribe to Christian doctrine? He speaks in two ways about *dogma.* He first describes dogma as "the church's proclamation, insofar as it truly corresponds to the Bible as the Word of God."[147] Barth stays within the vicinity of traditional Christian notions with this definition. But as we have already seen, Barth is very critical with regards to what man contends to know about God, for whoever knows something no longer stands empty-handed. A second definition of dogma is understandable in terms of Barth's hammering on this insight, a definition which we encounter on the very same pages as the first. Dogma here is not a substantial, but a 'relational concept'; it indicates the relation obtaining between the church's proclamation and the Word of God to which Holy Scripture testifies, or more particularly, it indicates its *correspondence* to it.[148] For Barth, dogma in this sense contains all particular dogmas; the concept points to the absolute truth, to the perfect knowledge of God's Word in the eschaton. People know the teaching of the church, the doctrines and dogmas; these point toward the full truth. The full and absolute truth is

---

[143] *Ibid,* I/2, 387 ff.

[144] See H. Berkhof and H. J. Kraus, *Karl Barths Lichterlehre* (Zürich 1978), esp. pp. 35 ff.

[145] H. Kraemer, *The Christian Message in a Non-Christian World* (London 1938).

[146] H. Kraemer, *Godsdienst, Godsdiensten en het Christelijk Geloof* (Nijkerk 1958), e.g., pp. 266 f.; see A. Wessels, "Dialoog of Getuigenis," in *De Dialoog Kritisch Bezien,* ed. A. W. Musschenga (Baarn 1983), pp. 162 ff. J. M. Vlijm, *Het Religiebegrip van Karl Barth* (Den Haag 1956), pp. 14 ff., 31 ff., gives a description of Kraemer's affinity to and emendation of Barth, and of three passages in which Barth speaks concerning religion, pp. 49 ff.

[147] Barth, *K. D.,* I/1, 283, see also p. 280.

[148] *Ibid,* I/1, 284; see Vroom, p. 103.

God Himself in His Revelation, Jesus Christ. Dogma is therefore an eschatological concept. What Barth says about dogma corresponds to his remarks regarding truth. The 'truth of Christianity' does not consist in an ecclesiastical doctrine of a religious organization which is true in itself. The following statement is characteristic for Barth's view:

> The one decisive question which confronts the Christian religion, or its adherents and representatives, in respect of its truth, is this: who and what are they in their naked reality, as they stand before the all-piercing eye of God?[149]

Doctrine too is only 'true' if it establishes this relation to God. Barth calls Christianity the only true religion. This it is only because and insofar as God Himself makes it true and just-ifies it.[150] "What is Truth, if it is not this divine Yes?"[151] Christian doctrine is only 'true' in a very limited sense of the word. The doctrine or the preaching of the church is used by God to justify man; herein lies its real truth. Christian faith can be called the true religion because God so uses and chooses the Christian religion. This can never become a quality which Christianity *has,* or which can be established by universal human standards.[152]

The heading above the section which Barth devotes to the relationship between Christian faith and other religions is: "Religion as Unbelief."[153] His thesis is that all religion is unbelief. This is true of other religious traditions; it is more seriously true of the Christian religion. Of itself, Christianity is not a true religion. It only becomes that in the name of Jesus Christ, when God speaks His Word to people.[154] It is not possible to further defend or explain this in universal human terms.[155] Even the most sublime expression of culture and religion are the work of sinful people who are trying to realize their own salvation and who create idols to that end.[156] We can accordingly understand the recapitulating thesis which Barth wrote at the top of his section on "The Revelation of God as the Abolition of Religion:"

> The revelation of God in the outpouring of the Holy Spirit is the judging but also reconciling presence of God in the world of human religion, that is, in the realm of man's attempts to justify and sanctify himself before a capricious and arbitrary picture of God. The church is the locus of true religion, so far as through grace it lives by grace.[157]

---

[149] *Ibid*, I/2, 391.
[150] *Ibid.*
[151] *Ibid*, I/2, 384.
[152] See Barth, I/2, 356; also the debate with H. Scholz, "Wie ist eine evangelische Theologie als Wissenschaft möglich?" (1931) in *Theologie als Wissenschaft*, ed. G. Sauter (Munich 1971), pp. 221-64; Barth, *K. D.*, I/1, 7 f.
[153] Barth, *K. D.*, I/2, 324 ff.
[154] *Ibid*, I/2, 376.
[155] *Ibid*, I/2, 364.
[156] *Ibid*, I/2, 344 f.; see Vlijm, p. 62.
[157] Barth, *K. D.*, I/2, 304.

This view has had a great deal of influence in Protestant missions circles. In the following section (§ 4) we will return to the Christian view of other religions as it has been developed within the World Council of Churches. First, however, we will now focus our attention on a Roman Catholic theologian, Karl Rahner, whose view has had great influence in Catholic circles.

3.6 Karl Rahner

Karl Rahner (1904–1984) is one of the most influential Roman Catholic theologians of our time. He took ahold of thoughts from Thomas, gave them an interpretation which was other than customary in Catholic 'scholastic theology,' and related them to the spirit of the Second Vatican Council — the *aggiornamento,* seeking to link up to the current times.[158] Two of the themes which have particularly exercised Rahner are the relationship between nature and grace and, in connection with that, the evaluation of other religious traditions in terms of Christian faith. We will spend some time on this. We will then examine his view of the value of religious knowledge. By way of introduction, we will present a short characterization of Rahner's view of Christian doctrine. He notes that Christianity more than other religions makes a claim to absolute truth.[159] At the same time, Rahner places major emphasis on the perception that the purpose of God's activity in the world is to save all people. He gives the following characterization of Christianity:

> Christianity is the outward and socially ('ecclesiastically') articulated confession that the absolute mystery which inevitably directs and governs our existence and which we call 'God,' communicates itself to us as forgiving and sublimely divine in the history of Spiritual freedom, and that God triumphantly reveals himself, historically and irreversibly, in Jesus Christ.[160]

This expresses what is decisive for Christianity, in Rahner's opinion. In this definition, we recognize the role of the church community; the element of doctrine and confession; the nearness of Creator and creature; the work of the Holy Spirit in church and world; and the special revelation of God in the climax of his merciful turning to this world in Jesus Christ. In his salvific and merciful nearness God remains the mystery before which a person inevitably finds himself placed. The person who responds positively to God's presence knows God, but he can never say who God is in adequately pure statements; the mystery of God surpasses

---

[158] See K. Rahner, "Die Wahrheit bei Thomas von Aquin," *Schriften zur Theologie,* X (Einsiedeln 1972), pp. 21ff.; "Die Heilsbedeutung der nichtchristlichen Religionen," *Orientierung* 39 (1975): 243ff.

[159] Rahner, "Das Christentum und die nichtchristlichen Religionen," *Schriften,* V (1962), p. 137.

[160] Rahner, "Intellektuelle Redlichkeit und christlicher Glaube," *Schriften,* VII (1966), p. 66.

human possibilities for cognition and designation.[161] Man does have his own responsibility, however, since one can reject God.[162] Rahner stresses that God's grace is not automatic. It is free grace, which God offers benevolently. Rahner therefore considers it necessary to discuss human nature independently of God's free grace.[163] Man is still responsible even without having obtained grace.

Actually, however, God mercifully turns to every person, whether the person is aware of it or not. Rahner's intention here is to indicate something which is universally true for all human beings; he expresses this by speaking of an *existential,* or a structural characteristic of human existence.[164] It is not an existential determinant of the natural person, however. Rahner therefore speaks of a supernatural existential characteristic of human existence, a supernatural existential determinant. God's merciful turning to man in general is therefore a fact. The human response to this grace of God, however, is not a universal human fact. Seen in terms of man, this grace of God offers the possibility for a saved and responsible human existence within the luminous circle of God's grace. Since human existence can only find its fulfillment in the acceptance of God's grace, Rahner speaks of the *entelechy* (purpose, teleology) in everyone's life history, or of the *finality* of man. Man, thanks to God's grace, is inclined towards immediate communion with God:

> Without detracting from its supernatural and voluntary character, it can be conceived of universally as a permanent, always and everywhere present *existential determinant* of man —of humanity and its history, as a perpetually present possibility for a salvific relationship in freedom to God, as the inner *entelechy* [purpose] of the history of individuals and of humanity as a whole, in which the merciful communion of God with the world, though unmerited, is nevertheless the ultimate finality and dynamic of the world and its history, equally true whether each human individual accepts or opposes it in his freedom.[165]

Rahner conceives of this receiving of grace by man as supernatural salvation history and as revelation history. Thanks to this undeserved grace, man is the object of God's revelation. Vandervelde states that in

---

[161] This is discussed more elaborately below; Rahner, "Was ist eine dogmatische Aussage?" *Schriften,* V, 68 ff.

[162] Rahner, "Die anonymen Christen," *Schriften,* VI (1965), p. 550; "Anonymer und expliziter Glaube," *Schriften,* XII (1975), p. 80.

[163] Rahner, "Natur und Gnade," *Schriften,* IV (1960), pp. 233 f.

[164] Rahner borrows this term from Heidegger to suit his own purposes, cf. "Die Heilsbedeutung...," p. 244; "Die anonyme Christen," VI, 546; consult "Natur und Gnade" concerning 'Formalobjekt' and transcendence, IV, 224 f.; compare with what he had written in 1938 with respect to Thomas Aquinas, concerning an apriori formal principle of the mind, in *Schriften* (1938), X, 32. See Rahner, "Existentiaal: Het theologisch Gebruik," in K. Rahner and A. Darlap, eds., *Sacramentum Mundi,* Dutch tr. J. Mertens and S. Gentilis (Hilversum 1968), IV, 67 ff. Also compare our use of the term in Ch. IX.

[165] Rahner, "Die Heilsbedeutung...," p. 244.

Rahner's view, grace is God Himself in relation to man.[166] God actually makes Himself known to man, even if man is perhaps unaware of this. The creation is fulfilled in free divine self-communication in groundless Love. The relation between Creator and creature is an ineradicable element in the structure of reality.[167]

Man is predisposed towards the fulfillment of this propensity. The transcendence of man implies that man is characterized by an a priori structure of expectation, for a person is predisposed towards a fulfillment of existence which still awaits him.[168] Rahner speaks in this connection of the searching anticipation of man, who is predisposed towards the bearer of salvation, or more particularly, the absolute bearer of salvation.[169] This God has made Himself known in human history, in a special, unsurpassable manner, namely in Jesus Christ, 'the definitive, irrevocable, self-fulfilling self-promise of God, originating in God Himself, to the world and its history.'[170] The possibility and desirability of recognizing the revelation of the Word of God who became flesh as such is based on the fulfillment of the predisposition in man as he has been defined in terms of the supernatural existential determinant.[171] The church's proclamation does not direct itself to a person who is thereby for the first time brought into contact with the reality concerning which the proclamation speaks, but it is an address which produces awareness of that which was always inexpressibly present as a reality, as grace.[172]

From there, Rahner reaches his view of anonymous Christianity. He develops this view from an emphatically Christian position. It is an a priori position; he gives a view of non-Christians which he considers to be implied by Christian doctrine.[173] His point of departure is the church's doctrine. Ever since the Second Vatican Council, the church recognizes that God extends His salvation to non-Christians.[174] This is the first perspective in terms of which Rahner operates: God's universal salvific intent.[175] There is another doctrine of the church, however, to wit, the old rule that there is no salvation outside of the church: *extra ecclessia nulla salus*.[176] In addition, Rahner sometimes refers to the ecclesiastical

[166] G. Vandervelde, *Original Sin* (Amsterdam 1975), pp. 111 f.

[167] Rahner, VII, 68 f.

[168] Rahner, "Jesus Christus in den nichtchristlichen Religionen," *Schriften*, XII (1975), p. 379; see also IV, 231.

[169] Rahner, XII, 381.

[170] Rahner, "Über den Absolutheitsanspruch des Christentums," *Schriften*, XV (1983), p. 177.

[171] *Ibid*, VI, 548 f.

[172] *Ibid*, VI, 549; IV, 228 f.

[173] *Ibid*, XII, 370 f.; V, 143 f. For Rahners views, J. D. Gort, "Buitenkerkelijken als 'Randkerkelijken'?" in *Buitensporig Geloven: Studies over Randkerkelijkheid*, ed. J. M. Vlijm (Kampen 1983), pp. 142 ff.

[174] Rahner, "Die Heilsbedeutung," p. 243.

[175] Rahner, XII, 79; VI, 546 (I Tim. 2:4).

[176] *Ibid*, VI, 545 f.

proposition that faith is a prerequisite for participation in salvation.[177] Man must respond positively to God's silent yet still operative offer of grace. The combination of these two insights (1. God's universal offer of salvation, and 2. the necessity of faith and belonging to the church) prompts Rahner to express the proposition that a great many people actually have faith and may be regarded as Christian, even though they themselves are unaware of it. He defines anonymous Christian faith as follows:

> By anonymous faith we understand a faith which, on the one hand, is necessary for and leads to salvation (presupposing thereby what is necessary for justification and definitive salvation: hope and love of God and one's neighbour), and on the other hand, occurs without awareness of an explicit (conceptual and verbal, that is, objectively defined) relation to the Old and (or) New Testament revelation of Jesus Christ, and without an explicit awareness of God (in terms of an objective conception of Him).[178]

The salvation which has definitively appeared in Christ is thus already a reality among people who have no awareness of it as such.[179] Salvation comes to expression in such things as responsible living and neighbourly love.[180] One's morality is fashioned, at least in part, by the influence of one's time and culture. The transcendental propensity of a person is always 'mediated' by historical cultural configurations of morality and religion, or outlook on life.[181]

The term 'anonymous Christianity' does not imply anything automatic for Rahner. Not every person is a Christian (anonymous or not). That is dependent on the free choice which man must make to accept the grace proffered him. This acceptance takes the form of an acceptance of morality.[182] Or, if we understand Rahner well, of the searching, anticipatory character of human existence. In other words, one accepts the finality which is given in human existence.

It is understandable that Rahner is capable, in terms of this view, of open-mindedly acknowledging the value of many elements in other religious traditions. Although not free of defects, a religion is only illegitimate if its deficiency is intrinsically related to it.[183] This appreciation for other religious traditions does not just extend to movements which acknowledge the existence of God or of a higher power. Although the atheist explicitly denies the existence of God, he too can implicitly accept the finality of his existence and the grace which elevates him above the purely natural.[184]

---

[177] *Ibid*, VI, 546; XII, 77.
[178] *Ibid*, XII, 76.
[179] See Rahner, VII, 73; XII, 375.
[180] See Rahner, V, 146.
[181] *Ibid*, V, 152; XII, 373.
[182] See Rahner, XII, 83.
[183] *Ibid*, V, 149f.; "Die Heilsbedeutung," p. 245.
[184] Rahner, XII, 80; 83.

As long as a person has not been adequately brought into contact with the preaching of Christianity, he can be an anonymous Christian.[185] The value for other people of other traditions on life may be acknowledged up until the moment of an adequate confrontation with Christian doctrine.[186] Other outlooks, says Rahner, are mediators of real acts of salvation in the historical and cultural situation in which they are vitally present.[187] If, however, one has been adequately confronted with Christianity, but rejects it, and one also fails to heed the voice of conscience, then this repudiation is *schuldhaft* (culpable).[188]

If our analysis is correct, two things are determinative for Rahner's view of *religious knowledge*: (1) the fact that the reality of God is a mystery which can never be entirely known by people nor perfectly designated;[189] (2) the fact that human knowledge is dualistic by nature; knowledge is reflexive and immediate; it rests with 'itself' (the subject) and with the other (the object).[190] Linked to this is the fact that cognition is historically and culturally determined.[191] An articulation is never the thing itself. People know things by naming them. Cognition and will go together in one's view of reality, says Rahner, and religious knowledge is therefore more than purely theoretical.[192]

Faith is a fundamental datum of human existence which determines all of life;[193] faith contains an intellectual moment.[194] Knowledge is transmitted within the Christian tradition. What is the nature and the value of this knowledge?

Christianity, says Rahner, is not really a 'castle of truth' with many rooms which must all be inhabited in order to 'be in the truth.' On the contrary, it is the one opening which leads out of all particular truths (and errors) to *the* Truth, that is to say, to the *one* Incomprehensibility of God.[195] The truth concerning Jesus Christ is the fulfillment of a human being's transcendental propensity, but the reality of God in Jesus exceeds human comprehension. The deepest relationship to the one Truth therefore surpasses explicit human knowledge. Explicit religious knowledge is sustained by basic trust.[196] This primordial trust is the core of religious belief, but it never exists on its own, without opinions and verbal formula-

---

[185] *Ibid*, V, 143.
[186] What is 'adequate,' however? By comparison: When the whole church is being opposed, God can gain the victory through his secret grace, V, 157.
[187] Rahner, "Die Heilsbedeutung," p. 245.
[188] For the expression 'schuldhaft,' Rahner, XII, 80.
[189] *Ibid*, V, 72f.
[190] *Ibid*, V, 81.
[191] *Ibid*, XV, 172.
[192] *Ibid*, VII, 55f.; "Kleines Fragment 'Über kollektive Findung der Wahrheit,'" VI, 107f.
[193] *Ibid*, VII, 64f.
[194] *Ibid*, VII, 59.
[195] *Ibid*, VII, 67.
[196] *Ibid*, "Bietet die Kirche letzte Gewissheiten?" X (1972), pp. 288ff.; see also VI, 110.

tions of particulars.[197] Grace kindles man's basic trust.[198] Religious confidence is also anchored in this basic trust. The assurance which a person has about certain points of doctrine is derived from this deepest certainty, Rahner says.[199] The deepest confidence is given in grace; grace carries in itself its own confirmation.[200] It is necessary to justify belief as much as is possible; in the last analysis, however, confidence does not depend on this legitimation, but on grace and on basic trust.[201]

Rahner mitigates the importance of Christian doctrine somewhat in this fashion. Certain doctrinal positions of the Christian church are of central significance, however, and must be accepted by all who become familiar with the Christian proclamation. With certain caveats, Rahner assents to a statement by the Second Vatican Council about the hierarchy of values.[202] In so doing, he acknowledges that the authority due to ecclesiastical —or biblical— doctrines is not always similar. Certain perceptions are essential for Christian faith. These the church teaches; with respect to these true statements, the church is infallible.[203] Next to these insights which must be accepted by Christians as infallible, there are other matters about which different conceptions exist and about which no fixed doctrine exists.[204] Just as is true of all church doctrine, however, so too the fundamental true statements must be constantly interpreted and articulated anew within the cultural horizon of the times in which people live.[205] Real knowledge of the truth is nevertheless possible in this time-bound manner.[206] The terms used might be one-sided due to the historicity of this knowledge, and since they refer to God, they are never univocal.[207] One should therefore rather speak of effectiveness than of truth with respect to the terminology of Christian doctrine.[208] The words refer to the subject matter of which they speak; they are not the matter itself. We see, then, that Rahner would rather not speak of the *definite truth* of dogmatic formulations, on account of the historicity of knowledge and the inadequacy of human language for describing the reality of God.[209]

Rahner has written an extensive article about Thomas Aquinas' conception of truth. It is an early article; Rahner regards it as particularly

[197] *Ibid*, X, 290f.
[198] *Ibid*, X, 293.
[199] *Ibid*, X, 294.
[200] *Ibid*, VII, 63.
[201] *Ibid*, VII, 59, 62.
[202] *Ibid*, "Hierarchie der Wahrheiten," XV (1983), pp. 163ff.
[203] *Ibid*, X, 296f.
[204] *Ibid*, X, 299f.
[205] *Ibid*, V, 67f.; X, 302.
[206] *Ibid*, VII, 64.
[207] *Ibid*, V, 68f.
[208] *Ibid*, V, 69.
[209] E.g., "Auch das letztverbindliche Dogma ist nach vorne offen," X, 303. For Rahner historicity does not mean that the truth cannot be known, VII, 64; see X, 3.

important for an understanding of his own deepest intentions.[210] He is in agreement with Thomas when the latter points out that the knowledge of things ultimately stands in a broad context: *"Omnia cognoscentia implicite cognoscunt Deum in quolibet cognito."* (All knowledge is implicitly knowledge of God).[211] Knowledge of things ultimately points to God. In this early piece, Rahner subsequently discusses the coincidence of logical and ontological truth in God.[212] Pure knowledge is the "unquestioning conjunction of Being with itself."[213] Man is predisposed to such a knowledge of God. This propensity of man is manifested in the fact that man —who already stands in the expanse of God's free grace— seeks to do what is good and to say what is true. Apparent in this is the predisposition towards the *finis,* the goal of all things — in which God will be all in all. This 'supernatural existential determinant' pervades all of life, and thus, knowledge too. And so, knowledge and being are interrelated.

§ 4   The attitude towards other religions within the Vatican and the World Council of Churches

The relation between Christianity and other religions or philosophical traditions has been under discussion since Christianity's inception. Since the Enlightenment, views of other traditions have often been marked by the idea of the progress of culture in the course of ages, in the sense that Western culture is the most advanced form of development. This did not automatically imply a favourable judgment in the Western philosophical tradition about any actually existing form of Christianity. Sometimes the restoration of *natural religion* was sought amidst all the religious differences, the actually existing religions being seen as outgrowths and deformations.[214] Around the beginning of this century, many ascribed value to other religions; the culmination of spiritual development, however, was seen in certain forms of Christianity.[215] Next to the liberal views, there was the orthodox point of view that all other religions are idolatry. We encountered this view in Barth, though in an original and self-critical version. The developments within the mission organizations of the Protestant churches in the World Council of Churches have been described many times.[216] What is remarkable in Catholic circles is the open minded

---

[210] *Ibid,* X, 21.
[211] *Ibid,* X, 37.
[212] *Ibid,* X, 39.
[213] *Ibid,* X, 38; see the section on Thomas.
[214] E.g., W. Stoker, *De Christelijke Godsdienst in de Filosofie van de Verlichting* (Assen 1980), pp. 58ff.
[215] See E. Troeltsch, *Die Absolutheit des Christentums und die Religionsgeschichte* (1902; rpt. Tübingen ²1912), pp. x, 111f.
[216] See C. F. Hallencreutz, *New Approaches to Men of Other Faiths* (Geneve 1970); Vlijm, *Religiebegrip van Karl Barth.*

acknowledgment of truth, salvation, and grace beyond the actual Christian church on the one hand, as we have seen with Rahner, and on the other hand, the retention of the unique position of Christianity. The encounter with followers of other religious traditions has obtained an organizational and procedural position in Christianity. The pope established a secretariate for non-Christians in 1964. The World Council of Churches appointed Samartha in 1968 as study secretary for the church's view of other living religions. By 1971, a department was instituted for dialogue with adherents of other religions and ideologies.[217] Both ecclesiastical organs have brought forth statements. In this section, we will address the outlook voiced by those statements, for they do not represent purely personal sentiments on the part of the authors, but are the result of rather long and broad reflection within both Christian traditions. One should recall that the 'dialogue' is disputed in both churches. The most prominent objection made is that the dialogue, or 'conversation,' with followers of other ideas means a decrease in Christian witness, and therefore conflicts with the missionary task of the Christian church. The necessity of further theological reflection on other religions, the *theologia religionum*, is acknowledged in circles around both commissions for the dialogue.[218]

In the declaration of the Secretariate for non-Christians, *The Attitude of the Church towards the Followers of Other Religions*, in conjunction with the declarations by the Second Vatican Council and of later papal decrees and statements, the dialogue is defined as follows: "It means not only discussion, but also includes all positive and constructive interreligious relations with individuals and communities of other faiths which are directed at mutual understanding and enrichment."[219] It is the task of the secretariate to find ways for suitable dialogical communication with people from other religious traditions. Just as in the document from the World Council of Churches, it is pointed out that simply the presence and the hopefully eloquent life of Christians amidst followers of other ideals will have the value of a witness. Witness can adopt many forms.[220] One of the objectives of the dialogue remains to inform others about Christian beliefs, and to thus bring people to the point of conversion.[221] Other objectives also come into perspective here. Justification for the Christian hope towards others is related to the dialogue "... thanks to which Christians meet believers from other religious traditions, to continue

---

[217] See D. C. Mulder, *Ontmoeting van Gelovigen* (Baarn 1977), pp. 21 ff.; also S. J. Samartha's volume, *Courage for Dialogue* (Geneve 1981), and, by the present secretary for dialogue, W. Ariarajah, *The Bible and People of Other Faiths* (Geneve 1985).

[218] *My Neighbour's Faith — and Mine: Theological Discoveries through Inter-faith Dialogue.* See also "The Attitude of the Church Towards the Followers of Other Religions," *Bulletin of the Secretariatus pro Non-Christianos* 19 (1984): 127, point 6.

[219] "The Attitude," point 3.

[220] *Ibid,* point 13.

[221] *Ibid,* points 11 and 37.

further along the road together, seeking the truth, and together dedicating themselves to the common interest."[222] Here we again encounter notions which we have already seen many times, when people from one tradition expose themselves to other traditions. One does not have exclusive title to the truth; one cannot see everything; and one can learn from others. "Mutual affirmation, reciprocal correction, and fraternal exchange lead the partners in dialogue to an ever greater maturity which in turn generates interpersonal communion. Religious experiences and outlooks can themselves be purified and enriched in this process of encounter."[223] With regard to knowledge, the concern of the dialogue is to learn from others; they too have their insights and experiences. One can appreciate those, since every individual is redeemed by Christ.[224] That is why elements of truth are to be encountered everywhere. There is much that is of value in the religious traditions.[225] One can learn about the ideas of others in the dialogue and discover what treasure God has distributed among the nations of the world. It is the task of Christians to shed light on these treasures in terms of the light of the Gospel.[226] This Gospel witness will arise by itself in the dialogue. If the experience of prayer, contemplation, faith, and action is shared at a deep, personal level, and acquaintance is made with the assorted expressions of the ways along which people have sought the Absolute, then the reasons which people have for their own faith will be mutually discussed.[227] The proclamation of the Gospel can take place within the context of such dialogue.

In summary, one can say that the Secretariate believes that Christians can learn from followers of other traditions in their own articulation and reflection of faith despite the sometimes deep differences dividing their traditions, because in His great love, God is mercifully present among them, and they have sought the Absolute and have experienced It too.

A declaration has also appeared from the World Council of Churches' department for dialogue regarding the attitude of Christians towards followers of other traditions, *Guidelines on Dialogue with People of Living Faiths and Ideologies.* The drift of the piece is displayed by the central terms, *dialogue in community.* Both the concepts of dialogue and community cannot be exactly defined; they first of all involve a lifestyle, an open attitude by which one accommodates others, speaking and living with them. A little further in the report, the following description of dialogue can be found: " ... witnessing to our deepest convictions and listening to

---

[222] *Ibid*, points 13 and 16; cf. I Peter 3:15f.
[223] *Ibid*, point 21.
[224] *Ibid*, point 23.
[225] *Ibid*, point 26.
[226] *Ibid*, point 27.
[227] *Ibid*, point 35.

those of our neighbours."[228] Just as with the Catholic report, the basis of the dialogical attitude, is Christian neighbourly love and the " . . . awareness of the richness of the diversity of humankind which Christians believe to be created and sustained by God in His love for all people."[229] It is pointed out that the dialogue must not be carried out in terms of religious systems, but much more in terms of people meeting one another as concrete believers and unbelievers.[230] The Christian witness is possible in this dialogical fashion, together with respect for others.[231] The purpose of the dialogue cannot be to reduce all religions to the lowest common denominator, nor to discuss concepts and symbols; the aim is ". . . the enabling of a true encounter between those spiritual insights and experiences which are only found at the deepest levels of human life."[232] The commission acknowledges that a number of questions arise, such as the problem of biblical guidelines in the encounter with people of a different faith; these and other questions demand further reflection.[233]

It is apparent that both commissions assume that God mercifully works among all people, that religions can sometimes differ enormously from one another, but that people can nevertheless learn about the reality of God from each others' experiences. The view in the Catholic document shows tangible affinity with Rahner's thought; the tone of the World Council of Churches' work betokens the spirit of Wilfred Smith (and others), with his emphasis on personal faith.

It is now in order to draw some conclusions. There is no one 'Christian' view of 'other religions,' not one *theologia religionum*.[234] Calvin had a different view than Barth; Rahner's view was different again. It is apparent that the attitude which one adopts towards other individuals and their beliefs depends on the basic convictions which one has. Within the totality of the Christian outlook, divergent accents may be placed, on, for example, the unity of God, the measure and incomprehensibility of the divine mystery which is the deepest ground of our being, the person of Jesus Christ, the atonement by his death on the cross, or the coming of

---

[228] *Guidelines on Dialogue* (Geneve 1979, ²1982), p. 16, see Part I, point 17. See also the essay by the former World Council's librarian, A. J. van der Bent, "The Coming Dialogue of World Religions," in his volume, *Theology — Miserable and Wonderful* (Madras 1982), pp. 62ff.

[229] *Guidelines*, I, point 5, see II, point 16; see Ariarajah, pp. 10ff.

[230] *Guidelines*, II, point 20.

[231] *Ibid*, II, point 19.

[232] *Ibid*, II, point 22.

[233] *Ibid*, II, point 23.

[234] For the texts, *Attitudes Towards other Religions*, ed. O. C. Thomas (London 1969); for a description of modern views in Christian theology, A. Race, *Christians and Religious Pluralism: Patterns in the Christian Theology of Religions* (London 1983). On Christianity's role amongst the major world religions, see the volume *Concilium* 22 (1986/1); also A. Camps, *De Weg, de Paden en de Wegen: De Christelijke Theologie en de Concrete Godsdiensten* (Baarn 1977; Eng. edn. by Orbis Books).

the Kingdom of God. Each of these accents implies —both psychologically as well as 'logically'— a certain evaluation of other (religious) traditions. To put it more concretely, activist Christians who believe they are now already working for the coming of the Kingdom of God feel more affinity with those who want this world to be better, whether they are believers or not, than they do with esoteric traditions. More pietistically inclined Christians who find personal piety and serenity important feel more affinity for the contemplative Sufies and the restrained lifestyle of certain other traditions. For someone who assigns to Jesus Christ a pivotal role as the exclusive revelation of God in a world which is ultimately in flight from God, the heart of faith threatens to vanish from view when too much discussion occurs over what is worthwhile in other religions. Every posture towards followers of other traditions betrays one's own *interpretation* of the Christian tradition. Since Christianity includes so many currents, one cannot speak of a single Christian view of other religious traditions.[235] In this section we have discussed more or less official documents from the Vatican and the World Council of Churches concerning dialogue. They pursue the challenge implied by the encounter with people from various religious traditions in our global culture. Alongside of this, there is a current which thinks very exclusivistically; still others speak in terms such as 'the many ways' to God, all of which are considered to be of equal value.

The crucial point within Christianity is the exclusivity which the role of Christ in God's revelation and in His plan of salvation brings with it. If the position of Christ is emphasized, a critical posture towards other traditions is almost inevitable; recall here the views of Calvin and Barth. If one puts more weight on the breadth of God's love, greater margins emerge for more 'inclusive' conceptions; compare the former with Rahner and the documents just discussed.

---

[235] For some opinions from currrents within the Christian tradition other than those being described in this section, see, for example, *Christianity and Other Faith: An Evangelical Contribution to our Multi-Faith Society* (Exeter 1983); also J. Burtness, "Thinking About Evangelism," in *A Monthly Letter on Evangelism*, edited by the Commission on World Mission and Evangelism of the World Council of Churches, April/May/June 1987.

Chapter VII

The Concept of Truth in
Islamic Tradition

§ 1 Introduction

1.1 Preamble

As in the previous chapters, we will begin by presenting some of the
main ideas of Islam and then sketch some of the main lines in its the
historical development. In the second section (§ 2), we will examine its
beliefs in somewhat more detail, inasmuch as this is of significance for
interreligious relations and the question of truth. The third section raises
the question of truth itself: What is understood by 'truth'? What is the
role of knowledge within Islam? The fourth section then asks how other
religions are viewed in Islam.

1.2 Islam: religious commitment and surrender

The word *islām* means 'subjection' (of someone or of a person to
God); the Arabic word is often translated as 'religious surrender.'[1] This
immediately brings us to the core of the Islamic faith. In relation to God,
only obedience and subjection is proper. If one worships God and does what
God has charged, then one can live in trust of Him, having peace with God
and man. God is just and merciful. Since days of old, God has sent
prophets. The last of these prophets is Mohammed (Muḥammad), to whom
God gave the Koran (*Qur'ān*) via the angel Gabriel. What is written in the
Koran is thus literally the Word of God. If one believes that word and
performs the duties which the Koran specifies, one will survive the
judgment on the Last Day and be admitted to paradise.

---

[1] W. Montgomery Watt, *Bell's Introduction to the Qu'ran*, rev. enl. edn. (Edinburgh 1970),
p. 119; H. A. R. Gibb, *Mohammedanism: An Historical Survey* (London [2]1961), p. 1.;
L. Gardet, "Islam," in *Encyclopedia of Islam* (Leiden 1960–), IV (Leiden 1978), pp. 171f.

God is portrayed as the Creator of the earth and of humankind. Mohammed taught strict monotheism; his opposition to idolatry was very severe. Islam has no monasticism — religion must be enacted in ordinary life. The whole of life is marked by the duties which every believer must perform. Five duties form the core of the religious life. The Koran also contains more detailed regulations circumscribing these five duties. Since Islam shapes, or desires to shape, the whole of life, it has, like Judaism, great concern for the application of law in new situations. The legal scholars and the actual rulers of the various Islamic countries form two different groups of people. The interpretation problem of the Koran has to be dealt with in circles of legal scholars: How is one to apply old rules to new situations and cultures? In addition, there are political issues: To what extent should Caliphs and later government leaders actually implement the ideas of the legal scholars?

1.3   Developments in the Islamic tradition

Mohammed was born in Mecca around 570 C.E.[2] He grew up there, became a camel driver, married a rich widow, and was trusted and successful in the flourishing business life of Mecca. The tradition relates that he regularly sequestered himself in a cave situated in a mountain near Mecca, known as Mt. Ḥirā'. There he sought God. Though he lived amidst polytheistic tribes, Mohammed apparently abandoned polytheism. During a retreat to the Ḥirā' cave in 610, he was visited by the angel Gabriel who called him to be a prophet. Since that time, Mohammed preached what he had been told. He acquired a small following — the poor and slaves, it is said. The rich of Mecca ridiculed him. Since they were wary of the possible consequences of his monotheism for the position of Mecca, a city with many religious sanctuaries, they boycotted him and made life miserable for him. In 622, Mohammed fled to the place which has been called Medina ever since. There he could give concrete form to his theocratic ideas as a leader, at the invitation of the population. The Islamic calendar reckoning thus starts at July 16, 622 C.E. After a series of clashes, Mecca was conquered in 630. By the time of Mohammed's death in 632, the whole of the Arabian peninsula had already been brought under Muslim control.

Mohammed was succeeded by Caliph Abū-Bakr (632–634 C.E.).[3] The first of the additional conquests (Syria, Palestine, Egypt, Iraq, and Persia) took place under Caliph Omar (634–644). The Caliphs were the governing leaders of the Muslim community. They were not prophets, however, for the Koran had been given to Mohammed. The fourth Caliph, Caliph Ali (656–750), despite being the son-in-law of the prophet, found himself

---

[2] Watt, pp. 9 ff.; Gibb, p. 1.

[3] For the following, K. Wagtendonk, "De Islam," in *Antwoord*, ed. J. Sperna Weiland (Amsterdam [2]1982), pp. 165-72.

opposed by another Caliph, Mu'āwiya. The latter ultimately obtained power and established a kind of kingship, the 'Omayyaden Caliphate' (661–750), with Damascus as its capital. The followers of Alī, known as the Shī'ites, continued throughout the centuries to resist the mainstream of Islam.

The conquests continued at high pace. The Muslims crossed over to Europe at Gibraltar in 711. In the East, India was reached. The expansion was checked in 732 at Poitiers (France). Islamic culture flourished in Spain right up until the Middle Ages.

Science and culture blossomed in the 9th and 10th centuries. Plato and Aristotle were studied and provided with commentaries. The wisdom of Aristotle was transmitted to Judaism (Maimonides) and Christianity (Thomas) via Arabic scholars. The philosophical approach to religious perceptions led to a more rational formulation of Muslim theology.

The political unity of the empire was lost. In the eastern part of the empire, Shī'ite Caliphates emerged, such as in Persia/Iran. The conquests in northern India (Punjab) continued in the 11th century. Bengal (Bangladesh) was reached around 1200. Since the end of the 13th century, Islam has been spread to Indonesia, where Islam has remained mingled with the old folk religions as well as Hindu and Buddhist elements. The Christian Byzantine Empire was increasingly driven back, starting from the 11th century onwards. The Muslims conquered Constantinople in 1453. The Muslim advance was called to a halt near Vienna in 1683.

One of the more vital factors in the continuing expansion of Islam, aside from military power, was the mystical Ṣūfī movement. Simple artisans and other adherents of Sufi groupings spread Islam further to parts of Africa, India, Central Asia, and some portions of Southeastern Europe, according to Gibb's reports.[4]

In connection with the period starting in the 11th century and lasting up until the 16th or 17th century, Wagtendonk speaks of a period of spiritual ossification.[5] Differing judgments prevail on this score, of course; Corbin points to numerous of developments, especially in the more mystical traditions of Iran.[6] Islamic countries suffered under Western colonialism, as did many other lands. At the end of the previous century, a current emerged in Islam which strives for 'pan-Islamism,' or the restoration of theocracy in a pure Islamic form. Since the sixties there is talk of 're-Islamization' in the Muslim world. Mosque attendance has risen in many places. The old Islamic system of justice is implemented more rigorously in a number of countries. The influence of Western society makes itself strongly felt in many countries. In some, opposition has

---

[4] Gibb, pp. 13f.
[5] Wagtendonk, p. 168.
[6] H. Corbin, *Histoire de la Philosophie Islamique*, I (Paris 1964), p. 342; cf. his *Spiritual Body and Celestial Earth: From Mazdean Iran to Shi'ite Iran*, tr. Fr. Pearson (Princeton 1977).

arisen to less strict conceptions of Islam and the Islamic legal system, especially on the part of fundamentalist groups, which can be quite radical.[7]

§ 2 Central insights

2.1 Monotheism

There is no God but Allāh, and Mohammed is His Prophet — this is the principal Muslim confession, pronounced daily by millions of Muslims in their prayers.[8] Monotheism was the substance of Mohammed's preaching among the polytheistic Arabic tribes.[9] Just as the Jewish prophets had preached that there is one God who made heaven and earth, and just as the Christians believe in this one God, so Mohammed proclaimed to the Arab peoples that God is one and that He alone is God. Initially Mohammed could count on the sympathy of Jews and Christians,[10] but later it became apparent that the Jews did not recognize him as a prophet and that Christians do not regard Jesus as merely a great son of God. Mohammed discovered that they were less attentive than he had initially expected. Portions of the Koran which are regarded by Western Islamologists as originating from a somewhat later period show an altered posture towards Jews and Christians. Mohammed still regards them as believers, but he opposes them as well, especially the Christian doctrine of the Trinity — at least in the interpretation often given to it in the Koran.[11] The chief sin of people is that they give 'partners' to God and therefore do not accept his divinity in a rigorously monotheistic sense.[12]

This God has deigned to speak to man in earlier times through prophets. Mohammed refers chiefly to the Jewish prophets and to Jesus. The revelation of God which Mohammed received thus confirms earlier revelations. As the final and definitive revelation, however, the Koran also supplies the standard by which other revelations must be measured; what is written in the Koran is true, and everything which deviates from it in Jewish and Christian writings has been wrongly presented or distorted.

---

[7] See Wagtendonk, p. 172; E. Sivan, *Radical Islam: Medieval Theology and Modern Politics* (New Haven 1985).

[8] See Watt, p. 25.

[9] Gibb, p. 53; cf. D. S. Attema, *De Koran: Zijn Ontstaan en Zijn Inhoud* (Kampen 1962), pp. 66 ff.

[10] See Attema, pp. 113-26; also A. Wessels, *De Moslimse Naaste: Op Weg naar een Theologie van de Islam* (Kampen 1978), pp. 20 ff.

[11] See Wessels, pp. 105 f., and pp. 127 ff.; also the Index to the Koran, *s.v.* 'Trinity,' *The Koran: Interpreted*, tr. A. J. Arberry (1955; rpt. Oxford University Press 1986).

[12] See the *Koran*, sūra 9. 4-12 (the numbers of verses refer to the so-called Eastern version of the Koran; if different, the numbering of Arberry's edition has been added between brackets; the page numbers of Arberry's translation are noted as follows: OUP pp. 179 f.

In His revelation, God makes Himself known as the Merciful and the Compassionate. He is praised in many ways. The faithful call Him by His ninety nine names.[13] His holiness and unassailability have the utmost primacy. He is compassionate in the sense that He makes Himself known to people and provides them with rules to live in a way which pleases Him. There is also much that He forgives. Great emphasis is laid on God's power and His governing of life. He appoints a place and station to people which pleases Him, and people can feel secure in that trust. He will judge all people on the last day, rewarding good deeds and punishing the bad.

The chief of sins —and this is of utmost importance for interreligious relations— is that people do not accept Him as God. Gibb states that,

> True belief demands *iklās*, the giving of one's whole and unmixed allegiance to God, and its opposite is *širk*, the ascribing of partners to God and the worship of any creature. This is the one unforgivable sin: 'Verily God forgiveth not the giving of partners to him; other than this will He forgive to whom He pleaseth, but whosoever giveth a partner to God hath conceived a monstrous sin.'[14]

2.2 The Koran

The Koran (and the other revealed books, such as the Bible), in the traditional representation, stem from a heavenly original, the *umm al-kitāb*.[15] The divine revelation was given to Mohammed piecemeal, one part at a time. The prophet announced these prophecies. Upon his death, according to tradition, the revelations were committed to pieces of parchment and leather, camel ribs and pieces of wood.[16] Disciples knew many of the divine words by heart. From these —according to the rendition of Western Islamologists— the chapters (*sūras*) of the Koran were 'composed.' After the introductory chapter, the remaining *sūras* follow in order of length. Transitions in the *sūras* are explained in terms of this process of composition.

Approximately a century later, the text was largely fixed, barring small variations in reading and spelling.[17] To solve the minor problems of variation in textual form, a group of seven famous 'reciters' were declared canonical; their readings were accepted as orthodox. In this century, a single reading is practically general custom in the Islamic world.

Given the fact that the Koran was given literally to Mohammed, the Arab language is no incidental matter. A translation is inferior to the

---

[13] Watt, p. 152.

[14] Sūra 4:(51) 48; OUP p. 80. This translation is Gibb's, p. 55.

[15] Wagtendonk, pp. 163f.; M. Fakhry, *A History of Islamic Philosophy* (London [2]1983), pp. 62f.; cf. Watt, pp. 179f.; R. Paret, *Der Koran* (Graz 1979), p. 34.

[16] See Watt, pp. 18-39.

[17] Gibb, p. 50; cf. Watt, pp. 47f.; J. H. Kramers' Introduction to the Dutch translation of the *Koran* (Amsterdam [3]1969), pp. xvff.

Arabic original not only for linguistic reasons, but also for religious reasons.[18] The transcendental origin of the Koran is the reason why those portions of the Koran which parallel biblical stories are always regarded as the true version of what happened, in the event of discrepancy.[19]

In the Koran, as we have noted, there are many statements about biblical prophets and about Jesus, Mary, the Holy Spirit, and the Christian faith. Jesus is honoured very highly; it disputes that He is (literally) the Son of God, however, and that He —being a good man— died on the cross. The Christian doctrine of the Trinity is opposed.[20]

The Koran contains no systematic exposition of Muslim faith, Gibb notes, but it does form a "consistent body of doctrine and of practical obligations."[21] The recitation of the Koran fills an important place in worship.

2.3　The five pillars of Islam

Religious obedience marks the whole of life, not in the least due to the fixed habit of periodic religious obligations. It is not enough just to believe in God. The following five obligations have to be observed.[22]

(1) *Faith (īmān)*: Muslims accept God, and Mohammed as His prophet; they regard the Koran as God's word and the angels as instruments of His will.

(2) *Prayer (ṣalāt)*: one may always pray; ritual prayer five times daily is an obligation.

(3) *Alms (zakāt)*: one is duty-bound to give alms.

(4) *Fasting (ramaḍān)*: one ought to fast once a year during the month of *ramaḍān* between sun up and sun down; the lunar month *ramaḍān* shifts throughout the entire calendar year.

(5) *Pilgrimage (ḥajj)*: everyone ought to fulfil the *ḥajj* to Mecca once in their lifetime (or more often); an assembly around the Ka'ba in Mecca —built by Abraham and Ishmael according to tradition— is the high point.

More detailed rituals have been established around these five 'pillars,' also containing exceptions for special circumstances. Next to these five general religious obligations, other legal rules for life are in force, together with their elaboration in Islamic jurisprudence, particularly in states where the majority of the population is Muslim.

---

[18] Paret, p. 36.

[19] Watt, pp. 156f.

[20] Wessels, pp. 105ff.; 114-31; cf. Watt, p. 158; see G. Parrinder, *Jesus in the Qur'ān* (London 1965), pp. 30ff., 126ff., 133ff.

[21] Gibb, p. 53.

[22] Wagtendonk, pp. 183ff.; see Gibb, pp. 62ff.; Watt, pp. 162ff.; *Enc. Isl.*, s.v. 'īmān' and 'ḥadjdj.'

The prayers can be performed anywhere as long as one cleanses oneself before prayer. In the mosque, where the preaching takes place, one is required to attend the afternoon *ṣalāt* on Friday, the holy day. Priests are unknown in Islam, and all believers are equal,[23] but there is someone connected to the mosque as *imām* to lead in common prayer.[24] In addition, there are specialized judges, legal consultants, and teachers in the Koran schools. Every Muslim who demonstrates suitable competence can in principle exercise these functions. There is no ordination, nor is there any hierarchy.

2.4 Tradition and interpretation

No sacred book can go uninterpreted. In Islam, there is already mention of further explanation of previously given revelations in the Koran itself, where we can discover signs of shading in and sometimes development with regard to certain ideas, due to the influence of circumstances (such as the attitude towards Christians and Jews).[25] Various groups give their own interpretation of the Koran (*tafsīr*); Wagtendonk lists them: Mu'tazilites, orthodox, Ṣūfies, Shī'ites, philosophers, and modernists.[26]

In addition to the Sacred Book (*kitāb*), tradition (*sunna*) plays an important part. The honouring of the *sunna* stems from the role of custom and tradition in pre-Islamic Arabia.[27] The Islamic *sunna* is honoured within Islam. As in other religious communities, discussion arose over the scope of the *sunna* and the authority which the *sunna* is permitted to develop or retain. *Sunna* means customs of the (Islamic) community which have not been recorded in the Koran. The tradition began to evolve in various directions after the spread of Islam over greater areas. The necessity thus arose for distinguishing between valid and invalid *sunna*. The tradition scholars of the first centuries objected to the accretion of tradition; only traditions stemming back to the prophet himself were considered valid. An extensive body of literature arose called the *ḥadīṯ* (story or declaration about an event). It mentions situations in which the prophet had settled or said certain things. Due to the steady expansion of the *ḥadīṯ,* the need arose for testing the authenticity of the tradition. A kind of *ḥadīṯ* scholarship emerged to establish which traditions were reliable.[28] According to Gibb, the people who prevailed were those who counted only those customs as tradition which Mohammed had himself instituted. The term

---

23 See Gibb, p. 48 (cf. sūra 57:27); Wagtendonk, p. 189.
24 Wagtendonk, pp. 189 ff.
25 See Watt, pp. 86 ff.
26 Wagtendonk, p. 175.
27 Gibb, p. 73.
28 *Ibid,* p. 76.

Sunnites is used for Muslims who observe the 'customs of the community.'[29] The other important current in Islam the *Shī'a*, or the *Shī'ites*, are the 'party of Alī'; they believed that the actions of the Muslim community were illegal; they advocated a more rigorous implementation of the *sunna*. Originally, the Shī'ite segregation was actually primarily a political movement which wanted to restore the Caliphate to the house of Alī.[30] 'Quasi-Shī'ite' sects arose in later times, who, in addition to the ordinary literal interpretation of the Koran, also had a concealed interpretation. This concealed interpretation was supposedly known to the *imāms*. That is why an absolute personal authority is ascribed to the *imām* in these communities. Arkoun points out that the allusion to charismatic leadership revitalizes the awareness that revelation pervades actual historical life, since life is related to the transcendent in this manner.[31]

2.5 The development of law and doctrine

Gibb begins his treatment of the law (*Sharī'a*) with the following comment: "It is characteristic of the practical bent of the Islamic community and of its thought that its earliest activity and most highly developed expression is in law rather than in theology."[32] Although various circumstances may have played a role in the thorough-going development of Islamic law, the real incentive for the study of law must be sought in Islam itself. The study of law is a natural consequence of Islam. Practical life had to be arranged in agreement with Islam. Legal scholarship was distinguished from theology, and *fiqh* (jurisprudence, legal scholarship) exists alongside of *'ilm* (positive, descriptive study, theology).[33] It was assumed that the prophet had received not only the *kitāb*, but also the *ḥikma* (wisdom) to interpret and apply what is written. It is therefore understandable that all kinds of hermeneutical issues arose, and still arise, corresponding to the aforementioned (§ 2.4) interpretational problematics. Approval was granted to the principle that the view which enjoys general acceptance is valid. The principle of 'general agreement' (*ijma'*) is the cause, according to Gibb, of the fact that the Islamic conception of law has a somewhat fixed and rigid character.[34] Infallibility was ascribed to the consensus of the Islamic community, although the methodological problem of establishing whether a 'universal consensus' on an issue exists soon made itself felt.[35] *Ijma'* is valid not only within the domain of legal

---

[29] *Ibid*, p. 74.
[30] *Ibid*, p. 74.
[31] *Ibid*, pp. 122f. Moh. Arkoun, "Comment lire le Coran?" in *Le Coran*, tr. Kasimirski, preface M. Arkoun (Paris 1970), pp. 28f.
[32] Gibb, p. 88.
[33] *Ibid*, p. 90.
[34] *Ibid*, p. 95; see J. Schacht, *Enc. Isl.*, II, 891 col. 1, *s.v.* '*fikh*.'
[35] Gibb, pp. 97f.; see M. Bernand, *Enc. Isl.*, III, 1024, *s.v.* '*idjma'*.'

developments, but also in the area of dogma and politics. Thus, certain decisions made in the 2nd and 3rd century of Islam have become irreversible.

Concerning the *Sharī'a* (the precepts of law), it is held that it articulates the will of God. The law encompasses the whole of life, 'religious' obligations (in the secularized, Western sense) as well as everyday conduct. The primary rule within Muslim law is liberty. Due to human weakness and greed, however, limits were established in the form of legal stipulations. Gibb notes that the standard definition for law runs as follows: "The science of law is the knowledge of the rights and duties whereby man may fitly conduct his life in this world and prepare himself for the future life."[36] Actions about which no stipulations exist are thus permitted; they are indifferent in legal terms. Five classes of action may be distinguished: (1) actions obligatory for believers; (2) non-obligatory actions which are desirable or recommended; (3) actions which are indifferent; (4) actions which are questionable, though not forbidden; (5) actions which are prohibited.[37] Four orthodox schools of legal interpretation emerged. The interpretation of law was not in the hands of the Caliphs but of legal scholars. The Caliphs were to create facilities for the study of Islamic law. Of course the problem of how religious legal rules were to be implemented in policies of state arose time and again. Gibb calls the *Sharī'a* the "epitome of the true Islamic spirit, the most decisive expression of Islamic thought, the essential kernel of Islam."[38]

Tolerance was a primary characteristic of Islam in the development of doctrine. The limits of tolerance were set as widely as possible, even though there was little appreciation for certain theological methods, and some schools garnered little support.

A more scholastic form of theology emerged within the Mu'tazilite School through the study of Greek philosophy, which formed the impetus for the development of the more philosophical Mu'tazilite Schools.[39] This current of thought was no longer recognized in later times; perhaps its influence remained slim. One nevertheless speaks of a high point of Islamic civilization in connection with the work of Medieval Arabic philosophers such as al-Kindī († 873 C.E.), al-Fārābī († 950 C.E.), and Ibn Rushd († 1198 C.E.).[40] The philosophical current did leave traces in more orthodox theology, however, since there too a more rigorous form of argumentation started to hold sway.

---

[36] Gibb, p. 100.

[37] *Ibid*, p. 101.

[38] *Ibid*, p. 106. Compare Isma'īl R. al-Faruqi, "The Essence of Religious Experience in Islam," *Numen* 20 (1973): 95, "At the core of the Islamic religious experience ... stands God Who is unique and Whose will is the imperative and guide for all men's lives."

[39] Gibb, pp. 113 ff.

[40] *Ibid*, pp. 118 f. (see below, § 3.4).

Gibb believes that theological thought did not play such an important part in the development of Islam. In his view, the influence of philosophical thought waned in the later development of Islam. In his overview of the history of Islamic philosophy, Fakhry comments that the views which theology and philosophy advanced from the 13th century onwards tended to be less original, mainly producing commentary on older writings.[41] After treating the thinkers from the 14th century, Fakhry passes on to a discussion of some prominent Islamic thinkers from the 19th century. This observation does not in any way entail a judgment about the value of traditional theology and philosophy. Institutions for theological education mostly pass on traditional theology, according to Gibb.[42] As already mentioned, he believes that theological thought did not play such a significant role in later Islam. Believers felt more drawn to a living relationship between God and man, as the Koran sketches it. Popular religion in Islam is closely related to the history of Islamic asceticism and mysticism, Gibb notes. The Sufies transmitted this tradition, strongly emphasizing the inner experience of religion and sometimes stressing mysticism. Religious experience rather than rational scholarship ('ilm) is deemed as the way to knowing God. Within Sufism, the worship of holy predecessors obtained a legitimate status. Al-Ghazāli († 1111 C.E.) contributed to the fact that Sufism was able to obtain a permanent place in Islam.[43] Confrontation with the Western world starting at the beginning of the 19th century has produced many new movements. In continuing, we will consider a modern Islamic thinker, Hossein Nasr, from Iran. At the end of § 1, we have already mentioned in passing the enormous ferment resulting from the confrontation with Western technology, values, and norms; fundamentalist groups, sometimes very radical, criticize people who seek a synthesis of modern society, as it has developed in the West, with Islamic values.[44]

§ 3 Truth

3.1 General remarks

As a revealed religion, Islam insists on the correct knowledge of God. Knowledge of God occupies a prominent position. God has revealed himself so that man could know and serve Him. Both words and deeds are important

---

[41] Fakhry, p. 322, see pp. 333 ff.

[42] Gibb, pp. 145 f.; for a survey of the various theological schools, Gardet, s.v. "ilm al-Kalām,' Enc. Isl., III (1971); he says that the period of flourishing lies between the 9th and the 15th century C.E. (p. 1150).

[43] Gibb, pp. 140.

[44] Sivan, Radical Islam, offers insights into the motivation of rather fundamentalistic groups, in their reaction against what in their opinion is a superficial adaptation of Islam to the spirit of modernity.

('*ilm* and '*amal*). Rosenthal comes to the conclusion that knowledge is valued more highly than action within Islam, in his ample study about the role of knowledge in the first centuries of Muslim tradition. This is apparent, for instance, from the discussion of whether it is adequate for true faith to recognize God or whether it is also necessary to show the right conduct. This discussion had practical significance, of course; the boundaries of the Islamic community had to be established. The community's view of the relation between faith and action becomes apparent from this discussion. The majority of Muslims were proponents of a conception of *īmān* (faith) in which faith is conceived of as a combination of *taṣdīq* (the discernment of belief as true)[45] and *iqrār* (explicit recognition of God).[46] Rosenthal refers to one of the old confessions, the *Waṣīyat Abī nīfaha*, which in its first article describes faith as follows: "Faith consists in confessing with the tongue, believing with the mind, and knowing with the heart."[47] The concern of Islam is knowledge, in the sense of personal knowledge; not so much knowing about God, but the acknowledgment of God as GOD — knowledge of the heart. Such knowledge of God is what makes a Muslim a Muslim. A Muslim who fails or who does not heed his obligations remains a Muslim, albeit a deficient one. The faith in God which religious commitment implies and which comes to expression in one's conduct is of central importance to the entire Islamic tradition.[48]

3.2 In the Koran

In his *Knowledge Triumphant*, Rosenthal points out that the Arabic word for knowledge, '*ilm*, occupies a conspicuous place in the Koran. The way in which '*ilm* comes to prominence is very influential and revealing. "Mohammed's concept of 'knowledge' set intellectual life in Islam on its basically unchangeable course," is Rosenthal's appraisal.[49] The root '-*l-m*, together with its derivatives, is one of the most frequently occurring words in the Koran.[50] There is major emphasis on God's omniscience: "And not so much as the weight of an ant on earth or heaven escapes from thy Lord, neither is aught smaller than that, or greater, but in a Manifest Book."[51] God's knowledge of things is qualitatively different than human knowledge.[52] Since all human knowledge comes from God, a person cannot

---

[45] F. Rosenthal, *Knowledge Triumphant: The Concept of Knowledge in Medieval Islam* (Leiden 1970), p. 101; see also Gardet, *Dieu et la Destinée de l'homme* (Paris 1967), pp. 361 ff.

[46] Rosenthal, pp. 103 f.; see A. J. Wensinck, *The Muslim Creed: Its Genesis and Historical Development* (London ²1965), pp. 125, 194, 32 ff.

[47] In Wensinck, p. 125. On this confession, different views of the nature and development of faith, and on the relation between faith and works, Gardet, p. 375 (353-81).

[48] See Gardet, p. 372.

[49] Rosenthal, p. 19.

[50] Rosenthal, pp. 20 f.

[51] Sūra 10:(62) 61; OUP p. 204.

[52] Rosenthal, pp. 28 f.; e.g., sūra 6:59; 11:(33) 31; OUP pp. 127 f., 214.

know more than God. "Knowledge is only with God."[53] Man is completely dependent on God for his knowledge.

Knowledge is explicated in Scripture as "a guidance and a mercy unto people who believe."[54] The knowledge which comes from revelation is the most important knowledge which can be imagined, and it is the precondition for belief.[55] A mortal can answer to his eternal destiny through such faith. A limited number of cardinal religious truths are emphatically repeated in the Koran, spread among the practical directives, remembrances of former prophets, and such. The heart of *islām* is the acceptance of these cardinal truths of faith, experiencing them and testifying to them in obedient conduct.[56]

This scope of the revelation qualifies the nature of knowledge. The only knowledge which really matters is the knowledge of God —knowledge in religious commitment— and the knowledge of God's will.

In the Koran it says that when he gave the Scriptures, God summoned the former prophets to believe in a later Messenger who would come to them, "confirming what is with you."[57] 'Confirming the truth' here apparently means, to say that things *really are thus*. Knowledge here is knowing reality as it really is. "God has spoken the truth" means to say that God has furnished knowledge of things as they are.[58] The truth about man and the world is disclosed by revelation. It hardly seems possible to speak of a special concept of truth in the Koran. *ḥaqq* has the prima facie meaning of 'knowledge which corresponds to things as they are.'

What man knows about God therefore comes from revelation. That is how one learns to know God as the Omniscient One, as the Just Judge, but also as the Pardoner who mercifully and mildly forgives many transgressions.[59] It is of vital importance for man to know this. God is so exalted above His creation that "they comprehend Him not in knowledge."[60] The Koran does not speak about human knowledge of God in any theoretical sense. The Koran never speaks of knowledge (*'-r-f*) 'about' God, according to Rosenthal.[61] Knowledge of God comes from revelation and therefore is of a mysterious origin; it is not speculatively or rationally acquired reflective knowledge, but emotional, religious knowledge. Only knowledge (*'ilm*) revealed in such a way serves to enrich man's inner understanding

---

[53] Sūra 46:(22) 23, OUP p. 524; see 2:(134) 140; 2:(256) 255, OUP pp. 18, 37; Rosenthal, p. 29.
[54] Sūra 7:(50) 52, OUP p. 149.
[55] See Rosenthal, pp. 30ff.
[56] See Gardet, pp. 395, 406.
[57] Sūra 3:(75) 81, OUP p. 56.
[58] See sūra 3:(89) 95, OUP p. 58.
[59] See sūra 1:(1) 2, OUP p. 1.
[60] See Rosenthal, pp. 130ff.; Gardet, p. 397; they refer to a sūra of which the interpretation is a matter of discussion, 20:(109) 110, OUP p. 319.
[61] Rosenthal, p. 134.

and to direct the prayers, thoughts, and actions of man 'on high.'[62] The Word of God generates a form of cognition which Arkoun characterizes as *l'être-au-monde-créé* (being in a created world).[63] Arberry speaks of a general revelation contained in the visible signs of God's omnipotence and mercy in creation. He refers to the following portion of Scripture:

> And of His signs
> is that He created you of dust; then lo,
> you are mortals, all scattered abroad.
> And of His signs
> is that He created for you, of yourselves,
> spouses, that you might repose in them,
> and He has set between you love and mercy.
> Surely in that are signs for a people who consider.
> And of His signs
> is the creation of the heavens and earth
> and the variety of your tongues and hues.
> Surely in that are signs for all living beings.[64]

This passage and related ones enabled the use of reason with respect to religious truths long before theological controversies arose, as Arberry notes.[65]

3.3 Later developments

In later centuries, the question arose whether man can attain knowledge of God apart from revelation. The majority understanding which developed, according to Rosenthal, was that God can be recognized in His works, but that essential knowledge of God is impossible.[66] He mentions an interesting distinction which Ahmad b. 'Atā made. He distinguished between the *ma'rifa* (knowledge) of truth (*haqq*) and the *ma'rifa* of reality (*haqiqa*). Knowledge of the truth is knowledge of God's unity by knowing His names and attributes; this knowledge is within the reach of mortals; the other kind of knowledge, knowledge of God's reality, is unattainable for human beings.[67] We shall see how the relationship between reason and revelation exercised later Islamic thinkers. The conception of the Koran is that man can only know what God wants him to know.[68]

Sufism went beyond this in later times. They pursued a deeper relationship with God, and even unification with God in which revelation and reasoning are left behind. The first great mystic was al-Hallāj, executed in 922, who claimed to possess immediate knowledge of the truth:

---

[62] Arkoun, pp. 16f.
[63] Arkoun, p. 17.
[64] Sūra 30: (19-21) 20-22, OUP pp. 412f.
[65] Arberry, *Revelation and Reason in Islam* (London, 1957), pp. 14f.
[66] Rosenthal, p. 135.
[67] *Ibid*, p. 141.
[68] *Ibid*, p. 135.

> Now stands no more between the Truth and me
> Or reasoned demonstration,
> Or proof, or revelation . . . [69]

His is the statement: *'anā'l-ḥaqq'*, "I am the absolute truth," or, "I am God."[70]

Differing conceptions about knowledge were reached within this movement. Sometimes the importance of knowledge was toned down; sometimes it was esteemed very highly. True reality (*ḥaqīqa*) was sometimes even seen as being equal to knowledge. Rosenthal gives as an example a statement by al-Abharī (915–16 C.E.): "All true reality is knowledge, and all knowledge is true reality."[71] Ibn 'Arabī (1240 C.E.), the great Sufi master, taught the unity of all that had being. In terms of this notion, one can understand that true knowledge of God implies union with Him — knowledge, object, and subject must be considered as one.[72]

3.4 Medieval philosophy

In this section we will examine somewhat more closely two Islamic thinkers who were influenced by Greek philosophy, especially the philosophy of Aristotle: al-Kindī and al-Fārābī; the view of al-Ghazālī, who was critically disposed towards philosophy, and who lead the wandering existence of a Sufi in the last years of his life, will be subsequently sketched; finally, the last great Arab philosopher of the Middle Ages will be mentioned, Ibn Rushd. Assessment of the value of philosophical systems varies, as appears already from the above. Arkoun points out that the principles of Aristotelian logic were applied to the explanation of the Koran — no matter how contrary "à l'intention vivificatrice de la Parole de Dieu qui dynamise l'histoire" (to the intention of the Word of God which bringeth life and movement in history).[73]

a) Al-Kindī

In his history of Islamic philosophy, Fakhry calls al-Kindī († ±866) the first Arab philosopher.[74] His thought was characterized by a rational approach to the revealed texts. According to Fakhry, al-Kindī's work must be placed in the mainstream of theological thought, which is commonly associated with the Mu'tazilites, at the beginning of scholastic theology

---

[69] Arberry, p. 29.
[70] *Gärten der Erkenntnis: Texte aus der islamitischen Mystik*, German tr. Annemarie Schimmel (Düsseldorf 1982), p. 10.
[71] Rosenthal, p. 175.
[72] Rosenthal, p. 188; see Fakhry, p. 251.
[73] Arkoun, p. 26.
[74] Fakhry, p. 66.

in Islam.[75] Al-Kindī believed that the truth of the Islamic revelation could be proven by means of syllogisms in a manner which only incompetents could oppose.[76] He conceived of philosophy as "the knowledge of the reality of things, commensurate with the human faculties of apprehension."[77] Rational analysis cannot but agree with the revelation in the Koran.[78] He could, accordingly, adopt the perceptions of Greek philosophy in his thought. There are different ways to knowing; by sense perception and by reasonable analysis. Reasonable knowledge comes about by abstracting the forms of intelligible objects (i.e., species and genera), so that reason becomes identical with its object in the act of thought.[79] In his treatment of reason, al-Kindī gives an Aristotelian view of the intellect. He distinguishes between four meanings of the term reason (*'aql*) in Aristotle: the actual, the potential, the habitual, and the manifest. The centre of this epistemology is that "realized knowledge coincides with its object," as Aristotle himself had written. The soul becomes identical with the object of cognition when the intellect makes the transition from a state of potentiality to a state of actuality.[80]

In addition to normal, human, reasonable knowledge, al-Kindī also accepted super-human, prophetic knowledge given by God to His Messengers. The distinguishing trait of such knowledge, according to Fakhry, is the extraordinary clarity and comprehensiveness with which it is expressed.[81] In this way, al-Kindī relates his loyalty to the Koran to his assimilation of the Greek philosophical tradition.

b) Al-Fārābī

Al-Fārābī (872–950 C.E.), one of the greatest of Arab philosophers, was a deeply religious and mystical thinker.[82] He was influenced profoundly by Greek philosophy. Like other Muslim thinkers, al-Fārābī regarded Greek philosophy as a unity, in which not only Plato and Aristotle were placed within a single framework, but in which Neo-Platonist emanation theories also occupied a prominent position.[83] The Highest and the Primary which forms the foundation of all that exists is the *intellectus intelligens intellectum.*[84] Al-Fārābī examines the concept of reason (*'aql*) in a separate work.[85] In addition to some other meanings of the word *'aql*, al-Fārābī

---

[75] *Ibid*, p. 68.
[76] *Ibid*, p. 69.
[77] *Ibid*, p. 70.
[78] Arberry, p. 35.
[79] Fakhry, p. 87, see pp. 71 f.
[80] Fakhry, p. 87; Aristotle, *De Anima*, 431. a.
[81] Fakhry, pp. 92 f.; Arberry, pp. 36 f.
[82] Corbin, *Histoire*, p. 223.
[83] D. C. Mulder, *Openbaring en Rede in de Islamitische Filosofie van Al-Fārābī tot Ibn Rusd* (Amsterdam 1949), pp. 35 ff.
[84] Fakhry, p. 117.
[85] Mulder, pp. 43 ff.; Fakhry, pp. 121 ff.

mentions Aristotle's concept of reason in *de Anima*, with its distinctions between *intellectus in potentia, intellectus in effectu, intellectus adeptus, and intellectus agens*.[86] As soon as the potential intellect adopts the forms for itself, it becomes actual (or effective) intellect. The forms of the *intelligibilia* in the actual intellect can be the object of thought, that is, for a higher form of thought, the *intellectus adeptus* (acquired intellect).[87] These immaterial forms are "perceived" immediately.[88] Above this, al-Fārābī posits the *'aql fa"al (intellectus agens,* or Agent Intellect) as the highest, an immaterial form which never has been nor will be materialized.[89] This highest form of reason effectuates the transition from *intellectus in potentia* to *intellectus in effectu,* and is responsible for making actual forms of potential ones, "just as the sun makes it possible for the sight to see and for the colors to be seen."[90] The order of knowledge thus corresponds to the order of being. The thinker rises from cognition to the Primary; in cosmology, one descends from the Primary down to earthly reality. The reason cognition is so important is that man's *happiness* consists of participation in the immaterial nature of the Highest, the Agent Intellect.[91]

Al-Fārābī's view of revelation is also determined by his philosophical system. The *'aql fa"al (intellectus agens)* operates directly on the imagination of the prophet.[92] By means of the revelation, the prophet is able to teach the masses the eternal truths in the form of sensuous representation.[93] The revelation interprets the truth which is thought in philosophy into vivid and persuasive images for the masses. Al-Fārābī articulated the thought which would remain essential to all of Islamic philosophy: revelation and reason do not contradict one another.

c) Al-Ghazālī

Al-Ghazālī (1058–1111 C.E.) is considered as one of the most important and profound thinkers Islam has produced.[94] Al-Ghazālī opposes the synthesis of Greek philosophy and Islamic thought in the philosophical school of Medieval Islam. He criticizes thinking in terms of emanation and stresses the will of God.[95] In his later years, al-Ghazālī wandered about as a Sufi in order to find peace with God along this path, rather than via the route of intellectual cognition. Although al-Ghazālī appreciates the importance of theology, true knowledge is not to be obtained in that

---

[86] Mulder, p. 44; Fakhry, pp. 121 f.
[87] Mulder, p. 45.
[88] Fakhry, p. 122.
[89] Mulder, p. 45.
[90] Fakhry, p. 122.
[91] Fakhry, p. 126; Mulder, pp. 51 f.
[92] Mulder, p. 51.
[93] Mulder, p. 55.
[94] Fakhry, pp. 217 ff.; Mulder, p. 75.
[95] Mulder, pp. 78 f.

way, but along the route of mystical religious experience.[96] Al-Ghazālī reports in his autobiography that he was driven by a fervent desire for truth even before he was twenty; he detested the image of "conflicting beliefs and creeds" and the passivity and credulity of those who blindly rely on the authority of their parents. He went out in quest of *certain* knowledge, "that knowledge in which the object is known in a manner which is not open to doubt at all."[97] Where can such knowledge with such certainty be found?

It is apparent that sensory knowledge is deceptive. But if knowledge based on perception, which seems so certain, is actually uncertain, with what right can one attach credence to the knowledge of 'necessary' propositions? Al-Ghazālī found a solution for this doubt in the "light which God poured into his heart."[98] This light was not a matter of argumentation but of grace. Such illumination is accompanied by renunciation of the illusory world and a turning to the world of reality.[99]

According to his report, al-Ghazālī examined four groups of people who appeared to have the truth at their disposal: the theologians (the *Kalām*), the Ismāʿīlīs, the philosophers, and the Sufies. The Kalām assumes the authority of the Scriptures or the consensus of the community; these premises are not insusceptible to doubt.[100] The Ismāʿīlīs require faith in an infallible *imām*. The Prophet is deceased, however, and the *imām*, although not dead, is hidden, and is thus equally inaccessible, any observer would have to admit. Al-Ghazālī discusses the works of the philosophers in detail; he warns against errors, especially those of the Muslim Neo-Platonist thinkers.[101] He focusses primarily on their view of the eternity of the world, the will of God, God's knowledge of things, the mutations within God, and the resurrection of the body.[102] Al-Ghazālī believes that reason can give no verdict on the immortality of the soul. In order to know that with certainty, one must have recourse to the authority of Scripture or revelation. Reason must be aided.[103]

As mentioned, al-Ghazālī finally found certainty in the mysticism of the Sufi movement. In two of his main mystical works —despite al-Ghazālī's criticism of platonizing Muslim theologians— the Neo-Platonic hierarchy of being forms the metaphysical basis for his mysticism.[104] The metaphor of light plays an important role. The hierarchy of luminous beings in the spiritual world is determined by their degree of proximity to the Highest

---

96 Mulder, p. 90.
97 In Fakhry, p. 218.
98 *Ibid*, p. 219.
99 *Ibid*, p. 220.
100 *Ibid*, p. 220.
101 *Ibid*, p. 223; Arberry, p. 62.
102 Fakhry, pp. 225 ff.
103 *Ibid*, p. 233.
104 *Ibid*, p. 248.

Light, which is God. For only God truly exists; everything else, taken by itself, is non-being.

This view has consequences for epistemology. Human perception starts with the senses and culminates in Reason. A special faculty has been given to prophets and saints, however, by which they have the capacity to obtain knowledge of the future, of future life, and of super-natural and divine things.[105] The highest type of knowledge, al-Ghazālī says, is not reasonable knowledge or knowledge on the basis of faith, but is knowledge by direct experience. Thus it is also true of the knowledge of God that it is 'experiential.' Al-Ghazālī believes that one person achieves a more exalted experience of God than the next. Most privileged are those people who are completely absorbed in the Highest One.[106] Mulder presents a division of the sorts of knowledge to which al-Ghazālī was led. The lowest rung of knowledge is the knowledge of the masses, which rests on the acceptance (taqlīd) of the literal sense of the revelation. The reasonings of the Mutakallimūn are higher, "useful for refuting the heretics, but insufficient to conduct one to true knowledge." Thereupon follow the speculations of the philosophers, whose heresies must be resisted. The highest knowledge is the knowledge of the mystic and of the prophet, which they have obtained through inspiration and revelation.[107]

d) Ibn Rushd

The last of the great Medieval Islamic thinkers was the Spanish philosopher, Ibn Rushd (1126–1198 C.E., in Latin, Averroes). Ibn Rushd developed into one of the pre-eminent commentators of Aristotle in the Middle Ages. He was able, due to his vast knowledge of Aristotle, to develop a new position in respect of the old question of how faith and reason could be related. He opposed al-Ghazālī, but was able to side with him in his criticism of al-Kindī and Ibn Sīnā (in Latin, Avicenna) because he himself gave a different interpretation to Aristotle. Ibn Rushd is regarded as the best among the Arabic interpreters of Aristotle.[108] Fakhry notes that in his philosophical labours, Ibn Rushd chiefly engaged himself with three areas: commentaries on Aristotle; criticism of al-Fārābī and Ibn Sīnā in connection with their interpretation of Aristotle; and the relationship between philosophy (properly understood) and Scripture.[109]

Ibn Rushd is the only Islamic philosopher who explicitly deals with the relationship between revelation and reason, according to D. C. Mulder. Mulder describes just how widely the interpretations of Ibn Rushd's

---

[105] *Ibid*, p. 249.

[106] *Ibid*, p. 250.

[107] Mulder, p. 92; Arberry, claims that his critique has been corroborated, and that no important philosophical works appeared thereafter in Eastern Islam, pp. 64 ff.

[108] Fakhry, pp. 274 f.

[109] *Ibid*, pp. 273 f.

thought on faith and reason diverge.[110] Ibn Rushd believed that faith and reason were in harmony with each other.[111] He thereby joins a long series of Islamic thinkers before him, who all assume that the truth, in all its manifestations, is ultimately one.[112] Whoever accepts that the results of philosophical thought and the explanations of Scripture agree will not be able to take the anthropomorphisms in the Koran literally, but must interpret them metaphorically. Support for this is to be found in the Koran itself, which somewhere distinguishes between 'proper signs' and 'ambiguous' ones.[113] Kramers takes the expression 'proper signs' to mean 'clearly formulated verses.' Fakhry translates the passage as follows: "some of its verses are unambiguous . . . and the others are ambiguous." To this is added that only God and those confirmed in knowledge know His interpretation (*ta'wīl*). This text apparently indicates that there is an interpretation problem with certain texts; not everyone knows how the texts ought to be understood. In Ibn Rushd's conception, the philosophers are the people who are confirmed in knowledge. He finds here a take off point for a deeper, figurative interpretation of anthropomorphisms. He can accordingly harmonize explication of Scripture and philosophical analysis.[114]

There is yet another ground for the legitimacy of philosophical reflection; in Sunnite Islam, the teaching office is not clearly circumscribed: Who represents the majority voice of the Koran interpreters? This is where philosophical reflection has its task. Fakhry here recalls the difference between Sunnites and Shī'ites in respect of doctrinal authority. For the Sunnites, this lies in the consensus within the community (*ijma'*); while in the *Shī'a* the *imām* has infallible authority, as mentioned. According to Fakhry, now, this difference in respect of the interpretation of authority is the explanation for the fact that the relationship between philosophy and Scripture was not a serious problem in Shī'ite circles between the 10th and the 17th centuries.[115]

Ibn Rushd thus attributes to philosophy a task in the explication of Scripture, but he believes that not all people should be confronted with the results of such philosophical reflection. In His goodness, God has made Himself known to the great mass of people through metaphorical language. It is legitimate and good that the great mass of people understand the metaphorical expressions of Scripture just as they are.[116] At this level of understanding, the rhetorical method of argumentation is used. Theology employs another type of argumentation, the dialectical, whereas philosophy

---

[110] Mulder, pp. 113-17.

[111] Fakhry, p. 274.

[112] *Ibid*, pp. 276f.

[113] Sūra 3:(5) 7, OUP p. 45.

[114] Fakhry, pp. 278ff.; Mulder, p. 120.

[115] Fakhry, p. 278.

[116] *Ibid*, pp. 279f.; Mulder says that even here the point is not faith on the basis of authority, but a special kind of religious evidence, p. 137, see also p. 139.

follows the demonstrative method.[117] This method involves coming to self-evident conclusions by way of demonstration from self-evident premises.[118] One finds these three methods in the Koran itself, according to Ibn Rushd.[119] Mulder points out that the distinctions between these three methods in the context of the relationship between revelation and reason are replaced in Ibn Rushd's later work by the distinction between 'practical' and 'theoretical.' We will pass over this further elaboration.[120] Acceptance of faith at any of these three levels is sufficient to convey a person to salvation.[121] There are three cases in which philosophy has occasion to resort to a non-literal interpretation of the text of Scripture: (1) passages where no consensus (*ijma'*) about the legal or doctrinal meaning of that passage is possible; (2) passages where various Scriptures apparently contradict each other; (3) passages where Scriptures appear to be at odds with the principles of philosophy or natural reason.[122] Ibn Rushd himself is concerned with the third category of problems; as long as one explains Scripture correctly, it is not in conflict with proper philosophy. Ibn Rushd wants to be true to the content of revelation as well as to the principles of philosophy.[123]

The salvation of the philosopher too depends on believing what is necessary for happiness in this life and in the next. Ibn Rushd sums up the doctrines which are necessary for salvation, both for the philosopher and theologian as well as for the ordinary man: (1) the existence of God, the Creator and Governor of the world; (2) the unity of God; (3) the attributes of His perfection (knowledge, life, will, hearing, seeing, speech); (4) His freedom from imperfection (in consequence of sūra 42:(9) 11, 'No thing is equal to Him,' often regarded as the ground for the *via remotionis*); (5) the creation of the world; (6) the validity of prophecy; (7) the justice of God; and (8) the resurrection after death.[124] One may differ concerning the *manner in which* one views these matters, but it is incumbent upon every person who covets salvation to believe in them. Each group has the right and the duty to assimilate beliefs at their own level; thus, it is the duty of the majority to accept the metaphorical language as it is; attempts to explain the hidden meaning of the metaphors to the masses is objectionable.[125] The substance of faith does not differ, only the form in which it is expressed. For matters about which philosophy cannot judge, one must

---

[117] Fakhry, p. 278.

[118] Mulder, p. 135.

[119] Sūra 7:(184) 185; 6:78; 88:17 (among others) exhorts man to look upon the wonders of creation, OUP pp. 165f., 130, 642.

[120] Mulder, p. 162.

[121] Fakhry, p. 279.

[122] *Ibid*, p. 280; on a case of conflict between the Koran and philosophy, Mulder, p. 135.

[123] Mulder says his thought is 'synthetic,' because of this combination of philosophy and revelation, p. 165.

[124] Fakhry, p. 282.

[125] *Ibid*, p. 283; Mulder, pp. 124f.; see also pp. 133f.

rely on Scripture for insight.[126] For, to Ibn Rushd, revelation is instruction in true knowledge and in right action.[127]

In the area of competence belonging to science, the philosopher must accept the way of philosophical demonstration. How exactly does the sophisticated understanding of Scripture which the philosopher attains differ from the understanding of others? The philosophers supply a different content to the concepts; the concepts themselves are not denied. They merely deny that our concepts are univocally applicable to God.[128]

Finally, we pose the question as to Ibn Rushd's view of the nature of knowledge. True knowledge —in Fakhry's presentation— is essential knowledge of the causes of things.[129] God's knowledge is the cause of all things. In his self-knowledge, God knows all things.[130] It is the nature of knowledge that object and subject are completely identical. Thus, we again run into the fundamental notion of Aristotelian epistemology here, now in Ibn Rushd's case. Why is so much significance attached to knowledge? Because by means of knowledge one participates in and becomes one with the object of knowledge.

Ibn Rushd is the last of the great Medieval Islamic philosophers. In the second section of the introduction (§ 1.2), it was already pointed out that philosophy never occupied a very important position within the Islamic tradition. We will now move on to a discussion of a modern author.

3.5 Seyyed Hossein Nasr

To conclude this exposition on truth and knowledge in the Islamic tradition, we will examine a modern Islamic thinker, Nasr. From the end of the fifties up until the Khomeiny period, Nasr was one of the pre-eminent Islamic thinkers in Iran. In his publications, he tries to show how the traditional Islamic accent on religious surrender is of essential significance in modern times too, and especially in confrontation with Western culture. Nasr tries to show how people find their destiny in the experience of God's nearness. The Sufi movement tries to help people to achieve this experience.

We will begin by presenting Nasr's view of Islam and Sufism in general, and then deal more elaborately with his thoughts on the relation between God and man, and of the role of knowledge and reason within it.

The fundamental insistence of Islam is the unity of God, the unity of human life, and the fellowship between God and man. The Koran is the clear revelation of monotheism; the law (*Shari'a*) orders all of existence and integrates all aspects of life into a unity; the spiritual way (*Tariqa*)

---

[126] Fakhry, p. 284; see Mulder's summary, pp. 161 ff.
[127] Mulder, p. 134.
[128] Fakhry, p. 284.
[129] *Ibid*, p. 286.
[130] *Ibid*, p. 285; Mulder, pp. 143, 157.

leads people to unity with God. Islam is comprehensive — not religion adjacent to the rest of life, as many people conceive of religion, but ...

> also a socio-political order, a world view and a way of life in which all aspects of man's physical, mental, and spiritual needs are considered and fulfilled.[131]

The ordering of life specified in the law, and knowledge of the Unity and the Greatness of God known from revelation, have a purpose. This purpose is not extraneous to religion, in a secularized life, in material prosperity or outward appearance. On the contrary, the purpose of religion is and remains to bring people closer to the fulfillment of their existence, the nearness of God:

> The heart of the religious life resides and will continue to reside in traditional forms and practices, in the inner being of individuals for whom Islam means an approach to the Divine and a sanctification of human life, and not a mere asset with which to further particular worldly causes, whether they be political, social, or economic.[132]

Nasr insists on the experiential in religion. This does not mean that he detracts from the more objective side to religion. He forcefully repudiates (Western) subjectivism:

> Islam is a religion which rejects individualistic subjectivism. The most intelligible material symbol of Islam, the mosque, is a building with a space in which all elements of subjectivism have been eliminated. It is an objective determination of the Truth, a crystal through which radiates the light of the Spirit. The spiritual ideal of Islam itself is to transform the soul of the Muslim, like a mosque, into a crystal reflecting the Divine Light.[133]

In this quote, we encounter emphasis on *objectivity*, on *experience*, on *purification* and transformation of the person, and on the pure *reflection* of the divine Light. These notions are essential for Nasr's view. We will pursue them.

First, then, *objectivity*. This is presupposed by Nasr when he insists that inwardness is intrinsic to religion. Religion has an outward and an inward aspect. To the outward belongs doctrine, organization, and behaviour. Doctrine has been given by God in the revelation. "Moslems continually have the innate feeling that they possess in the purest form the doctrines which all religions proclaim," Nasr remarks.[134] The outward is also to be discovered in the organization, for example, the mosque and art. Islam not only embraces the way of knowledge to come closer to God, but also the way of art, of that which one makes. People can therefore give expression to the unity of things and the Unity of God in art and in the buildings

---

[131] S. H. Nasr, *Islamic Studies* (Beirut 1967), p. 1.
[132] Nasr, *Islam and the Plight of Modern Man* (London 1975), p. 95.
[133] Nasr, *Plight*, p. 141.
[134] Nasr, *Sufi Essays* (London 1972), p. 132; see *Plight*, p. 131, "... the Prophet of Islam asserted the Truth in the most straightforward and naked manner."

which they make. Behaviour is another visible aspect of religion. The *Shari'a* helps people to live according to the divine will.[135] Since the Law encompasses all aspects of life, life in conformity with the Law already confers a certain degree of unity to life.

Nasr's chief purpose is to point from the outside of religion to the inside. His concern is *experience*. The integration of life which can be reached by observing the Law must be deepened. Alongside of the *Shari'a* stands the *Tarīqa*, the contemplative way, which a person can follow in order to come closer to God already in this life. No opposition exists in Islam between the active and the contemplative life; contemplation is also the meant for people who stand in the midst of life.[136] Action and contemplation go together; *al-'ilm* and *al-'amal* are connected, for Islam embraces the whole of existence. Nasr is primarily concerned with the inside of faith, how it is experienced. He uses the word mysticism on occasion, but notes that he uses that word in its original meaning, which in his view is, "in relation to the divine mystery," or, knowledge combined with love, which is far from irrational; mysticism alludes to the inward aspect of revealed and orthodox religion; it remains firmly secured to the paths which that religion indicates.[137]

One needs such paths to *purify* and to *transform* oneself. The condition of mankind is not as it should be; it is deficient. The basic error is that man is separated from God; man has fallen into the earthly condition of disintegration and distance from his origin, which consisted in unity with God. To be sure, man is never separate from God, but he does not realize that. That is why man does not experience existence in full unity with God.[138] Two things are implied by human nature, the awareness or representation of perfection, and an "experiential certainty of separation within himself."[139] Nasr adds here that these eternal characteristics of human nature are more important than properties which change with the times. Life is dependent on the bond with God which is sensed. The divine pervades and sustains this world. Believers have a relation to this divine power which sustains their existence. If there were no people who consciously sense this bond, then the earth would cease to exist, Nasr states. A very narrow relationship exists between *being and knowing*; life comes from Being; the relationship between Being and its earthly manifestations would cease to exist if there were no *conscious ontological nexus*: "It would fall into the abyss of nothingness."[140] Increased understanding can be acquired by knowing God and his Will. Knowledge is obtained from the Koran, that is, awareness of God, of the coming world, and of the

---

135 Nasr, *Plight*, p. 77; *Sufi Essays*, pp. 49, 45.
136 Nasr, *Sufi Essays*, p. 50; *Plight*, p. 69.
137 Nasr, *Sufi Essays*, p. 26 n. 5.
138 *Ibid*, p. 43, see p. 50.
139 *Ibid*, p. 25.
140 *Ibid*, p. 27.

return to God.[141] By observing the law man is protected from all pursuits which lead away from God. By using one's reason, it is possible to arrange life in conformity with the understanding received and with the commandments; one is then approaching God. If reason is not used well ('reason' conceived broadly: *'aql*), the passions will not be conquered; reason will then be pressed into the service of wrong desires, and it will start to function as a veil which prevents discerning what is and what is not important. People live as though imprisoned; Sufism wants to free them from the constraints of an illusory prison.[142] Ultimately, a deformed culture will ensue, a consequence which is borne out, for example, by the problems facing the technologically and economically oriented Western societies.[143]

In order to sanctify oneself, one must have an understanding of revelation and observe the precepts of the *Shari'a*. A person must learn virtues, for the learning of virtues transforms a person; virtues are a way of being.[144] To become more God-like, one must follow the *Tariqa*, the spiritual path. To this end, one must subject oneself to the guidance of a Sufi master. The master is connected to the other masters by the golden chain of initiations. To understand the role of the Sufi masters properly, according to Nasr, one must bear in mind the position which the twelfth, hidden *imam* occupies, especially in Persia. This *imam* is the spiritual axis of the world in a hidden way, the pole to which all Sufi masters are inwardly related.[145] Nasr mentions an example of a tractate in which spiritual development is described in forty stages.[146] If one goes through all these stages, one achieves the full realization of life, the purpose which all religion pursues.[147] One is then related to God, the Truth (*al-haqq*).[148]

Seen in terms of man, these stages are developmental phases in a process for which a person must exert himself. They can also be viewed from another perspective, however; they are then seen to rest on God's gift of mercy.[149]

We now come to the purpose of the spiritual journey: the crystal clear reflection of the Truth, or, put differently, of 'Universal Intellect,' which is the realization of Unity, both of *man* ('Universal Man') as well as of God.[150] One is so focussed on what is permanent and enduring in creation that one becomes 'man': "Universal Man is the mirror in which are reflected

---

[141] *Ibid*, p. 54.
[142] *Ibid*, pp. 33, 54.
[143] *Ibid*, pp. 152 ff.; 43; compare *Plight*, p. 49.
[144] Nasr, *Sufi Essays*, p. 70.
[145] *Ibid*, p. 66.
[146] *Ibid*, pp. 77 ff.
[147] *Ibid*, p. 82.
[148] *Ibid*, p. 69.
[149] *Ibid*, pp. 29, 76.
[150] *Ibid*, p. 35; see also p. 33; *Plight*, p. 74.

all the Divine Names and Qualities."[151] Then being man in the fallen state
has been overcome, and eternal unity with God is realized. One reflects
Divine Knowledge like a clear mirror; the full realization of 'Universal
Man' is therefore the full realization of the Truth.[152] One can understand,
then, why Nasr says of the 'gnostic path of spirituality' that it is not
merely one rational form of knowledge alongside of others, but is a
theosophy, a *ḥikma,* a help unto spiritual realization.[153]

What role does rationality play in this process? The answer is that
reason plays a different role at various levels, so that the concept of
truth also receives a different content each time. Nasr says somewhere
that one cannot achieve any true insight into religion(s) unless one realizes
that there is a *hierarchy* of knowledge. There are at least four fundamental
levels of knowledge: the sensory, the rational, the representative (the
'imagination'), and the intellectual.[154] We will leave the category of purely
sensory experience for what it is in the present context. Although the
description below has been compiled from a number of different articles,
we trust that it conforms to Nasr's intentions.

(1) At the level of the *truths,* we find the doctrines which are propagated
by Islam; they ultimately originate from the Koran. Many will regard
doctrine as 'true' at this level, in the common sense meaning of 'truths'
— statements which correspond to reality. Recall that reality itself still
lies behind a 'veil' at this level, so that its true nature is unseen, and
indeed cannot yet be seen.

(2) A *transformation* of the person is necessary for deeper knowledge. Grace
is necessary to effectuate this, as well as exertion, initiation in the
methods of the spiritual way, and a master who can guide one on this way.
More and more one learns to see the world as it is — related in a
mysterious fashion to God. Nasr speaks of the *eye of the heart.*[155] This eye
takes one further than discursive reason alone.[156] Philosophy is traditionally
familiar with two approaches to the transcendent, the affirmative and the
negative way. The affirmative way deals with unity and manifoldness,
cause and effect, potentiality and actuality, substance and accident. The
negative way entails the denial of every definition of Being, of its
composition, or of its participation in anything else.[157] Discursive, purely
affirmative reason is transcended. Nasr states that on the one hand,
Being is beyond the manifest order; on the other hand, there is nothing
outside of Being; all qualities of being are derived from Being and return
to it. Nasr points out that the proclamation, *Lā ilāha illa'llāh,* is interpreted

---

[151] Nasr, *Sufi Essays,* p. 35.
[152] Nasr, *Plight,* p. 75.
[153] *Ibid,* p. 110.
[154] *Ibid,* p. 31.
[155] *Ibid,* e.g., p. 31.
[156] Nasr, *Islamic Studies,* p. 134.
[157] *Ibid,* p. 137.

by the Sufies not only in the traditional sense as 'there is no divinity but God'; but also as 'there is no being other than Being itself.'[158] All being derives its existence from Being itself, which transcends all beings. This deeper knowledge apparently requires the transformation of the person as well as the surpassing of discursive cognition. The truth, if we may articulate it thus, is no longer purely rational at this level, but (let us say), intuitive.

(3) The highest knowledge —knowledge in the proper sense— is the intellectual knowledge, the contemplation, or better yet, the *reflection*, of Being:

> For the intellect, which is the only faculty within man capable of knowing Being qua Being, no concept is clearer than Being because the sense of being is inherent in the intellect.[159]

In this gnosis, reality is thought in its pure, non-manifest and undetermined state, beyond existence and beings.[160] Of concern here is "sapiential knowledge, based upon the direct and immediate experience of the Truth."[161] The human mind is actually emptied, remote from the passions of this world, and purified by (1) observance of the commandments of the *Sharī'a*; (2) thoughtful consideration of the revealed truths in the Koran; (3) adherence to the *Tarīqa*; (4) surmounting of discursive thought. The outcome of such purification is that one is capable of 'perceiving' the only true reality. Nasr speaks of a *passive reflection of the universal Intellect.*[162]

> The contemplative 'sees' the Truth and knows it through the process of identity. At the end when he has reached the state of 'union,' through the effective realization of the Truth or through gnosis (*ma'rifa*), his knowledge becomes perfect, and because knowing is essentially being, his being also partakes of the 'perfume' of the divine knowledge thus acquired.[163]

Such reflection amounts to oneness with God (and, one will recall, since God is Being and Being is one, it is unity pure and simple). Being is the Truth; the realization of this Truth is thought, love, and being. This realization does not stand apart from the religious tradition in which a specific route to this realization is indicated.[164] Such, in our opinion, is Nasr's vision of the highest truth.

In conclusion, we will present his view of the relation of Islam to other religions. Nasr's appraisal of other religions follows from his view of elements in them which correspond to the esoteric tradition of the

---

[158] *Ibid*, p. 140 n. 4.
[159] *Ibid*, p. 159.
[160] *Ibid*, pp. 134f.
[161] Nasr, *Plight*, p. 29.
[162] Nasr, *Islamic Studies*, p. 135; see *Sufi Essays*, pp. 43f.
[163] Nasr, *Islamic Studies*, p. 142.
[164] Nasr, *Plight*, p. 30; see Nasr's remarks on comparative philosophy.

Sufi movement, for this esoteric way is intrinsic to being human; the pursuit of the integration and the unity of existence is inherent to human existence. This does not imply that the way of the Sufies entirely corresponds to the way which spiritual currents in other religions follow. According to Nasr, every valid esoteric path is determined by the objective framework of the revelation to which such a path belongs.[165]

Muslims believe that God has sent many prophets to the nations — traditionally it said 124,000. It is obvious that there are other religions on the basis of the 'universality of revelation.'[166] The later prophets were able to link up with the earlier ones. The great prophet was therefore able to link up with what the prophets before him had said, especially in the Abrahamitic religions.[167] Every prophet, Sharī'iatic Muslims believe, proclaimed monotheism.[168] This idea was determinative for the practical posture of Islam towards adherents of other religious traditions. Nasr describes the attitude towards various groupings somewhat more elaborately.[169] What has been written in the Koran about the same person or events as narrated in the Bible or Talmud, has not been derived from such accounts, but from the archetype of these three revelations.[170] The relationship of Islam to the Indian religions is more difficult, given the different cultural climate. The Hindus in India were certainly not regarded as simple heathen; Muslims were aware that the Hindus also realize that the One resides behind the many.[171] Other religions were always regarded as a form of the Divine Law. The most profound encounter is possible at the level of religious experience, the esoteric level. The Sufi penetrates to the Ground, the One; all forms become transparent through this.[172] The inner unity of all religions lies in loving gnosis.[173] All peoples are underway as though to the Ka'ba. At the Ka'ba, people understand that the diversity of religions does not have to produce tensions.[174] Those who truly love God understand that the Ka'ba is in reality God himself. Nasr also gives the familiar image of the mountain on which people ascend to the Highest along many paths; God himself has chosen various paths for various people.[175]

The concept of truth naturally occurs at the various levels of cognition. Nasr speaks of the 'truths' of the Koran, or, in other words, of doctrinal truth. For him, this is indisputably given in its purest form in Islam; this

---

[165] Nasr, *Sufi Essays*, p. 17.
[166] *Ibid*, pp. 131, 169.
[167] *Ibid*, p. 130.
[168] *Ibid*, p. 132.
[169] *Ibid*, pp. 133 ff.
[170] *Ibid*, p. 134.
[171] *Ibid*, pp. 140 f.
[172] *Ibid*, p. 146.
[173] *Ibid*, pp. 146 f.
[174] *Ibid*, pp. 149 f.
[175] *Ibid*, p. 151.

truth must be confirmed and defended.[176] At a higher level a certain
relativity of articulated knowledge is achieved, as we have seen; one might
speak of 'intuitive truth.' At the highest level, truth is participation,
unity, and passive reflection of God who himself is the Truth, *al-ḥaqq*,
who on the one hand transcends all determinations, but who on the other
hand, reveals himself through his names and qualities, and so in his
mercy enables the possibility of knowledge at lower levels.[177]

§ 4   Attitude towards other religions

4.1   Tolerance towards followers of other religions

In his study on the tolerance of the Islamic community towards
followers of other religions, Adel Khoury sketches the developments which
have taken place. He begins with the stipulations in the Koran respecting
the attitude towards adherents of different religions; he subsequently
deals with later developments. He appeals to legal stipulations and
contracts, chiefly from Arabic countries.[178] The Islamic community was
faced with a problem in relation to followers of other religions, since
Islam requires *total* religious surrender, marking the whole of life.[179]
According to Khoury, the highest principle of Islam is that God guides
people; it is an absolute norm that one directs himself to God's will. That
is done as a community, and that yields a problem if a portion of the
population doesn't belong to the Islamic community and does not feel
obligated by the *Sharī'a*. It was necessary to regulate the rights and the
duties of non-Islamic population groups. What was written in the Koran
formed guidelines for this process; its application was determined by
circumstances.

The foundation of tolerance towards non-Muslims is that *compulsion
is inappropriate in religion.*[180] The prophet allows for the recognition of
the relative authority of other prophets, particularly the prophets of ancient
Israel and Jesus. There is one basic revelation, though there are differences
between the Koran, the books of Moses, and the books of the Christians.
This produced a certain feeling of affiliation with Jews and Christians on
the part of Mohammed. As we have seen, he initially counted on more
support from Jews and Christians than he later received. His attitude
towards people with generally different convictions was altered when he
ran across resistance and threats on the part of his Mecca opponents.
This led him to take a more rigid posture, and according to Khoury, this

---

[176] *Ibid*, p. 55; *Plight*, pp. 131, 148.
[177] See Nasr, *Sufi Essays*, pp. 57, 69, 91; *Islamic Studies*, p. 137.
[178] A. Khoury, *Toleranz im Islam* (Munich 1982).
[179] *Ibid*, p. 17.
[180] *Ibid*, p. 20; sûra 2: (257) 256, OUP p. 37.

harder stance became the foundation of later legislation.[181] Recall here that from the beginning, there were two prime interests: first, the protection and spread of the faith, and second, the protection and establishment of the religious community's unity.[182] Unbelief and every other impediment to Islam is dangerous for the community, since *islām* is its foundation. Recall again here that the Islamic view is that knowledge of God belongs to the natural aptitudes of man, and that revelation has come via many prophets to *all* people.[183] There is thus something strange about people's refusal to accept the revelation. Within this setting, it is understandable how a differentiated attitude towards religious freedom developed:

(1) Muslims were not permitted to repudiate their faith.
(2) Polytheists were not to be excused since God does not abide 'partners,' nor were they tolerated.
(3) People of the book were permitted relative freedom of religion; they themselves were responsible for their conduct in life.[184]

It was prescribed that Muslims were not to commune with unbelievers, and certainly not with heathens.[185] This attitude towards others must be understood against the backdrop of the struggle which would be conducted, in the first instance, against the polytheistic tribes. In later times, Mohammed also ordered an expedition against Christian tribes in the north of the Arabian peninsula.[186] Despite reservations on the part of Mohammed towards Jews and Christians, they nevertheless received a relative freedom in respect of their religion; they were obliged to pay tribute, but could count on protection. Persecution of Jews sometimes occurred; such persecution coincided with the spirit of the times. *That* others were not allowed to integrate into Islamic society was a stipulation which came from the Koran. *How* this was worked out in later times depended on the interpretation given to the Koran.[187] Khoury offers many interesting examples of treaties and ordinances, from many areas of life. Of interest, among others, is the treaty (probably from 638) which tolerated Christians in Jerusalem and which guaranteed a relatively high degree of religious freedom, but which forbade Jews to live in Jerusalem.[188] A stipulation which is to be found repeatedly, is that the *Dimmīs* ('the protected') are not permitted to practise too publicly elements of their religious or other customs which could give offense to Muslims, such as the transport of pigs through Muslim neighbourhoods and the sale of

---

[181] *Ibid*, p. 24.
[182] *Ibid*, p. 24.
[183] *Ibid*, pp. 28f.
[184] *Ibid*, pp. 29ff.
[185] *Ibid*, p. 35.
[186] *Ibid*, p. 45.
[187] *Ibid*, pp. 52f.
[188] *Ibid*, pp. 77f.

alcoholic beverages.[189] The priority of safeguarding the Islamic community is also strongly conveyed by the prescriptions surrounding marriage and education.[190]

Khoury calls the posture adopted by Islam towards the _Dimmīs_ a blend of tolerance and intolerance.[191] Islam reigns; it submits to no one. Such was the theory, and often the practice as well, with all the sad excesses thereof. The cause of this lies in Islam's claims to absoluteness. Islam is the definitive form of religion; there can therefore be no legitimate reason not to belong to Islam. Recall, Khoury adds here, that instances of intolerance occur in the Bible too, as well as in the history of the Christian church.[192] Fundamentalist circles within modern Islam still insist that all people must be brought to Islam.[193] Such is the import of Khoury's presentation of the Islamic attitude towards those of a different persuasion.

4.2 Nasr: the Islamic view of Christianity

We have presented Hossein Nasr's view in § 3.5. Nasr himself has presented the Islamic view of Christianity in an article published in the journal _Concilium_. Where his own view is advanced in this article, it is an extrapolation of what we have earlier described. Since he does not just give his own view, however, but writes in a more general sense on the Islamic view of Christianity, we will present some points from this article here. It becomes apparent from what he says that Muslims proceed towards an approach of other religions in terms of their own understanding.

Nasr points out that not all Muslims have, nor had, the same view of Christianity. When there was peaceful cohabitation with Christians, matters lay differently than when crusaders had to be confronted in combat. People who merely keep the law view things differently than those who have more spiritual merit.[194] Such variation does not diminish the fact that the Islamic view is rooted in certain chapters of the Koran which deal mainly with Jesus and Mary.[195] Christians were regarded as people of the book (_ahl al-kitāb_); as a consequence, they had a protected status when living under Islamic government.[196] The Islamic view of Christianity comprises a doctrine of its own concerning Jesus, Mary, and the unity of God. The differences between Islam and Christianity primarily concern the unity of God, which Christianity violates according to traditional Islamic

---

[189] _Ibid_, pp. 82 ff.

[190] _Ibid_, pp. 153 ff.; 144 f.

[191] _Ibid_, p. 177.

[192] _Ibid_, pp. 178 ff., 181 f.

[193] _Ibid_, p. 183.

[194] Seyyed Hossein Nasr, "De Islamitische Visie op het Christendom," ['Islamic View'] tr. H. Wagemans, _Concilium_ 1986/1 (Hilversum 1986), pp. 12-20, see esp. p. 12.

[195] _Ibid_. See also A. Johns, "De Islam als Uitdaging aan het Christendom," in _Concilium_ 1986/1 (Hilversum 1986), p. 25.

[196] Nasr, "Islamic View," p. 13.

conviction. A conflict exists between Christianity and Islam on this point.[197] Much religious art also poses major difficulties, as does the hierarchy within Catholic Christianity. In Islam, each person is his own priest.[198]

In the course of history, a further elaboration of the doctrine in the Koran has taken place. The *abolition* of former revelations by a later one was taught.[199] Such a view is less accommodating to a positive appreciation of Judaism and Christianity. This view never became universally current, however. Nasr describes the view generally accepted in Islam, as he sees it, as follows: "the divine origin of Christianity must be accepted and ... Christians (shall) be saved ... if they practice their religion."[200] In addition, says Nasr, the general feeling exists ...

> that, in any case, changes have occurred in the holy Scriptures of the Christians which have lead them to doctrines such as those about the Trinity and the incarnation, which could never have been proclaimed by a prophet of God, according to the Muslim view of the prophetic function in its entirety, from Adam to the prophet of Islam.[201]

Of importance is that objections are advanced against Christianity, says Nasr, for providing insufficient social and economic regulations, and thus being directed in a virtually exclusive manner towards esoteric religion. Christianity makes too high demands of people, demands which only people who live spiritually can meet.[202] The ideals preached have often not been put into practice.[203] Nasr refers to a current within Islam, usually designated in the West as fundamentalist, which assumes a sharper stance towards Christianity.[204] In addition, he mentions the positions of Muslims who believe that God has willed both religions and uses both to save people; Nasr then recapitulates his own view, which we have already described.[205]

4.3 Conclusion

Within Islam, we will conclude that:

(1) Monotheism is pivotal — there is no god but God. The central concern, therefore, in a fashion somewhat similar to Judaism, is with faithful living, with the *lived truth*, or, in the terminology of the subsequent chapter, *religio vera* (true religion). This religion ideally marks the whole of life.

---

[197] *Ibid*, p. 14.
[198] *Ibid*, p. 17.
[199] *Ibid*, p. 14.
[200] *Ibid*, p. 15.
[201] *Ibid*, p. 15.
[202] *Ibid*, p. 15.
[203] *Ibid*, p. 16.
[204] *Ibid*, p. 18.
[205] *Ibid*, pp. 18f.

(2) This life attitude of religious surrender and obedience presupposes that the beliefs are true. Isma'īl R. al-Faruqi states:

> To my knowledge, no Muslim thinker has ever denied that his religion has an essence. Granted that the question itself is a modern question and that the thinkers of the Middle Ages did not raise it in the manner we do today, we can still say with certainty that for all of them Islam was religion, religion *par excellence*, indeed 'the religion'; that it was a coherent, autonomous system of truths about reality, of imperatives for action and of desiderata for all kinds and levels of human activity. All of them affirmed that at the centre of this system stood God, the knowledge of Whom they called *tawhid*; that the whole rest is a hierarchy of imperatives (*wājibāt*), recommendations (*mandūbāt* and *makrūhāt*), prohibitions (*muharramāt*), and desiderata (*hasanāt*) — collectively called the *sharī'ah* and knowledge of which the Muslims called *fiqh*.[206]

This quote confirms our appraisal. Beliefs do not always have to be conceived of very theoretically; reflection on faith often did not, and does not, occupy such an important position, as other authors have noted. One must recall that Islam is concerned with a number of central religious truths. Islam does not have complicated beliefs, such as the designations of *śūnyatā* in Buddhism (if one may be permitted to call these beliefs), or like Christology and the Trinity in Christianity. They do believe that God has given the complete revelation to Mohammed; this (exclusive) belief is mostly conceived very literally. The truth of these central beliefs, in the sense of correspondence with the nature of reality, is always presupposed.

It is remarkable that the word *haqq* can apply both to truth as well as to reality. *True* knowledge is knowledge of the *true* nature of *reality*.

(3) An appraisal of the beliefs of other religions is achieved on the basis of *basic convictions*. As an example, we have described the attitude in respect of Jews and Christians. It is not difficult to understand how this approach works out with respect to other religions. A less exclusive approach to other religious traditions appears to be possible in terms of Sufism; then too, however, which religious currents are considered to be higher and which lower is determined in terms of one's own religious disposition and therefore one's own beliefs.

---

[206] Isma'īl R. al-Faruqi "The Essence of Religious Experience in Islam," p. 186.

PART 3

ANALYSIS

Chapter VIII

Truth in Religion

§ 1 Multiplicity in discourse on 'truth'

It became apparent in the previous chapters that the word 'truth' is used in more than one way when people reflect on religion. In this chapter we will attempt to outline the usage of the word 'truth.'

We will proceed from the notion that the philosophy of religion (insofar as it endeavours to orient itself impartially) must find links with the philosophical and theological thought of the major religious traditions, as this has been raised in Part 2 of this study. We will return to the status of the philosophy of religion in more detail in our last chapter. For our present purpose, we will proceed from the presupposition that a *philosophical understanding* goes beyond strict *empirical description,* in the sense that it is not wholly demonstrable in empirical terms, although it does spring from experience of what is empirical. We will not at this point go into the problem of whether a neutral description of facts is possible. In what follows, we will attempt to develop a view of various aspects of the theme of *religion and truth* which is capable of being argued by referring to individual exponents of religious thought.

Discourse concerning truth in respect of religion is characterized by multiplicity. We will distinguish between *five* ways of using the word truth. (1) As we have seen at various occasions, truth can be used to designate the more or less public teaching of a religious tradition, the *doctrina,* accessible to everyone. (2) The former can be distinguished from that teaching which is actually comprehended, the *truths* which one knows not only from hearsay, but which generate a degree of insight: the *veritates.* (3) Truth can mean the *true religion* in the sense of faith in practice, the *vera religio.* (4) The word can be used to denote *true religious understanding,* the *intellectus verus.* (5) The concept of truth can also be applied to the Highest, to God. *God is the Truth,* or, to put it differently, the Truth is God — *Veritas.* In the remainder of this chapter we will elaborate these distinctions which we have now made between

301

these five usages of the word truth. The least obvious distinction is perhaps that between *doctrina* and *veritates*; this is raised in §§ 2-4. Four uses relate to human knowledge (in whatever form); the fifth pertains to the transcendent.

It is difficult to speak of 'the concept of truth' in respect of religion, due to the multiplicity attaching to use of the word in this context. The meaning of the word truth is thought of differently within the various religious traditions. There are important differences of accent between the religions with respect to the position and role of doctrine as well as other truth; stated concisely, use of the word 'truth' is characterized by multiplicity. We will explore this area more closely, and try to clarify somewhat the use of the word 'truth' in religion. We will proceed from the distinctions given between five different contexts in which the concept of truth is applied.

1. *doctrina*   (public knowledge)
2. *veritates*   (comprehended knowledge)
3. *vera religio*   (practised knowledge)
4. *intellectus verus*   (the moment of understanding)
5. *veritas*   (the transcendent)

Consider here the fact that not every religious current recognizes the (legitimate) existence of all five 'truths.' On the contrary, we have seen the kinds of reservations which are held. In some traditions, such as Judaism and Islam, the emphasis rests with living faithfully, the *vera religio*. In some traditions within Christianity, all emphasis lies on the acceptance of the objective truth, the *doctrina*. In Zen Buddhism one attains true understanding (*intellectus verus*) in *samādhi*, which is inaccessible to normal, discursive reason. Thus, although the accents differ from tradition to tradition, and although not all five uses of the word truth occur in each of the traditions discussed, we can nevertheless distinguish five meanings in this *model of the concept of truth*. We will now better illuminate this, and will accordingly start with the first usage, *doctrina*.

§ 2 Initial, public teaching (*doctrina*)

Every religion (necessarily) has an *introduction*, by which the uninitiated are initiated into the tradition. All sorts of other elements can also belong to the introduction, but it always includes an exposition of the tradition's doctrines and a rationale which makes it clear why people should engross themselves in this teaching. Such a doctrinal exposition is a guide to a deeper understanding of the tradition, as well as a *recapitulation* of the doctrines, particularly for 'beginners.' Buddhism has the Four Noble Truths; many Hindus point to portions of the holy books as essential to

Initial, public teaching (doctrina)   303

any acquaintance with Hinduism, such as the *Bhagavadgītā*; in Judaism
there are central confessions, such as the *Shema* and Bible stories which
are told to the uninitiated; the Christian tradition has the *catechismi* and
confessions of faith; Islam has confessions such as in *Al-Iḫlāṣ* (112th
sūra), and the summary of the *five pillars*. We call such guiding summaries
initial doctrine. The term isn't especially winsome, but it is suitable for
expressing certain aspects of these *doctrina*. (1) The *doctrina* plays a role
in the initiation into a tradition. (2) The ultimate purpose of *doctrina* is
a deeper comprehension which is seldom, if ever, immediately realized by
the hearer. (3) The possibility exists that the initial doctrine no longer
plays a significant role for the more fully initiated. (4) Viewed from the
position of the 'adept,' in some traditions, the initial doctrine is, strictly
speaking, 'untrue.' Those are the aspects which we mean to designate by
the term *initial*: it is doctrine for beginners.

The initial doctrine can contain any or all of the following five
parts, but does not necessarily include them all.

1. An exposition about the true nature of 'ordinary life' as it is
   viewed in the perspective of the tradition.
2. An exposition about reality as it really is, and as it could be
   more adequately experienced.
3. An exposition about why there is a difference between
   apparent and genuine reality, and between an adequate and
   an inadequate experience of reality.
4. An exposition about the manner in which one can train
   oneself to see reality as it is.
5. An exposition about alternative views of reality.

For illustration and elucidation, reference will first of all be made to the
Buddhist doctrine, the *dharma*:

1) It describes the ordinary world as *dukkha* (unsatisfactory) and *anitya*
   (transitory); it is stressed that man is *anātman*.
2) The Second Noble Truth indicates the cause of suffering as *craving*;
   usually reference is made to the chain of dependent origination
   (cf. point 3 above).
3) The Third Noble Truth makes it plain that suffering can cease; a more
   adequate experience of reality is possible (cf. 2).
4) The Fourth Noble Truth indicates ways by which suffering can be
   overcome on the eight-fold path and in the 'realization' of *anitya*.
5) By articulating the *anātman* doctrine, Buddhist teaching opposed the
   belief that man has a substantial self. We have already seen that
   there is always query and scrutiny of other traditions in terms of
   one's own view, such as Christianity's belief in God.

In the second place, reference will be made to Jewish and Christian
doctrine; this too basically contains all five elements.

1) 'This world' is portrayed as unrighteous, or as 'of the flesh' and as passing away.
2) This world is God's creation, and, because of God's work of salvation, it is *en route* to a better destiny.
3) The teaching about sin.
4) Directives for conduct and for practising a better disposition.
5) The rejection of error, already to be found in the Bible, vehement in some periods, lukewarm in others.

Simply compare the Heidelberg Catechism by way of example: Part I deals with the misery of man (cf. points 1 and 3); Part II, the redemption of man (cf. 2); Part III, gratitude towards God for redemption (with an exposition about the Law, cf. 4). Within the Christian culture of Middle and Northwestern Europe in the 16th century, there was no need for an apologetic, but, after the schism, there was need for an exposition on the Roman Catholic Church, and this is indeed to be found in the Catechism.

It is not difficult to elaborate such confirmation with illustrations from Islam and Hinduism. For Islam, all these elements are to be found in the consideration given of Nasr's views.

1) People live wrongly, materialistically, only seeing the world exoterically.
2) The world is God's creation and must be experienced in terms of its centre.
3) A variation on the doctrine of sin.
4) The five pillars of Islam regulate holy living; the *Tarīqa* teaches how one can attain a more adequate experience of reality.
5) Polytheism is wrong; objections to Jews and Christians are already to be found in the Koran.

Within the Hindu view, certainly within the *Advaita* tradition, one finds that:

1) The world is *māyā*.
2) The world is fundamentally Brahman.
3) Attachment and ignorance are the causes of evil and are obstacles on the path to *mokṣa*.
4) Being without attachment and guidance.
5) Expositions with respect to Jainism, and later Buddhism.

In summary, we will designate the five elements of the initial doctrine as follows:

1. the doctrine of the fallen world
2. the doctrine of the real world
3. the doctrine of the barriers
4. the description of the path
5. the apologetic.

§ 3 Barriers

We will now delve into the barriers which prevent people from seeing through this world as a fallen world, and from accepting the doctrine of the real world. These barriers yield difficulties peculiar to 'religious epistemology.' It is our perception that these difficulties have not been sufficiently discerned throughout large segments of Western thought, both inside and outside of the Christian tradition. Of course consideration has been given to human failure, but the epistemological consequences of this have not always been gauged properly. One can speak of "das radikal Böse" as Kant does, but that is not enough. 'Religious epistemology,' as a rule, teaches that this 'evil' makes its effects felt precisely in the area of knowledge. Knowledge is not seen as being free of value. There is a profound difference on this point between most (or all?) of the views of knowledge discussed so far and the Western philosophical tradition. Influenced by the Greek philosophical tradition, it was believed possible to elude incompetence and imperfection through knowledge. Access to perfection was sought in analysis. It was assumed that analysis leads to permanent and true understanding. The awareness, however, that certain obstacles must be overcome on the path to deeper understanding belongs to the fixed elements of religious epistemology.

The barriers to religious insight as we have encountered them up till now, have two aspects. In the first place, there is the issue of ignorance (*avidyā*). People do not realize how the world really is; it must be explained to them. They do not know what has happened; they must be told. The second factor lies in the moral defects of man. Reference is generally made to the perverting role of attachment, greed, and egoism. Insight into egoism is necessary, of course, but one ought also to overcome it in order to attain deeper insight into doctrine. To speak in terms of the Christian tradition, holiness of life is a condition for seeing the (deeper) truth and for understanding doctrine. We will see what radical consequences this has below.

We have stated that the barriers have two *aspects*, as religious epistemologies describe them: ignorance and attachment. The difficulty resides in the fact that there are not two separate barriers which one can surmount the one after the other. If that were the case, the person to be initiated could then first go through a written or oral course of instruction in the *doctrina*, and, upon being acquainted with them and accepting their truth, could subsequently be advised about a rule for living. Such a straightforward course of action in clearing the obstacles appears impossible, however. Ignorance and attachment are interwoven. Overcoming attachment must keep stride with acquisition of insight. Liberation from 'sin' and insight into the truth go hand in hand. This is the reason why one reads over and over that it is not the doctrine itself which is of concern, but life, viz. lived faith, which we have called *vera religio*.

It is pointed out in various religious traditions that a deepening of insight is both possible and desirable. This is to be found most clearly in mystical currents. It is sometimes taught that every person must go this route, through a cycle of many lives. Sometimes the teaching can also state that such deeper insight is not ordained for everyone; ordinary folk may suffice with keeping the *Sharī'a*, while the Sufies proceed on the path of insight and sanctification through the *Tarīqa*. In many religious currents, less emphasis falls on the possibility of deepening insight. These notions do not allow of being suppressed altogether, however, for the central insights of the various religions imply that a twofold obstacle must be removed: ignorance and attachment. The descriptions of the spiritual path in particular indicate to people how they can make headway.[1] The entire pattern of life which a religious tradition recommends is not intended only to enable people live a good life, but also to further guide them in love, compassion, understanding, and wisdom. We have given expression to this in the distinction between *doctrina* and *veritates*; between the initial doctrine of the catechization and introduction, and a true grasp of the 'condition humaine' and of the real nature of things. Two examples will be given to elucidate this distinction. First, within Christianity it is taught that Jesus died a humiliating death on the cross and that He bore the sins of humanity. This belongs to the *catechismus* of the Christian faith. In the Gospel according to John, however, we encounter the image of Jesus as lifted up on the cross. This inversion of the view which is customary in this world has to do with a deepened insight into the destiny of man, the depth and function of God's love towards mankind, and the seriousness of sin. In order to surmise something of the depth of meaning of this inversion in the gospel according to John —lifted up on the cross instead of humiliated— it is needful that one looks at reality, including one's own life, with different eyes. Second, Nishitani describes how one can ultimately attain a good experience of one's self and the world upon assimilating the doctrine of *anātman*. Purging and deepening have the effect of teaching one to see differently. This in turn enables deeper insight. These two examples can serve to make it clear that one must distinguish between the initial doctrine and the real doctrine, or, in the terms in which we have phrased it, between *doctrina* and *veritates*. Sometimes deeper insight will bear on what is also stated in the *catechismi*, but then in a deeper and more comprehensive grasp of what was formerly known only superficially and without fathoming the consequences. Then too, the initial doctrine is sometimes considered untrue from a more advanced position, and other terms are used to express this vision of

---

[1] See H. de Wit, *Contemplatieve Psychologie* (Kampen 1987), esp. pp. 47ff., 116ff.

what reality is.[2] Recall here the Christian stories of the virgin birth of Jesus, for example, which are explained by many Christians as an expression of a deeper truth, or the Buddhist stories about the function of Buddha, while the famous Zen proverb is: If one meets the Buddha, one must kill him. This manifests a deeper understanding of the *dharma*.

The intention of the initial doctrine is to effectuate a *shift of perspective*. The mentor who must initiate another attempts to get him to see with new eyes, and to experience and feel reality differently. This shift in perspective stands between the preliminary doctrine and the insight of the 'adept.' In terms of religious epistemology, the problem which we encounter here is that the new perspective not only demands the acquisition of knowledge, but also transformation of the person.

§ 4 Appropriated doctrine (*veritates*)

Religious traditions pursue interiorization of faith. Even if the *doctrine* is stressed, the intention is the experienced doctrine; not the initial doctrine, but doctrine as the *truth* which one holds fast. A beautiful example of this is the Heidelberg Catechism. This gives a summary of Protestant Christian doctrine, as previously cited. What strikes one immediately at the very beginning is the personal tone.

> *Question 1*: What is your only comfort in life and in death?
> *Answer*: That I, with body and soul, both in life and death, am not my own, but belong unto my faithful Saviour Jesus Christ; who with his precious blood has fully satisfied for all my sins, and delivered me from all the power of the devil; and so preserves me that without the will of my heavenly Father not a hair can fall from my head; yea, that all things must be subservient to my salvation, wherefore by His Holy Spirit He also assures me of eternal life, and makes me heartily willing and ready, henceforth, to live unto Him.[3]

The tradition holds out the doctrine as truth to be personally experienced. Islam, similarly, tries to not merely pass on doctrinal truth, but 'interiorized truth,' personal faith. In the next section (§ 5) we will examine more closely lived faith, the *vera religio*. Here we will limit ourselves to appropriated religious truth (*veritates*). The examples which we gave from Christianity and Islam could be supplemented with countless illustrations from other traditions. The evening of Sēder is counted as a repetition of the evening of the Exodus from Egypt, since the dogmas of Exodus and Election are brought to presence and interiorized by celebration and narrative. Experience is so tied up with 'doctrine,' that further examples from Hinduism and Buddhism would be superfluous.

---

[2] H. de Wit, pp. 46f.; cf. pp. 123f.

[3] Heidelberg Catechism, see *Bekenntnisschriften und Kirchenordnungen der nach Gottes Wort reformierten Kirche* (Zürich ³1938), p. 149.

The background for our distinction between *doctrina* and *veritates* is that the *doctrina* is 'valid' or 'true' in a different manner that the *veritates* are. The truth of the *doctrina* is related to the shift in perspective which is the aim of the *initial doctrine*. The truth of the *veritates* is related to the new perspective which one has assimilated. This has consequences for the concept of truth.

In the Introduction to this study (Part 1), we have seen that some authors follow a rather obvious line of reasoning: A believes assertion p, because A assumes that p is true. What is meant is, "I believe it because it is true"; and not, "it is true because I believe it." Belief applies to reality in some way; religious belief is not optional. Doctrine must be true if one is to believe responsibly. Trigg reasons along these lines. We have seen that Kuitert states that doctrine must be open to discussion to a certain extent; for him too, doctrine must be true in advance, if someone is to believe responsibly. The element of truth in these views seems to be that the truth is always *transcendent*. Man does not make the truth, but acknowledges that a perception or statement is true. The acknowledgment that something is true presupposes a *norm*. This norm exceeds the criteria —as we shall elaborate further— and is therefore called transcendent. If this is what authors means when they say "p must be true, before A can believe that p is the case," they are right, in our opinion. Our enquiry seems to point in the direction of serious complications, however. These complications issue from the modifications of perspective which ensue when one assimilates the doctrine through an increase of knowledge and 'sanctification.'

For an elucidation of the nature of such alterations in perspective, links can be explored, in certain regards, to philosophical traditions which stress the contextuality and perspectivity of knowledge and language: Heidegger and Gadamer, Wittgenstein and, for the philosophy of religion, D. Z. Phillips, and the (neo)-Marxist tradition. Such philosophical currents and their exponents have on many points reached divergent conceptions, yet they agree on one point. They do not wish to divorce the question of meaning completely from the question of truth. We must elaborate this somewhat further. It will then become apparent that the *doctrina* is not true in the same manner as the *veritates* are. If we state that the question of meaning and that of truth cannot be separated, we deny one of the most fundamental premises of an important current within analytical philosophy (of religion).[4]

The meaning of concrete statements by people is in part dependent on the situation. Thus, the sentence, "The door is open," can have very different functions. Yet assertions also have a certain independence. Consider

---

[4] It is stated that the question of meaning logically precedes the question of truth; thus W. Blackstone, *The Problem of Religious Knowledge* (Englewood Cliffs, N.J. 1963), p. 2; V. Brümmer, *Theology and Philosophical Inquiry* (London 1981), p. 220.

the well-known example: "New York is a large city," defining truth as:
" 'New York is a large city' is true, if and only if New York *is* a large
city."[5] One could also consider the following: "Some Buddhists believe that
the Buddha was omniscient." This statement has a certain meaning. One can
communicate it to other people. People can understand it, even if they
merely grasp it in a superficial manner. This dogma is capable of communication within a generally shared perspective on reality; it is made at the
level of *initial doctrine*. The word 'omniscient' yields a problem, however.
What is its meaning? At the first level, people will think that the Buddha
knows more than another person. Something similar applies for the
expression 'the Buddha.' In the first instance, one would hear no more
than in any another designation for prince Gautama. If one wishes to
better understand the sentence, "Buddhists believe that the Buddha was
omniscient," then one must be able to comprehend it within the context
of Buddhist doctrine. It is known that Buddha means the Enlightened One.
To understand that, one needs to understand what Enlightenment involves.
That cannot be understood so easily — if, indeed, one can ever grasp it
without being enlightened oneself. The expression 'omniscient' also means
more than one would ever realize merely by reading a primary introduction
to Buddhist thought. It is not just a quantitative concept, but also
qualitative. It means to say, "knowing more than another," but also,
"appraising things for their true value." One could also ask oneself what
exactly Buddhists are doing when they 'believe' this. The sentence,
"Buddhists contend that the Buddha was omniscient," can apparently be
understood superficially and more deeply, depending on one's grasp of the
Buddhist tradition, one's insight into life, and one's imagination. The
concern, in the first instance, is a *deeper* and more *comprehensive*
understanding of a religious statement. One obtains more insight and sees
better 'what all is involved' (just as more insight can be obtained into all
that which is connected with executive authority by speaking with the
captain of a large airplane). In the second place, a *change of perspective*
is involved. It is therefore not only a matter of expanding and deepening
insight, but also of *change*. In this connection, we can understand —to
carry on with a previous example— that the crucifixion of Jesus can be
seen as humiliation in the first instance, but also as a lifting up in the
second.

This can be somewhat clarified in Gadamer's terms.[6] Gadamer chiefly
discusses the interpretation of (classical) texts, but his insights are valid
for understanding in general. The text once stood within a certain
horizon of understanding. The reader reads the text with the aid of his
own horizon of understanding; this helps him on the one hand, but on the
other, it can be an impediment to the interpretation of the text. The

---

[5] D. W. Hamlyn, for instance, in *The Theory of Knowledge* (London 1971), p. 127.
[6] H. -G. Gadamer, *Wahrheit und Methode* (Tübingen [2]1965), esp. pp. 250-360.

meaning of the text lights up when the horizons of the text and the reader fuse. Consider here that (a) the horizon of a text or a reader can never be made completely explicit, and that (b) the horizon of the reader is in motion, dependent on the life of the reader, and that (c) one knows the horizon of the text only within a paradigm which one constructs oneself as reader, and that (d) the fusing of horizons —no matter how methodically prepared and legitimate the scientific interpretation— is ultimately an event which eludes the grasp of the interpreter: the meaning of the text lights up, truth transpires. What Gadamer, and Ricoeur and David Tracy in his tracks, say about the fusing together of horizons and the changes in somebody's horizon, can aid us in understanding religious shifts in perspective.[7] Increase of knowledge is not purely quantitative, certainly not in religion. According to the religious traditions, it is related to being without attachment, to commitment, and to sanctification, as we have seen. It has the character of a journey, of a path which one travels; that is how it is designated in spiritual traditions. Whoever travels a certain distance, gets another horizon. A different horizon yields a different perspective. This notion can be found in Hare, who spoke of religion as a *'blik'* (perspective) on the world.[8] Wittgenstein said in the *Lectures,* that whoever believed in a last judgment, lived in a different world. It is continually a matter of a different *perspective* on reality, designated by such terms as horizon of understanding, world-view, outlook, context, frame of reference, etc. The influence of this on one's view of the constituents of reality is usually denoted by such terms as presuppositions, (philosophical) choices, etc. From the Neo-Marxists we can learn that one's manner of life and the society of which one is a member is of influence on this perspective. This insight accords to a great degree with the emphasis which religious traditions put on the necessity of transformation for the person (and sometimes society).

In summary, we could say that the *doctrina* of religious traditions offer a perspective on reality. The introductory *doctrina* shows reality as being untrue; through a process of development, a person learns to see and experience the world differently; little by little, one learns to free oneself of attachment, and thus to gradually overcome disaffection. Transformation of cognition and the person work together in a dialectical process: on the one hand, the person is sanctified and estrangement is reversed, on the other hand, a deeper, altered understanding is achieved. The *veritates* of a religion are not merely a broadening of the *initial*

---

[7] See P. Ricoeur, *Hermeneutics and the Human Sciences,* ed. & tr. J. B. Thompson (Cambridge 1981), esp. pp. 131 ff.; D. Tracy, *The Analogical Imagination* (London 1981), esp. pp. 124 ff.

[8] R. M. Hare in A. Flew et al., "Theology and Falsification," in *The Philosophy of Religion,* ed. B. Mitchell (Oxford 1971), p. 16.

doctrina, but entail a further alteration of perspective, in addition to a deepening of understanding.

This change in perspective has consequences for the meaning of the words which are used by a religious tradition. In the Part 2 of this study, we saw many times how religious language usage is subject to many qualifications. Nāgārjuna undermines the meaning of concepts through a 'negative dialectic' with the aim of conducting the reader to the point where only Emptiness remains. Nishitani's purpose is to engender —by means of dialectical reasoning— an understanding which cannot be described in a discursive fashion. Maimonides regards terms applied to God as being homonymous. Saint Thomas spoke of analogy. Much is being written today in the West about the expressive power of stories and about metaphorical religious language.[9] Religion is concerned with a perspective on reality. But the terms used in describing this (in doctrine, the *veritates),* are not univocal. With respect to the concept of truth, this means that a simple 'correspondence' of word and reality cannot be looked to for the truth of religious statements. Religious statements do refer to reality; but their significance cannot be isolated from the context of the religious tradition and from the perspective of the believer. The truth of the *veritates* is, in a certain sense, valid of the entire perspective within which they have obtained their meaning. We will return later to the concept of truth in more detail. In this chapter we want to sketch the five contexts in which this concept functions within religious traditions.

§ 5   Lived Truth (*religio vera*)

We have repeatedly seen that the 'truth' of a religious tradition is often sought not so much in the doctrine, as in the religious experience of a life which conforms to the rules of that religion. The accent in Judaism rests on being Jewish and on living in accordance with the Torah. We saw how Fackenheim also bestows significance on secularized Jewishness on this basis. The 'truth,' to be perfectly consistent, is then a matter of being, and not truly a matter of knowing. Similarly, it has often been said that the truth of Christianity is doing *ĕmeṯ*; the truth is not situated in the doctrines. In Islam too, it is the *islam* which is stressed: living a life of religious commitment and obedience. The life of an enlightened person is sometimes depicted as a lasting condition. We have seen that a similar tack is often taken in religious traditions right across the board; the importance of doctrine is qualified and mollified in favour of religious life. For the sake of comparison, recall the view of Wilfred C. Smith. We have related how he conceives of faith as generic,

---

[9] See J. J. van Es, *Spreken over God: Letterlijk of Figuurlijk?* (Amsterdam 1979).

as a human universal, common to all religions. Doctrine, or the beliefs themselves, are secondary in this view. We will return yet to the problem of the position of doctrine in religion. Wilfred Smith has in any case touched on something essential with his emphasis on experience. It seems that the importance of doctrine can indeed be somewhat mitigated without undue disregard for the question of the truth of doctrine.

With the aim of distinguishing between religious experience and religious knowledge, we will distinguish between the following aspects of religion.

1. experience
2. conduct
3. knowledge
4. co-operation.[10]

The fourth aspect has to do with the religious community and with tradition. The other three aspects call to mind the traditional *transcendentalia*: beauty, goodness, and truth, which are all ultimately one according to Plato. There is therefore something to be said for the aforementioned fourfold division right from the start; it dovetails with aspects of existence which have always been distinguished. For conduct, one should think in terms of rituals and other religious customs as well as morality. This distinction brings us a little closer to determining the relationship between *doctrine* and the *religio vera*. We will proceed from the assumption that one cannot isolate these four aspects from one another. In Part 2, we discovered that none of these four aspects was omitted in any major religion, although there were differences in accentuation regarding which aspect of religion is ascribed the most importance. On this score there are major differences between religions as well as between the various currents within religions. Some traditions stress the acceptance of doctrine. In others, conduct is placed in the foreground, such as in orthodox Judaism and in orthodox Islam. Others are focussed primarily on the inward experience. But no matter where the accents lie, experiences always play a role; and conduct is a significant factor, both in the sense of moral action as well as religious custom; knowledge of rituals and an understanding of man and the world always play a background role in a person's behaviour; religious communities are the guarantors of the tradition. In this way, all four of the aspects always occur together.

---

[10] See D. J. Hoens, J. H. Kamstra, and D. Mulder, *Inleiding tot de Studie van Godsdiensten* (Kampen 1985), Chapter V. Some important phenomena: 1. On evil and salvation (Over onheil en heil); 2. Individual – social; 3. The aspect of knowledge; 4. The aspect of acting; 5. The aspect of emotions. In "Wie kan nog een Christen genoemd worden?" in *Buitensporig Geloven: Studies over Randkerkelijkheid*, ed. J. M. Vlijm (Kampen 1983), pp. 118 ff., I referred to five aspects of Christian belief: conduct, participation in the church community, bearing witness, experiencing life in faith, and knowledge. The four aspects, mentioned in the text are applicable to religion generally. Salvation (in one form or another) is the end of religion as a whole.

Together they constitute faith. Accordingly, a *formed faith* also contains such knowledge as we have described in the previous section as appropriated doctrine. The knowledge which plays a role in religious life is always a matter of appropriated knowledge.

We must now try to determine more closely the status of knowledge in lived religion. We shall see how a number of central religious truths, the *veritates,* are of primary concern with respect to the experience of religion, giving direction to behaviour and fostering mutual recognition within the religious community. Following Brümmer's lead, we will call these central truths basic convictions, although he uses the term in the singular. These basic convictions furnish the believer with assurance; they sustain experience and conduct. In the articulation and elaboration of doctrine, one cannot be as sure as in the experience of reality itself, which is what the basic convictions denote. It is therefore quite possible to explain why people can be very certain in their *religio,* but gropingly uncertain in their 'theology.'[11] Brümmer offers the following elucidation of basic convictions:

> ... first, they all define a certain x (an object, or metaphysical entity, or ideal, or person, or something else) as distinct from all other entities. That x is unique in the sense that the attitude appropriate to it differs from attitudes appropriate to any other reality. Secondly, the attitude we ought to adopt to any other thing or situation or event, etc., is ultimately determined by its relation to x. The meaning of all things is therefore determined by their relation to x. In short, in the conviction fundamental to a view of life, a certain x is deemed to be unique because it is the primary determinant of meaning for all other things.[12]

The final chapter (Ch. XII) about the mutual relationship between religions defends the notion that it is better not to speak of one basic conviction in each religion; we shall introduce some nuances, which we will here only indicate summarily. A number of matters are fundamental to each religious tradition. They are —in a manner which must yet be further explicated— *'primary' determinants of meaning,* the quotation marks enclosing 'primary' indicating our reservation with respect to the idea that every religion (without qualification) has one centre. They are related to what we will call basic experiences. These are *existential experiences*; we will elaborate them in the next chapter (Ch. IX). These basic experiences are partially determined by the *accumulated experience* of the tradition and its *being nurture* in the rituals and way of life which the tradition passes on. The way recommended by a religious community refers to ritual and spiritual directives as well as to moral tutelage. Together we can call them instructions for living. Just as there are certain conceptions which are fundamental to any knowledge, there are certain *main rules* which are fundamental to the religious life. In their

---

[11] See I. T. Ramsey, *On Being Sure in Religion* (London 1963), p. 90.
[12] V. Brümmer, p. 132.

mutual relation, the primary determinants of meaning, the basic experiences, and the instructions for living, afford life meaning and orientation. A religious current actually contains a more or less coherent whole of 'rules of interpretation' (only in part explicit) for the explanation and application of instructions on how to act. Religious traditions endeavour in this way to effectuate a certain *disposition* in a person, which in turn has consequences for somebody's posture towards the world. We thus again discover the four aspects of religion which we distinguished.

1. experience   — basic experiences
2. conduct   — basic rules
3. knowledge   — 'primary' determinants of meaning, basic insights
4. cooperation — nurture of traditions and religious community.

In terms of the above, it is possible to explain why people in various religions are certain (or believe they are) of certain main issues, while at the same time, there is room for discussion and even different perceptions with respect to more derivative issues. People are in fundamental agreement about the chief issues, even though people differ about the implications, and might therefore be (somewhat) uncertain. Some religious currents demand a large measure of unanimity about rather elaborate doctrines and well defined rituals; others admit more freedom. The fact that the 'primary' determinant of meaning cannot be ascribed without further qualification to one certain 'x' is precisely what opens up the possibility for different interpretations of the religious inheritance, and thus for conflict between various currents, for dissent, heresy, and schisms.

An important constituent of personal faith is the assimilation of the truth of the religious tradition in which one stands. Absorption always entails *interpretation*. An interpretative element is already lodged even in the *appropriated doctrine*. People communally reach a certain interpretation and assimilation of customs, rituals, moral directives for action, and the *veritates* passed on by a tradition. This process harbours both a collective, group-related element as well as a personal one. According to Wilfred Smith's familiar saying, "every religion is new every morning."[13] The collective element of renewed interpretation tends to be lodged in the *veritates* of a religious community, as well as in its rituals and customs; the personal element in interpretation tends to be lodged in personal religious life, the *religio vera*.

§ 6 Experiencing Truth (*intellectus verus*)

There is apparently a growing *towards* the truth in religion, truth now understood in the sense of experiencing the Truth. When we write

---

[13] W. C. Smith, *Questions of Religious Truth* (London 1967), p. 75.

'Truth' with a capital letter, we mean the Transcendent. In this section we will pause at the experience of the Truth in the narrower sense. This experience is conceived of in disparate ways by the various religious currents. According to many religious currents, though not all, this experience is what is most profound, and wherein religion reaches its fulfillment. We have in mind here mystical currents, for example. There is debate about whether all religion ultimately has as its purpose the same mystical experience. Since there is a close connection between the framework of a religious tradition and the experiences which that tradition nurtures, we should take notice of the differences between what are known as mystical experiences in the various traditions. This is not to say that there are no points of contact between the mysticism of one tradition with that of another. Yet whatever understanding we might have of mystical experiences, we cannot avoid recognizing experiences in every religious tradition which amount to some form of encounter with the transcendent — whether they wish to speak of union with the transcendent or not.

We will now make a number of remarks about such experiences.

(1) Specifically religious experience does not coincide with *religio vera*. It can be a single experience; sometimes it is interwoven with the religious life, as for instance the Buddhist *arhat* who has realized *nirvāṇa*.

(2) What is of concern is the experience of salvation. What is understood by salvation depends on the religious tradition; the conception of salvation is related to a certain view of life and of the defects which appear to be normal in this world. Salvation is conceived of in different ways. It can be seen as well-being in this world consequent upon God's favour and moral perfection; in the inner experience of being accepted by God through grace; in the peace of knowing that one pleases God by living in conformity to the *Sharī'a*; in the awareness of being related to Brahman; or in the experience of *śūnyatā*. What is seen as the (nature of) salvation differs. The most important differences relate to (a) the measure in which one retains one's personal individuality and —in connection with this— (b) the relation between the salvation experienced and worldly reality. To give an example and counter-example of (b): *mokṣa* is remote from this world, which is *māyā*; *shālôm*, to the contrary, is the peaceful experience of this world, which is God's creation.

(3) The experience of salvation in the strict sense is always seen as an experience of harmony and unity. One cannot simply equate the unity of all things in Brahman with the experience of the harmony of God's purposes in *shālôm*. Still, the more profound experiences agree in admitting of characterization in the following terms: serenity, peace, harmony, meaningfulness, happiness. Irrespective of the fact that for many people, —or in some traditions, for all people— only experiences of limited duration are involved, it is still an experience of salvation.

(4) Many traditions relate this experience to the truth. The experience of salvation is broader than merely cognitive; we have already referred to the relationship of the four aspects of religion in the previous section (§ 5). The cognitive does not stand on its own. And yet *insight* is an aspect of the experience of salvation. This experience appears always to involve seeing things as they really are, related to the experience of the Transcendent. Due to this moment of insight, it is possible to speak of *satya, ĕmeṭ, alètheia*, etc. What is also of key significance for many traditions is that a person attains his destiny in the experience of salvation, as, for instance, when the Christian tradition speaks of 'being in the truth,' and the Buddhist tradition of *paramārtha satya*.

(5) This experience of salvation is portrayed as non-discursive, as we have seen repeatedly. A distinction ought to be introduced at this point. Non-discursive is not the same as non-dual. We will first deal with 'non-discursive.' What is in any case intended by this term is that the reality experienced in salvation cannot be entirely explained in universally understandable words. In Part 2 of this study, we continually met up with qualifications in respect of the use of language: negative dialectic, paradoxes, koans, enigmatic proverbs, analogy, metaphor, and even homonymy. Time and again, it is stated that the truth cannot be grasped at this ultimate level with the 'logic' of the fallen world and the understanding of fallen man. The qualifications have two sides: (a) the transcendent cannot be understood by discursive reason, and the experience of the transcendent cannot be articulated in words; (b) fallen man is unable, or at best only scarcely so, to understand it. We discussed this twosome in § 3 as the 'barriers.' Conflicting views prevail about the importance of doctrine. We will return to this question in Ch. x.

(6) The ultimate experience is sometimes portrayed as being non-dual. We ran across the thesis of non-duality in connection with the Advaita Vedānta, as an experience of Union between *ātman* and *Brahman,* and in connection with Zen-Buddhism, as the experience of *śūnyatā,* (or, in Nishitani's terms, *ego/non-ego*). Medieval Aristotelian exponents of Judaism and Islam confronted us with a view of salvation as pure *understanding,* in the sense of a *reflection* of the transcendent. Nishitani too presented us with such a notion of reflection. The pure reflection of experienced (transcendent) reality is then salvation and Truth. In the Jewish, Christian, and Islamic Middle Ages, pure knowledge was not conceived as absorption in God. This experience can be articulated as, pure '*awareness*' of the transcendent.

(7) This deepest knowledge is not detached knowledge, but is accompanied by strong commitment. We have repeatedly discovered that this knowledge is related to love and to bliss, as in the formulation, *sat-cit-ananda,* and with respect to such thinkers as Maimonides, Augustine, and Nasr. In Buddhism, the highest insight is accompanied by compassion for all beings.

We have already pointed out that the increase of knowledge and the transformation of the person are consistently interwoven.

(8) The moments of this highest insight are not conceived of by the various religious traditions as though common to all believers. Neither are they reserved for the learned. Factors mentioned as being of influence in whether someone participates in such moments are: mercy, freedom from attachment, moral perfection, spiritual discernment, and insight. This is not to say that all these factors are always mentioned, for such is not the case.

(9) Definitive and final salvation is not attained in a single life, at least not according to any major religion. A person must strive to this end in a series of many, many lives, or must receive bliss in the hereafter. What is possible in a certain life (or, if one prefers, in this life) are moments of happiness and an abiding awareness of relationship to the transcendent (momentarily leaving aside here the different conceptions of the transcendent).

(10) It is to the element of *insight* that we owe the right to designate this ultimate experience of salvation by the term *intellectus verus*. What is here involved is a truth by which a person is made true or good, and whereby true insight and salvation are realized.

§ 7　The transcendent as Truth

God is often called the Truth. Sometimes this is related to the notion that God is perfect knowledge, as for example by thinkers who were influenced by Aristotle. Sometimes it means that God knows all things. Sometimes the connotation is more that God acts truly. The meaning can therefore embrace true Knowledge, true Being, and true Action. Much thought has been given to the question of how God knows, particularly about the relation between the unity of God's knowledge viewed as non-dual, and His knowledge of particulars. We need not delve into this issue in this enquiry. Certain consequences can be inferred for our topic from such identification of the transcendent with the truth. In the first place, when it is stated that God (alone) is the Truth, then the implication which that statement might be suggesting is that human knowledge is never completely true. God is then seen as the Absolute (and normative) Truth, human knowledge being partial and fallible; sometimes the intimation seems to be that 'human knowledge is untrue, strictly speaking.' It is not rare that a view of the fragmentariness and complementariness of religious traditions is developed in such terms. Gandhi and Wilfred Smith think along such lines. Secondly, one does well to bear in mind that calling God or the transcendent 'the Truth' does not exempt one from the question as to what in human claims to knowledge about the transcendent is actually true. The question of truth does not allow itself to be shunted. The same holds true with respect to those who want to exclusively relate truth to life, with what we have called *religio vera*. Even if we call to mind the so-called Hebrew concept of truth, the question of truth in relation to knowledge and understanding still does not allow of being repressed. Our enquiry so far bears out the fact that there is always a kind of perception of which it is claimed that it is sound, and often too, that it is sounder than any other understanding. One cannot circumvent analysis of the concept of truth within religious epistemology.

§ 8   Five ways of speaking about 'truth' in religion

We have distinguished five ways of speaking about truth in religion in this chapter. We will now summarize the results of this chapter.

We first spoke of religious knowledge in the sense of what people can come to know about specific beliefs in their initial acquaintance with a religious tradition. This concerns more or less public knowledge. Viewed in terms of deeper religious knowledge, this is an *initial doctrine,* which enables one to attain a relatively simple religious understanding. The question of what is meant when it is said that this doctrine is true will be raised later. We subsequently discussed deeper religious understanding, the *veritates* of religions, appropriated doctrine. Here the concern was no longer with guidance towards a religious understanding, but with 'true' insight into reality. What is meant by this will be raised in Ch. X. In the third place, we discussed 'lived truth,' the *religio vera.* One of the problems which arose in that connection was the extent to which the importance of doctrine can be made a relative matter in terms of the *religio vera.* Is it possible for someone who does not have a profound faith —in terms of understanding— still to have a 'true' religious experience? We spoke fourthly about the inadequacy or even inability of articulating rationally (salvific) religious awareness. And fifthly, we briefly discussed the portrayal of the transcendent as the Truth. The first four meanings refer to knowledge, the fifth to the transcendent.

We have based these distinctions between five usages of 'truth' in respect of religion on the descriptions of religious epistemologies in Part 2. We repeatedly encountered a twofold division of knowledge, such as that between discursive and non-discursive truth; dual and non-dual truth; or *saṃvṛti satya* and *paramārtha satya.* Such division are familiar to the literature of the philosophy of religion. Recall W. C. Smith's distinction between *faith* and *belief* for purposes of comparison. All sorts of terms have been coined to isolate religious knowledge from knowledge in ordinary life and the knowledge of the natural sciences. The distinction which Pascal made between the reasons of the mind and the reasons of the heart has become classic.[14] In Nasr's case we encountered terms such as esoteric and exoteric knowledge, and J. H. Newman speaks of "notional and real assent."[15] There are more of suchlike divisions. They do not always overlap. Sometimes two cognitive routes to knowledge are being designated, but only one concept of truth is being assumed. Other distinctions aim to denote a different kind of truth, a knowledge which refers to the reality described in an unconventional way. Even in the case of people who distinguish sharply between truth at the initial level and at the level of deep religious insight —the fourth level in our discussion— intermediate levels emerge to mediate, as it were, between the initial knowledge of a tradition and true understanding. We spoke in this connection of appropriated or true doctrine, the *veritates,* while the relation between insight and inner growth comes to expression better (although in part) in what we have called *religio vera.* Distinguishing between five ways of speaking about truth in religion helps us to obtain a better overview of the use of the concept of truth in respect of religion than does a twofold division.

The distinguishing of five meanings as discussed in this chapter does not amount to a theory of true religion. As yet, we are concerned only with giving an account of the meanings of 'truth' as we have encountered them. It is a model, in the sense that it sums up usages, distinguishing them and showing their mutual correlation. Not every religious current actually needs to exhibit each of these five uses of the concepts which are usually 'translated' as 'truth.' Seen as a description, it is a model. It is worth considering whether not all true religion yields such a fourfold division within human religious knowledge.

This fourfold division in religious knowledge (*public knowledge, appropriated knowledge, lived knowledge, and the moment of insight*) implies some further perceptions, which possess a certain relevance in view of contemporary discussion within the philosophy of religion. They will be indicated in summary fashion here. We will later return to them in more depth.

(1) If deepening religious knowledge is not only a question of study but also of personal growth, then the question arises: Can religious truth be established by means of argumentation? If the demonstration concerns not only the rigour of the argumentation, but also the surmounting of barriers

---

[14] "Esprit de Géométrie" and "Esprit de Finesse," by B. Pascal, *Pensées,* ed. J. Chevalier (1936; rpt. Paris 1962), p. 23 (fr. 21); see also in *Pensées et Opuscules,* ed. M. L. Brunschvicg (Paris[11] n.d.), p. 317 (fr. 1); "Le coeur a ses raisons, que la raison ne connaît point; on le sait en mille choses" (fr. 277); see G. E. Meuleman, "De Apologetische Methode van Pascal," *Gereformeerd Theol. Tijdschrift* 64 (1964): 2 f.

[15] J. H. Newman, *An Essay in Aid of a Grammar of Assent* (1870; London 1930), pp. 98 f., 36 ff.

which prevent a person from attaining insight, question arises as to the value of argumentation and the univocal usage of terms and inferences.

(2) If religions possess insight into a way of living which can help people attain more understanding, then it is unnecessary to assert that nothing can be stated regarding religious truth, that it must be 'given' to a person, or that it is based on enlightenment from God, etc. One can still take pains to introduce someone to a particular faith even if that tradition holds that faith, seen in terms of a deeper understanding, is a gift.

(3) If real insight into religious truth can only be attained at a later stage, the question arises: How can one be convinced to accept the initial doctrine and to live in conformity with the rules for living which a tradition provides? In some traditions one must abandon oneself to the good graces of a master, as appears within the esoterically oriented currents of various religions. Trust plays an important role here, particularly in some Buddhist currents.[16] On what is that confidence to be founded? The initial doctrine, including the five constituent parts mentioned (§ 2), plays a role in this foundation, One must think of the initial doctrine more as a guide towards religious understanding than as a profound exposition of it.

(4) Furthermore, question arises as to the relationship between initial understanding, the authority of the master, and the truth of a religion.

In the next chapter (Ch. IX), we will examine the experiences which sustain religion. In Ch. X the doctrine will again be brought up; Ch. XI will discuss the applicability of criteria for valid faith; and the concluding chapter deals with the relationship between religious traditions.

---

[16] See H. de Wit, pp. 36, 168ff.

Chapter IX

Religious Convictions and Experiences

§ 1 Religious experiences and basic insights

1.1 The problem

A religious view of life is commonly regarded as a whole. In this chapter we will pursue the question of whether, and too what extent, a philosophy of life forms a single entity, and with what human experiences religion dovetails.

It is commonly assumed that a religious view of the world ought to manifest unity and coherence. Indeed, for many, the degree of coherence is one of the criteria by which the truth of a religious tradition should be assessed. It is demanded that a religious persuasion be consistent or even coherent. The issue of the unity of a philosophical or religious life-view seems to us less simple than is often thought. The proposition that a religious persuasion exhibits and/or must exhibit unity is in need of further elucidation and nuance. We will show that religious views are not necessarily sustained by one central religious truth, but that they can have *several central or basic insights*. Such insights are sustained by *basic experiences,* and are indeed derived from them. For this reason they do not necessarily from a coherent philosophical system. We will characterize religious views of reality as *multi-centered belief-systems*. This view is developed more elaborately below. In this chapter we will pursue the notion of basic experiences in more detail. In the following chapter (Ch. X) we will discuss the role of doctrine within a religious tradition. A view of religion as a 'multi-centered belief-system' is of critical importance for an analysis of which criteria apply to religious truth (Ch. XI); within the context of this view, it is possible to develop a position on 'inter-religious relations' which avoids the implausible alternatives of relativism and exclusivism (Ch. XII).

The insight that religious teaching is a *multi-centered belief-system* is essential to a proper understanding of various aspects of the theme, 'religion and truth.' That is the reason why we bring it up here, subsequent to the introductory chapter of the analytical Part of the study.

We will begin by mentioning objections which should, in our view, be made against the view of a religious persuasion as a unified entity (§ 1.2). We will then demonstrate how the belief-system of a religion is formed by a conjunction of a number of fundamental insights (§ 1.3).

1.2   Objections to the concept of religious persuasions as independent and unified entities

a)   Religion as a 'belief-system'

W. C. Smith has justifiedly pointed out that the concept of religion has undergone changes in the Modern Period. The propositional element has become increasingly prominent, wrongly so according to him.[1] For this reason, beliefs have increasingly become independent entities in their own right as opposed to what is properly religious, namely *faith*. Religion was increasingly conceived of as a *belief-system* to which a logical analysis could be applied and which was ultimately expected to be (more or less) susceptible to scientific scrutiny. The basis of religion is then conceived of as adherence to a *belief-system* which ought to be consistent, public, and verifiable.[2]

In the previous chapter, we made a distinction between five ways of using the word 'truth' in religion. Lived faith (*religio vera*) is not identical to doctrine conceived of either as initial teaching (*doctrina*) or as appropriated doctrine (*veritates*). If it is stated that religion entails at least that one accept the *doctrina*, or the *veritates*, of a tradition, the experiential element of lived faith is neglected. An objectification of doctrine vis à vis experience takes place because one thus starts at the wrong end, i.e., with doctrine and not with experience. To regard and scrutinize a religious persuasion as more or less akin to a scientific theory is only possible after such an objectification of doctrine has occurred. A degree of unity and consistency is then sought in religious conviction which religions usually does not pretend to possess and which they indeed cannot possess in accordance with the nature of religion. It is inadmissable to derive a view of what 'unity' and 'consistency' is in a religious persuasion from phenomena which are not intrinsic to religion, rather than from an understanding of the *nature* of religious conviction itself. A religion *is not* a *belief-system*; a belief-system is a component of a religious tradition; the nature of the belief-system is determined by the religious tradition.

---

[1] W. C. Smith, esp. *Belief and History*, see above Ch. II § 3.2.

[2] D. Wiebe, see above, Ch. II § 3.4, the text at *nn* 296-300; also H. M. Kuitert, above Ch. II § 2.2., the text at *n.* 126.

b) Religions as separate language-games

D. Z. Phillips regards religions as a (separate) language-game, as we saw in Ch. II. One sometimes gets the impression that he sees each religion as a (separate) language-game. If this is indeed what he intends to say, the consequence would be that each religious tradition forms a *unity*. A religious view is regarded —following in the footsteps of the late Wittgenstein— as a *world-view*. This seems correct as long as such a *world-view* is not conceived of too rigorously as a unitary entity. We will leave it an open question here whether such rigour is D. Z. Phillips' intention — probably not.

Earlier in this enquiry, it became sufficiently clear that a religious tradition always acclaims certain beliefs. It is another question whether these beliefs can be arranged in a consistent doctrine. If the view that religious traditions have a certain world-view is elaborated in such a way that religion is construed as a consistent or coherent, explicit belief-system, then this conception of a belief-system owes more to the notion of a world-view or language-game than to the facts concerning religion.

It seems almost too obvious to say that a religious tradition involves a certain world-view —and implies a certain language-game— but this statement suggests a certain degree of coherence and unity in a religious persuasion which is apparently not present, and which, in our view, need not be present. It therefore does not seem useful to characterize a religious tradition as a separate language-game. Phillips' tendency in this direction is strong. H. Kraemer too has emphatically pointed out that religions must be understood as comprehensive entities wherein the terms used by various religions obtain their meaning.[3] This is only partly correct. Of course the tradition is the context within which religious terminology acquires meaning; but the context is not a systematic unity; moreover, the context in which terms are used is broader than just the religious tradition which coined them.[4] Notions such as world-view, view of reality, and belief-system suggest more unity and coherence in a religious tradition and a world-view than is actually present.

c) Basic convictions

A third approach to religion assumes that a certain idea is basic to each religion. This view occurs in several ways. People have spoken of the religious root, of the centre of a religious tradition, and of basic convictions. As an example of such a view we refer to the conception of V. Brümmer, who characterizes a view of life as follows, as we have already seen:

---

[3] H. Kraemer, see above Ch. II, *n.* 192.

[4] Compare with the discussion concerning the so-called contextuality of belief in Christian theology.

> A view of life ... involves a responding to whatever inspires one as being
> more important or more determinant of meaning than anything else.[5]

Brümmer stakes out more exactly what is determinant of meaning, as we
have shown in a quote in Ch. VIII § 5. He speaks of *primary determinant
of meaning* and of *basic convictions*. Each religious tradition indicates, on
the basis of impressive experiences, a certain *x* as unique and *determinant*
of the meaning of all other entities, situations, and events.[6] The task of
religious reflection within a tradition is then to interpret entities,
situations, and events in terms of this *determinant of meaning*, x.

Brümmer's view is of value in this connection for two reasons. First,
because of his reference to impressive experiences; and second, because
of his analysis of the primary determinant of meaning. It appears necessary
to introduce some nuance into this view. We will mention two points.

(1) If one proceeds in terms of impressive experiences, it is unnecessary
to settle on a single central religious insight. It is also possible to settle
on different foci. If one imagines a religious tradition as a circle with a
central point, then it is possible to imagine a tradition with two basic
insights as an ellipse with two foci. These centres of religious tradition
could be called foci of meaning or *basic insights*. A religious persuasion
has one or more basic insights.

(2) The basic insights are central due to impressive experiences. It is
important to note here that an experience can be impressive only when it
touches on basic levels of human existence. We speak here of *basic
experiences* to express this. Human existence has a number of characteristics
which are essential to being human: *existentials*. These *existentials*
correlate with experience. We shall see that this involves a relatively
modest number of fundamental human experiences with which people must
of necessity come to terms within the course of their life. Due to the
relationship of religious faith with human *existentials,* a religion has a
number of basic insights which are, on the one hand, related by their
reference to the transcendent, but on the other hand, can be in tension
with each other. People often endeavour to arrive at a coherent view of
reality in a religious tradition. To this end, basic insights are probed to
find the relationships between them; we will return to this in Ch. X.
Simple reference to the transcendent does not guarantee the unity of a
view of life and, furthermore, is not specific enough to serve as a
distinguishing feature of different religious traditions.

We have now examined three views of religious persuasions as unities.
We believe that the reasons for regarding religious views as coherent
entities are a priori philosophical constructions which perhaps appear obvious
within Western culture but which are not based on the 'facts,' at least

---

[5] V. Brümmer, *Wijsgerige Begripsanalyse*, p. 142; see also above Ch. II § 2.1.

[6] Brümmer, p. 132; see also above, Ch. VIII § 5

not the facts as we have come to know them in Part 2. How can we view this differently?

1.3 Numerous fundamental insights in a religious tradition

In this section we will elaborate the proposition that a religious persuasion has more than one basic insight. We will begin our demonstration of this by referring to various traditions.

(A) The Hindu tradition, as we have seen, has six philosophical schools. Each has different accents. Some put all the emphasis on analysis, others on personal training via yoga and meditation for the purpose of making a spiritual journey. There are religious currents with a strong element of personal worship of the divinity —the *bhakti*— but there are also currents like the Advaita Vedānta which pursue transcendence of the personal element in a non-dual experience of the Whole. The Hindu tradition thus has a variety of basic insights; the assorted religious sub-currents apply different accents, put different basic insights at the centre, and view the relationships between the various basic insights differently. It has been suggested, on the basis of this diversity, that Hinduism is not a religion but a conglomerate of religions; such a view presupposes a certain conception of the unity of 'a religion,' however.

(B) We will mention four points on which the ideas of the Buddhist tradition seem adjacent to each other rather than being logically coherent or issuing from one centre. (i) The Buddhist tradition regards the world as *dukkha* and *anitya*. This does not entail the notion that one must relate to others with compassion. The notion of compassion nevertheless forms an essential part of Buddhist teaching and of its attitude. The idea of Buddha-hood is based on the comprehensive compassion of the Buddha(s) towards all people. The experience of the neediness of fellow beings apparently exists next to the basic experience of the transient and unsatisfying nature of things. (ii) On the issue of the cause of suffering, one also sees two things existing side by side, ignorance (*avidyā*) and attachment. We discussed the dialectical relationship between overcoming ignorance and attachment in the previous chapter. There are apparently two deficiencies; their relation and the best way of surmounting both flaws is apparently open to discussion. Everyone must find their own way on the basis of their experiences and with the help of a guru. (iii) On the one hand, Buddhists have the doctrine of rebirth, and on the other, the doctrine of *anātta*. The question thus arises as to the identity of the person who, upon death, is reborn in a different manner of existence. This question, for example, with regard to the *pudgala* doctrine, formed the occasion for the dispute between early Buddhist schools, as we have seen. We have already mentioned that Nishitani regards the doctrine of rebirth as mythology. (iv) The earliest strata of Buddhism already taught both the animation of things as well as the perishable nature and non-being of all things. Nishitani speaks of a 'field of force' as well as of *śūnyatā*. Here too one runs across a paradox.[7] Thus Buddhist teaching too apparently encompasses several insights whose mutual relationship is debatable.

(C) The Jewish tradition also displays multiple insights. (i) We would first of all point to the twin central thoughts of the closeness and the exaltation of God. These notions are not merely contradictory to thought, but these insights spring from different experiences. The doctrine of *ha-Šāmāyīm* is based on the experience of the exaltation and greatness of God, while the doctrine of *ha-Māḳôm* and *Šeḳīnāh* are based on the experience of an inimitable nearness. Both insights could be characterized as basic insights; their mutual relationship is disputed. (ii) Another ambiguity to be found in Judaism is the link between universality and particularity. God is the Creator, the God of all people; and yet he chooses a particular nation as his people. Within this awareness, the other nations are viewed as 'nations which do not know the law,' or as nations which exist under the Noachite covenant. (iii) A third point at which it becomes evident that several insights exist next to one another comes to expression in Facken-heim's struggle to relate faith and Jewishness. Fackenheim describes how Jewishness —to have to be and to wish to be a Jew— has become an act of faith after the Holocaust. There is apparently a basic experience of being called on to do God's will, and an experience of belonging to a certain, oft persecuted, empirical nation. Consistency of doctrine is secondary to fundamental experiences in these three ambiguities. In reflecting, one seeks how the one is or can be related to the other.

(D) It is not difficult to indicate differing basic insights in Christianity which cannot be accommodated in a seamless dogmatic system. (i) On the one hand, believers speak of the creation and regard God as Creator; on the other hand, God is the Covenant partner, and believers speak of the calling of Israel and the Church. The relationship between the Creator and the Covenant Partner is open to discussion; it is not simply an intellectual problem that is involved here; the problem has its basis in two fundamental experiences.[8] (ii) Believers speak of a God who has power over all things, on the one hand; on the other hand, they recognize the enigma of evil and suffering. (iii) In the New Testament, the person of Jesus is central; on the other hand, his life is in service to the coming Kingdom of God. The centre of Christianity is thus indicated either in Jesus Christ, or in the Kingdom of God to which Jesus was entirely

---

[7] See T. Vetter, "Weltgespräch der Religionen: Eine Rezension," *Zeitschrift f. Miss. Wiss. und Rel. Wiss.* (1987), pp. 137f. Concerning the field of force in Nishitani's thought, compare H. M. Vroom, "Aan het Nihilisme voorbij: De Godsdienstfilosofie van Nishitani," *Nederlands Theologisch Tijdschrift* 40 (1986): 151.

[8] Compare with the discussion which followed upon the appearance of G. von Rad's *Theologie des Alten Testaments.*

subservient.[9] Christianity as well is based on several *impressiva*; it has several *basic insights* which have never yet been poured into a flawless dogmatic system. The number of ambiguities and mutually 'complementary' insights could easily be expanded.

(E) Islam has, on the one hand, (i) the belief in the power of God and of the determination of man's destiny; on the other hand, man is assumed to have a certain freedom to observe the commandments of God. (ii) God's dealings with other religions which possess a (certain form of the) Holy Book are recognized, but so is the uniqueness of the Koran. Value is ascribed to the holy books of Jews and Christians, but these can also be regarded as distortions of the scriptures entrusted to Moses and the apostles. Some acknowledge God's dealings with all people and the goodness and truth of the insights which they attained; on the other hand, the uniqueness of the Koran's doctrine is confessed, as well as the greatness of art which is in complete accordance with *Islam*. Some Muslims thus struggle with the relationship between two fundamental experiences in their religious reflection, the impressiveness of their own *Islam* and of the Koran on the one hand, and the experience of the goodness and value of other traditions on the other.

The thesis that a religious tradition has several basic insights is most easily elucidated by the ambiguities within the various traditions. The reasons for this are obvious. Precisely in the ambiguities, it appears:

(1) that a religious persuasion is a 'conglomerate' of insights
(2) that a persuasion is not based on one central insight or centre but on fundamental, or basic, experiences, which find expression in *basic insights*.

Together these basic insights refer to the transcendent.

Insofar as religious traditions refer to historical events or persons, these events or persons have significance, since they have enabled or brought about a certain interpretation of basic experiences.

By basic insight we thus understand an *insight* that is fundamental to a religious tradition, that is founded on fundamental human *experiences*, that is articulated and transmitted through beliefs (which are sometimes tied to historical events or persons), and that is *nurtured* in the liturgy and the manner of life which a religion commends.

We are thus brought to our next point. The examples of basic insights which we have just given do not need to be exclusive to a particular religion. Thus, the issue of the relationship of God's power to evil and suffering is present in all three of the Abrahamitic religions (existentially as well as intellectually), and Hinduism is acquainted with the question of

---

[9] Referring to such texts as John 14:6 and Acts 4:12, Jesus is very often assigned a central position. For many Christians, the Kingdom of God is the centre of Christian faith; Jesus, then, is or points to the way of the Kingdom.

'theodicy' as well. It is precisely the recognition that a religious tradition does not have to be determined by a single determinant belief which sheds light on interreligious relations. It can accordingly be understood that traditions which are for the remainder very different can touch on each other in cognate basic insights.

A religious tradition ventures to do justice to the fundamental experiences of being human by means of basic insights, even when systematic problems emerge concerning the mutual relationships between various basic insights on account of this.

In terms of this diversity of basic insights, light is also cast on the nature of the historical developments which religious traditions undergo. What is of concern in this process —as far as doctrine is involved— is not just the elaboration of one basic insight or focus of meaning (as primary determinant of meaning), but an uninterrupted hermeneutical process in which at least four factors are linked together: (1) writings and traditions; (2) fundamental human experiences (*existentials*) and their interpretation; (3) new fundamental insights, derived from changing contexts; (4) reflection on the mutual relationships between the tradition's insights. The hermeneutical process is therefore not just 'saying old things differently,' but is also a creative process of interpretation, modification, renewal, re-utilization of old insights from tradition, taking account of new experiences, and adoption of insights from other areas of life and from other traditions.

This understanding of a *religious tradition as a living hermeneutical process* clarifies the developments which religious traditions undergo — for better or worse. One can also understand how very divergent currents can emerge within a religious tradition; they have often related the various basic insights to each other in different ways. Insights which are considered central in one current are regarded as relatively secondary to other insights by another current. Often the importance of certain beliefs will not be denied, but a different weight will be ascribed to them. There is, in other words, a *hierarchia veritatum*; the manner in which the *hierarchy* is constructed can differ from one current to another within a religious tradition. Within religious currents, insights are passed on in a complex network of transferring tradition, in which such factors as religious education, religious gatherings, liturgy, and presentations in the media play a part. Depending on the appreciation for certain basic experiences and basic insights, a religious current focusses primarily on *nurturing* certain basic experiences. The mutual relationship of basic experiences and basic insights is a matter of a permanent process of tradition in which reflection largely follows on life rather than offering initial guidance.

In reflecting, people seek —as appears from the study of classical exponents of the various traditions— the unity in the religious convictions of a tradition. People are not satisfied with a fragmented world view which consists in isolated basic insights. People aspire to relate them to one another and to bring them into agreement. The world view and the religious persuasion which thus emerge do not form a static unity; it is continually in flux, being modified, revised, and moderated; it is a *precarious* unity, to put it in words; it is a conglomerate of insights in which people attempt to do justice to fundamental human experiences, understood in a continual hermeneutical process. In the following section we will begin by examining more closely the basic experiences on which religious convictions are based.

§ 2   Basic experiences

2.1   General Remarks

In our consideration of basic insights we have seen how experiences are fundamental to religious convictions. A religious persuasion remains *alive* as long as it is sustained by experiences. It can tolerate inner tension or even contradictions if the experiences on which it is based are sufficiently impressive. The impressiveness of religious experiences is decisive for the durability of religious traditions. Religious traditions therefore *nurture* the fundamental experiences on which they are based. In the customs of the religious community, they possess the means to pass on impressive experiences, or, to put it better, to actualize certain experiential possibilities and to teach people to start looking at and experiencing things in a certain manner. Meditation, *yoga*, *ṣalāt*, preaching, and religious devotions in the home environment as well, all belong to these means.

We have stated that the experiences which are decisive for religion are fundamental human experiences. We have designated this with the term existential experiences since these *existential experiences correlate with essential characteristics of human existence, 'existentials.'* These are aspects of life which remain more or less the same throughout the ages. The manner in which these aspects of life are interpreted and in which the accompanying experiences are assimilated is largely determined by context and history. What one undergoes is experienced and thought within one's horizon of understanding — as people such as Gadamer, Ricoeur, and Tracey have elucidated.[10] Despite the historical (including the contextual) conditioning of knowledge and experience, a relatively concise range of experiences is involved in these basic experiences which —as mentioned earlier— are entailed by the nature of human existence in the world. Below is a brief

---

[10] H. -G. Gadamer, *Wahrheit und Methode* (Tübingen ²1965); P. Ricoeur, *Hermeneutics and the Human Science*, ed. & tr. J. B. Thompson (Cambridge 1981); D. Tracy, *The Analogical Imagination* (London 1981).

list of these experiences. It has not been derived from anthropology, but from our description of religious traditions in Part 2. If it is incomplete, it must be augmented.

2.2 Basic experiences

It appears from our enquiry that religions pay much attention to the following aspects of life:

(1) the finitude of human existence
(2) human responsibility and human failing
(3) the experience of the good, of happiness, peace, well-being, and meaning
(4) the receiving of insight
(5) evil and suffering.

It is very much the question whether an additional separate religious experience in the very specific sense of an immediate experience of the divinity must be spoken of. An immediate experience of God —if at all possible— is highly exceptional according to religious traditions. According to most traditions, this is not a separate, immediate experience, but a mediated experience of God which— according to some traditions— comes about through basic experiences in concrete circumstances. One can think here in terms of the experience of happiness (bliss), well-being, and peace. If one takes these terms very precisely, one can see why true happiness, true peace, and true well-being can only be experienced in the 'nearness of the transcendent' or in a 'transcendent state,' according to religious traditions.

The aspects of life mentioned (actualized in the experiences of daily life) are designated diversely by various religious currents. *Doctrine* (*dharma, veritates*) must be understood as an *interpretative description* of human existence. One learns to experience these aspects of existence in a certain way by means of the teaching and the life-forms correlating to them. Human experience is always interpreted experience. A religious persuasion offers a framework within which experiences can be interpreted, in conjunction with a religious life-style. Our investigation teaches that experiences which are crucial for religious traditions concern those aspects of existence which have been mentioned. On the basis of the fact that religious traditions are again and again concerned with the same *existentials,* it can be understood that religious traditions exhibit similarities and pursue the same existential questions.[11] Religions take account of the fact that human existence is always threatened; they all assume man's relative lack of freedom in ordinary life, and that actual life does not answer to its intention. We will examine the five aspects.

---

[11] D. C. Mulder, "Alle Geloven op één Kussen?" in *Religies in Nieuw Perspektief,* Essays for D. C. Mulder (Kampen 1985), pp. 145 ff.; cf. Brümmer, Ch. II, the text at *n.* 105.

2.3 Experiences of the finitude of existence

The experience of the finitude of human existence is fundamental to all philosophies of life. People cannot find an answer to the question of the *meaning* of life without taking into account the finitude of life.

Buddhism, more than other traditions, puts the finitude of existence in the foreground. All things are perishable, transient, *anitya*. The realization of this insight is a first step on the path to freedom from attachment. In Hinduism, as far as we can se°, the experience of finitude tends to be the experience of the insignificance of humanity in the greatness of the universe of which man forms an essential part. The experience of insignificance resounds differently in Judaism and Christianity, where there is a vital awareness of the greatness of God, the Creator of humankind. Humanity is no less than the image of God, on the one hand, but is tiny and fragile on the other: "What is man that Thou art mindful of him?" (Psalm 8). Islam emphasizes the finitude of man over against the greatness of God who knows and governs all things.

Finitude as the mortality of man has come to the fore in all these traditions. Also prominent in all traditions is the idea of finitude as human existence beleaguered and threatened by many dangers. These existential characteristics of human life receive a designated place in terms of the whole of a religious persuasion. The manner in which one can come to terms with difficulties is also indicated, be it through freedom from attachment, be it through an experience of the Whole, be it through trusting God, or be it through the anticipation of a blessed hereafter, or a cycle of rebirths. There is something fundamentally intrinsic to human existence which apparently undergirds religion, and which we designate as the finitude or limitation of human existence. This limitation appears in the confrontation with the superior forces of nature, which, hence, provide the material for much religious symbolism. This is an experience of quantitative finitude, of being smaller than what is great.

There also appears to be a qualitative experience of finitude in which existence as such is experienced as limited and precarious. This experience is interpreted within the context of a religious frame of reference. This frame of reference is formed by the cluster of basic insights which a religious tradition provides. The context provided by a cluster of basic insights can exhibit great variance. This can be seen in the Buddhist tradition, for example, in which a broad current that assumes a cycle of (predetermined) rebirths exists alongside a different interpretation of the doctrine of rebirth. The designation and interpretation, and, subsequently, the experience of 'finitude,' is contextual in the sense of being determined by tradition and situation. The *finitude* of existence, however, vis à vis which religions must determine their attitude, is fundamental to human existence. We can therefore state that a religious tradition must do justice to the finitude which is intrinsic to human existence, and must find a *modus vivendi* for coming to terms with finitude and limitation. The interpretation of human finitude is an insight which is basic to a religious tradition.

2.4 The experience of failure

The second *existential* experience which obtains prominence in the religions discussed is the experience of inadequacy, guilt, and failure in exercising responsibility and in the realization of ideals. The concept of failure presupposes the idea of a *purpose* to which one should ideally answer, or a state of goodness in which people should dwell. On the one hand, it presupposes a norm which the present *condition humaine* does not meet. On the other, the concept of failing presupposes human responsibility for shortcomings; the present condition is not a kind of doom which hovers above human existence. Religions point out the nature of failure. The blindness of man for the transcendent is generally pointed out, caused by egocentric attachment to what is worldly, especially property and esteem. No matter what words are used —attachment, sin, service to Mammon, egoism— ego-centeredness and materialistic behaviour are always mentioned. The aspiration for a good life always contains a certain degree of being free from care and attachment. We could designate this failure with respect to man's purpose or to a condition of blessedness as a *metaphysical deficiency*.

In addition, there is a *social deficiency*: human failure in responsibilities towards others. Buddhism connects egoism to shortcomings in compassion towards other beings. Hinduism emphasizes that all people are brothers and sisters, since they share in the same nature (Brahman). In the Abrahamitic religions the emphasis is on injustice and lovelessness. The exact relationship between these shortcomings in compassion, justice, and neighbourly love fall outside of the bounds of our enquiry. We can, however, ascertain that a person's relation to fellow beings, and particularly (in some religions) a person's relation to fellow human beings, is regarded as essential to being human, even though in the present situation people are deficient in this regard. In the major world religions, a correct attitude with respect to human purpose is accompanied by a proper attitude towards fellow beings and fellow man.

The relationship of these two obligations —realization of human purpose and maintaining good relations with one's neighbours— is subject to discussion. The commandment of love for God in Christianity is the equal, though not the same, as the commandment of neighbourly love. In Buddhism, the aspiration to attain *nirvāna* and *satori* exists next to the obligation to be compassionate. Within Hinduism, there are various ways which lead to *mokṣa*, among which the way of knowledge and the way of action. The way of action simply means that one fulfills one's duty, or *dharma*, while being without attachment. We can thus establish that human failure has two aspects, the one metaphysical and the other social. The relationship between both aspects is generally regarded as very close.

As with other experiences, further interpretation of the experience of human failure is determined by the whole of the respective religion's convictions. This does not diminish the fact that these traditions (endeavour to) do justice to the impressive experience of the metaphysical and social deficiency of man.

2.5 Experiences of the good

We have grouped together a variety experiences under 'experiences of the good.' Different traditions stress different things with respect to the importance of various experiences. We will allow the *existentials* to guide us in grouping a variety of experiences.

a) Strength: resistance to injustice and suffering

The experience of suffering, enduring injustice, or being exposed to the temptation to take wrong actions, can all give rise to another experience — the experience of having the strength to deal with the situation or to bear it. This strength is not considered the natural possession of man, but is regarded as something which must be either acquired or received. One must in any event prepare oneself to achieve or to receive this strength. Religious traditions have a common basis in this existential characteristic of human existence. People end up in situations wherein they must endure things or wherein they must arm themselves against the temptation of retreating from their purpose or from shirking their duties. On the one hand, religious traditions present ways towards spiritual growth which make people stronger and less dependent on material well-being and esteem from (alienated) society. On the other, religious currents across the board point out that the actual strength which is involved is not truly the possession or achievement of man, but simply that which occurs when one surmounts egoism, or, alternatively, grace. Nishitani describes the field of force which is present in the experience of *satori* and *ego/non-ego*. Hindus obtain strength from their belief in the unity of *ātman* and Brahman. The three Abrahamitic religions speak of duty and religious exercise on the one hand, and of grace on the other.

b) Peace, liberation, and happiness

The *condition humaine* entails the experience of disquietude and unrest in living amidst other people. Human existence is being-with-others. People's desires and the ideal image they have of themselves do not tally with reality. People cannot control their emotions and focus on the good. They are like a vessel full of contradictions. The dynamics of daily living are kept going largely by the dissatisfaction and agitation which people have; they are discontented with the situation in which they live; they want to 'get ahead,' they covet a larger share of the pie than they have. Dissatisfaction is allied to attachment to ego, social esteem, etc. Religious traditions all teach that this belongs to alienated human existence. Relief can be found by minding the *true value of things,* focussing on the will of God, or man's purpose, *dharma,* etc. This requires a liberation from attachment — described in the Christian gospel as freedom from worry, in Hinduism as *mokṣa,* and in Islam as obedient surrender to the will of God.

Such experiences of being free from constraints, and thus of peace and happiness while one is in the midst of life, are reckoned to be religious experiences. The existential, universal, human yearning for happiness and peace is fulfilled in this religious experience. Here again an essential characteristic of human existence is fulfilled by a religious experience — leaving aside the differing interpretations given to it by different religious traditions. It is again striking that various religious interpretations of this *existential* exhibit family resemblances. *Mokṣa* is not something totally different than Christian freedom from worry or than Jewish unconditional trust in God, even though it certainly is not the same. These religious experiences and attitudes of liberation exhibit many similarities. They correspond and yet differ. The explanation for these similarities lies in the fact that the various religions give an answer to and offer a solution for the fundamental human need for certainty, permanence, serenity, peace, etc. Religious traditions indicate ways in which people can meet these needs. How they 'colour in' a need or the solution to it depends on the religious persuasion, that is to say, on the entire cluster of basic insights which form a religious persuasion.

c) Well-being, prosperity

Well-being and prosperity is considered to be a gift of God in some religious traditions, especially as a result of the fact that God blesses someone's work. This notion is to be encountered primarily in the Abraham-itic religions, but —as we have seen earlier— in Hinduism too many believers are primarily interested in a prosperous life. One can safely state that this idea particularly plays a role in popular religion. More sophisticated forms of religion tend to introduce qualifications into what is represented as a good life and as prosperity.

Material life is valued more highly in the Abrahamitic religions than in certain Hindu and Buddhist currents. People may freely enjoy God's good gifts. But the notion of moderation and self-control comes into play here too. A kind of middle way is chosen between asceticism and hedonism. It is stressed time and again that well-being does not just have a material side but also an inward side, of well-being no matter what happens. For many centuries Jewish rabbis lived very soberly in order to spend as much time as possible studying the holy books.

Religious traditions all posses a certain appreciation for material prosperity. It is an essential trait of being human that one provide for oneself. An important part of social life which appears as strength in 'this world' is connected with this: success in relations, finances, and career. Most religious movements which aim to guide people to a more mature experience of religion adopt a skeptical stance towards material gain and social esteem. Concern with material success easily distracts one from the deeper values as these are seen by especially the more spiritual traditions. A number of traditions point to the possibility of leading a life free of attachment even while standing in the midst of society life. We encountered this idea in the *Bhagavadgītā*; it is also taught by elements in other traditions. By way of conclusion we will state that religious traditions are widely concerned with attitudes towards material prosperity and material deprivation; they —certainly the more spiritual traditions— are ambivalent with respect to worldly success, but (a certain measure of) prosperity is sometimes experienced as a blessing. The difference between the initial teaching and a deeper understanding of a religious tradition plays an important role with respect to this *existential* characteristic. Economic and social success are viewed differently in 'this world' —which lies beneath a veil of ignorance— than in terms of the *religio vera,* or lived faith — no matter in what tradition one finds oneself.

d) The good and just life

Other aspects of social life meet sympathy without any reserve, namely charity and justice. Being-human is being-with-others, and all five of the major world religions include currents which heavily emphasize that. People of various religious traditions are committed to the struggle for the liberation of humanity from structures which are experienced as injust. The motivation for this can lie in neighbourly love, in compassion, in respect for all life, in the awareness that all people share in Brahman, or in the need not only to give *zakāt* but also to provide justice.

Here too, religious traditions decide their attitude with respect to an *existential,* for it is an essential feature of human existence that society is ordered in such a way that it provides some with the opportunity to be more privileged than others. This universal human fact is 'placed,' as it were, by a religious tradition; it is interpreted in terms of that tradition, and people are thus led to a certain experience of it. The attitude which people take towards inequality in economic, legal, and cultural matters differs with and within each religious tradition. Poverty or birth in a poor environment can be explained in terms of the *karma* of previous lives; it can also be ascribed to social disfigurement, incidental factors, egoism, or ineptitude. Religions differ in their insights in these matters.

It is also apparent that an *existential* which is of central significance to one religion may be less important to another tradition. Each religion determines its own attitude with respect to *existentials*. These attitudes exhibit variance due to influences by the total framework of a life view. Thus, certain elements within Judaism and Christianity put so much emphasis on social justice that historical episodes in which people were freed from restraining bonds are interpreted religiously. The experience of the liberation from slavery in the Jewish Bible was one of the most significant religious experiences, for in the Exodus, the Jews experienced the hand of God. This notion is currently also being assimilated in Christian circles; in earlier times, belief in an ultimate settling of all inequality in the hereafter often moderated many aspirations for improving 'this world.' All religions, then, must determine their attitude with respect to the essential features of human existence; they each do that in their own way. How they decide their attitude, depends on the manner in which they forge their basic insights into a whole. It is often a matter of a different approach between the one religious tradition and the next, rather than a matter of being diametrically opposed. They overlap each other, as it were. What the one considers to be important is not regarded as unimportant in another, but perhaps as less important. It thus seems to us that if all things are considered to be determined by *karma,* or if one believes that man must pursue an experience of *ego/non-ego,* then the idea of the essential equality of all people will be considered self-evident, even though it will be interpreted rather differently, and the struggle for political and social 'liberation' will not be given the highest priority. The *configuration of basic insights* is determinative for the religious value which is ascribed to certain existential experiences, and for the priority of various forms of conduct.

e) Experiences of meaning and totality

We will mention separately here experiences of totality. Such an encompassing experience is actually already included in the experiences of the good which we have just mentioned. The experience of inner strength, of well-being, and of serenity, peace, and freedom has profound significance for life as a whole. The experience of life *as a whole* is sustained by a number of experiences within the *religio vera*. In this sense the experience of totality is implied in every 'religious experience.' The reason for speaking here of experiences of totality in a stricter sense is that all the major religions include movements which are acquainted with more or less direct experiences of the totality of existence, or at least the totality of existence as it is intended. Recall in this connection the *śūnyatā* experience, the state of bliss of the Advaita Vedānta, and the awareness of living before the face of God in certain currents of Judaism and Christianity, as well as of Islam.

The fundamental characteristic of being human which is at issue here is the need to feel that one can live *meaningfully* and that one has a place in the total scheme of things. The experience of meaning involves the most fundamental facet of being human. People can have everything and still be apprehensive because they cannot make sense of life or of their own life. The meaningfulness of existence is presupposed by all remaining experience. It is, as mentioned earlier, present in all kinds of experiences. Just as experiences of serenity, peace, and liberation support and sustain the experience of meaningfulness, so the experience of meaningfulness provides a certain measure of inner quiet and freedom, even if the situation in which one finds oneself is disquieting.

The existential need for meaning is recognized by all traditions, but is —again— interpreted in divergent ways. We will present a few examples. When Nāgārjuna equates *saṁsāra* to *nirvāna,* this indicates an immersion in the whole. According to Nishitani, the loss of an ego-centric ego leads to the experience of absorption by a field of force as ego/non-ego. In Hinduism there is the awareness of being related to the whole. In the Abrahamitic religions, the meaning of life is secured by the context of the creation, in God's will for man, and in his gracious mercy. According to some traditions, the experience of meaning is an immediate experience of the totality of experience — no matter how it is experienced. Others do not speak of such an experience of totality or even regard such experience as impossible. In the latter case, the experience of totality is an experience in which the miscellaneous aspects of existence are assigned a place within the whole, and in which life —lived in a certain way— is interpreted as meaningful.

f) Experiences of beauty and awe for nature

It is said that philosophy begins with wonder at the fact that there is something rather than nothing. Awe at the beauty, complexity, and regularity in nature plays an important role in religion, given that this too is experienced within the framework of a tradition. Buddhists sometimes try to train themselves in such a way that they see all things with an open mind, as though for the first time. Buddhist teaching speaks of the order in the world. Religions with a doctrine of creation praise the beauty and complexity of the world. The starting point for proofs of God lies in the experience of the order in the world. These experiences are linked to lasting features of being human, namely the sensitivity to beauty and the need for regularity in the order of nature.

The possibilities which the natural order presents to man have been approached in divergent ways. The Western Christian tradition especially has for many centuries been oriented towards the managing and exploitation of natural resources. Hinduism and Buddhism lean much less in this direction; some traditions primarily pursue an increased mastery of human possibilities and the exercise of what is known in the West as paranormal gifts. If one were to express it briefly —and clearly, though rudimentarily— one could say that Hinduism and Buddhism focus more on the mastering of the inner person, while Judaism and Christianity, and Islam as well, focus more on mastery of what is outward, on behaviour, and on the world. The contrast is not absolute, but does serve to indicate a difference in accentuation. In both cases *existentials* are involved: people must explore their own possibilities and learn to master themselves. They must live in the order of nature which they must use with wisdom in order to provide for their needs (true or alleged).

g) Experiences of goodness and of being good

Experiences of human goodness occupy an important position in religious traditions. The *existential* at issue here is that of dependence on other people. This represents a further step than being-with-others, as mentioned earlier. A particular way of being dependent on others is dependence on religious authorities. In the revealed religions one must rely on the religious insight of the prophets and of the authors of holy scriptures. In Hinduism and Buddhism one needs to rely on gurus and masters. Upon closer examination, one discovers that in the Abrahamitic religions, religious leadership also plays an important role; it receives form in the functions which are fulfilled within a religious community.

The experience of the goodness of certain people is generally given a religious significance. The capability of conquering oneself, of helping others, compassion, and neighbourly love have religious significance. Depending on the remaining religious convictions, people will speak here of grace, God's guidance, or, of having proceeded further on the spiritual path.

2.6 Insight

People are in need of insight into the reality which surrounds them in order to orient themselves in life. This too is apparently an *existential*. Religious insight is closely tied to religious experience. In acquiring religious insight one is confronted by the same ambiguities as was the case with the strength to endure things. On the one hand, people must take pains to acquire insight. People must surmount obstacles which prevent them from attaining true insight. On the other hand, it is recognized —particularly by the revealed religions— that insight is a gift. Some Buddhists speak of sudden enlightenment and of grace by which one receives insight. True religious insight, the *religio vera*, is counted as religious experience.

2.7 Experiences of evil and of suffering

Since misery, suffering, and evil belong to the normal experience of the world, it is incumbent upon every religious current to 'clarify' the existence of suffering and evil, and to point out a way of coming to terms with it when one must endure it. The religious traditions we have studied arrive at different views of affliction. Within the Abrahamitic religions woe is sometimes regarded as willed by God; God sometimes puts such obstacles in peoples' way to test them, and to teach or punish them. Others within these traditions maintain that the relationship between God and evil is unclear, or that God never wills evil. This view can often be heard in modern Judaism and Christianity. Protests against evil are often to be heard. The experience of suffering is exceedingly important for the initiation of people in Buddhist doctrine. The world is sketched as *dukkha* and *anitya,* full of sorrow and perishable by nature. Some monastic traditions help their novices to appropriate this view of the world by concentrating on the less savoury sides of life. The experience of suffering which formed the occasion for the Buddha to turn his back on 'ordinary' life is a beginner's truth, according to the understanding of people more advanced on the religious path, and serves to motivate people to abandon the 'ordinary' view of life and to exercise themselves in the realization of *śūnyatā.* Hinduism too struggles with the problem of the presence of evil, but a concomitant awareness of the goodness of the Transcendent preclude directly tying Brahman to evil.

All traditions must determine their attitude with respect to the experience of affliction and evil. Many share repulsion at the idea that evil has a transcendental origin. Others, primarily within Islam and certain Christian groups, stress the close relationship between God and all things, even evil. The theme of suffering and evil arises in all religions. An attempt is made to help people come to terms with their experiences with the aid of teachings or the narration of classical stories.

2.8 Basic experiences and *existentials*

Fundamental human experiences correspond to fundamental characteristics of being human. We have summarized such fundamental features, or *existentials,* and have shown, sometimes with the aid of examples, how the correlated experiences play a role in the major religious traditions. A whole string of *existentials* were reviewed: the pursuit of happiness; being vulnerable to the temptation of betraying one's own purpose and duty; yearning for peace, liberty, and justice; the need for providing for oneself; sensitivity to beauty; awe at nature and wonder at the good; the experience of meaning; undergoing suffering; the presence of evil; being dependent on the warmth and assistance of others; seeking insight and orientation in life. People have experiences on all these scores. This state of affairs secures an experiential basis for religious traditions. They interpret experiences; they evaluate the various aspects of human existence. Some experiences are singled out as impressive, others as misleading.

Basic experiences are correlate to these *existentials*. They are experiences in which the possibility of the deep, existential experiences entailed by human existence become actual. Sometimes such experiences are discussed as *borderline experiences*. This term expresses the notion that these experiences refer beyond the boundaries of 'ordinary' human existence towards the transcendent. Furthermore, the term *borderline experiences* indicates that such experiences are rather difficult to define; one runs into the limits of what can be articulated.[12] Since the core of one's existence is touched on here, we speak of *basic experiences*.

Basic experiences are obtained via *concrete experiences,* of which they form the depth dimension, as it were. To give an example, when one reaches a mountain ridge and suddenly sees the rugged snowcapped peaks on the other side, one does not simply experience the beauty of those mountains, but the beauty of nature as well as one's own insignificance; in the beneficence of another person, one experiences goodness; a gesture can mean friendship, but it also implies dependence on others; in concrete failure one experiences guilt; futile work tends to lead one to the question of the meaning of things. Such is the manner in which basic experiences are entailed by concrete experiences. Concrete instances bespeak the deeper, the real, or, if we may be permitted, that which is encompassing and decisive. That is why basic experiences are impressive. Since they are impressive, they require interpretation. Religious traditions present such an interpretation. We will discuss this in the following section.

§ 3   Religious views of life as configurations of basic insights

3.1   Religion and basic experiences

The traditions associated with a view of life offer interpretations; they help people to experience impressive experiences in a specific way. They are in pursuit of the *correct* interpretation of basic experiences. Uninterpreted experience does not exist; it is furthermore an anthropological necessity to interpret impressive experiences which touch on the basis of human existence. Since these are basic experiences which are at issue, people are inclined to pose the question of truth: How can the real significance of these experiences be designated? If we define a view of life as an interpretation of basic experiences, then it follows from this that every person who is consciously confronted by such basic experiences necessarily

---

[12] E.g., D. Tracy, *Blessed Rage for Order* (New York 1978), esp. Chapter 5; see also I. T. Ramsey, *Religious Language* (London 1957); J. Macquarry, *God-Talk* (London 1967); P. M. van Buren, *The Edges of Language* (London 1972).

has a view of life, either explicit or implicit. Interpretations by earlier generations emerge as the traditions of a world-view. Wilfred Smith says that they are the precipitate of a cumulative process of interpreted experience. Kuitert speaks of a search paradigm. There is indeed an element of interpretation, of formulation, which is at work here. One gives an interpretation of impressive experiences which affect man in an essential way because they correlate with *existentials*.

Religious traditions interpret the significance of basic experiences in the light of a decisive reality, which is different from the empirical world at hand. They believe that one comes into contact with the transcendent in such basic experiences. The transcendent announces itself in experience as that which is of real concern, that which provides meaning, peace, and reassurance, and which thus answers to man's deepest longings and aptitudes. The experience of the transcendent implies that 'ordinary' life comes to be illumined by a different light, and that many of its elements will be seen as misleading and wrong.

Various religious traditions give disparate interpretations of the transcendent. The reason for this is that people are fundamentally affected by different concrete experiences. In the biblical narrative of the Exodus from Egypt, for instance, the experience of liberation from constraints is related to the liberation from slavery and the promise of a peaceful and just life. The fundamental experience of liberation is obtained in Buddhism by relinquishing one's egocentric desires and needs. The concrete experience is experienced as impressive because it connects with the *existential* of longing for freedom and serenity. On the one hand, the *existential* is the 'point of contact' for the impressive experience, but on the other, is itself interpreted by the concrete experience. The interpretation of concrete experiences —with the basic experiences in the background— is usually determined by the religious tradition within which one lives. The entire interpretational outline of a religious tradition is not completely fixed, however. People can therefore reach different interpretations than former generations did, and in this sense there is a *history of interpreting* fundamental experiences. Insofar as people reach a personal understanding of their tradition and have a personal interpretation of basic experiences, religion is new every morning, to use Smith's expression. Certain interpretations have become classical within religious traditions. In this connection one could speak of the *operational history* ("Wirkungsgeschichte") by classical interpretations, to use Gadamer's term; classical interpretations mark the experience of many generations.[13]

---

[13] D. Tracy, *The Analogical Imagination*, pp. 99 ff., 154-338.

3.2 The unity of religious world-views

The conception of religious views of life as multi-centered belief-systems raises the question: In what does the unity of a religious tradition consist? If it is assumed that a tradition has one centre or designates one 'object' as its primary determinant of meaning, then the question as to the unity of a religious tradition does not at first glance seem difficult to answer. The unity of a religious tradition is then secured in the primary determinant of meaning. In actual fact, however, matters are more complicated. This became apparent when we quoted Brümmer's description of the four things which Christians think of when they hear the term, 'works of God': God as Creator; God as the origin of order and regularity in the world; revelation in history; God's renewing grace in the present.[14] The comment we made then was that a Muslim could articulate matters in like manner; many a Hindu would assent as well. It therefore seems to us that not much is being said when God is called the primary determinant of meaning in a religion. Smith would say that God is present in all religions. Religion is focussed on the transcendent, but experience of the transcendent is mediated by other experiences through which people believe they experience the transcendent. The unity of a religious world-view consists in the fact that all mediating experiences are related to the (one) transcendent. Its unity is therefore transcendent (in a certain sense). People experience this unity more as an ideal than as a visible and comprehensible reality. In traditions with relatively more doctrinal development, it is considered the task of religious reflection to explicate such unity systematically. No one has ever succeeded at this yet, however. The reason is that such unity is not anchored in an elaborate theory, but in the communal relationship of people to the transcendent in their concrete human experiences. This relationship is mediated by experience, however. On the part of believers, the basic experiences which we have discussed are fundamental. The interpretation of these basic experiences, however, and the configuration of basic insights which constitutes a religious persuasion, is accomplished by the tradition. The tradition passes on a way of experiencing and interpreting experiences which has emerged in the course of history, often at the instigation of the founder of a religion. Stories about the Buddha and an exposition of the *dharma* help a believer to structure his or her experiences. That is how the central insights or cores of tradition come about. The unity of a tradition lies in the (stipulated) reference by all religious experiences and basic insights to 'the' transcendent. It is precisely this reference to the transcendent that marks a certain concrete experience as religious. Religious traditions can be seen as configurations of basic insights, that is, concrete experiences and basic insights of whatever sort are connected

---

[14] See above Ch. II § 2.1, the text at *n.* 109.

with each other to form a more or less explicit view of life. In the following chapter we will examine more closely the status of doctrine, and give a more specific definition of the concept of truth in relation to religious doctrine.

Chapter X

Truth and Doctrine

§ 1 Basic insights and doctrine: summary and problems

In this chapter we will examine more closely the nature of truth and the role of doctrine. We will begin by recapitulating the view of religion just developed (§ 1). In § 2 we will attempt to establish what value is ascribed to doctrine in various traditions by referring to Part 2. We will also summarize the manner in which it was thought that religious truth could be assessed. In § 3 we will draw conclusions about the *incongruency of religions with regard to the role which doctrine plays.* Finally, we will examine the extent to which it is possible to speak of a single religious concept of truth with respect to doctrine in all religions across the board (§ 4). The issue of assessment will be brought up in Ch. XI.

We will now recapitulate the view developed in the previous chapter, where we distinguished five elements.

(1) *existentials*
(2) basic experiences
(3) basic insights
(4) the tradition
(5) doctrines (*multi-centered belief-system*).

We will elucidate these in what follows below.

1.1 *Existentials*

Existentials are permanent, universal characteristics of human existence. One could speak of *religious existentials* to express the fact that elements from human existence which are (or can be) interpreted religiously are involved. The need for food and drink, sleep and exercise, etc., are permanent elements of existence. Such elements do play a role in religion, but only in relation to religious experience. An *existential* is *religious* if an experience which is connected to that *existential* refers to the transcendent. 'Ordinary' experience is then interpreted religiously: the dependence on food is experienced religiously as dependence on a higher power; the receipt of food produces gratitude towards the gods; enduring injustice as being in conflict with God's purposes, etc. The *existentials* were described in the previous chapter. Concrete situations in life can be experienced as *impressive* due to their relationship with these religious *existentials*.

What Kant said about the 'Dinge an sich,' and what Gadamer notes of the 'Welt' of which people speak is applicable to *existentials*: they are never experienced without interpretation. Every human being interprets experience within the context of a view of life — no matter how unarticulated, implicit, or disjointed one's view of life may be. If certain concrete experiences are impressive, then one 'actualizes' a religious *existential*. We spoke of basic experiences in this connection.

1.2 Basic experiences

Basic experiences lie at the basis of religious traditions and personal religious experience. Only if people experience situations as impressive, as related to the transcendent, will they have faith. It has been said that some people have faith without being aware of it. It is perhaps possible that someone is acquainted with impressive experiences without being handed an explicit outline of interpretation by a tradition. In that case a person has —in whatever way— reached his/her own interpretation of impressive experiences. An interpretational outline for basic experiences is usually proffered by a religious tradition, however. The tradition appeals to people in terms of the existential characteristics of their life which are actualized in certain situations and which are interpreted in impressive experiences.

1.3 Basic insights

Basic insights are religious insights which are fundamental to a tradition. The basic insights of a tradition offer a person interpretations of basic experiences. Recall, for instance, the insight that the world is *dukkha,* or that the world is *meaningful, purposeful, and created*; that the happiness and liberation of a person in the deepest sense are not effectuated by the 'I,' but by *non-ego* or *grace*; that *love, compassion,* or *justice* are ultimate.

Basic insights are interwoven with a tradition and with the beliefs of a tradition. Basic insights are more fundamental than teachings, however, including the doctrinal reflection on basic insights. The basic experiences and basic insights together are the plane on which the *religio vera* takes place, as we have described it in Ch. VIII § 5. The *initial doctrine* is focused primarily on the basic insights. Although people who are untrained in religious reflection can have a clear awareness of these basic insights, we are not dealing with what has been called a historical faith in Protestant

Christian theology, or with a knowledge *about,* but with lived faith. In actual practice, such insight is nearly always attained in relation to a certain religious tradition.

1.4 Tradition

Traditions contribute an interpretational outline for basic experiences. They do this via rituals, celebrations, and religious exercises, via the narrating of stories and the reading and exposition of holy books, and via education. The *initial doctrine* belongs to elementary education. In a few traditions the holy books are the most important component of the tradition, and the tradition derives its identity from them. To state the matter trenchantly, no one reads the literal Bible or Koran. A person always reads the interpreted holy scriptures. Living tradition contributes the interpretational outline for the holy books. The tradition is the hermeneusis of the holy books, just as it is itself the *operational history* ("Wirkungsgeschichte") of the holy books. Basic insights are central in this hermeneusis. Within Buddhism, for instance, the accent is sometimes placed on overcoming attachment. Sometimes it was, and is, placed on overcoming ignorance, effectively ascribing salvific power to *discerning insight.* Within Islam, much value is assigned to obedience, to faith in the prophet, but also to the inward experience of God's nearness. The variety of currents within religious traditions stress certain things, nurture certain impressive experiences, and thus reach their own scheme of interpretation for their religious tradition. This scheme is comprehensive, encompassing insight, as well as experience and how to act. The community of believers sustains the tradition and carries it ahead in new circumstances. One aspect of a tradition is religious reflection. And this brings us to beliefs.

1.5 Beliefs

Every religious tradition has its own beliefs and religious reflection. To a great extent, the same questions are posed everywhere: What is the broader context in which life stands? What is the origin of suffering? How ought a person to orient himself? The attempt is made —in terms of the tradition, in which certain insights are fundamental (the basic insights)— to fathom the cohesion in a view of life, and to formulate responses to the philosophical questions people have. Doctrine arises due to both factors: the inner need of a religious tradition to experience the world as a unity of meaning, as well as the need to provide answers to people's fundamental questions. The unity of a religious view of life lies in the focus of the tradition as a whole on the transcendent. There is a need to experience and understand this unity. Some currents put more emphasis on experiencing, others on understanding, but what is present everywhere is the pursuit of insight into reality, that is, reality as a unity in relationship to the transcendent, and of actually experiencing this unity.

According to what was said in Ch. IX § 3, doctrine consists of configurations of basic insights. All religious traditions must give an interpretation of the existential characteristics of life, and, with a view to this purpose, of the world. They offer disparate accounts of this. Different currents are present within traditions, and these reach divergent configurations of basic insights. To give a few brief examples, within the Christian tradition, the Eastern Orthodox Church emphasizes the experience of salvation; the Western Church traditionally places more emphasis on the atonement; the Roman Catholic Church has stressed obtaining salvation through good works for ages, and on the experience of the sacred in the Church, the offices, and the mass; Protestants put more emphasis on the 'by grace alone' and on personally living before the face of God. What is believed in one current need not be denied in another. The primary phenomenon is the differing accentuation which leads to different configurations of doctrines, and, at least partly, to different forms of religious experience. Contradictions can also arise from this differentiation. Groups which place more emphasis on acting properly, or on the right inner experience of true insight, or the achievement of enlightenment, can be found in all religions right across the board. These differences in accent reappear in the doctrines. Since a tradition does not spring from a single basic conviction and one impressive experience but is sustained by a variety of basic experiences and insights, numerous configurations are possible. And since doctrine —as a process of configuring— is not fixed, doctrines can undergo developments which lead to yet more configurations. Recall here what Thomas Kuhn noted about paradigmatic shifts. One could speak of 'religious revolutions' in this connection.

The above applies generally. Account must be taken of the fact that doctrine does not occupy a similar position in all religions. The role of doctrines is also related to the basic insights. If it is believed, as is the case in a number of currents, that there is no way in which the deepest truth can be adequately articulated, and that ineffable true insight can only be received when one has morally and meditatively prepared oneself for it, then doctrine will be assigned a different status than if it is believed that discriminating insight itself is already beneficial, purely as analytical knowledge. The role of religious reflection is therefore not always similar, and there are important differences on this score. The importance of initial doctrine and of appropriated doctrine is viewed differently. It is precisely such differences which are important for the dialogue between adherents of different religious traditions as well as for comparative philosophy of religion. We will therefore pursue the issue in more depth in the following section.

§ 2   The role of doctrine in the various traditions

With regard to the role of doctrine in various traditions, one must take account of the fact that each religion has many currents. Just as there are differences in terms of the substance of doctrine, there are also differences in respect of the value ascribed to doctrines and to religious reflection. It is nevertheless possible to point out a few matters. We will also pay attention in this summary to the issue of the criteria by which it is believed religious truth can be assessed in order to avoid repetition. In this way we will avoid covering the same ground again in the following chapter.

(A) The unity of all things in the divine is central for Hinduism. The transcendent is not a different reality as it is in the Semitic religions, but it is immanent. It is important with respect to this chapter's line of questioning to note that the Whole embraces opposites. Śiva is not only the creator but also the destroyer. Several important perspectives spring from this reconciliation of opposites in the Whole and in immanence. (1) This unity is outside the reach of the intellect. This unity cannot be thought since thought operates in terms of distinctions, hence the expression *neti, neti* (not thus, not so). There are different paths and ways of considering things which do not exclude one another. This idea is quite central to the Neo-Hindu approach. (2) At the end of Ch. III we have seen that differences of opinion between Hindu thinkers and currents do indeed exist. We mentioned Hacker's characterization of the Hindu approach as being *inclusive*. To this we appended the remark that the nature of doctrine and the nature of conflicting views are *different* in Hinduism than, for instance, in the more scholastic traditions of Western Christianity. (3) Since the ultimate religious truth is not doctrinal, philosophy stands in close rapport with life; religious truth is not so much formulated as lived truth and truth which must be 'realized' in life. (4) Since the bond with the Divine lies in *ātman*, knowledge of the external world is of less weight than concentration on the self in relation to Brahman.

These central insights —that the Divine encompasses all things, brings them forth, and causes their disappearance; that it transcends plurality and is not accessible to discursive thought; and that true reality (*sat-cit-ananda*) is not so much something to be known as to be attained in self-realization— are determinative for the role and nature of doctrine in large segments of the Hindu tradition. Doctrine has a two-sided function. It describes reality as it is in the deepest sense, and it aims to focus the attention of people on the Divine reality. Just as the worship of one or more gods is a means to the inward experience of religion, so learning to know the doctrines is more a means of attaining insight and happiness than a way of establishing 'the' truth. All five uses of the term 'truth' which we distinguished in Ch. VIII occur in the Hindu tradition.

We will now return to the criteria for valid knowledge. Hinduism —like all revealed religions— recognizes the testimony of others as a valid means of cognition (Ch. III § 3.2.a). According to Satprakashananda, *śabda-pramāṇa* (verbal testimony) is bound to certain requirements which boil down to the demand that a statement be clear and intrinsically consistent. It must, furthermore, be externally consistent; it may not contradict other valid knowledge. Satprakashananda regards the principle of non-contradiction as crucial to the Vedānta, as we have seen; but we have also seen that religious truth lies on a different plane than empirical knowledge, according to Satprakashananda, which means that the problem of consistency between religious and empirical knowledge does not really arise. Comparison is recognized as a valid means of cognition; the door is thereby set ajar for a qualified religious usage of language. The expression of truth is plural, however, since truth is comprehensive.

(B) Within Buddhism, the *dharma* is subservient to salvation. To be sure, some schools ascribed much weight to *discerning insight*. Vetter, as we mentioned, says that the value of theoretical understanding was hereby emphasized at the expense of the Buddha's meditative 'middle way.'[1] In general it can be stated that the ultimate purpose of all reflection is to guide people to the point at which reality is experienced differently. Zen stresses meditation and renunciation, which are prerequisites for attaining *samādhi*. The doctrine here is essentially initial doctrine and this is determinative for the role of doctrine in the Buddhist tradition. Even so, claims to truth are being made: Reality as it is ordinarily perceived is *dukkha* and *anitya*; a basic insight of the Buddhist tradition is here involved. The difficulty here is that the truth of this doctrine cannot be fully fathomed from the 'ordinary,' universally human, inter-subjective point of view; many Buddhists therefore regard the doctrine as of meager value and insist on the transformation of a person through meditation. For the same reason, they try to break through the ordinary way of thinking with proverbs and *kōans*. Someone like Nishitani likewise gives dialectical arguments which are intended to guide the reader or discussion partner to another perspective on reality. Expressions such as '*saṁsāra* is *nirvāṇa*' serve to indicate that the principle of non-contradiction no longer applies with regard to *appropriated doctrine*. We conceive of this as follows: The criteria which apply to the 'worldly' perspective are no longer valid without qualification within the religious perspective on reality. At the level of ordinary life the normal rules for communication apply. One cannot say in ordinary life, "The Peace Palace is located in the Hague and in Tokyo," or, "The Peace Palace is located neither in the

---

[1] See T. Vetter, cf. above Ch. IV, *n.* 6.

Hague nor in Tokyo." In order to achieve profound religious insight, however, qualified, non-literal descriptive language is necessary. The normal criteria for communication as these apply in daily life and in scientific cognition are then no longer valid without reserve. An attempt is made to conduct people to the point where deeper insight emerges by means of dialectical reasoning and alteration of perspective.[2]

(C) It is often claimed that doctrine has a subordinate position in the Jewish tradition. This is understandable against the backdrop of the nature of Judaism as a religion of a chosen people with a calling and mission of their own. Given the emphasis which accordingly falls on the law, a person is relatively free with regard to doctrine. A certain confession of religious truths is nonetheless connected with the acceptance of the Jewish Bible. There are *loci* in the doctrines: the creation, the covenant, the nation, the assigned duty of fulfilling the *Torah,* and the perspective of the coming Messiah. The doctrines cannot be separated from life; nonetheless, it is assumed that certain states of affairs are true. Here too one encounters the qualifications with regard to religious language usage. The *haggadah* contains more narrative than rigorous exposition. Despite all the argumentation of his philosophical reflection, Maimonides emphasizes that religious knowledge must employ *homonymous* terms. The Jewish tradition is pervaded by the awareness that the reality of God exceeds human thought. The rules for valid knowledge which pertain to 'ordinary' life are no longer applicable in a strict sense when speaking of God. Aspects of the divine reality are then mentioned which cannot be unified in any strict theological/philosophical scheme.

(D) Doctrine plays a more prominent role in the Christian tradition. The first dogmatic developments occurred in the ancient church, especially the elaboration of the doctrine of the Trinity and the two natures of Christ. Both doctrines are related to the role which is ascribed to Christ as the one who reveals God, and, indeed, who *is* God. The role of the Holy Spirit remained a matter of dispute for a longer time. The impetus for the development of Christian doctrine which culminated in its classic formulation by the ancient church at the Council of Chalcedon (451 C.E.) was to a great extent provided by the position which the Christian church would assign to the person and work of Christ. A continuing development of Christian doctrine has taken place ever since the Middle Ages. This in part reflects the influence of Aristotelian thought, which formed the basis for Scholasticism — true knowledge is knowledge of (the four kinds of) causes. Whereas for Thomas this knowledge was still situated within a broader framework —just as is the case with the Arabic philosophers and Maimonides— an objectification of doctrine occurred in

---

[2] E.g., dialectics, as discussed with respect to Mahāyāna Buddhism; see above Ch. V §§ 3.4 and 3.5.

the later development of Western theology. The real concern of Christianity is the appropriation of salvation; doctrine as a description of reality, however, has obtained a value all of its own in broad currents. This is related to the fact that faith is based on beliefs with respect to the nature of reality. Since the Christian view of life is true, one can live according to it and trust in God — this is also the position defended by several of the philosophers of religion discussed in Ch. II. Christianity too puts a lot of emphasis on the qualified nature of religious language usage. It is often pointed out that the chief doctrinal declaration of the ancient church concerning the 'mystery of the person of Christ' is expressed in negative terms only: the divine and human 'nature' are "undivided and inseparable, without confusion or change." The ancient church did not state 'how it is' but fenced this deep insight off from misunderstandings. Precisely because it is a problem for human thought to comprehend how a finite person could at the same time be (infinite) God, Christology has always preoccupied Christian thinkers. The issue here is a surplus belief, as it were, which Christianity has, in contrast with Judaism or Islam; it is an additional issue to the problems surrounding the creation and the doctrine of God. The opinion in Christianity too is generally that religious truth cannot meet the criteria for human knowledge as these have come to prevail in Western culture. A classical solution to this problem is the distinction between natural and supernatural truth. Another view is Barth's, who regarded the normal human criteria for valid knowledge as inapplicable to religious reflection.

(E) Ch. VII showed that doctrine does not play such an important role in Islam. In similarity to Judaism, the emphasis is on a life of religious surrender and commitment, or *islām*. The substance of belief is concentrated in monotheism: there is one God, creator, and governor of the world; God has revealed His Will to the prophets, the last and clearest among whom was Mohammed, to whom the Koran was given; someday the deeds of all people will be judged. These basic insights are claimed as true. God surpasses thought; access to God lies in the Koran. The knowledge of God (and as a result, of man and the world as creation) is central; of concern, again, is lived insight, the *religio vera*. This is transcended in the mystical traditions in the *intellectus verus* (as mentioned in Ch. VIII), the surpassing of doctrine in the experience of the extraordinary nearness of God, or even union with God (as in Nasr). The range of discursive reason must be transcended to partake of this lofty knowledge of God.

§ 3   The substance of doctrine and its role

We will now first draw a few conclusions with respect to the role of doctrine in the various traditions.

(1) Each tradition has initial doctrine and makes a claim to truth for their basic insights. These truths can exclude one another or overlap.

(2) In some traditions the initial doctrine is considered to be true; it must still be deepened, but is itself true. In other traditions, the initial doctrine is merely *relatively* true, leading to a higher truth, and, when viewed in terms of a higher perspective, such initial doctrine is untrue, for articulated knowledge simply cannot be counted as real truth (*intellectus verus*).

(3) In some traditions the emphasis lies on the way one lives and/or the transformation of the person. In Judaism, for instance, doctrine is less important than the *halakah,* while in Islam, religious commitment and obedience is central (given the relatively terse dogmatics). Many currents in Hinduism and Buddhism also accentuate meditation and one's manner of life, and have little stress on doctrinal reflection.

One could articulate the fact that doctrine does not play a similar role in various traditions and that it is not ascribed equal value by them as follows: *there is an incongruency between religions with respect to the role and the value of doctrine.*

We have seen that various religious traditions all give an interpretation of human *existentials.* Certain themes therefore reappear time and again: hope, relationships to other people, human failure and setting things right again, the origin of life, etc. Such themes are strikingly recurrent. As the phenomenology of religion demonstrates, the similarities between religions are striking. This can also be seen with doctrines. The same *loci* necessarily arise in the religious reflection of various traditions. One should recall here that Buddhism has no theism; if one substitutes 'God' with 'the transcendent,' and revelation with 'liberating insight,' then the parallelism spreads to Buddhism as well. Several *loci* reappear everywhere, although always within the *configuration* of a particular religion. In addition, every religion also has its own *particularia.* Whereas Judaism speaks of the election of the Jewish nation, Christianity speaks of Christ and the church, Islam of Mohammed and the Islamic community, Hinduism of the Vedic scriptures, and Buddhism of Buddha's enlightenment and Buddhahood. Next to such *particularia* there are common *loci,* however. The common point can be tracked down if one takes into account that religions respond to the same questions, as D. C. Mulder notes.[3] These questions can be formulated as follows.

(a) What is the nature of the *transcendent?*

(b) What causes and purposes lie at the foundations of the *world* and what laws govern the world?

(c) What is *humanity?* What is its destiny, defect, freedom, responsibility, etc.?

(d) *What gives life meaning?* In what relationship does humanity stand to the transcendent? "How do I find salvation?"

---

[3] See Ch. IX, the text at *n.* 11.

(e)   How can one *act* in accordance with the nature of reality? and possibly, How can one come to know (the will of) the transcendent?

(f)   What is the *future* of man and the world?

Responses to these six questions are to be found in the initial doctrines of religions. These six questions which the tradition of a life view must answer one way or another in fact concern the classical components of philosophy: (a) metaphysics and theology; (b) ontology and cosmology; (c) anthropology (including teachings regarding estrangement); (d) philosophy of religion; (e) ethics (and social philosophy); (f) utopia/eschatology. The difference with philosophy as this has developed in 'Western culture' lies primarily in the question of salvation which *(d)* includes. This is the central question in popular religion; in religious reflection, the other questions also play a role. Not only must religious persuasions give answers to these questions but non-religious views of life also delve into these questions. In Marxism, for instance, answers are given to questions concerning the laws which lie at the foundation of the world, and concerning what is characteristic of man; there is a teaching about 'salvation' and about 'sin,' and there are social ethics; declarations are made about a better future; the question of transcendence is dealt with. Belief in God is repudiated —just as in Buddhist currents— but Neo-Marxists such as Block and Adorno, leave room for transcendence, each in their own way.[4] Every persuasion must inquire into these matters. Each persuasion, as a *multi-centered belief-system*, has its own 'centres of gravity.' Certain fundamental experiences and basic insights function as 'hermeneutical keys' for acquiring insight into the whole of experience. We will give an example to elucidate. Given the Islamic religious experience and its doctrine of God, Islam will regard the question of the transcendent as the most consequential, though in many Buddhist currents, anthropology will be considered as most vital. Marxism will seek its centre of gravity in questions concerning the economic laws in the world since they are profoundly determinative for people. In other words, which questions the tradition of a persuasion will regard as most significant will depend on its particular *configuration* of basic insights. Since persuasions and traditions are constantly in flux, the same questions need not always be most prominent.

The fact that it is the same questions which continually arise can be explained in terms of the basis of persuasion in existential experiences. The experiences of finitude and limitation, of success and failure, the experience of happiness, peace, welfare, and goodness, of enduring evil,

---

[4] Concerning the floating, inexpressible, non-identical, Th. W. Adorno, *Negative Dialektik* (1966; rpt. Frankfurt 1970), pp. 91, 112ff.; E. Bloch, *Religion im Erbe*, ed. J. Moltmann (Frankfurt 1967), pp. 189f., 193f.

injustice, and suffering, the awe for beauty, and the breakthrough of insight — these experiences evoke the questions mentioned.

Several similarities can also be pointed out in the responses given by the religions discussed to these questions. In philosophical reflection on faith, people everywhere (pretty well) encounter certain emotional and intellectual problems which cannot be completely resolved, such as the following issues.

(1) The unsuitability of language in speaking about the transcendent, and furthermore, the necessity of saying something nonetheless, or at least of focussing attention on it.

(2) The relationship of transcendence to immanence.

(3) Unclearness in the response to the question of the origin of the world ('dependent origination,' decrees by God, *līlā*).

(4) The relationship between human freedom and determinism.

(5) The origin of evil.

(6) The relationship between the necessity of human exertion for realizing the good on the one hand, and, on the other, the feeling that insight and salvation cannot be produced but must be received.

There is a large number of issues which —if reflection is permitted— have everywhere been pondered, but which have nowhere been completely resolved.

It is precisely these recurring problems of religious reflection which form the basis for our assertion here that belief-systems spring from fundamental insights which have been arranged into a (multi-centered) view of life by traditions; religious reflection attempts to relate various basic insights with one another. The necessity for religious reflection is created by the problem of the coherence of these basic insights within the whole of a view of reality. The intuition that diverse fundamental experiences cannot be unified plays a significant role in this. Religious currents which want to surpass thought in the experience of the Whole or of the unity of God stress the impossibility of achieving —by way of reflection— a coherent view in which opposing experiences are related to each other in a plausible fashion.

Although differences between traditions are significant, these can (in part) be explained in terms of the fact that different basic insights have become the hermeneutical key for their view on the nature of reality. The greatness of God and his mercy are most prominent in Islam; in Christianity it is the experience of the goodness of God which is believed to be experienced in a unique way in and through Christ. Buddhism presents a certain interpretation of the experience of suffering, and offers insight into how suffering can be surmounted and enlightenment attained. These basic experiences are interpreted on the basis of special experiences of extraordinary people; basic insights are the key to an understanding of reality within a religious persuasion. A tradition's configuration of basic insights can be modified by new experiences, either through a long process of accommodation or in a revolutionary manner.

Up to this point we have been giving a rather detailed consideration to the nature and role of doctrine in various traditions. We will now deal with questions pertaining to the 'truth' of doctrine.

§ 4   Doctrine and the truth

In Ch. VIII we distinguished between five ways of speaking about truth in religion. We gave a model; not all five ways of speaking are present in all religious currents. This model nevertheless indicates a pattern which can be found in many currents. It does not apply rigorously to all traditions, however. The incongruency in the relative status of doctrine is the primary cause of this. Despite all the differences, all traditions are concerned with a true understanding of reality. In our presentation of the extant literature on this subject we have seen that discussion exists on the question of whether there is a specific religious concept of truth. This question could be split in two parts.

(1) Is the religious concept of truth clearly distinct from a general epistemological concept of truth?

(2) Is there a single 'religious concept of truth' (for all religions) or does every religion have its own concept of truth (along with its own criteria)? We will now pursue these matters.

In Ch. I § 2.2 we distinguished between a number of elements in the concept of truth. We proceeded in terms of person A (or possibly a community) who says something about the nature of things to person B who does not (yet) know this. We will now examine whether the same elements are present in the communication of religious understanding. We primarily have in mind the initial doctrines of a tradition here.

(a)   In the first place there was A's commitment: A confirms 'p'. Commitment also plays a prominent role in religion. People often speak of the commitment which a person has with respect to reality as he knows it, or at least believes he knows it.

(b)   If A states something, he implicitly possesses *authority* to speak about the matter, (x). With respect to religion it is equally valid that someone must himself/herself be in a position to inform another about his/her beliefs on the basis of personal experience and (some) reflection.

(c)   In general, communication of insight presupposes a *personal knowledge* on the part of the speaker with regard to the matter which is concerned. We have spoken at length about the personal character of the experiences from which religious insight springs.

(d)   Communication presupposes, furthermore, a *provisional knowledge* which listener B has of the issue. The preconditions for the comprehension of religious matters lie in the link of religious experience to human *existentials*. Every human being poses certain questions about the nature of man and the world in connection with borderline experiences, or at least can pose them.

(e) The passing on of knowledge takes place within a *communication situation*. Religions have developed their own means of communication for conveying religious insight and for promoting religious experience.

(f) Communication presupposes common *language conventions*. Two things must be said about religion in this connection. Firstly, that religions reforge the language. They often use ordinary words, but their meaning is qualified in such a way as to refer to the transcendent. People speak of analogies, metaphors, and even homonymy. Secondly, the initial doctrines attempt to communicate religious insight within the context of 'ordinary' language usage. In connection with language use, we should bear in mind that physics, the area of science which is reckoned to be a paradigm of valid knowledge, also speaks in models and metaphors.

(g) Communication presupposes a broader context in which an exposition has value. We have spoken of frames of reference in this connection. A religious view of life offers such a context in which statements are meaningful. The exercise of religion nurtures a certain manner of experiencing reality. Religious traditions explicate the *traditum* and relate it to the rest of experience.

(h) It is normally demanded of the communication of knowledge that an assertion really say something about the matter under discussion; this is what truth is according to the idea of correspondence between a statement and the matter at hand. The idea of correspondence is not completely clear, however. If this idea means to say that an assertion 'manifests being,' then room must be allowed for a more evocative (religious) use of language.

(i) As a final point, we mentioned criteria. We will examine that issue in Ch. XI below.

The matters of concern in the various traditions are not univocal and easily accessible. The difficulties lie in (a) the qualified use of language, and (b) the necessity of overcoming obstacles which hinder people from discerning the truth. This does not diminish the fact that all nine of the elements from the theory of truth, which we summarized in Ch. I § 2.2, play a part in the religious concept of truth. It therefore seems incorrect to view a religious concept of truth as being completely separate from a more or less ordinary or universally valid concept of truth. Even though there are exceptional sides to religious epistemology, a religious concept of truth which is completely disconnected to all other epistemology is not present.

How can this concept of truth —which is applicable to religious doctrine— be defined? It is often said that a (religious) statement is true if reality is as the statement says. This expression has resurfaced in shortened form many times, in Part 1 as well as in Part 2: 'as it is.' This is actually not a definition of 'truth,' but a common sense synonym for it. It must be supplemented. The concern in religion is not with a simple description of 'how things are.' Almost without exception, all religious traditions point out the obstacles which people must surmount to attain insight. The expression *as it is* must therefore at least be augmented to *as it really is*. Then the opposition between appearance and reality would be expressed; one must free oneself from illusion and misunderstanding. That is of course valid in general, and is not distinctive for religion. In this definition the question as to the manner in which doctrine presents 'how things really are' remains urgent, also for the problem of truth in religion. Taking cognizance of the qualifications surrounding the religious use of language, it would be better to say: **true doctrine indicates how things really are.** True doctrine is not simply ascertaining the pure experience of reality, but is a suggestive, evocative description of it. If it is assumed that the formulation, 'true statements are statements which indicate how things really are,' also applies to knowledge in general, then this concept of truth, though applied to religious doctrine, is not specific to religion. What is distinctive of religion is that the essential being of things is seen in relation to the transcendent (as this is conceived in various traditions).

The second problem which we brought up at the beginning of this section was whether there is a concept of truth for each religion or whether there is a universal concept of true doctrine. Phillips defends the notion that each religion recognizes its own concept of truth and criteria. Phillips is undoubtedly right in the sense that it would be inadmissable to prescribe a Western secularized theory of truth for religion, or to derive a specific religious concept of truth from an a priori epistemology. One must indeed observe the adage, 'look and see.' That is the manner in which we have conducted our enquiry. It became apparent, however, that there were striking similarities between various traditions. In distinguishing five ways of speaking about truth we have taken a route midway between a stipulative conception of 'religious truth' and a pluralist approach. There is too much correspondence between religions to conclude that there are as many concepts of truth as there are religions and that these are inherent in a religion. One similarity is that concepts such as *satya, ĕmet,* and *ḥaqq* all pertain to true knowledge as well as to true reality. This is not, in itself, so remarkable. People seek right knowledge of what *is real*. Yet there are too many differences to conclude that the usage of the word truth is the same in religious traditions right across the board. With respect to the doctrine of traditions, however, we have concluded that it is possible to give a single definition of 'true doctrine.' The elements of this definition are: (a) Doctrine does not contain the 'truth' in itself, but in its reference to reality (i.e., man and the world in relation to the transcendent). (b) The concern of religious doctrine is with genuine reality, which is "generally and commonly" not perceived as it really is. (c) Since it is concerned with the transcendent, religious language usage is full of metaphors; religious argumentation is not apodictic — it is dialectical. (d) In this connection we should bear in mind the fact that religious knowledge is of value in itself; true doctrine conducts one to an experience of reality; in addition, insight into true reality provides knowledge of possibilities for action and of desirable conduct, given reality as it manifests itself.

The concept of truth thus outlined applies to doctrine. In Ch. VIII we distinguished between the initial doctrine and appropriated doctrine. The accent in initial doctrine is more on guidance, whereas in appropriated doctrine, there is a heavier accent on the result: appropriated doctrine is insight into true reality. Since one is referred to (genuine) reality time and again by the 'truth' —as long as one does not yet completely apprehend transcendent reality, knowledge is mediated by doctrines and stories, etc., — this moment of guidance is also retained by appropriated doctrine. The description given is therefore applicable both for the *initial doctrine* as well as for *appropriated doctrine*.

I will make a short remark yet about the other ways in which the concept of truth is used in religions. The concern in the *religio vera* is with living in faith, including the elements of experience, knowledge, and conduct (in community). This implies a different concept of truth than applies with regard to doctrine. What is at stake is not so much true knowledge or true insight, but being true. The *intellectus verus,* as we have seen, is conceived of as non-discursive experiencing of the Truth, that is, True Reality. This form of union occurs in some religious currents, but not in all. What is involved here is no longer showing what true reality is, making it visible and manifesting it, but rather immersion in it. Knowing the truth in this state coincides with being true. This is the third concept of truth. The concept of truth as we have described it in connection with *doctrine* is not applicable when one has the *religio vera* or the *intellectus verus* in mind.

Chapter XI

Assessment and Criteria

§ 1 Preamble

In both of the first two parts of our study we encountered remarks about the assessment of religious doctrine many times. We will now begin by formulating several of the issues which are under discussion in the philosophy of religion.

(1) The first point concerns the possibility for a completely inter-subjective verification of doctrinal statements. Inter-subjectivity is the first demand for scientific knowledge; scientific knowledge must be well-founded and systematic and must be coherent with experience. The manner in which the other criteria are conceived is dependent on inter-subjectivity; coherence with experience is a standard which must be accessible to other people, that is, to experts; others must be able to verify the reasoning on which it is based and to understand its systematic character. If it were to be declared that scientific knowledge serves as a paradigm for all forms of knowledge, then one would demand that religious claims to truth (beliefs) be inter-subjectively verifiable. Wiebe and Kuitert confronted us with this demand. Others deny the possibility of inter-subjective verification of *beliefs,* either because religion does not make a real claim to knowledge (and therefore has no beliefs in the strict sense), or because the ultimate ground for a religious world-view is personal rather than inter-subjective, or because religious truth lies in an area of knowledge which does not admit of demonstration and reasoning. The view which is adopted regarding the possibility of inter-subjective assessment of religious truth claims also implies that the validity and applicability of universal human criteria for valid knowledge is being either acknowledged or denied.

(2) The second issue is whether there are criteria which all true religion must meet. Are there criteria which religious traditions (at least those traditions which we have discussed) have in common? If one were, for instance, to state —as we have done in the previous chapter, following

the example of Mulder and Brümmer— that religions respond to the 'same questions,' then it seems an obvious course of action to investigate whether the criteria which true religion must meet can be inferred from those 'same questions.' Some people state that such criteria exist, while others deny it.

(3) The third issue is whether religions have internal criteria which other religions do not recognize. Some people deny this possibility; they only take into account universal human and/or universal religious criteria. It is also conceivable that such particular criteria are recognized but that they are regarded as supplementary to the previously mentioned criteria. Finally there are people who believe that such criteria are the only true religious criteria. Each religion has its own view of reality within which certain rules are valid. Each religion, it is then said, has it own rationality, its own concept of truth, and its own ways of assessing beliefs. D. Z. Phillips confronted us with this last notion.

There are thus three possible sorts of criteria: (1) universally human, epistemological criteria; (2) universal religious criteria; and (3) particular religious criteria.

If only criteria of the first kind are recognized, then assessment of beliefs is fundamentally public and *inter-subjective* (in principle). If the first as well as the second kind of criteria are recognized, assessment is public to a certain extent, and furthermore, is inter-subjective among adherents of various religions (*inter-religious*). If all three kinds of criteria are recognized, then assessment, though inter-subjective and inter-religious to an extent, is ultimately reserved for the adherents of a religion (*intra-religious*). If only the second and third forms of criteria are recognized, assessment is inter-religious up to a certain point, but ultimately intra-religious. If only criteria of the third kind of criteria are recognized, assessment is purely intra-religious.

Judgments with respect to the problem set out here spring from the conclusions which we reached in the previous chapters. It was apparent that religions have much in common, also in respect of 'religious epistemology.' Discussions about criteria arise everywhere; there are striking parallels with respect to the concept of truth; religions indicated certain general characteristics of man and the world. We will examine whether certain criteria are also common to all. The conclusions reached in this chapter are determinative for the problematic of the concluding chapter — the relationship between religions in terms of their beliefs. If religions were to have no common rationality and criteria whatsoever, then no inter-religious enquiry and comparison would be possible, and it would be incomprehensible how dialogue about beliefs could be possible. But if, to the contrary, certain rules are generally heeded, then this would provide common ground on the basis of which discussion is possible.

The distinction between necessary condition and sufficient reason should be kept in mind with respect to the issue of assessment. *Necessary conditions* are demands which religious belief must always meet in order to be eligible as true belief. If a belief meets such demands this does not yet establish that it is true, but only that it remains a candidate for further assessment. In order to be able to accept a belief reasonably one must be convinced that *sufficient reasons* exist to do so. By sufficient reasons, either a chain of arguments or an apodictic demonstration could be meant. It has already become apparent from this enquiry that no incontrovertible proofs are available to religion; what remains therefore is to regard a certain sequence of argumentation as adequate.

It became plain from earlier parts of this enquiry that two problems immediately arise in connection with the assessment of religious beliefs. To begin with, one is confronted by the difficulty that religious language usage is always subject to qualifications. The *meaning* of statements only becomes clear within the framework of a religious tradition, it is often asserted. We have already discussed the relationship between the question of meaning and the question of truth (Ch. VIII § 4). Since the meaning of appropriated doctrine is not inter-subjectively apprehensible in its entirety, no wholly public discussion about the substance of belief is possible. In the second place, the question of personal growth in religion arises here, since religious traditions require personal transformation of their adherents. The question is therefore to what extent unconverted, untransformed people are capable of verifying religious beliefs. In this chapter we will begin by examining the criteria which are attendant upon religion as such. We will subsequently deal with the other two kinds of criteria.

§ 2 Criteria derived from the nature of religion

2.1 Religious beliefs must deal with transcendence

It is specific to religious beliefs that they are related to the transcendent. Even when a religion makes statements about features of being human, the state of the world, or about events, these stand in relation to the transcendent. Such statements are connected to the transcendent within the context of religion. The transcendent itself is ineffable, however. It is known via mediating experiences. When one speaks of God, the Absolute, or the transcendent one employs words derived from the finite reality of experience. This means that religion necessarily uses language in a qualified manner. In order to open the truth of religion to discussion, it is requisite to admit that language cannot be used only in a literal way, for religion relates all things to the transcendent. Religious statements must be adequate to their topic. A first criterion for religious statements as *religious* statements is, consequently, that they not deal with finite things as though they were transcendent, but that they continually relate the finite to the transcendent. Religious beliefs must be concerned with what is truly ultimate and transcendent. We should bear in mind, however, that the various religious traditions differ about the nature of the transcendent.[1]

2.2 Religious beliefs must integrate experiences

Religious belief not only presents finite things in relation to the transcendent, it also presents them in an encompassing framework. Religion is always concerned with the experience of reality as a whole. The interpretation of individual things and experiences takes place in terms of an encompassing whole. This was the thrust of the previous chapter, and in other chapters as well, we have encountered several authors who likewise discuss religious world-views as an interpretational framework within which the meaning of things is seen in a certain way, and who discuss beliefs as valuations of things. Kadushin spoke of valuing, connecting concepts (in contradistinction to discursive, scientific concepts; see Ch. V § 3.2). Whether religion integrates people's manifold experiences was regarded by Pannenberg as a criterion of religious truth. The integration of experiences occurs in different ways. Buddhism concentrates in the first instance on the transformation of the human world of experiences into a consolidated experience of 'dependent origination'; this is a distinctive, specific form of integration. The Semitic religions, in contrast, teach people to see reality in first instance as creation. Hinduism nurtures the experience of the unity of all things. Despite the differences in the type of integration, the purpose always remains to construe a totality of relations among the many experiences which people undergo.

The concern of belief with reality as a unity reappears in the following criteria which we noted in Ch. II: coherence of religious beliefs; integration of experience (Pannenberg, Kuitert); unity of religious views of life (Brümmer); and, self-consistency (Christian).

In Part 2, however, it appeared that complications arise if this criterion is framed too rigidly. There are important traditions which deny the possibility of thinking and articulating such unity. Beliefs can never express the all-encompassing as unified precisely because thought always involves thinking in dualities. Some currents of Hindu philosophy contend that the Absolute transcends the oppositions present in thought and in everyday reality. In order to attain awareness of such unity, one must pass beyond beliefs, so it is said. Satprakashananda does recognize the principle of non-contradiction, and even states that this principle is fundamental to the Vedānta philosophy. It only applies to the relative world, however, and must be transcended for absolute knowledge. If we

---

[1] Cf. P. Tillich, *Religionsphilosophie* (1925; rpt. Stuttgart ²1962), p. 44.

have understood it correctly, this means that for the Advaita Vedānta the demand for integration and coherence is a *task* which, although it should be pursued, can never be attained in thought. The limitations of reason are emphasized by other traditions as well, even when they do not speak of all-transcendent experiences of the Whole in *samādhi* or *mokṣa*. Judaism too stresses the limitations of human comprehension. Beliefs are fragmentary. They are not related in an (almost scientific) systematic coherent theory; people seek inter-relationships, but emphasize different things at different moments (Kadushin). People have an intuition of unity but cannot articulate it in words (Heschel). Maimonides mentions the homonymy of concepts used for God; thought must be emptied. One wonders how such conceptions are to be related in a coherent system. In Christian doctrine —and certainly not just there— one encounters contradictions: God is good and omnipotent, yet it is acknowledged that the world is not wholly good and that much evil persists — how can this be?; people speak of Christ as both God and man without being able to make it clear how a finite human being can simultaneously be infinite God. Brümmer demands that beliefs be free of contradiction. He himself points out that in the event of contradictions, people will tend to explain that only apparent contradictions are involved; despite the semblance of discrepancy, such statements nevertheless do amount to declarations, without the one statement rescinding the other.[2] Statements which seem (and remain) contradictory for the intellect are nevertheless capable of transferring knowledge. In such cases it remains a fact that the demands of the intellect for comprehensible coherence are not met, yet it is still possible to have an appreciation for the reasons why both statements are made within the context of a tradition. The reasons that lead people to make seemingly contradictory statements can be understood even though the relationship between them cannot truly be grasped. An enormous broadening of the concept of coherence is admitted by allowing paradoxes which, though they cannot be resolved, can be illumined. At the same time, however, such generosity somewhat threatens the concept of coherence with blurring.

It is, all the same, generally accepted that religious doctrine should seek coherence. The pursuit of this is anchored in the idea of a transcendence, which sustains *true* existence and consolidates it in some way. This unity cannot be wholly apprehended in terms of the 'unreal' world. Three factors are responsible for this: estrangement, the deficiency of (discursive) human cognition, and the multitude of different experiences. The reference to the multitude of experiences returns us to the basis of religion in the basic experiences which characterize being-human. Fundamental experiences partially contradict one another. People experience goodness and strength but cruelty and suffering as well. Religious traditions, because they must

---

[2] V. Brümmer, *Wijsgerige Begripsanalyse*, p. 138, see also p. 35.

relate all experiences to the transcendent, face the task of connecting different kinds of experiences with each other. Emotional as well as theoretical difficulties emerge as a result. Doctrinal reflection is not wholly successful in amalgamating all experiences in a coherent whole. This is experienced as a problem, however, and makes it apparent that people do aspire to have a coherent view. The demand that religious doctrine be coherent is therefore recognized. It cannot be met, though, and that is why there are paradoxes, mysteries, riddles, proverbs, puzzles (Thakur), images, surprising narratives, and the lingering fascination with a reality which can never be contained by a theory. This too is the reason for the emphasis on the fact that knowledge can be secured from (apparent) paradoxes (Brümmer), that people speak in models and metaphors (Ramsey), and that dialectical argumentation can focus attention on what cannot be said *clare et distincte*.

In terms of the above, it is viable to acquiesce in the demand that religious doctrine must integrate human experience. By mutual inter-relating basic insights, people seek to secure a view of reality which is as consistent as possible. Successful integration of the many experiences is not of itself decisive, however, since the experiences are of differing weight. We will return to this point. One must also in this connection take into account the Neo-Hindu view, which suggests that the indescribability of the Absolute not only makes numerous approaches possible, but *requires* them — without such approaches being wholly capable of consolidation. On the basis of the above, it must be said that Western philosophers of religion often ascribe more weight to the demand for coherence than it receives in the major world religions.

On the basis of this consideration of inter-religious criteria for religious truth, we will now draw conclusions with respect to the customary demands for truth: a persuasion must show internal consistency and coherence; it must not contradict the facts of ordinary experience, nor those of science (i.e., external consistency); it ought to integrate the diversity of experiences.

(1) *internal consistency and coherence*: This demand is recognized in the fact that a coherent view is sought, that contradictions are recognized as such, and that ways are sought to reconcile them or to let them refer beyond themselves. At the same time, it is recognized that no indisputable theory regarding the transcendent can be given, nor one regarding our reality in relation to the transcendent.

(2) *external consistency*: The 'hard' data of general human experiences is honoured.[3] Religions do not make particular demands of what could be called 'relative knowledge,' but they place the 'relative world' in a different perspective. Scientific knowledge concerning man and the world,

---

[3] For the taking into account of 'hard data,' see above Satprakashananda, Ch. III, § 3.2.d, and Jayatilleke, Ch. IV § 2.3; compare P. Sherry's four sorts of facts, Ch. II § 1.3.

and, for instance, knowledge concerning a tradition's own history and development do form the impetus for new developments within religious persuasions. What is distinctive of religion is that it construes experiences in relationship to the transcendent. *External consistency* is, consequently, only a necessary condition of the truth of religious beliefs and never a sufficient reason for them.

(3) *integration of experiences*: Religions aspire to an integrated experience of reality. The nature of the integration which they believe they can attain differs depending on the substance of belief. (To give a single example, while a Māhayāna Buddhist might say that he has achieved an experience of oneness, many Christians are unable to integrate the experiences of suffering and affliction with their belief in God.) One must therefore conclude that there is an *aspiration* for integration of experiences but that the nature of such integration depends on the substance of belief. This criterion is thus not universal to religions in a straightforward way. The aspiration for integration is inter-religious, but the manner and degree in which it is believed that integration can be achieved is intra-religious. Finally, the demand for integration of experiences is not a definitive criterion; it is always necessary to consider whether a certain belief-system meets this demand sufficiently. There is thus no 'master-norm' for settling religious truth claims.[4]

2.3 Religious beliefs must claim universal validity

Since religious beliefs are concerned with the world *as the world really is,* they must be regarded as universally valid by those who accept their truth. A person is thereby confronted by the question of how one's own faith is related to alternative views; we will discuss this in the following chapter. Someone who regards his view as universally valid must have reasons for this. Since religion stems from experiences, such a view requires legitimation with reference to those experiences (Kuitert). If one gives account of oneself (or at least to a certain extent), this implies that there is room for discussion, differences of opinion, and consensus forming (Christian). We have seen that all religions contain expositions with which they try to make their beliefs clear to outsiders (i.e., the initial doctrine). We have also seen that all religions consider their own beliefs better than those of alternative views — no matter how tolerant their stance is, for whatever reasons. Someone like Gandhi is very open-minded; yet since he favours the Hindu view of the nature of religious truth and the nature of the transcendent, he regards the more particularistic beliefs of Jews and Muslims as incorrect. Another problem which one encounters in connection with the universality of beliefs is that religions declare estranged humanity to be incapable of discerning the deeper

---

[4] Compare with W. A. Christian's view, above Ch. II § 3.1.

truth. We have discussed this in detail. This does not diminish the fact that religions do usher people to deeper insight and do claim truth for the initial doctrine (even if this is only holds for the relative world, and is intended as education). The claim to universal validity fundamentally implies the obligation to pursue inter-subjective justification. The value which is actually ascribed to such inter-subjective legitimation depends on the substance of belief and on a number of rather different factors, such as one's position of power within a culture.[5] In view of the nature of religious belief, that is, concern for an intangible transcendent reality, one must, with respect to inter-subjective justification, be content with the fact that it is recognized as a perpetual task, even when inter-subjective agreement remains unrealized.

2.4 Religious beliefs must help a person to become truly human

This demand stems from the function of religious belief. Faith leads to experiencing reality as it really is: Truth is *that which indicates how being really is.* This holds for being human too. It is therefore understandable that a criterion of true religion which is repeatedly mentioned is that it must help people to become truly human. The term 'being truly human' condenses a variety of designations. Whether one speaks of man's purpose, of the fulfillment, integration, or wholesomeness of life, of liberation and liberating insight, or of salvation, there is always a relationship between true beliefs and the way in which people live and experience things — a reality which we have denoted as *religio vera.* What is actually required by many in assessing a religion is to test its effect. This desire corresponds with the demand that a theory be tested by the *praxis* (practice) that it implies.

In our discussion of views within the philosophy of religion in Ch. II, we repeatedly discovered references to the function of religion. Smith appeared to believe that true religion puts people in a right relation to God, to the world, and to their neighbour. Thakur believes that religion must helps people in "coming to terms with the world." Phillips says that true faith helps people to love. It is pointed out that true religion makes people God-centered instead of self-centered. This could be summarized as follows: true religion helps people to (a) acquire an attitude and (b) to realize a perspective on reality which enables them to experience reality and to act in accordance with the true nature of reality. In the case of the religions discussed, this experience of reality implies a benevolent disposition towards one's fellow man and fellow beings. The term 'benevolent disposition' signifies kindred and yet somewhat differing attitudes such as

---

[5] See A. F. Droogers regarding the role of power and dominance in dialogue, in his opening article in the Volume of essays for the workshop on *Dialogue and Syncretism,* Amsterdam, May 17-19, 1988, published in *Currents in Encounter,* no. 1 (Amsterdam/ Grand Rapids 1989).

compassion, neighbourly love, and uprightness. Not all religions gauge conduct by the same moral instructions, yet the ethics by which they gauge, and the attitudes for which they desire to liberate people and to which they summon them often display family resemblances. Moral ideals are not always the same but frequently not contradictory either.

Considerations regarding *praxis* as the criterion for true religion can be found in divergent traditions. Religion must help people to live well. Both Hindu thought as well as Christian theology are familiar with this criterion. Judaism strongly insists on living a just life, both for Jews as well as for the righteous from other nations. Buddhists regard compassion as the rule of life, and Muslims must honour justice and *zakāt*. People are continually being admonished to be considerate of the interests of other people. Since religions summon people to personal transformation, it could be said that *praxis* is a criterion which often reveals whether someone has understood the doctrines of a religion.

There are a number of problems connected with the teaching of *praxis* as a criterion to which we wish to draw attention here. If a certain doctrine does not help a person to become, or desire to become, a better person, then the cause of this failure should not necessarily be sought in that doctrine. It could also be that the obstacles which must be surmounted in internalizing the doctrine were too difficult for that person. The defect could lodge in estrangement and not in the doctrine. We have seen that every religion possesses a certain teaching of sin which deals with the difficulties which people encounter in comprehending the teachings and in living according to them. Yet other difficulties are tied to the teaching of *praxis* as a criterion, as we have discussed in more detail elsewhere. One of these problems is that people who believe in something nonsensical can lead exemplary lives. A person's manner of life need not say anything about the truth of a persuasion. Another problem is that religions imply a *particular* view of what desirable behaviour is and therefore of what true *praxis* and "heil" is. What is regarded as true *praxis* is therefore not a neutral criterion.[8] Since all the major religious traditions do, however, summon people to benevolent behaviour it is safe to state that according to the major religious traditions, true faith must meet the requirement that it commends and motivates benevolence.

The reference to the (possible) estrangement of the person who does not discern the truth of certain beliefs yields an additional complication. If it is stated that some people are further along the spiritual path and have attained more insight and maturity than others, this means that they are better capable of judging. Those who are less advanced are therefore less competent. The problem in a discussion free of domination ('*herr-schaftsfrei*') is how to settle who may and who may not make pronouncements. In some cases it is relatively clear that a person has some awareness

---

[8] See H. M. Vroom, *De Schrift Alleen?* pp. 168 ff.

of the deeper truth. Some people speak from their experienced truth (*religio vera*) with an authority which others sense and recognize (at least to some extent). The consequence of this is that it must be recognized that not everyone has equal understanding of religion. That is why religion needs to *help* people to become truly human. The difficulty with this criterion is that any view of who is a true person is related to the entire multi-faceted pattern of a religious world-view.

The criterion that religion *is efficacious* is therefore not a very convenient criterion, and does not allow for straightforward theoretical application. Assessment of religion with this criterion in actual practice is a different matter, however. Several authors point out that there is, in effect, a practical testing of religion in the course of history. Thakur speaks of a 'subterranean' assessment; Kuitert stated that people continue to believe as long as they continue to *find* with the aid of their search paradigm. This practical testing runs its course via the basic insights. As long as religious traditions can help people to obtain salutary existential experiences by means of the religious inheritance which they pass on, they will presumably continue to exist. If certain matters are no longer experienced, then a part of the tradition dies off. The problem of estrangement arises again here. It could well be that people are unable to perceive the truth because they are too attached. 'Subterranean assessment' is therefore also not a criterion which tells all about the truth of beliefs. It is true, however, that the influence of shifting culture subjects the major traditions to tremendous developments. A process of adjustment and assessment of beliefs is indeed at work; religions are implicated in a hermeneutical process in which their 'tradition' is confronted by external experiential data and by other philosophical currents. What is involved here is practical testing and adaptation of beliefs (and customs and morals) on the basis of the experiences which people undergo. Some religions fall away in this process, when they are no longer credible. Here again, the remark must be made that the fact that 'people' no longer believe in something does not necessarily mean that it is not true. However, on the basis of what religious traditions tell people regarding compassion, righteousness, and love, it can be categorically stated that beliefs are not truly religious if they promote a selfish attitude and hate or indifference towards other people. Beliefs that promote the cause of some at the cost of others are not authentically religious. We may thus require of religious beliefs that they help people to become truly 'human.'

2.5 Religious beliefs must be rooted in basic experiences

Since faith is based on fundamental experiences, it is to be expected that the relationship between beliefs and experiences be clarified.

I. T. Ramsey spoke of religion's *empirical fit*.[7] We ought to recall here what was said in Ch. IX about the nature of doctrine. Doctrine summarizes basic insights (which are in turn underpinned by basic experiences) into a complex theoretical network or multi-centered conceptual scheme. All religions appear to have such doctrine, although its value is appraised differently by one religion than by another. We stated that religious traditions regard certain basic experiences as decisive (and 'nurture' those experiences), while other experiences are not singled out as root-experiences. Radical discrepancies emerge between traditions on this account, inter-religious differences as well as intra-religious ones. The manner and degree in which the diversity of experience is interpreted differs depending on the experiences which are considered to be central in giving transcendental meaning to life. The statement that every religious tradition has its own principles for constructing a world-view is therefore partially correct. The configuration of basic insights (and their entwinement with experiences obtained from nature and history) is specific to a religious tradition; it forms a part of its identity. In addition, a general religious criterion is entailed by the demand that religions exhibit empirical fit, or in other words, stem from basic experiences.

We may conclude that religious beliefs must be supported by fundamental experiences. Moreover, examination of how various existential characteristics of man are interpreted in religious traditions is possible. Religions must, accordingly, offer a plausible interpretation of these experiences. They therefore admit of comparison, yet this does not imply that an impartial judgment can be attained in this manner.

2.6 The value of inter-religious criteria

What are these five criteria (§ 2.1-5), which are acknowledged to a certain extent within the religions discussed, worth? Can the truth of religion be demonstrated or refuted by them? In cases where religion speaks of worldly facts matters are simpler. Issues such as the age of the world, the material constitution of man, and historical facts are fundamentally easier to decide than questions as to the nature of the transcendent. We wish to recall here the three difficulties involved in formulating and assessing religious convictions. (a) The qualified nature of religious language use. (b) The obstacles which people must surmount if they are to achieve insight. (c) The comprehensive character of speaking about the totality of existence. Making theoretical constructions in religion —of which the value is not estimated equally in all traditions— is a subtle and refined undertaking, given the nature of the problems to which religion must respond. One must be aware of these difficulties in the study of religions as well as in dialogue between religions.

---

[7] Compare to I. T. Ramsey, as described by W. A. de Pater, *Theologische Sprachlogik* (Munich 1971), pp. 35 f.

Such difficulties accompany any theorizing about religion. This is balanced by the fact that religions do show family resemblances on many points; all take the same *existentials* into account; all introduce qualifications with respect to the religious use of language; all point out kindred imperfections in humanity, obstacles, etc. In mutual dialogue, participants are more or less accustomed to the manner of thought inherent in religion thanks to their own tradition. Views from another tradition therefore can, to a certain degree, be grasped, and discussion is possible. These five points comprise the common ground between religious traditions with respect to criteria for assessment.

§ 3   Criteria derived from universally valid knowledge

The criteria which spring from the nature of religion were discussed first. In doing so, it became apparent that this discussion is fundamental to the question of whether the truth of beliefs can be established inter-subjectively. We will now extend the lines of the problem of inter-religious verification to the question of whether neutral, universal human assessment of religious persuasions is possible.

It seems almost obvious that for a universal human assessment of the truth claims of religions we should consult that paradigm of valid knowledge, science. Of course there is also discussion within the theory of science concerning the criteria which scientific theories should satisfy. Numerous summations of the criteria which scientific knowledge ought to meet have been given, but they can be condensed into the following five conditions. Valid knowledge ought to be: systematic; well-founded; inter-subjective; discovered in freedom; and presented with a critical mind.[8] We will examine these criteria and will see that though it is possible for religion to recognize these criteria in part, it must also introduce reservations which spring from the nature of the subject matter, that is, the totality of experience in relationship to the transcendent.

---

[8] Lists of criteria are found, for instance, in H. Scholz, "Wie ist eine evangelische Theologie als Wissenschaft möglich?" (1931) in *Theologie als Wissenschaft*, ed. G. Sauter (Munich 1971), pp. 231 ff. Generally accepted criteria are: 1. proposition with a truth-claim, 2. coherence (i.e., in an area of science), 3. intersubjective judgment should be possible; criteria which are subject to discussion are: 1. independence from presuppositions, 2. compatibility (=without contradiction of the fixed data of physics and biology). Scholz further added deduction from principles as a possible criterion. Compare also E. Troeltsch's three principles of historical critique in "Über historische und dogmatische Methode in der Theologie" (1898), in *Theologie als Wissenschaft*, ed. G. Sauter, pp. 107 ff.; cf. a summary of criteria, in R. F. Beerling et al., *Inleiding tot de Wetenschapsleer* (Utrecht ²1972), pp. 14 f., 'well-founded, systematic, and intersubjective.'

3.1   Systematic

Scientific theories must be systematic. Religious traditions, as we have seen, do recognize the demands of consistency and coherence but claim that the nature of the transcendent does not admit of rigorous theoretical constructions. Religious truth is fragmentary. At the same time, we concluded, contradictions are discerned as such, puzzles as puzzles, etc. The principle of coherence is recognized, but as we have shown in § 2.2, this requirement can only be satisfied to a certain extent.

3.2   Well-founded

Religious views are rooted in basic experiences. For believers, this is an existential ground. The rootedness of beliefs in basic experiences and their relationship to *existentials* as well as to concrete historical and natural data can be investigated by the philosophy of religion (conceived of as neutrally as possible). If the question of truth cannot be decided in inter-religious study, one cannot reasonably expect that such would be possible at the universal human level.

3.3   Inter-subjectivity

Religious traditions recognize inter-subjectivity but, again, point out limitations. Justification of beliefs is intended for others; the more important currents within religious traditions engage in reflection and mutual apologetics. In situations during the course of history where religious traditions ran into each other, debates were frequent; people studied each others' scriptures, and gave arguments and refutations. Inter-subjectivity is apparently recognized, but, given the difficulties inherent to religion with its qualifications regarding language, the comprehensiveness of the topic, and the personal commitment involved, a debate between believers and unbelievers does not yield univocal conclusions. (According to many unbelievers, this testifies against the truth claims of religion in general; according to believers, however, this stems from the nature of religion.)

The consequence of this inter-subjectivity is that justification should be provided inasmuch as this is possible, that the greatest possible degree of public openness should be pursued, and that religious views should be explicated in terms of experiences which people have obtained in the area of religion and philosophy. This does occur in modern culture. The problem, though, is again that a concise exposition of doctrine does not, without further ado, lead to deep insight.

3.4   Freedom

Great emphasis is placed by European and North American culture on the demand that scientific investigation must be free. All the same, the problems on this score are significant, just as was the case with the other criteria we discussed. One need only call to mind the way technology, the economy, and scientific research are intermeshed. All religious traditions would furthermore point out that people are "generally and commonly" not free, being attached to many things in life, primarily to their own *ego*. Religious traditions point out that one must be spiritually and morally free of all attachment if one is to apprehend the deeper truth (beyond the initial doctrine). Religious traditions in effect thus give a critique of scientific thought as soon as this transgresses its own boundaries and arrogates powers of judgment on ultimate questions. This also means that all the major world religions subscribe to the demand that people must be 'free' in order to learn the truth.

3.5 Critical

Religions stimulate —it would seem to us, in view of what has become apparent in the second Part of this enquiry— an exceedingly critical disposition. This is evident not only from the thinkers which they have produced, but is intrinsical to religion. Not everything is held to be true; very intelligent people with integrity have reflected about their faith thoroughly. Even though none of them would assert that they have come to know the whole truth, they nonetheless believe to have seen something of the Truth, and to have said something about it, though only by way of intimation. Religions are sometimes portrayed as uncritical in 'Western' culture. If one examines these traditions more carefully, however, it is apparent that people in them are very critical, particularly of their own imperfections. The thrust of this critical disposition is aimed at the person who is estranged and does not intend to face the truth. With regard to self-criticism, which is an essential part of religious insight, it could be stated that religious traditions sometimes manifest a disposition which is still more critical than that of science.

The importance of ideological critique has been pointed out during the last few decennia in view of the misuse of religion to the advantage of some group interest. Religion may not serve unjust interests or occasion wars. Insofar as the moral norms by which religious traditions are thus assessed are external to those traditions, adherents of those traditions might well ask on what grounds the moral standards of such ideological critique are based. As far as we can tell, the major religious traditions would be able to concur to a great extent with such ideological criticism; religious traditions nearly invariably demand an attitude of love and compassion towards one's fellows. Questions might be posed of certain religious currents in this regard, such as concerning the caste system. We will pass over them because a comparison of the morality promoted by various religions would require a separate study. We merely wish to point out that religious traditions across the board admonish people not to be egocentric and materialistic, and proclaim that happiness is to be found in the pursuit of the nearness of a just God, or the realization of liberation, or emptiness.

Among the things which belong to a critical disposition are readiness to account for new experiences, openness to criticism, and being prepared to legitimate one's views to outsiders, inasmuch as that is possible. This is not the case in all religious currents or with all thinkers. Yet there are many people in the various traditions who endeavour to provide legitimation for their belief, not only with respect to others but also with respect to themselves.

We conclude that the demands made of scientific knowledge in modern culture are not foreign to reflection on religious claims to truth. These criteria are, however, less stringently applicable here in connection with the nature of religious knowledge than in many areas of scientific research.

One should call to mind the discussions in the modern theory of science in which all sorts of nuances have been introduced in respect of the neutrality and objectivity of the practice of science. Since this enquiry is not concerned with a justification of religious belief, we will leave this discussion at rest.[9] We merely wish to ascertain that universal human criteria for valid knowledge such as these are to be found in the criteria for scientific knowledge are recognized by religion in its own way, although application is complicated.

§ 4 Criteria derived from particular religious traditions

In addition to the criteria discussed, religions generally have criteria of their own which are directly related to their own identity. Christianity, for instance, speaks of Jesus Christ as the criterion for all theology, and as the way, the truth, and the life. We are here faced by a condensed manner of speech, in our view. Christ is the converging point of basic insights for Christians; in what Jesus said and did, people experienced transcendence — for Christians, God; the Christian view of man and the world was profoundly determined by Jesus' experience of reality. Something similar could be said of Buddhism. The Buddhist experience was profoundly determined by Buddha's middle way. The Islamic view was likewise profoundly determined by Mohammed's experience of God. Nevertheless, the fact that these persuasions emerged in this way leaves undiminished the fact that traditions appeal to people on the basis of their basic experiences, and that the traditions structure their experience of the world in a certain way. Reference to the founders of religious traditions

---

9 Think here of the discussion concerning M. Polanyi, Th. Kuhn and others.

is a criterion internal to a religion. It is not, as far as we can see, an extra criterion in addition to those we have mentioned, but an abbreviated manner of speech which has authority and appeal for adherents of the religion concerned, and which fosters community.

In addition to the founders, there are the writings of a tradition. In the religions known as the revealed religions, it is required that ideas be in agreement with the holy books. The Hindus have the Vedic scriptures and the *Bhagavadgītā*, the Jews the (Jewish) Bible and the Talmud, Christians the (Christian) Bible, and Muslims the Koran. These writings do not all possess equal authority. Each tradition does have a certain form of appeal to authority, however, as well as a hermeneutic to adapt the tradition to new circumstances. We have pointed this out repeatedly in Part 2. The acceptance of the authority of the revelation also occurs via the basic experiences; appropriated doctrine is based on internalized knowledge of the tradition; this internalization is based on certain existential experiences, experienced within the interpretation which a particular religion has given it. An appeal to the scriptures of a certain tradition is naturally valid within that tradition. To explicate and justify one's views for outsiders, it is necessary to appeal to general criteria rather than internal ones.

In this chapter we have seen that there are a number of necessary conditions which religious claims to truth must meet. The most important criteria are empirical fit and the integration of experiences into the broader context of reality in relation to the transcendent. Reflection on the coherence of a persuasion plays an important role, just as do critical deliberation and adaptation of insights to new experiences. Religious insight is not purely neutral and inter-subjectively accessible due to the twin difficulties that effectively prevent a public discussion: qualified use of language and ego barriers which must be surmounted. The initial doctrine is accessible to a certain extent; but comprehending it requires a change of perspective which alters the way a person looks at himself and at the world. The interpretation of basic experiences (and the concrete experiences within which these are actualized) depends on the individual religious tradition. Every verification must come to an end somewhere — as has been said in analytical philosophy. In religion, that point is reached when people state that a particular interpretation of life seems right to them. For the truth of a tradition, an appeal is made to an interpretation of experiences, yet the significance of those experiences depends on an interpretation which attaches to those experiences only within the confines of precisely that tradition. Allusion has been made to circular reasoning in this regard. This is partly correct, since experiences obtain a particular interpretation within a certain tradition. It is, nevertheless, no more than partially true, for it is doubtful that this is truly a matter of circular reasoning. An appeal is being made to the experiences and not to the tradition. Basic experiences are fundamentally open to discussion because they are rooted in general features of human existence, even though it must be conceded that the question of truth continues to be faced by the difficulties which we have repeatedly pointed out.

Chapter XII

Exclusivity and Universality: Interreligious Relations

§ 1 Four models for interreligious relations

One's view of the nature of religion, the beliefs which are honoured, and the conception of the role of knowledge in religion is determinative for one's view of the relationship between the truth claims of the various traditions. If it is said, for instance, that religion does not contain any *cognitio* (knowledge), then no contradictions will exist at the level of propositions. If the hermeneutical problems with respect to (the qualifications of) religious language usage are denied, and all religious statements are regarded as *clare et distincte,* then it must be assumed that people advocate clearly definable opposing views of ultimate reality. If, on the contrary, it is said that all knowledge concerning the Whole is fragmentary and approximate, then all religions can be characterized as more or less equal approaches to the Whole. If one regards one's own religion as founded in the exclusive revelation of God, then no room will be allowed for moments of truth in other traditions. In short, a certain view of the nature of religion and religious knowledge is determinative for the scope which there is for developing a particular view of other religions. With the aid of the conceptions described in Ch. II, it can be easily demonstrated that a particular view of the nature of religion has implications for one's view of the relationship between religions. In Ch. IX § 1.2, we have already mentioned several conceptions which regard religious world-views as unified entities, and have noted the objections to them. In this chapter we will draw conclusions from the above with respect to the relationship between religions, especially in respect of religious claims to truth. We will not pursue the mutual relation of religious experiences, rituals, and injunctions for conduct. Four views will be distinguished. We will reject the two implausible alternatives that (a) all religions boil down to the same thing, and that (b) all religions are mutually exclusive systems. We will do so in order to develop a model with more nuance, an aspiration which is a distinct possibility if religions are conceived of as multi-centered belief-systems. If justice is done to the fact that a number of basic experiences play a role in religion, and that faith is a complex phenomenon which is related to a number of human *existentials,* then it is possible to achieve a differentiated approach. Such an approach is to be preferred above the inclusivist and exclusivist conceptions, which are implausible on account of both the striking similarities and differences between religious traditions.

We will recapitulate the results of our enquiry with respect to the truth claims of religions in § 2. In the final section of this chapter (§ 3) we will examine the status of a theory of religion such as we have been describing in the third Part of our enquiry. What is the relationship of a philosophy of religion to the data obtained through religious studies? Can such a theory be formulated independently of the author's world-view? Does such a theory imply a theological position? These questions as to the status of the philosophy of religion, as approached in this study, will be raised at the close. In so-doing, we are reaching back to Ch. I § 1.5, where we discussed the conditions for the possibility of this enquiry.

1.1   Model 1: All religions are essentially equal

The first model of the relationship between religions which we will raise is one in which it is assumed that all religions stand in relation to the same transcendent reality, that is, to God. Contradictions between religions arise due to the limitations of the human intellect and the multitiplicity of human experiences of the transcendent, it is then said. This model could be represented by a circle whose centre is formed by the transcendent, and in which the various religions are segments of the circumference. They represent different approaches to the Absolute, partial truths of the Inexpressible.

This model entails that the exclusivist *particularia* of other traditions cannot be accommodated. Gandhi could be regarded as an exponent of this view, declaring that all religions concern God, the Truth; the exclusivity of Judaism, Christianity, and Islam, however, are based on incorrect claims to absoluteness on the part of these traditions. Hick goes a long way in this direction; he relinquishes, for the sake of interreligious relations, the exclusive claims of Christianity with respect to the person of Christ. Hick nevertheless allows for the possibility that one religion is better than another or contains more truth. Smith too goes far in the direction of the circular model; the heart of faith is the relationship to the transcendent; Smith nonetheless acknowledges the differences between religious traditions. The significance of beliefs is not completely clear in Smith's case. We believe we can do justice to his real intentions and also to his view of religions as cumulative traditions in the fourth model which we will develop. The relativist model corresponds, in effect, to the Neo-Hindu view of other religions. Religions are essentially the same, yet people approach the Highest by many paths, and indeed ought to do so, for the Absolute is inexhaustible. This model is unconvincing. We will mention two objections. (1) Thakur, who goes a long way in this direction, points to the contradictions between religious traditions (see Ch. II §3.4). An example is the doctrine of reincarnation. Such contradictions cannot be erased. (2) If all religious traditions are examined for common beliefs, one is left with purely *formal* perspectives: religion is concerned with the transcendent, with the integration of experiences, and with the purpose of humanity. In the previous chapter we have derived criteria for true religion from these general perspectives. In terms of the substance of belief, differences exist between religious traditions about the nature of the transcendent, the manner in which experiences are integrated, and man's purpose. These objections are critical. Whoever elects the circle model either chooses for the Neo-Hindu view (perhaps severed from the Neo-Hindu view of reincarnation), or for one's own construction of true religion. To our mind, one then exceeds the possibilities of the philosophy of religion (which ought to be as neutral as possible). One then chooses sides; this is permissible, as long as it is acknowledged.

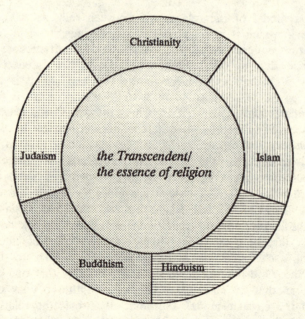

Figure 1

common essence—non-essential particulars.

1.2 Model 2: Religions as alternative world-views

The second model of the relationship between religions can be represented by five independent circles. Religions are independent entities, in the sense of language-games or cultures. The whole determines the parts; the components of a religious culture are completely and thoroughly determined by that religious culture. All phenomena and concepts within a religion therefore possess *significance* only within that particular religion. Even concepts which correspond to concepts in other religions bear their specific meaning only within the whole of the individual religions. They are therefore incomparable. When, for instance, Christianity, Amida-Buddhism, and *bhakti*-religion speak of *grace*, they mean entirely different things (and not related matters which have acquired different connotations within the various traditions). This model is an extension of an understanding of religious traditions as world-views (compare Wittgenstein); Phillips goes a long way in this direction, but also introduces nuances (Ch. II § 1). Kramer presents a Christian version of this model, connecting it to Barth's theological ideas (Ch. VI § 3.5).

Figure 2
religions as separate entities.

This model is implausible as well. (1) There are simply too many striking similarities between religious traditions. It cannot, accordingly, be maintained that religions are incomparable independent entities. Just as the first model absolutized the similarities between religions, the present model likewise absolutizes the differences. In religions which believe that God created the world, people are impressed in a rather similar fashion by the majesty of nature and marvel at life in a mutually recognizable way. In traditions which teach that being truly human cannot be attained until a person loses his (ego-centric) life, people are struck by the unearned character of the experience of serenity. It would be easy to continue in like manner, listing examples which manifest similarities. It must at least be ascertained that much overlap exists between religions. (2) Moreover, the fact that religions are not unified entities to the degree suggested by terms such as 'Hinduism,' 'Buddhism,' etc. must be taken into account. Smith has pointed this out emphatically, as have others. To also allow the variegation present within religions to come to expression, we have devoted several pages of each chapter in Part 2 to a sketch of the developments within each religion; we have often used 'religious traditions' instead of (the shorter) 'religions' for the same reason. Religions are implicated in a hermeneutical process, in which universal human experiences play a part alongside of the religions experiences which people have, and which is also influenced by the encounter with various traditions and persuasions. The intertwining of religion and culture is responsible for the fact that there are significant internal differences in religions which are spread over various cultures, and that these religions are subject to large-scale historical and cultural developments. The horizon of understanding of the time in which one lives influences one's religious understanding. Religions are not secluded entities.

1.3   Model 3:   Religions as bi-centered world-views

If religions are not related as circles which share a common centre, nor as separate, independent circles, we must consider whether they are not perhaps related as ellipses. An ellipse is a figure with two foci. Could it be that the major world religions share a common focus, while having an additional focus of their own? The common focus would then generate the similarities and overlap between religions; the other would engender the particulars of each tradition and its own identity.

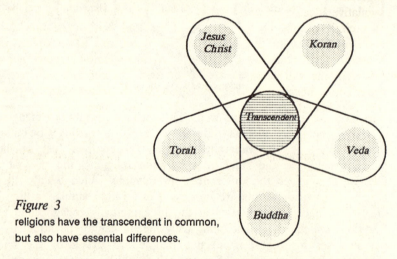

Figure 3
religions have the transcendent in common,
but also have essential differences.

This model is most easily clarified by looking at the Semitic religions. They have a common focus in God, the Creator and sustainer of the world. In addition, they each have their own focus: the covenant between God and Israel (and the *Torah*), Jesus Christ, and the Koran. The *particularia* colour in the image of God in each of the three traditions; this leaves undiminished the fact that a number of elements within these religions correspond, or are at least related. God is seen as Creator; He is Merciful; He demands justice; He gives people responsibility, but is at the same time capable of accomplishing His will. These are common elements; they stand within a certain framework within these traditions. Hermeneutical philosophy has taught us that the whole is determinative for the meaning of the parts. It therefore seems obvious to think that faith in the Creator is different within Islam than it is within Christianity, and different again within Judaism. The meaning of a particular element of belief must be established in terms of the whole of a person's horizon of understanding, or so one would think. This line of thought, though not incorrect, requires some shading in. The image of a horizon of understanding perhaps suggests a univocal whole; the term was coined, however, to indicate the fluidity of a person's horizon. A cultural horizon is not a fixed datum; nor is it a theoretical or psychological entity. Let us elaborate an example for a moment: Standing among the houses, the horizon is invisible. One has an idea of a town, but cannot see it. The picture which one has is determined by the memory of one's experience of the town. One does not imagine how the next street would look if the houses between one's own street and that street would disappear, but as one sees it when bicycling through that street. My image of the town is therefore determined by my perception of the town at various moments, even by impressions gained in houses which I have entered. My image of the town is not factual, but construed. The same is true of the world; we experience the world as a whole. The unity of experience is a kind of regulative idea. It is not some kind of mathematical unity, like the unity of a circle or an ellipse. It is an experiential unity constituted by *being-in-the-world.* The unity of a world-view is likewise not a rigid unity, but a more or less coherent accumulation of fundamental insights and experiences. If one will allow, it is a whole, with fissures and seams, and with connections between insights to which one is accustomed or which one has assimilated in one's manner of life. We have already given many examples: God is good and powerful, and still there is much misery for which people are not responsible; God determines all things, and yet man is free and responsible; God is complete in himself, and yet He wished something more — the creation of the world (this world, to be precise). Theistic religions grapple with these problems; in actuality, they are struggling to connect different experiences and the insights derived from them. The unity of a religions world-view is a regulative idea; unity is more a challenge than a fact within religious reflection. It is therefore incorrect to state that the Muslim's belief in creation is entirely different than that of a Jew or a Christian. Even if a Christian states that all things which were made were made by the Word, which is Christ (John 1), it is still the same creation. If a Muslim thinks of Moses in terms of the central position of Mohammed and the *kiṯāb,* then he is still thinking about Moses and the revelation of the book. The language games of the various religious traditions overlap; they do not coincide, yet they are not wholly contradictory either. The images of circles and ellipses are therefore too schematic.

1.4 Model 4: Religions as multi-centered world-views

We must therefore make matters a trifle more complicated. Judaism, Christianity, and Islam do not actually have two foci. It is not correct to say that in Judaism the concern is with God and with the covenant, in Christianity with God and with Christ, and in Islam with God and the prophet who received the Koran. Both foci are interwoven, for the way to God and the way of God run by way of the *Torah*, by way of Christ, and by way of the Koran. Ascertaining this does not have to return us to the circle model, however. The truth of the circle model is that the concern in all religions is with transcendence, as it is experienced by way of the basic experiences. One can concur with Smith and Hick when they state that one must not think religion-centered but *God-centered*. This centre is transcendent, however; there are different understandings of the nature of this centre — as we have stated with regard to the first model. That is why the first model is too simple. The ellipse model is too simple as well. With reference to what was said in Ch. IX about the basic experiences upon which the edifice of a religious world-view is founded, we can now sketch a fourth model — not mono-centered, nor bi-centered, but a *multi-centered view of religion*. In the fourth model we can do more justice to the reality of the major world religions.

Following on the circle, the circles, and the ellipse, a three dimensional figure displaying numerous centres should be drawn at the present place (if it were possible). The overlapping of the various religions would then no longer occur in the one focus — belief in a Creator. There would be many overlaps. The similarities all relate to such dimensions of religion as ethical injunctions, ways of experiencing community, interpretation of basic experiences, and the content of belief. It is apparent that religions can assimilate elements from one another which are subsequently more or less integrated into a particular tradition. Different currents within the various religions apply different accents. Similarities and differences with respect to other traditions exist, depending on the configuration of a tradition, as described by comparative religious studies and the phenomenology of religion. It is questionable whether one may speak of a single phenomenon as occurring in all religions right across the board. Van der Leeuw himself devoted study to the status of a phenomenon; a religious phenomenon is, to a certain extent, the construct of the investigator, but it is also, again to a certain extent, "what manifests itself"; the phenomena do not have 'being' in themselves (compare Ch. I § 1.5). How people reach comparable insights must nonetheless be clarified. We have in this connection referred to the existential characteristics of human existence in the world. People have an awareness of transcendence, they experience the unnameable in and by way of particular concrete experiences, and reach interpretations of them in basic insights. In the next section we will elaborate this view somewhat more with respect to the relationships between religious claims to truth.

§ 2 Truth Claims

We will summarize the results of our enquiry with reference to the issue of truth claims in interreligious relations as follows.

(1) It is incorrect to characterize religions in terms of a single basic conviction; there are a number of basic insights in which people believe they experience the transcendent. The truth claims of religions are therefore not monolithic and uncompromisingly opposed, but they display family resemblances, showing both similarities and differences.

(2) Each tradition has an idea of the transcendent, of humanity, and of the world, which has emerged from such basic insights. The configuration which the basic insights receive in a tradition is attained in a hermeneutical process which colours the basic insights. Corresponding beliefs from one tradition cannot, therefore, simply be equated with those from another tradition.

(3) Since people have different insights concerning the nature of the transcendent, man, and the world, the question of truth is at stake; people claim that they know reality as it *really* is.

(4) Conflicting views do not eliminate the fact that people agree on a number of points. Examples already mentioned concern the created-ness of the world, dependence on grace, the necessity to transform one's ego, and the emphasis on a benevolent disposition towards fellow beings. This mutual concurrence is often not a matter of assent, but of criss-cross family resemblances. Religious phenomena resemble each other closely, yet they remain different. One must take into account that such similarities do not always apply to each religion as a whole, but to particular currents within a tradition which may resemble a current in another tradition. To give a few examples: Christian Unitarians stress the unity of God; they repudiate the Trinity; they are closer to Judaism and Islam in this regard than Christians who place all the emphasis on the divinity of Christ. The mystically inclined tend to agree more with each other across religious boundaries than with other currents in their own tradition. *Bhakti* religion displays similarities to Christian currents that accentuate grace, as well as to Amida Buddhism. People who emphasize practical action as a form of *yoga* or religious experience find it easier to understand each other than to understand people in their own tradition who put all the emphasis on articulated truths. Conversely, currents in which formulated

doctrine is very important can often identify with each other on that point, perhaps better than with mystically inclined people in their own tradition.

(5) The verdict which one has about other religious traditions is implied in one's own view. If it is said, for instance, that the kingdom of God comes by love and self-sacrifice, there will be little appreciation for some Islamic currents which teach the idea of holy war. If it is believed, as in many Hindu and Buddhist currents, that every person must break his *karma* by way of many lives, one will not have much confidence in Christians who see the church as an 'institute of salvation.' One's own view naturally determines one's appreciation for other traditions. We have stated that the initial doctrine of a tradition contains (in principle) a determination of its position with respect to other religions.

(6) The criteria for the assessment of religious truth claims are not of such a nature that what is true and what is untrue can be established inter-subjectively. The criteria do, however, offer minimal requirements which religious claims to truth must meet (Ch. XI). The decisive demands are that they do justice to experience and that they disclose the fact that they speak concerning the transcendent. The problem is that religious experience pure and simple does not exist; experience is always interpreted. Traditions nurture certain interpretations. The discussion about the truth of religious insights is therefore concerned with experiences together with their interpretation.

(7) When discussing beliefs, the role which doctrine plays in a tradition must be taken into account, as well as the distinction between two levels of religious knowledge. All traditions possess beliefs, even though the heart of religion everywhere is lived faith (*religio vera*). The formulation of belief springs from lived faith and cannot be separated from this experiential basis. Discussion of beliefs which one has not lived retains something outward and superficial. As a consequence, those who state that interreligious dialogue is a process are right, and those who believe that the assessment of beliefs is a matter of public, philosophical, and academic study err, even though religious studies and the philosophy of religion can play an important role in such dialogue. Institutions for religious studies do not amount to a kind of Peace Palace for settling conflicts between religious insights. The most promising procedure for the evaluation of competing truth claims seems to be the consideration of whether a religious tradition gives due attention to all aspects of life (the *existentials*).

(8) Since people claim to know something about the nature of the transcendent in stating their religious beliefs, and about the right inter-pretation of the world and of man, they are not only different and (perhaps) in conflict, but can also be complementary. Just as religious traditions take stock of the reality presented by the exact sciences, they can likewise take into account each others' insights. They can, at least

partly, integrate interpretations from other traditions into their own world-view. This integration is not adaptation to a single centre of integration or basic conviction, but integration within a configuration of basic insights.

(9) Since religion has a number of aspects, differences of opinion about certain beliefs can be accompanied by agreement in respect of particular moral convictions. Differences of opinion do not exclude mutual respect and cooperation.

(10) The will to learn from one another implies that claims to truth and conflicting insights are not quelled, but are presented for a hearing, and are discussed inasmuch as that is possible.

§ 3 Concluding Remarks: inter-religious philosophy of religion

In closing, we will make a few remarks regarding the pre-conditions of this enquiry. We stated in Ch. I § 1.5 that a comparison of the concepts of truth in the five traditions to which we have limited ourselves was possible (1) because all people evaluate their beliefs and assume them to be true, and (2) because the same sorts of issues arise in diverse religious traditions. Religious traditions also have internal discussions about the nature of the truth and the position of doctrine. These points were raised in Part 2. In Part 3 we have sketched out several lines. What is the 'theory of religious truth' thus developed worth? We will offer a few considerations.

(1) The view developed here is based on a comparison of the epistemologies of the traditions discussed. We are aware that this enquiry is characterized by innumerable limitations. Only a few representative thinkers could be presented; religions are far more variegated than this enquiry can possibly demonstrate. This does not diminish the fact that a number of more or less —sometimes very— representative thinkers from the traditions have been described, who have generally left their imprint on currents within their own tradition. Hence, the view developed has not just been derived in terms of the culture and tradition of the author, that is, Western philosophy and Western Protestant Christianity. Dissatisfaction with views which have arisen in such a manner were precisely what formed the instigation for this enquiry.

(2) Some lines have been extended in terms of the views described in Ch. II. The view described is not a description of pure facts (assuming that this is possible), but a philosophical view. It was argued in terms of the facts, as these are known to the study of religion, but at the same time, it is an attempt to say how things *really* are. On one key point I have avoided taking a position. We have distinguished between five ways

of speaking about truth in religion, of which four pertain to levels of knowledge. A number of currents reserve a level at which one is absorbed in the Highest in non-dual awareness. No neutral statement can be made about the possibility of such an experience. If the possibility is allowed, one must rely entirely on the authority of those who (say they are) familiar with this experience. If the possibility of such an experience is denied, one effectively chooses a position with respect to the nature of the transcendent and of being human, and thus betrays a (theological!) taking of sides in favour of certain currents of thought. I have tried to abstain from such position taking. I have avoided including any immediate experience of the transcendent in summarizing basic religious experiences partly for that reason. I have likewise not addressed or considered the experiences of the founders of religious traditions, which sometimes bespeak revelation. Dealing with these matters would have needlessly introduced many qualifications which are not germane within the context of this enquiry. If this reticence has hampered this enquiry, then be it said that it was an attempt to be as neutral as possible.

(3) One could ponder whether the problem posed —the concept of truth in religion, and the relationship between truth claims— does not itself betray a particular cultural form of thought. Do people within tribal religions ask such questions? It can be assumed that people who implicitly or explicitly accredit certain beliefs will pose the question of truth when they come into contact with people who have noticeably different conceptions and customs. I have not maintained that people in all religions pose the question of truth, nor that they are interested to the same degree in theoretical consideration of this problem. It is a fact, though, that articulable mutual differences of opinion exist between Buddhists and Hindus, and between Jews, Christians, and Muslims, and that contradictions apparently exist between both clusters of religions — which have sometimes led (and still do lead) to violent confrontations. The question as to the nature of conflicting religious views, and the issue of how these disparities can be dealt with, therefore has practical significance. Furthermore, for someone who himself lives within a religious tradition, and perhaps also for people who are merely interested in the phenomena of religion, it is interesting to try to uncover how 'things really are.' An enquiry by the philosophy of religion is itself also motivated by the question of truth. Such enquiry comes about simply because someone desires to know what the the case is.

(4) It became apparent in this enquiry that the nature of religion does not allow religious beliefs to be easily discussed for a number of reasons: (i) because of the obstacles which prevent people from attaining insight; (ii) because of the qualifications to which religious language usage is subject; (iii) because of the fact that the beliefs of traditions always

stand within a broader context with which some familiarity must be gained in order to understand the importance of various beliefs; and (iv) because of the enormous variation of conceptions within the traditions themselves. If there are shortcomings in our presentation of the beliefs of these traditions, this is at least partly related to the these difficulties. Comparison of beliefs, and certainly comparison of the concepts of truth present in various traditions, lies at a certain level of abstraction. In principle, it is therefore possible to make general statements about religious truth. As a rule, such statements are made at the level of public knowledge, although the author hopes that they also reveal something of a deeper insight into the traditions discussed. The proposition that the question of truth cannot be definitively settled by philosophy does not mean that one is not permitted to try to obtain as much clarity within philosophy of religions as is possible.

(5) One of the problems which we noted at the end of Ch. II is the issue of whether all religious traditions have in mind a similar or even the same transcendental reality. It has become evident during the course of our enquiry that the abstract concept 'transcendental reality' takes on different meanings within the various religions. Some authors identify such transcendental reality in the various religions. *Nirvāṇa*, for instance, is then equated with the divine. Other authors, such as Nishitani, repudiate this identification of God or the divine with *saṁsāra sive nirvāṇa*. On the basis of the material described in this study, I would venture to say that it is incorrect to state that the traditions discussed all have one and the same lofty reality in mind. One can, however, conclude that each tradition has its own view of that most fundamental reality which everyone aspires to attain, or at least should aspire to attain. The appreciation which is held of other traditions, and indeed the possible scope for such appreciation, is determined in no small measure by the insight one has into this question of transcendental reality. All traditions claim that human existence is related to a transcendental ground or purpose; views of the nature of such transcendence, however, are marked both by differences and similarities. We will pass over the question of whether two or more of the traditions discussed have in mind the same transcendental reality, for this question requires a separate enquiry.

(6) We should pause for a moment at the distinctions between the philosophy of religion, as described in this enquiry, philosophical theology, and theology. By theology we understand reflection on faith (and giving an account of faith) within a tradition. By philosophical theology we understand the reflection on the beliefs of a tradition within that tradition, using philosophical methods. The whole field of the philosophy of religion contains more than a single approach to religion. In *this* study, the philosophy of religion has been practised as little as possible in terms of

a particular tradition, and hence, has been conceived of in a universal human and interreligious manner. Western students of religion have too often proceeded from Western (post-)Christian ideas concerning religion and truth, taking this position for granted. And, regrettably, the Western philosophy of religion has too often thought it could comprehend the phenomenon of religion without acquiring familiarity with the (epistemology practised by the) various traditions. Religious insight into reality and the barriers which —according to religious traditions— prevent people from perceiving the truth imply certain consequences for the practice of philosophy as a whole. Religious epistemology disclaims the possibility of neutral, detached access to reality, that is, reality as it *really* is. More than philosophical analysis is demanded in order to achieve true insight; obstacles must be overcome through a transformation of the person. Religious epistemology has fundamental significance for the whole of philosophy due to its insight into the preconditions for attaining true insight into reality. We therefore concur in Wilhelm Dupré's thesis —developed by way of a rather different problematic— that the philosophy of religion is 'fundamental philosophy,' for the concern of students of the philosophy of religion is with the fundamental questions of the whole of philosophy.[1] The basic questions of anthropology, cultural philosophy, ethics, and epistemology are raised in the most fundamental way.

This study is therefore not a theological but a philosophical enquiry. It does, however, have significance for theology. In order to arrive at a responsible theological appreciation (either positive or negative) of other religious traditions, it is necessary to be aware of what other religious traditions think about truth. Our enquiry is a contribution to this reflection. In so-doing, we have been specifically preoccupied with the theme which by tradition belongs to the central task of Western universities — out of a proclivity for wisdom and insight (*philosophy*), seeking truth: *veritas.*

---

[1] Wilhelm Dupré, *Einführung in die Religionsphilosophie* (Stuttgart 1985), pp. 10f., 162. On the relation between 'science of religion' and philosophy of religion, cf. H. G. Hubbeling, *Principles of the Philosophy of Religion*, (Assen: Van Gorcum/ Wolfeboro, New Hampshire, 1987), pp. 3, 27ff.